WHY THERE REALLY IS A GOD

AND WHAT YOU NEED TO KNOW ABOUT HIM

BIBLICAL CHRISTIANITY VOLUME 2

For TIM, a great helper

Why There Really Is a God, and What You Need to Know About Him

Believers Publications, P. O. Box 485, North Lakes, Qld, 4509, Australia, www.believerspublications.com

Image Credits:
Chapter 3: Socrates: Bust in Vatican museum, public domain, © Marie-Lan Nguyen / Wikimedia Commons
Chapter 6: The Cell: Malcolm Bowden: mbowden.info
Chapter 7: Müller glial cells: Franze, K., et al., "Müller cells are living optical fibers in the vertebrate retina", *Proc. National Academy of Sciences USA* 104(20):8287-8292, 15 May 2007 | 10.1073/pnas.0611180104, Copyright (2007) National Academy of Sciences, U.S.A., used by permission.
Chapter 8: Bacterial Flagellum: Malcolm Bowden: mbowden.info
Chapter 22: Eternity photo: Sardaka 09:13, 2 May 2008 (UTC) - Own work, CC BY-SA 3.0, https://commons.wikimedia.org/w/index.php?curid=3976888
Cover image: Carina nebula, the jewel of southern skies.

ISBN: 978-0994397751

Contents

Part Two: What You Need to Know About God

Part Three: Objections to God

Introduction

God?

The atheist Bertrand Russell was once asked what he would say if he found himself standing before God in the afterlife and was asked why he had not believed. Russell replied that he would tell God there was not enough evidence[1].

Contrary to what Bertrand Russell said, many famous people in history have believed there is good evidence for God's existence. In Part One of this book, we will look at sixteen arguments for God's existence. I have named these arguments after sixteen different people: Socrates, Albert Einstein, Sir Fred Hoyle, Stephen King, Sir Isaac Newton, C. S. Lewis, Blaise Pascal, William Shakespeare, General von Zieten and King George VI, among others. Most of these people became believers in God because of a particular piece of evidence, but others simply express or embody the argument for God so well that I name the arguments after them. The arguments in Part One come from ten main areas of evidence: intuition, creation, design, human dignity, conscience, Christ, providence, history, scripture, and personal experience – in other words, from a wide range of human interests. Different types of argument will appeal to different people: some arguments are scientific, some are logical, some are historical or cultural, some are personal stories, and some involve good old-fashioned common sense.

There is a story about an old man who met a young atheist. The young atheist fired off a list of arguments against God and then declared, 'I am an atheist'. The old man asked, 'Are you sure of that?', to which the young man replied, 'Absolutely. I am quite certain that there is no God'. The old man reached out his hand and said, 'Then would you please give

---

[1] Quoted in Wesley C. Salmon, "Religion and Science: A New Look at Hume's Dialogues", *Philosophical Studies* 33, 1978, p.176

me the great privilege of shaking your hand, because you are the most remarkable and outstanding person I have ever met'. The young man was a bit confused by this and said, 'There is nothing unusual about me. I am just an ordinary person, convinced that God does not exist. Why are you making such a song and dance about that?'

The old man said, 'Let me ask you some questions. If you have not been alive throughout all time, won't you accept that it is possible that God does exist, but that he revealed himself to humanity at some point before you were born? If you have not been everywhere in the universe, won't you accept that it is possible that God does exist, but that he is somewhere in the universe that you have never visited? And as you admit that you don't know everything it is possible to know, won't you admit that there may be evidence of God's existence that you don't possess?'

This had an immediate effect on the young man, and he said, 'I see what you mean, and you are right. It is *impossible* for me to be an atheist. I have just become an agnostic'[2].

Here is the sort of person this book is written for: someone who is open-mined enough to engage with the best arguments for (and against) God, and fair-minded enough to change their view if the evidence points in that direction.

The majority of Western people today still believe in God, or at least say they are open to God's existence. In Australia, Canada, the United Kingdom and the United States, only 12-13% of people are 'convinced atheists'[3]. Many people today are unsure, or agnostic, about God's existence – even people from a religious background.

The most important question I have for such readers is this: are you fair-dinkum (as we say in Australia)? Are you genuine, are you sincere, do you really want to know whether there is a God or not? Are you an open-minded agnostic, or a closed-minded agnostic? Here is another way of asking this question: are you ready to honestly weigh up the arguments for God's existence, and willing to believe in God if that is what the evidence shows?

---

[2] In John Blanchard, *Does God Believe in Atheists?*, Evangelical Press, 2000, pp.195-6
[3] Survey by Colmar Brunton in Australia, Leger in Canada, ORB International in UK (all for WIN-Gallup International) in November 2014, Gallup poll in USA in 2017

Introduction: God?

It does not really matter how much – or little – evidence there is for God if you are not truly willing to consider the possibility (and consequences) of believing in God. You have to start by being willing to follow the evidence wherever it leads.

It is important to understand that believing in God is not simply a matter of arguments and evidence. Blaise Pascal wrote: 'People almost invariably arrive at their beliefs not on the basis of proof, but on the basis of what they find attractive'[4]. That is why I encourage you to read Part Two of the book: what you need to know about God. It would not be fair to reject God until you know the full truth about what God is like.

It is true, however, that there are strong arguments against God's existence. Part Three of the book deals with some of the most common complaints against God: the problem of suffering and evil, biological evolution, the question of who made God, and the damage religion has done in the world. These are powerful arguments that require a response.

Ultimately, evidence alone will not decide the matter. You have to come to your own conclusion. Again we come back to the most important question: are you genuinely open-minded and willing to consider all the evidence, for and against God. It is not possible to definitively prove God's existence (for proofs belong to mathematics and very few other subjects), and some arguments for God are not conclusive, but just suggestive. As every juror needs to be reminded, there is a difference between evidence and proof. I encourage readers to treat the book as a cumulative case that offers different pieces of evidence for God's existence. Hear the entire argument out before passing judgment.

God's existence is one of the most important questions it is possible to consider. Rather than offering a one sided argument or simplistic presentation of arguments for belief in God, this book provides a fair, balanced and comprehensive examination of all the main arguments, both for and against God, leaving readers to weigh up the question for themselves.

---

[4] Blaise Pascal, *On the Art of Persuasion*, 1658

PART ONE:

Arguments for God

Chapter 1

The Alec Catchpole Argument: Intuition

Alec Catchpole was a good swimmer in his early twenties. As he swam out through the waves, the last thing on his mind was the question of whether God exists. Nor was he thinking this might be the last day of his life.

Alec was on holiday in the Caribbean. But the beaches were not the main reason for coming to Dominica. Having lost his motor vehicle licence for drink-driving, and his job as a milkman, he went to the island in February of 1987 for six months. Dominica was attractive because of the cheap drugs, but his real reason for coming was to start a socialist revolution. Three surprises were waiting for him in the Caribbean.

Alec had grown up in north London, England, in a middle-class family, but by his late teens he was involved in drugs and revolutionary socialist politics. During the turbulent years of Margaret Thatcher's conservative government, he took part in demonstrations and running battles against the riot police. He called himself an internationalist, and his dream was worldwide socialist revolution.

Alec's mum was Catholic, and his father a Protestant, both merely nominal Christians. Alec himself had embraced atheism, or as he called it, 'scientific materialism'. As he shared his atheism and political views with the islanders on Dominica, his first surprise was their faith in God. Despite constant poverty and mounting problems, their faith seemed to bring them peace, joy and hope. As much as he tried to deny the evidence, they seemed to have something that he didn't.

Alec became friendly with one of the island's leading athletes, who encouraged him to read the life and message of Jesus. Here was a second surprise: as they began to read the gospels together, Alec wasn't expecting what he found. He was impressed by how Jesus helped the poor and marginalized, and his courage to stand up to the political and religious leaders who abused their authority. As he read the pages of the New Testament, he started to reflect on how different the message of Jesus was to the violence and social revolution that he was promoting. Jesus' message changed the world by transforming the hearts of those that followed Him.

The third surprise was waiting for Alec in the surf. Alec had been on the island for a few months when he was invited to a party on a beach. After a while, he and his girlfriend left to go to an adjoining deserted beach. Wanting to show off, and against his girlfriend's warnings, he swam out about 100 metres. No sooner had he tried to return to the beach, than he felt the pull of a powerful current. He tried his best to fight against it, but it was too strong. He was now totally exhausted, and even further from shore. He realized he was in danger, and there was no way he could save himself.

What happened next is best described in Alec's own words: 'I cried out to God from my heart to rescue me, and something amazing happened. God spoke to my heart, telling me to put my feet down. As I did, although far out to sea, I found sand under my feet. I was overcome with relief and started taking little 'pigeon steps' to see how far the sand went before trying again to swim to shore. But I found there was no need to swim at all. There was a sandbar that allowed me to walk all the way back. As soon as I was safe to shore, I knelt on the beach to thank God and promise that I would seek him with all my heart'.

Over the following weeks, Alec kept his promise, reading the Bible, praying and going to church. In June of 1987, very simply, he surrendered his life to God, turning away from his old life to put his faith in Jesus Christ. God immediately freed him from his drug addiction and gave him a burning desire to help others come to know the same freedom, peace and joy he had found in Jesus Christ.

I first met Alec about five years later in London when I came to England from Australia in my early twenties. By a strange turn of events, I ended up in one of the last places I would ever have chosen to live. The north London borough of Tottenham might be famous to football fans, but apart from the football ground there were only large high-rise housing estates, dirty congested streets, and tension in the air.

Tottenham was the scene of race riots in the 1980s (when a policeman was hacked to death with a machete), riots repeated again in the early 21st century. In addition to a large West Indian immigrant population, Tottenham was an entry point to the United Kingdom for refugees from all over the world.

Here Alec was telling people about God in the community and in churches, reaching out particularly to young people from underprivileged backgrounds. For a year I helped Alec and others as they shared the Christian message. But Alec was already preparing to move to Italy, to work as a missionary in one of the most desperate and needy places in the world, Naples. Here was a city largely run by the mafia, where many people lived in fear, poverty, and addiction, trying to survive amidst the crime, corruption and violence. In the twenty-five years since, Alec has been working in Naples, and with God's help, many people have been rescued from these evils and turned their lives around.

Alec's Christian conversion was not a phase or a fantasy. His encounter with God shows all the marks of reality. He went from being a drug-addicted drop-out to someone caring for people in socially deprived and difficult places. Instead of a life of violent revolution, he is evidence of the very different revolution that Jesus produces, a life transformed by God.

But back to what happened at the beach. Why is it that most people, even militant atheists like Alec Catchpole, call on a higher power when they are desperate and in distress? In Alec's case, it was an instinctive reaction – there was no time for leisurely reflection upon the issue.

Belief in God

Prayer is a 'global phenomenon'[1], found among people of all religions, and even amongst some non-religious people. Is belief in God an instinctive, innate part of our make-up? Theologians refer to this deep-down, in-built belief in God as the 'sensus divinitatis', the God-sense. Augustine wrote, 'A sense of Deity is inscribed on every heart. Nay, even idolatry is ample evidence of this fact' (*Confessions*). John Calvin wrote,

---

[1] Timothy Keller, *Prayer*, Hodder, 2014, p.44

'There is within the human mind, and indeed by natural instinct, an awareness of the divinity'[2].

Belief in God seems almost 'hard-wired' in human beings. Oxford University psychologist Olivera Petrovich and her research assistants found that children they tested in Britain and Japan chose God as the explanation for natural objects (e.g. dogs, as opposed to man-made artefacts), despite significant cultural differences. Petrovich said:

'On forced choice questions, consisting of three possible explanations of primary origin, they would predominantly go for the word "God," instead of either an agnostic response (e.g., "nobody knows") or an incorrect response (e.g., "by people"). This is absolutely extraordinary when you think that Japanese religion — Shinto — doesn't include creation as an aspect of God's activity at all. So where do these children get the idea that creation is in God's hands? It's an example of a natural inference that they form on the basis of their own experience. My Japanese research assistants kept telling me, "We Japanese don't think about God as creator — it's just not part of Japanese philosophy." So it was wonderful when these children said, "Kamisama! God! God made it!" That was probably the most significant finding'[3].

Petrovich concluded that belief in God develops naturally among infants, while atheism has to be learned[4]. Many of the world's most prominent atheists, like Richard Dawkins, had an atheist 'conversion' experience sometime in their teens. Before that, they (naturally) believed in God.

Dr. Justin Barrett, a senior researcher at Oxford University's Centre for Anthropology and Mind, says that young people have a predisposition to believe in God, citing other studies which show that children have an instinctive understanding that the natural world, and

[2] John Calvin, *Institutes*, Vol. 1, 43, 43n.2

[3] Bryant, R., "In the Beginning: An Interview with Olivera Petrovich", *Science and Spirit*, 1999

[4] https://www.theage.com.au/national/infants-have-natural-belief-in-god-20080725-313b.html

everything in it, was designed for a purpose. Children appear to be born believers in an intelligent Being behind the universe and do not simply acquire a belief in God through religious teaching from parents or teachers[5].

Alison Gopnik, a Berkeley psychology professor, wrote in the *Wall Street Journal*, 'By elementary-school age [i.e. ages 5-11], children start to invoke an ultimate God-like designer to explain the complexity of the world around them – even children brought up as atheists'[6]. She reported that even pre-school children have begun to think in terms of design when they consider the natural world and suggested that educators need to intervene before the idea of design had 'become too entrenched'. Gopnik again shows us the intuitive nature of human beings' belief in a designing intelligence behind the world from the earliest ages, irrespective of whether we have a religious upbringing or not.

Virtually every human culture has been religious. The Roman orator and statesman Cicero asked, 'What people is there or what race of men, which has not some traditional teaching, some presentiment of the existence of God?' A human society without its own form of religion would be almost as strange as a culture without its distinctive dress or cuisine. Still today, the vast majority of people on earth believe in God.

The near-universal belief in God among human beings down through history is not proof of God's existence. But it raises an important question. Why is it that the vast majority of people on far separated continents, in different cultures and times have believed in God? Is belief in God more easily explained by some atheistic reason, or by the fact that there really is a God who created us? What is the reason for the prevalence and persistence of belief in God?

As we are about to see, the argument from creation is probably one of the most powerful reasons why the vast majority of people down through history have been believers in God. But before we turn to the argument from creation, we need to take stock of where the argument from

---

[5] M. Beckford, "Children are born believers in God, Academic Claims", *The Telegraph*, 24 November 2008

[6] Alison Gopnik, "See Jane Evolve: Picture Books Explain Darwin", *Wall Street Journal*, April 18, 2014

intuition leaves us. If we represent atheism and belief in God on a scale from 0 to 10, where 0 is atheism and 10 is belief in God, the strength of the argument from intuition would probably be rated at about 1-3 (by atheists) or 7-9 (by believers in God). That is, in terms of how persuasive it is as an argument for God's existence, it is far from conclusive (i.e. nowhere near a 10), but neither does it provide any evidence for atheism. We are going to split the difference and call it a 5:

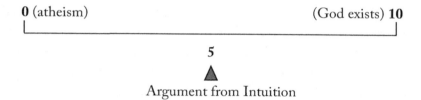

0 (atheism)   (God exists) **10**

5

Argument from Intuition

Whether you, as a reader, agree or not with this assessment of the strength of the argument from intuition is unimportant at the moment. Here is where I am heading: many atheists today argue that atheism should be the natural starting assumption for any discussions or debates about God. There should be no presumption that God exists. However, the argument from intuition suggests otherwise. The fact that humans are seemingly born believers in God, and the additional fact that belief in God has been the norm for the vast majority of human societies down through time, shows that an assumption of atheism does not reflect reality for most people. On the other hand, the argument from intuition hardly proves God's existence. What the argument from intuition does, I suggest, is to raise the issue of God's existence as a genuinely open question.

In the next chapter, we are going to see that the evidence from creation tips the scales decisively in favour of God's existence.

Chapter 2

The Albert Einstein Argument: Creation

Have you heard the joke about the Big Bang? First there was nothing, then it exploded. It doesn't quite add up, does it? The idea that the universe sprang into existence from nothing, with no cause and for no reason, defies all rational sense. It is just about the most ridiculous idea possible to believe.

The argument from creation asks where the universe came from. Another way to put it is: Why there is something rather than nothing? This has been called the most important question in philosophy. Gottfried Leibniz the great German mathematician and philosopher expressed it this way, 'Nothing happens without a sufficient reason … Assuming this principle, the first question which should rightly be asked will be "Why is there something rather than nothing?"[1]

I used to live in an area where there were many new houses being built. The first sign that a new house was about to be built was a bulldozer coming and flattening a block of land, leaving a pad of dirt. The second thing to happen was that a portable toilet would appear out the front of the block. The reason was simple: houses cannot build themselves – they need a builder – and a builder needs a toilet. Just as houses cannot build themselves, so the universe could not have created itself – it needs a creator. The Bible even makes this same argument: it says that 'every house is built by someone, so He who made all things is God'[2].

Common sense tells us that something cannot make itself. In fact, it is not just common sense, it is a scientific fact, true for every single thing we know of – without any exceptions. Cakes do not mix and bake

---

[1] G. W. F. von Leibniz, "Nature and Grace", in *Leibniz Selections*, ed. P. Wiener, Scribner's, 1951, p.527
[2] Hebrews 3:4

themselves, they need a baker. Books do not write themselves, they need authors. In the same way, the universe did not create itself; it requires a Creator.

James Clerk Maxwell (1831-1879) was one of the three greatest scientists to have ever lived (along with Newton and Einstein). He was responsible for our modern world of radio, television and mobile phones through his discoveries in electromagnetism. He wrote, 'Science is incompetent to reason upon the creation of matter itself out of nothing ... because matter cannot be eternal and self-existent, it must have been created'[3]. In other words, because matter is not eternal, and it cannot have created itself, it must have been created by God out of nothing.

There is a down-to-earth logic about the argument from creation. Everybody knows that we cannot get something from nothing. Magicians are only able to pull a rabbit out of a hat because they somehow managed to hide it there in the first place. The Bible expresses the logic of the argument from creation as follows: 'Know that the LORD, He is God; it is He who has made us, and not we ourselves'[4]. Nothing is able to make itself.

At the level of popular culture, this common-sense argument is expressed in *The Sound of Music*, where Maria sings 'nothing comes from nothing, nothing ever could'. (She thinks she must have done something good in her youth to deserve marrying the captain). This truth is expressed at a more theological level by the Latin expression, *ex nihilo, nihil fit*: out of nothing, nothing comes. The universe requires a Creator – God.

The biophysicist and philosopher Kirk Durston has formulated another version of the argument from Creation, as follows:

If we take 'nature' to refer to everything in physical reality (space, time, matter, energy, and laws of nature), then:
    1. the cause of nature is either natural or non-natural (i.e.

---

[3] W. D. Niven, *The Scientific Papers of James Clerk Maxwell*, Courier Corporation, 2003, p376
[4] Psalm 100:3, KJV

supernatural)
2. the cause of nature cannot be natural
3. therefore the cause of nature must be supernatural.

The only difficult part of this argument to understand is step 2, but this is obviously true, because just as a woman cannot give birth to herself, so something cannot make itself. Nature cannot create itself or be the explanation for its own origin. If nature refers to everything in the physical realm, then there is nothing natural left outside it to bring nature into existence. Thus, nature must have a supernatural origin.

Some objections to this argument may be quickly answered. Firstly, some might argue that nothing caused nature to begin. However, this is irrational, a retreat into nonsense. Everything we know in nature has a cause. Secondly, some might argue that maybe the cause of nature is something natural but it is so amazing that we have not yet discovered it. However, although there are probably many amazing things in nature that we have not yet discovered, we have already shown by the three-point argument above that the cause of nature itself can't be natural: something cannot create itself. Thirdly, at this point, someone will doubtless ask, "If this is the case, what caused God?" In reply, the fact that nature includes time means that the cause of nature must be outside time, or timeless, in other words, eternal, and therefore uncaused and supernatural – i.e. God.

We will deal with this question, If God created the world, who created God?, in more detail in Part Three of the book. Although this question is common today, it has many good answers. We have just seen one right here, and we will look at five ways of answering the question in Part Three.

Whatever way we look at the argument from creation, whether we appeal to logic, science, philosophy, common sense, popular culture or Scripture, the evidence points to God's existence. Because it is absurd to believe that something can create itself, creation requires a Creator: God.

Albert Einstein and the Evidence of Creation

Some of the greatest scientific discoveries of the twentieth century have reinforced the argument for God from creation. If you don't like science, this will probably not be your favourite chapter in the book. But please don't give up here, and don't worry if you do not understand all the scientific details. Here are the two main points to grasp: first, scientists have shown that the universe must have had a beginning and second, this strongly suggests that God is our Creator.

In 1905 a twenty-six-year-old Albert Einstein, working at the Swiss patent office in Berne, published a scientific paper, 'On the Electrodynamics of Moving Bodies', in which he advanced the mind-bending theory that time and distance are not fixed or constant but can vary depending on the relative motion of observers. This theory was called Special Relativity. In 1907 he went on to demonstrate that mass and energy can change into each other too, according to the equation $E = mc^2$, proof of which was seen later in the destruction caused by the atomic bomb. In 1915 he published his General Theory of Relativity, which incorporated gravity, arguing that gravity can distort time. This theory correctly explained the discrepancy in the orbit of the planet Mercury unaccounted for by Newtonian physics.

Einstein himself refused to be satisfied with his theory until it was proven true or false by a number of careful experiments. The first verification came from observations by Sir Arthur Eddington of a solar eclipse on the island of Principe off the coast of West Africa in 1919, showing that a ray of light had been bent at twice the gravitational deflection that Newton's theory had predicted. The next evidence came from the astronomer Edwin Hubble at the Mount Wilson observatory in California in 1923 who observed that other galaxies seemed to be moving away from us, and the furthest away seemed to be moving away the fastest.

This evidence was particularly significant because it indicated that the universe was expanding. In response to Einstein's theory, Alexander Friedmann and Georges Lemaître had already proposed that the universe was expanding. Therefore all matter must have been closer together in the past, and working backwards, all matter must once have been compressed into an very small and densely-packed point from which it rapidly expanded, a concept later named the Big Bang theory.

This was an aspect of his theory that Einstein himself was uncomfortable with because it suggested that the universe must have had a beginning. Einstein had introduced a 'cosmological constant' into his equations, a force which counteracted the universe's expansion (or contraction), making it static, and removing any need for a beginning. After examining the evidence for an expanding universe, Einstein said that adding the 'cosmological constant' to his theory was the 'biggest blunder' of his life.

Before Einstein, many people believed in a fixed, static, eternal universe. Aristotle the Greek philosopher argued that the world was eternal, and many other modern scientists, including Einstein, were uncomfortable with the idea that the universe had a beginning because it suggested that the universe had an outside cause, and pointed in the direction of divine intervention. Sir Arthur Eddington found the idea 'repugnant', and admitted, 'the beginning seems to present insuperable difficulties unless we agree to look on it as frankly supernatural'[5]. A beginning suggested a Creator – God. It sounded too much like the opening line of the Bible, 'In the beginning, God created the heavens and the earth' (Genesis 1:1).

In 1948, Fred Hoyle with others advanced the Steady State model of the universe, suggesting that matter created itself out of nothing to replace the matter expanding outwards, keeping the universe eternally in equilibrium, and removing any need for a beginning. However, apart from the problem of explaining how matter perpetually created itself from nothing, in 1965 Arno Penzias and Robert Wilson detected what was called the 'cosmic background radiation', the afterglow of the explosion of energy from the Big Bang. This effectively confirmed again that the universe had a beginning. Another theory that tried to get around the problem of a beginning was the Oscillating Universe theory, which argued that the universe 'bounces', expanding outwards then collapsing back on itself, only to bounce back out again, endlessly and eternally. But in 1970 Stephen Hawking and Roger Penrose demonstrated that a bouncing universe was impossible and that it must

[5] Arthur Eddington, *The Expanding Universe*, Cambridge University Press, 1933, pp.124, 178

have had a beginning in a 'singularity', an infinitely dense point of energy and matter where time had its beginning.

Other strong evidence for a beginning of the universe includes the first and second laws of thermodynamics, some of the most fundamental and experimentally-verified laws in all of science:

1. Energy can neither be created nor destroyed.
2. The amount of energy available for work is decreasing.

The first law states that matter and energy cannot be created. That is, they cannot be created *naturally*. Therefore, if matter and energy came into existence (i.e. were created at the beginning of the universe), there is nothing in nature capable of producing them. The cause of the creation of matter and energy must be outside nature or non-natural, i.e. supernatural.

The second law states that available energy is decreasing. For example, the sun is slowly using up its fuel-source. Another way to state this law is that entropy (or, disorder) tends to increase. We all experience this law in daily life: a suburban garden or a teenage boy's bedroom will not naturally become tidier and more orderly by itself. Other examples of entropy include the fact that a block of ice will spread out and form a puddle (i.e. become less orderly) as it melts, gas released from a bottle will tend to disperse in a room, and our bodies wear out as we get older. Entropy means that things tend to get messier and more chaotic, and systems run down. The result of this second law is that the universe is gradually running down, as its energy is used up and dissipated. Therefore, the universe cannot be eternal, for if it were infinitely old, it would have already used up all its energy and suffered heat death, the Big Freeze. Instead, the universe is like an old-fashioned pocket-watch, which although running down, is thankfully still ticking, and if it is running down, it must have once been wound up. It must have had a beginning.

By the way, despite some experimental successes, there are also many problems and unanswered questions with the Big Bang theory[6].

---

[6] Only 5% of the matter and energy in the universe can be scientifically detected. Nearly two-thirds of the universe is supposedly made up of 'dark energy' and another one quarter

Nevertheless, the observational evidence seems to suggest an expanding universe, a fact which the Bible also repeatedly mentions[7], and a beginning for the universe is also confirmed by the first and second laws of thermodynamics. Not only does observational evidence indicate a beginning of the universe, but all current scientific theories about the universe demand a beginning too[8]. Therefore, just on scientific terms, a creation event is required. This, in turn, points directly to the existence of a Creator.

Robert Jastrow, the Director of NASA's Goddard Institute for Space Studies, and himself an agnostic, writing in the *New York Times*, asked 'Have Astronomers Found God?' He concluded that the evidence for a universe with a beginning comes very close to providing a scientific demonstration that God exists:

'This is an exceedingly strange development, unexpected by all but the

---

is made up of 'dark matter', both 'dark' because they are invisible and not empirically detectable (despite being all around us), but required by the standard Big Bang theory. As someone put it, 'you cannot invoke two Fairy Godmothers'. Calling upon one mysterious factor (dark energy) to make the big Bang model work is dodgy enough, but calling in a second invisible factor seems truly desperate, and similar to Einstein's 'cosmological constant' 'fudge factor'. A third 'fudge-factor', 'cosmic inflation' at faster than the speed of light – called in to fix the 'horizon problem' of temperature uniformity across the universe – has no physical mechanism to cause it or stop it. This means that the current standard Big Bang model of the origin of the universe is a triple-decker fudge cake. Another problem is increasing evidence of anomalous red-shifts in quasars, casting doubt on the red-shift expansion evidence. Finally, the Big Bang theory is built on the assumption that the universe is infinite, without boundary or centre (because in whichever direction we look the universe seems to be uniformly populated by galaxies). Either the universe is infinite, or we occupy a special place near the centre of the universe. The assumption of an infinite universe is a philosophical prejudice against humanity occupying a special place. But it contradicts the theory itself, for the universe expanded from a point in space smaller than your little finger (i.e. not an infinite space), nor are there actual infinites in nature (e.g. the grains of sand on the world's seashores are not infinite, neither are the stars). Without this assumption, the standard Big Bang model turns out quite different.

[7] No less than ten Bible verses speak of God who 'stretched out the heavens'; see Ps. 104:2, Isa. 40:22, 42:5, 44:24, 45:12, 48:13, 51:13, Jer. 10:12, 51:15, Zech. 12:1.

[8] Lisa Grossman, "Death of the eternal cosmos … every model of the universe has a beginning", *New Scientist* 213(2847), 14 January 2012, pp.6-7.

theologians ... We scientists did not expect to find evidence for an abrupt beginning because we have had until recently such extraordinary success in tracing the chain of cause and effect backward in time ... At this moment it seems as though science will never be able to raise the curtain on the mystery of creation. For the scientist who has lived by his faith in the power of reason, the story ends like a bad dream. He has scaled the mountains of ignorance; he is about to conquer the highest peak; as he pulls himself over the final rock, he is greeted by a band of theologians who have been sitting there for centuries'[9].

Einstein himself believed there was a divine intelligence behind the universe. He said, 'My religion consists of a humble admiration of the illimitable superior Spirit who reveals himself in the slight details we are able to perceive with our frail and feeble minds. That deeply emotional conviction of a superior reasoning power, which is revealed in the incomprehensible universe, forms my idea of God'[10].

Modern science is telling us the same thing as ordinary common sense has suggested to the vast majority of humanity down through time: the universe had a beginning, and creation requires a Creator, God.

Stephen Hawking: the Universe can Create Itself

What do atheist scientists say in response to the argument for God from creation? Atheist Stephen Hawking, until recently the world's most famous living scientist, argued that 'spontaneous creation is the reason there is something rather than nothing, why the Universe exists, why we exist. It is not necessary to invoke God ... to get the Universe going'. He says that 'because there is a law of gravity, the Universe can and will create itself from nothing'[11].

However, Hawking's argument has several glaring logical flaws. He first says that the Universe created itself spontaneously. But how is it

[9] Robert Jastrow, "Have Astronomers Found God?" *New York Times*, 25 June, 1978
[10] L. Barnett, *The Universe and Dr. Einstein*, William Morrow and Company, 1957, p.95
[11] Stephen Hawking, *The Grand Design*, Bantam, 2010, p.180

possible for the universe to create itself? To repeat, can a woman give birth to herself, and be her own mother? Hawking's first statement is absurd. Then, second, Hawking contradicts his first statement (the universe created itself) by saying that the law of gravity created the universe. But this introduces problem three: where did gravity, or all the other laws of physics, come from?

Hawking's statement seems so illogical and self-contradictory that readers might think I am trying to make fun of atheism by inventing this argument and falsely attributing it to Hawking. But, no, Hawking actually wrote this in an attempt to explain, as an atheist, how he believes the universe can come into being without God.

Oxford Professor Peter Atkins also argues that the universe created itself out of nothing. He writes that 'space-time generates its own dust in the process of its own self-assembly'[12]. To re-phrase, the universe made itself in the process of making itself. Atkins calls this his 'Cosmic Bootstrap' principle. That is, the universe made itself in the same way as a man sitting on a chair might lift himself off the ground by pulling on his bootstraps or like a man might stop himself from drowning in a swamp by pulling on his own hair. Atkins argues that the universe is 'an elaborate and engaging rearrangement of nothing'.

Oxford Professor John Lennox's conclusion applies equally to Hawking and Atkins: 'what this all goes to show is that nonsense remains nonsense, even when talked by world-famous scientists'[13].

If Hawking and Atkins were not famous scientists, ordinary readers might be forgiven for thinking that they were comedians. But no – these famous scientists really wrote this stuff. They are showing the desperate lengths that atheists must go to try to answer the question of where everything came from if there is no God.

How to Get Something from Nothing

In 2012, Richard Dawkins was involved in a debate with Catholic Cardinal George Pell on the Australian Broadcasting Corporation's

---

[12] Peter Atkins, *Creation Revisited*, Penguin, 1994, p.143
[13] John Lennox, *God and Stephen Hawking*, Lion Hudson, 2011, p.32

Q&A program. On the show, Dawkins claimed it is possible to get something from nothing. Here is an excerpt from the transcript of their interchange[14]:

> Dawkins: Well, something can come from nothing and that is what physicists are now telling us. I could give you – you asked me to give you a layman's interpretation. It would be very, very layman's interpretation. When you have matter and antimatter and you put them together, they cancel each other out and give rise to nothing. What Lawrence Krauss is now suggesting is that if you start with nothing the process can go into reverse and produce matter and antimatter. The theory is still being worked out …
>
> Pell: What he [Krauss] says is [that] … nothing is a sort of mixture of particles and perhaps a vacuum with electromagnetic forces working on it. That's what Krauss is talking about under the heading of nothing …
>
> Dawkins: You can dispute exactly what is meant by nothing but whatever it is it's very, very simple.
>
> (*Audience laugh*)
>
> Dawkins: Why is that funny?
>
> Pell: Well, I think it's a bit funny to be trying to define 'nothing'.

Dawkins was referring to physicist Lawrence Krauss' book, *A Universe From Nothing: Why There Is Something Rather Than Nothing*. Dawkins himself wrote glowingly in the Afterword: 'The title means exactly what it says. And what it says is devastating'[15]. In fact, Dawkins praised this book for being as important for physics as Darwin's *Origin of the Species* was for biology.

Krauss says that the universe sprung into existence from a quantum field, but quantum fields are not nothing. In fact, quantum fields require lots of things: space, a quantum vacuum (which is not the same thing as absolute nothing), laws of nature, time (for the equations of quantum

---

[14] https://www.abc.net.au/qanda/religion-and-atheism/10661470

[15] 'Richard Dawkins, 'Afterword', to Lawrence Krauss, *A Universe From Nothing*, Free Press, 2012, p.191

physics to work), in addition to a multiverse (in Krauss' account). It turns out, then, that when Krauss says he can explain how to get something from nothing, 'nothing' turns out to be 'some very important things', rather than absolutely nothing.

Atheist philosopher and physicist David Albert, reviewing Krauss' book in the *New York Times*, writes:

> The fact that some arrangements of fields happen to correspond to the existence of particles and some don't is not a whit more mysterious than the fact that some of the possible arrangements of my fingers happen to correspond to the existence of a fist and some don't. And the fact that particles can pop in and out of existence, over time, as those fields rearrange themselves, is not a whit more mysterious than the fact that fists can pop in and out of existence, over time, as my fingers rearrange themselves. And none of these poppings — if you look at them aright — amount to anything even remotely in the neighborhood of a creation from nothing'[16].

The question Krauss does not answer is this: where do the particles, and the fields in which they are arranged, and the laws that govern these fields, and time itself, come from?

Krauss spends five pages towards the end of the book (pp174-178) explaining how his idea works. Here is a taste of his theory, from the final paragraph of that section:

> 'Something may always come from nothing. It may be required, independent of the underlying nature of reality. Or perhaps something may not be very special or even very common in the multiverse'.

Is this how to create a universe? Is this the 'devastating' explanation Dawkins was referring to? There are a lot of maybes and perhaps, but the one thing that is certain is that Krauss hasn't told us how the universe

---

[16] David Albert, "On the Origin of Everything", *New York Times*, March 23, 2012

created itself from nothing.

Krauss thus offers us a book with no real explanation for how the universe came into existence, or how to get something from nothing. Sadly you can't magic up your own copy of the book for nothing – you have to pay $24.99! Krauss' book is truly devastating, as Dawkins says – but only for the reputation of people who have attached their names to such claims.

Agnostic physicist Marcelo Gleiser, winner of the 2019 Templeton prize said in *Scientific American*, 'I get upset by misstatements, like when you have scientists—Stephen Hawking and Lawrence Krauss among them—claiming we have solved the problem of the origin of the universe, or that string theory is correct and that the final "theory of everything" is at hand. Such statements are bogus'[17].

If you have managed to read this far, congratulations! Even if you did not understand all the scientific details, I hope you got some comedy value out of watching all the contortions and contradictions involved in explaining how the universe created itself from nothing.

The Cosmic Cop-Out

Some atheists reply to the argument from creation by quoting Bertrand Russell, who said, 'the Universe just is'. However, this answer is irrational. The atheist philosopher Kai Nielsen writes: 'Suppose you suddenly hear a loud bang … and you ask me, "What caused that bang?" And I reply, "Nothing, it just happened". You would not accept that. In fact, you would find my reply unintelligible'[18].

Now, let's substitute 'Big Bang' (if we may) for Nielsen's 'loud bang' and see if it makes any more sense. Bertrand Russell's argument that there was no cause for the universe is unintelligible. In fact, the claim that the universe 'just is' does not even contain an argument – it is just a bald assertion. It is simply a debating trick, an atheist bluff. Russell is

---

[17] "Atheism Is Inconsistent with the Scientific Method, Prizewinning Physicist Says", *Scientific American*, www.scientificamerican.com/article/atheism-is-inconsistent-with-the-scientific-method-prizewinning-physicist-says/, March 20, 2019

[18] Kai Nielsen, *Reason and Practice: A Modern Introduction to Philosophy*, Harper and Row, 1971, p.48

dodging the question because his atheism cannot handle it. Richard Dawkins once complained of religion as 'the great cop-out, the great excuse to evade the need to think and evaluate evidence'. This describes what Bertrand Russell is doing here; by arguing that we do not need an explanation for the most important question of our existence – where everything came from. Dawkins also said, 'I am against religion because it teaches us to be satisfied with not understanding the world'. Bertrand Russell is perfectly satisfied with having no explanation for the fundamental fact of our physical existence, the universe – exactly what his fellow atheist finds objectionable.

Some atheists have argued that to suggest a cause for the universe is wrong-headed because time itself began with the start of the universe. Therefore, there was nothing in existence before the universe to create it. Stephen Hawking used the analogy of explorers trying to go further south than the South Pole. He argued that as we cannot go back past the beginning of universe, the universe 'just is'. However, we have already seen that the cause of the universe does not (and cannot) exist in time. It therefore must be outside time (i.e. eternal), as well as sufficiently powerful to create it: God. Since the idea that the universe came into existence without any cause is unreasonable, we must identify some cause for it that is beyond itself (and therefore beyond the dimension of time). The answer, if we may refashion Hawking's analogy, is that while Arctic explorers are not able to go further north than the North Pole, there is nothing to stop them (in principle) blasting off in a rocket towards the North Star if they wish. Similarly, the answer to the cause of the universe (God) must exist in a completely different 'dimension' to the universe and time itself.

This atheist objection mixes apples and oranges by confusing two very different things: the cause of the universe and time before the universe. It also (again) insists that there is no cause for the universe – an irrational position. It is just a more sophisticated version of Bertrand Russell's cosmic cop-out.

Conclusion

I started this chapter off with a joke about the Big Bang, but there is another joke I like even more. Here it is: an atheist is someone who believes that nothing made everything (Ray Comfort). The joke is teaching a self-evident truth: the universe requires a cause, a creator.

Creation is a powerful argument for God's existence. On a scale of 0 to 10, I rate it at 9. The reason it is not 10 is because science does not offer us final, mathematical proofs, for new evidence may emerge.

Both the ideas of (a) an eternal universe without beginning, and (b) a universe that made itself defy scientific fact, common sense and sound logic. If the universe made itself, there would surely be other things that could also just 'pop' into existence from nothing – more trivial and less gargantuan things than the universe – like books or bananas or teddy bears. It seems that, to atheists like Dawkins, Hawking, Atkins and Krauss, it is just a matter of believing hard enough and it becomes possible for universes (and other wonderful things) to magic themselves into existence out of thin air. But ordinary people with experience of the real world, and more than an ounce of common sense, do not believe this.

In the Bible, the apostle Paul writes that all people everywhere are aware of God's existence (even those who wish to suppress this knowledge) because of the world's creation: 'Because what may be known of God is clear to them, for God has shown it to them. For from the creation of the world His invisible attributes are clearly seen, being understood by the things that are made, even His eternal power and Godhead, so that they are without excuse'[19].

But what sort of God are we faced with, if He created the universe? To understand what creation tells us about God, we need to remember

---

[19] Romans 1:19-20, author's translation.

that at creation, not only did matter and energy come into existence, but also space, time and all the physical laws that govern the universe. None of these things existed before creation. It is impossible to have matter without space to put it in, and it is impossible to have matter and space without laws of nature to govern them, and it is impossible to have all these things existing without the clock of time starting to tick. Therefore, if God is the creator, He is outside creation. He is not made of the 'stuff' that makes up the universe – matter or energy. Otherwise He would be part of creation, rather than the Creator. God is thus non-material, that is, spiritual. Further, the God who created time is outside and beyond time – He is eternal. God is also, as the Creator of the laws of nature, superior to and beyond these same laws – He is supernatural.

Dinesh D'Souza puts it this way: 'As the universe was produced by a creative act, it is reasonable to infer that it was produced by some sort of mind. Mind is the origin of matter, and it is mind that produced matter, rather than the other way around. As the universe comprises the totality of nature, containing everything that is natural, its creator must necessarily be outside nature. As the creator used no natural laws or forces to create the universe, the creator is clearly supernatural. As space and time are within the universe, the creator is also outside space and time, which is to say, eternal. As the universe is material, the creator is immaterial, which is to say, spiritual. As the universe was created from nothing, the creator is incomprehensibly powerful or, as best as we can tell, omnipotent'[20].

---

[20] Dinesh D'Souza, *What's So Great about Christianity*, Tyndale House, p.128

Chapter 3

The Socrates Argument: It's Staring You in the Face

The ancient Greek philosopher Socrates (c. 469-399 BC) was the son of a stonemason and served as a foot soldier in the Athenian army during the wars against Sparta. Despite his humble background, Socrates is considered one of the great thinkers in the history of the world. He was the teacher of Plato, who was, in turn, the teacher of Aristotle, two of the great 'founding fathers' of Greek philosophy and Western civilization.

Socrates was famous for two things. First, he had a brilliant mind and second, he had an ugly face, with bulging eyes, a stubby nose and fat lips. Socrates seems to have spent his time mostly talking to people in the marketplace, encouraging critical thinking. His policy was to question everything and to follow the evidence wherever it leads. Instead of telling others what to think, like a normal teacher, he instead used questions to help people to understand matters for themselves. He cast doubt on traditional opinions and annoyed people by showing up flaws in their thinking. He compared himself to a gadfly that stings a sluggish horse, stirring it into action.

Socrates was brought before the Athenian council, who accused him of not believing in the Athenian city-state's gods and of corrupting the youth with his atheistic teachings. He was condemned to death for his 'atheism' and forced to drink the poison hemlock. It is probably true that Socrates did not believe in the gods of Greek mythology. He argued that while the gods cannot lie or commit wicked deeds, the gods of Greek mythology were guilty of all sorts of sins and crimes. On the other hand, it is clear that Socrates believed in some sort of god or gods.

Socrates and Design

Socrates argued that human beings are obviously designed by a Creator because of the position of our eyes and nose directly above our mouth to prevent that which is unacceptable for consumption.

This is one of the best one-line arguments for the existence of God in the history of the world. He also added this zinger: the parts of our body that eliminate waste are as far away as possible from the organs of smell, sight and taste.

Socrates' reasoning is simple, powerful, and staring us right in the face. Our mouth, eyes and nose seem to be intelligently positioned in exactly the right place, above each other, to enable us to inspect and accept (or reject) our food before we put it in our mouth. Did all these body parts accidentally take their correct position, or gradually acquire them? It would seem unlikely. Imagine if our organs had been placed in the body randomly. If that were the case, there might be eyeballs under our armpits, so that we had to lift our hands if we wanted to see.

Socrates' argument is all about coordination. Imagine if a man went to a second-hand furniture store and randomly chose any six items of furniture, took them home and put them in the lounge room. He would probably get a serious telling-off from his wife. We like our lounge room furniture to have matching colours, fabrics, styles, and to be in the right place. It is not good to have colours that clash, styles from different eras, or to have inappropriate pieces of furniture in the wrong place (like bunk-beds in the lounge). Part of being a good interior designer is knowing how to get things to match each other. Socrates' argument from coordination states that everything on our face matches and balances perfectly, and is in the right place. This, Socrates argues, is because we are the products of wisdom. We have been designed.

We have about a dozen different anatomical systems all coordinating perfectly on our faces: a visual system, a digestive system, an olfactory (smelling) system, a breathing system (which we need to smell), a taste system, a skeletal system (our hinged jaws which open and shut), a muscular system (allowing movement of our mouth), a skin system (with openings in the right places), an excretory (waste-disposal) system at the other end, and a nervous system connecting them all to the brain. Let's not forget other systems running in the background, like the cardiovascular system (blood circulation) and immune system (defending against harmful diseases). We even get a sound system (speaking and hearing) thrown in for free, and it would be hard to eat without our two arms with hinged elbow joints halfway down allowing us to bring food right to our mouths.

Socrates' argument is not so much about how each of the different systems works on its own, or how all these biological engineering marvels arose. His argument is much simpler and even more powerful. Socrates asks how it all came to be in the right place, each separate piece working together with the others. How do all the independent parts coordinate together without design?

Here is the entire passage in which Socrates argued that man has been specially designed by a Creator, as related by Socrates' student Xenophon:

'When Socrates noticed that Aristodemus the dwarf, as he was called, did not use prayer or divination and mocked those who did, Socrates asked him if he admired any human beings for their wisdom. Aristodemus named Homer, Sophocles, and the outstanding sculptor and painter of his time. Socrates asked him to compare the phantoms they created to living, intelligent, and active beings. Although he admired living beings more by far, he assumed that they were created by chance. Socrates asked if the creatures that serve a useful purpose were more likely to be the result of chance or design. He then pointed out how various aspects of man are useful in specific ways. We have senses to perceive – eyes to see visible objects, ears to hear sounds. What value would odours have if we could not smell with our nostrils? Similarly with tastes, what if we had no tongue to discriminate sweet from bitter and others? The eyeballs, being soft, are protected behind eyelids which open and close like doors, so we can see or sleep. Eyelashes filter the winds, and eyebrows keep forehead perspiration from falling in the eyes. The ears catch all sounds, but they are not choked with them. The front teeth are adapted to biting off, while the molars can do the grinding and chewing. The mouth is conveniently placed next to the nostrils and eyes, but the ducts of elimination which release the unpleasant matter are placed far away from the senses. Aristodemus was beginning to see the handiwork of a wise and loving creator' (Xenophon. *Memorabilia*. I, iv, 2-7).

. . .

'To show that man has special favor from the gods, Socrates delineated how man is the only creature to stand upright with a wide range of vision; we are endowed with hands, which are particularly useful, and with a tongue, which can articulate the voice and express our wishes to each other. Sex is not limited by a certain season [as in animals] but only by old age. Man has the noblest soul, which can understand the gods who set in order the universe; only humans worship the gods. Man provides against hunger and thirst, cold and heat, relieves sickness and promotes health, acquires knowledge by work, and remembers accurately all that is heard, seen, or learned. Compared to other animals, people live like gods, by nature without equal in body or soul. The gods have given man the two most precious gifts; reason for the soul and hands for the body' (Xenophon, *Memorabilia*. I, iv, 10-14).

There are many interesting observations and arguments that Socrates makes in these paragraphs. Man has been specially blessed by the gods, and is quite unlike the animals, having been given unique gifts both physical and mental. In this, Socrates echoes the Bible's opening page which declares that man was made in the image of God.

Here, then, is another piece of evidence for God's existence: every time you look at your face in the mirror you can see evidence of wisdom and design. Because design demands a Designer, you are therefore evidence for God's existence.

Other Ancient Thinkers on Design

As we saw in an earlier chapter, from a very early age, children hold the belief that living creatures have been designed for a purpose. This is a deep-seated reaction to the beauty and brilliance of nature.

The argument from design is different from the argument from creation. Just as a house cannot build itself – it needs a builder – so too, good houses need an architect who decides where everything is to be placed so that it fulfills its purpose in the best possible way. It would hardly do to have the kitchen, or bathroom, in the main entrance hallway of the house.

With design, the question is not why there is something rather than nothing. Instead, the question is why our universe is so brilliant and beautiful in the way it has been put together. While creation shows God's power (creating it from nothing), design displays the wisdom of God.

The argument from design is an intuitive, common-sense reaction to the marvelous mechanisms we see in nature. We could mention many ancient thinkers who argued that God must exist from the evidence of design in nature, but in this chapter we will focus on three.

Cicero

The Roman statesman Cicero (106 – 43 BC) was a lawyer, senator, and the greatest orator and philosopher of ancient Rome. He lived through the turbulent times of Julius Caesar and was eventually executed by his political enemies. In addition to a busy legal and political career, he also managed to write many books on a wide variety of matters, and by his elevated style of Latin, he is said to have created the language of the civilized world. Julius Caesar praised him by saying, 'it is more important to have greatly extended the frontiers of Roman genius than the frontiers of the Roman empire'.

Cicero argued at various places against the ancient philosophy of Epicurus (341-270 BC), who taught, among other things, that everything formed itself by chance collisions of particles, even the world in all its beauty.

Cicero, by contrast, argued that we are designed by God and that Epicurus' ideas were as unbelievable as the suggestion that if we threw the letters of the alphabet on the ground repeatedly they would eventually spell out the *Annals of Ennius*, the ancient Roman equivalent of Shakespeare's plays.

Cicero's analogy is amazingly up-to-date in view of the fact that modern science has discovered that the DNA molecule at the heart of all life is a digital code made up of chemical 'letters' which spell out the software instructions of life, and these 'letters' have to be in the correct order for the organism to survive and thrive.

Cicero further argued against the accumulated lucky coincidences of chance as the cause of all things by pointing out that if they could make the greatest things in the world, and indeed the whole world itself, then why could they not make much simpler things like a colonnade, a temple, a house, or a city – which everybody agrees were designed?[1]

In addition to arguing that the orderly regularity of the starry heavens could not have been created by random chance but by intelligence of a high order, Cicero argued for design in the plant and animal kingdoms:

'To come now from things heavenly to things earthly, which is there among these latter which does not clearly display the rational design of an intelligent being? In the first place, with the vegetation that springs from the earth, the stocks both give stability to the parts which they sustain and draw from the ground the sap to nourish the parts upheld by the roots; and the trunks are covered with bark or rind, the better to protect them against cold and heat. Again the vines cling to their props with their tendrils as with hands, and thus raise themselves erect like animals....'

We could add to Cicero's observations that not only do trees support their own weight, but they support us by providing oxygen to breathe, food to eat, and the most amazing building material known to man – wood: strong, durable, able to be cut and shaped to the size we want,

---

[1] Cicero, *On the Nature of the Gods*, Book II, chapter 93.

plentiful on earth, and with a naturally replenishing supply. Cicero goes on to speak about animals:

> 'Again what a variety there is of animals, and what capacity they possess of persisting true to their various kinds! Some of them are protected by hides, others are clothed with fleeces, others bristle with spines; some we see covered with feathers, some with scales, some armed with horns, some equipped with wings to escape their foes. Nature, however, has provided with bounteous plenty for each species of animal that food which is suited for it. I might show in detail what provision has been made in the forms of the animals for appropriating and assimilating this food, how skillful and exact is the disposition of the various parts, how marvelous the structure of the limbs. For all the organs, at least those contained within the body, are so formed and so placed that none of them is superfluous or not necessary for the preservation of life'[2].

Plutarch

The first-century Greek historian Plutarch likewise argued we are designed. Here is what he says in his essay, *On Chance*:

> 'But can it be that those things which are most important and most essential for happiness do not call for intelligence, nor have any part in the processes of reason and forethought? Nobody wets clay with water and leaves it, assuming that by chance and accidentally there will be bricks, nor after providing himself with wool and leather does he sit down with a prayer to Chance that they turn into a cloak and shoes for him'[3].

Plutarch's argument is again simple yet powerful. Shoes, though basic items of human technology, do not build themselves from leather and string, but require a designer. Shoes are so simple that old-fashioned

---

[2] Cicero, *On the Nature of the Gods*, Book II, chapters 44 and 47.
[3] Plutarch, "On Chance" in *Moralia*, Book 2.

shoemakers were considered one of the lowliest of tradesmen. Is it therefore possible that while the humble shoe requires a designer, the foot does not?

The foot is made up of 26 separate bones giving it structure and strength, more than 20 different muscles in four layers pulling in different directions, nerves which relay electrical impulses causing the muscles to contract and which transmit important sensory feedback to the brain, and fatty cushions positioned under the heel and ball for comfort. It forms a rigid yet flexible arch, enabling humans (alone among the 400 different types of mammals) to walk upright on two feet. The foot is of infinitely greater engineering brilliance than a humble shoe. The human foot's arch, rigid and yet also flexible, acts as a spring and enables us to balance, absorb shock and propel ourselves forward, allowing us to walk most efficiently. Did the foot just happen, by an accumulation of lucky accidents, to build itself over time, or was it designed? Plutarch opted for design.

Minucius Felix

The Roman Christian writer Minucius Felix (3rd century AD), in his dialogue *Octavius* argued the case for design as follows:

> 'If upon entering some home you saw that everything there was well-tended, neat and decorative, you would believe that some master was in charge of it, and that he was himself much superior to those good things. So, too, in the home of this world, when you see providence, order and law in the heavens and on earth, believe that there is a Lord and Author of the Universe, more beautiful than the stars and the various parts of the whole world'.

We will run into Minucius Felix's argument in another form in the next chapter when we see how modern science has been accumulating powerful evidence which demonstrates that the universe and our 'home' planet Earth have too many amazing coincidences to be the result of random chance, but are instead designed for human life.

Atheist Counter-Arguments

There are three responses atheists give to the argument from design:

1. Evolution explains biological design,
2. If God designed the world, who designed God?
3. Suffering and poor design argue against God as the designer.

We will mention all three briefly here, and deal with them in more detail in Part Three of the book. Virtually everyone, including most atheists, agree that the world appears designed. Richard Dawkins has written that 'Biology is the study of complicated things that give the appearance of having been designed for a purpose'[4]. So overwhelming is the appearance of design that Francis Crick, co-discover of the structure of DNA, has written, 'Biologists must constantly keep in mind that what they see was not designed, but rather evolved'[5].

Both Dawkins and Crick argue that the appearance of design in nature is just an illusion, a trick being played on our minds. Evolution is the true explanation for all the appearance of design we see in nature, not God.

Atheists tend to argue that we should nevertheless respect the great thinkers down through history like Socrates and Cicero. These people were giants in their own time. Their only misfortune was to live before Charles Darwin's great scientific breakthrough which explained how natural selection produced all the wonderful forms of life on earth.

Ancient thinkers produced different versions of 'design' arguments to prove the existence of God. However, they primarily relied on logical reasoning and intuitive common-sense rather than mathematical or scientific proofs. Atheists rightly point out that we cannot be content with such arguments any longer, seeing we live in an age of scientific exploration, which has unlocked many of nature's secrets and enabled us to understand what is really going on. This is the first atheist response to

---

[4] Richard Dawkins, *The Blind Watchmaker*, W.W. Norton & Company, 1986, p.1.
[5] Francis Crick, *What Mad Pursuit: A Personal View of Scientific Discovery*, Basic Books, 1988, p.138

the design argument: Darwinian evolution has shown that there is no need for a divine designer for life.

However, two lines of evidence converge to make this response increasingly inadequate. Firstly, surprising results of scientific discovery in the field of physics have uncovered powerful evidence that points to the universe itself being designed. In addition, in the field of biochemistry, at the microscopic level, amazing new evidence suggests that the living cell was designed. We will look at these arguments in the next few chapters. However, if the largest structure in existence (the universe) and the smallest living structure (the cell) show tell-tale evidence of design, it becomes more probable that living creatures in the amazing biosphere between these extremes were also designed.

As Antony Flew, one of the most prominent atheists of the 20th century (who renounced his atheism in 2004) argued: 'I myself think it obvious that if this argument (design) is applicable to the world of physics then it must be hugely more powerful if it is applied to the immeasurably more complicated world of biology'[6].

Further, if the argument from Creation in the previous chapter is correct, and God created the universe, the design we see in it is real, not an illusion. The fact that the universe had a beginning, and was therefore created by something outside nature (time, space, matter, energy, laws), i.e. a supernatural, eternal, all-powerful Creator, this means that the design argument is probably true by default. Whether the Creator designed merely the laws of nature which would allow life to appear, or whether He designed the actual creatures makes little difference to this argument. The creation of the universe not only demands a builder – it also suggests a designing architect. Creation implies a Designer.

There are two possible alternatives to this. First, if the universe was the result of an accidental, unplanned explosion with no purpose, i.e. as the result of a 'mindless' cause (e.g. an unknown, out-of-control 'force'), or secondly, as a result of a 'blunder' on the part of its creator, then we might say there is no design or purpose or plan behind the creation of the

---

[6] Antony Flew's review of Dawkin's book, *The God Delusion*, https://www.firstthings.com/article/2008/12/001-documentation-a-reply-to-richard-dawkins

universe. However, these last two options seem very unlikely once we stand back and observe the majesty of the universe: the glory of its spiral galaxies, the brilliance of the exactly-calibrated laws of nature that govern it, the beauty of biological life-forms flying and swimming, running and growing, and above all, the miracle of human minds able in some small measure to explore and comprehend it. This universe is no heap of junk or chaotic mess. Its laws show evidence of great intelligence; its structure is marvelous beyond any human architect's imagination.

Here is how Albert Einstein described the orderly intelligence seen in the universe:

'I am not an Atheist. I do not know if I can define myself as a Pantheist. The problem involved is too vast for our limited minds. May I not reply with a parable? The human mind, no matter how highly trained, cannot grasp the universe. We are in the position of a little child, entering a huge library whose walls are covered to the ceiling with books in many different tongues. The child knows that someone must have written those books. It does not know who or how. It does not understand the languages in which they are written. The child notes a definite plan in the arrangement of the books, a mysterious order, which it does not comprehend, but only dimly suspects. That, it seems to me, is the attitude of the human mind, even the greatest and most cultured, toward God. We see a universe marvelously arranged, obeying certain laws, but we understand the laws only dimly. Our limited minds cannot grasp the mysterious force that sways the constellations'[7].

The second atheist counter-argument to design is this: Who designed the Designer? Richard Dawkins uses this counter-argument nine times in his book *The God Delusion*. The repeated invocation is an admission of the increasing appeal of the design argument at the largest and smallest levels – of the universe and the living cell – in the spheres of physics and biochemistry. Dawkins cannot explain away design in these non-

---

[7] George S. Viereck, *Glimpses of the Great*, 1930, Macauley, 1930, pp.372-3

biological areas by invoking Darwinian evolution. As a result, atheists are forced to repeatedly fall back on a secondary line of defense with the question, Who designed the Designer?

This counter-argument is just a variant form of the question, Who made God? We will look at this question in more detail in Part Three of the book, where we will see that there are plenty of good answers.

The third atheist counter-argument is the oldest of all: if God designed the world, why are there bad things in it? This is the argument from suffering and evil, and it is without doubt the most powerful argument atheists have. We will look at it in more detail in its own chapter in Part Three of the book.

Another variant form of this argument points to examples of poor design in nature as proof that there is no God. If God is all-wise, so the argument goes, His designs cannot be other than perfect. However, this reasoning is false. Does the fact that the famous Venus de Milo statue in the Louvre has had its arms broken off prove that it was never designed? Of course not. Or does the fact that humans cannot fly like birds (which would make us perfect, or at least better than we are now) prove that humans were not designed? Again no. In fact, some so-called design 'imperfections' may represent nothing more than our ignorance of their true design purpose. There have been many motor cars over the last century, but the fact that some go slower than others, and the fact that many have had accident damage, do not prove that they were not designed. Not all cars were designed to be racing cars, and the manufacturer is not to blame for the poor driving abilities of some motorists, or for the fact that cars eventually wear out or break down.

Conclusion

This chapter is a bit like the first chapter of the book, the argument from intuition. The argument from design, as presented by ancient thinkers like Socrates, presents intuitive, common-sense evidence of design in nature. Just like the first chapter, at the moment we can only say that this evidence from design is suggestive but far from conclusive. We would have to rate it at a level of about five out of ten.

0 (atheism)   (God exists) **10**

5

▲

Argument from Design

Atheists might reply that this vastly over-rates the argument from design, because the fact of biological evolution shows that the intuition of design is nothing more than an illusion based on pre-scientific ignorance. Atheists might rate the argument from design at 1 or 2 out of 10, or even lower if they are feeling ungenerous.

But before any atheists throw this book at the wall in disgust, let me remind everyone that the subject of design is a highly controversial flashpoint in debates over God today. I am not using the ancient intuitions of Socrates or Cicero to decisively settle the issue. Instead, I am using the wisdom of ancient thinkers to open up the question of design in nature. Over the next few chapters, we are going to explore in more detail some of the modern evidence for design, from the fine-tuning of the universe, the living cell, and other biological structures.

The big question that we have to answer is this: does the up-to-date evidence we are going to explore in the next few chapters swing the pendulum strongly in favour of design, or are there good atheist counter-arguments that disprove design? Were the wisest and most down-to-earth people (like Socrates) simply able to see the evidence staring them in the face, and some clever people today are making elaborate excuses to evade the obvious, blinded by their atheism? Or do many people who still live in superstition and ignorance need to be set free from religion, because design in nature is an illusion? Is there really a God, the Mastermind of creation, or is God a delusion? The next few chapters will help us answer these questions.

Chapter 4

The Sir Fred Hoyle Argument: Fine-Tuning

Sir Fred Hoyle was one of the most important British mathematicians and astronomers of the 20th century. He established the concept of nucleosynthesis in stars (the formation of chemical elements within stars by the fusion of other elements), and his prediction that the Carbon-12 nucleus would have a certain energy level to enable helium to undergo fusion earned his co-worker William Fowler (and Subrahmanyan Chandrasekhar) the Nobel Prize for Physics in 1983. To the surprise of many, Hoyle himself was not awarded the Nobel prize. The reason why Hoyle missed out is not certain but was probably because he did not subscribe to the idea of the 'Big Bang' (he coined the phrase, in mockery, instead preferring a Steady-State model where the universe had no beginning) and because he considered a naturalistic origin of life a mathematical impossibility.

Hoyle was an atheist, but his scientific discoveries added to a growing realization in physics, often described by the term 'Fine-Tuning'. Over the last century, physicists have been gathering evidence of a designing intelligence behind the universe at large. Sir Fred Hoyle described it best:

'A common sense interpretation of the facts suggests that a super-intellect has monkeyed with physics, as well as with chemistry and biology, and that there are no blind forces worth speaking about in nature. The numbers one calculates from the facts seem to me so overwhelming as to put this conclusion almost beyond question'[1].

Agnostic physicist Paul Davies described it like this:

---

[1] Fred Hoyle, "The Universe: Past and Present Reflections", *Engineering and Science*, Nov 1981, pp.8-12

'Scientists are slowly waking up to an inconvenient truth – the universe looks suspiciously like a fix. The issue concerns the very laws of nature themselves. For 40 years, physicists and cosmologists have been quietly collecting examples of all too convenient 'coincidences' and special features in the underlying laws of the universe that seem to be necessary in order for life, and hence conscious beings, to exist. Change any one of them and the consequences would be lethal'[2].

Just imagine an old-fashioned radio with a tuning knob, which allowed you to find a radio station's frequency, as well as another knob which allowed you to fine-tune the radio so that the sound came through clearly. This is how scientists today refer to the fact that everything in the universe is set within a very narrow range of values, not only to permit life to exist, but for the universe itself to exist.

Simple Evidences of Fine-Tuning

Before we look at some of the more complex and technical scientific evidences of fine-tuning, here are ten obvious evidences of things set up 'just right' for life on earth.

1. We need the sun for life to exist on earth. But planet Earth must also be the right distance from the sun. The result is that the Earth is neither too hot nor cold. Earth also has a near-circular orbit, again ensuring that we neither freeze nor fry. We therefore have liquid water and a stable water cycle essential for life. 'The sun is at just the right distance to ripen tomatoes' (Ray Comfort). If we compare Earth with Venus (the next planet closest to the sun) and Mars (the next planet further away from the sun), we see the following:

---

[2] Paul Davies, "Yes, the universe looks like a fix. But that doesn't mean that a god fixed it", *Guardian*, June 26th, 2007

Planet	Venus	Earth	Mars
Distance to sun	107 million km	150 million km	228 million km
Average temp.	462 C	14 C	-60 C

It is easy to see what would happen if Earth was closer to the sun or further away: all water would boil off (because Earth's temperature went over 100 degrees Celsius) or freeze (because it went under 0 degrees Celsius). If Earth were 5% closer or 20% further away from the sun, life on Earth would not exist. Out of all the possible distances for planets from the sun, which range from 58 million km (Mercury) to 4497 million km (Neptune), Earth's orbit must fall between 142 million km and 180 million km from the sun (a 0.85% range). If Earth was anywhere else outside this narrow ~1% range, the change in temperature would be far more devastating than the 2 degrees of climate change that many scientists today predict will be catastrophic for life on earth.

2. Earth's atmosphere protects us from deadly radiation. Remember the ozone layer being depleted in the 1980s? Certain manmade chemicals pumped into the atmosphere are able to damage the ozone layer, increasing harmful UV light. This, in turn, can increase incidence of skin cancer and cause other problems. These chemicals were banned once the damage they were doing to the ozone layer was discovered. Earth's atmosphere also contains exactly the right combination of gases (78% nitrogen, 21% oxygen, 0.04% carbon dioxide) which not only allow life to exist but also are colourless and so allow clear skies that we may explore the universe.

3. Large outer planets like Jupiter and Saturn shield small, inner planets like Earth from being bombarded by too many comets. The gravitational pull of Jupiter and Saturn functions like a vacuum cleaner, dragging harmful comets out of our way.

4. Earth's rotation time is just right: every 24 hours the earth rotates on its axis, allowing every part of the earth to be heated and then cooled, again preventing us from extremes of freezing or frying.

5. Earth's axial tilt (23.5 degrees) provides us with temperate seasons. If earth's axial tilt was greater (e.g. 45 degrees), certain parts of the

earth's surface would be further from the sun in winter and closer in summer, leading to more extreme seasons. If there was very little axial tilt, there would be no seasons at all, and the earth's poles would not enjoy a warmer summer period at all but would get too cold.

6.   The sun and moon have the same 'apparent' size in the sky when we look at them from Earth – the sun is 400 times the size of the moon, but is also 400 times further away. This means that our planet has solar eclipses (when the moon obscures the sun), and lunar eclipses (when the earth blocks the sun's rays from shining on the moon). Solar eclipses allow us to discover important scientific facts which would otherwise be very difficult to investigate. We saw this in a previous chapter, where Einstein's theory of relativity was confirmed by evidence from a solar eclipse. Eclipses also allow astronomers to investigate the sun's outer atmosphere, which in turn allowed them to understand distant stars, opening up the science of astrophysics. It turns out that planet Earth is not just the only place for life to exist in the solar system, but also the perfect viewing platform for scientific discovery. We 'just happen' to live on a unique planet that enables intelligent life to explore the mysteries of science and the universe.

7.   The oceans cover about 71% of the earth's surface, but if the water surface of the world was much greater, we would be flooded with rain, while if it were less, we would not have enough rain to be able to grow enough food to support life. The Bible puts it this way: God has 'measured the waters in the hollow of His hand' (Isaiah 40:12).

8.   The moon is also just the right size for ocean tides which wash our shores clean, oxygenate the oceans and keep them moving. But if the moon was much bigger, or if the moon were much closer to the earth, the gravitational attraction would be greater, causing massive tidal waves to crash over the continents, destroying much life. On the other hand, if the moon were further away or smaller, the waters of the oceans would stagnate and die, with only the top few feet being able to support life.

9.   Our sun is the right mass (if larger, there would be too much high energy radiation; if smaller, planets would be closer and disrupt

rotation) and the right colour for photosynthesis (yellow, not blue or red).

10. If Earth were smaller, its gravitational pull would be weaker, and the atmosphere and the oceans would be stripped off by the sun's solar wind, leaving a barren rocky planet. On the other hand, if the Earth were larger, its gravitational pull would be stronger, and we would be bombarded by more asteroids. Earth would also be more volcanic, and stronger gravity would mean that any life forms would be shorter, heavier and slower. Earth's magnetic field, which protects us against charged particles flying through space, if weaker, would result in more cancer and damaged DNA. Either way, Earth would be inhospitable.

There are many other factors like these, each of which needs to be within a range of parameters for the existence of life on any planet in the universe. Even if we set the odds of these 'habitability' factors at just 1 in 10 (a very conservative estimate), the chances of one planet fulfilling any thirty factors are 1 in 10^{30}, that is, 1 followed by 30 zeros. Considering that there are only 100 billion (10^{11}) stars in our galaxy, we would need billions and billions of galaxies to find just one other planet that is life-permitting. In short, the odds of any planet fulfilling all of these factors are so small as to make planet Earth's habitat amazing, even miraculous. Earth is the only known life-friendly planet in existence, filled with a tremendous variety of creatures.

The Fine-Tuning of Physical Constants

In addition, there are evidences of fine-tuning at an even deeper, cosmic, level. Stephen Hawking writes:

'The laws of science, as we know them at present, contain many fundamental numbers, like the size of the electric charge of the electron and the ratio of the masses of the proton and the electron ... The remarkable fact is that the values of these numbers seem to have been very finely adjusted to make possible the development of life'[3].

Here we will give a few examples of the way the fundamental physics of the universe has been finely-tuned to precise values to permit the universe (and life) to exist.

1. If the force of gravity were too weak, stars would not be stable or hold together, while if gravity were too strong, stars would burn up their fuel too quickly. This is because gravity pulls hydrogen atoms together inside stars, causing nuclear fusion and the release of energy. The physicist Brandon Carter has shown that if the gravitational force were greater or smaller by one part in 10^{40} [1 followed by 40 zeros] then life-sustaining stars like our sun could not exist, and life would not be possible[4].

2. Electromagnetism, on the other hand, causes protons (which are positively-charged) to repel each other inside atoms, just like the two 'north' poles of a magnet. Walter Bradley writes, 'the electromagnetic force is 10^{38} times stronger than the gravity force. It is the force of gravity that draws protons together in stars, causing them to fuse together with a concurrent release of energy. The electromagnetic force causes them to repel. Because the gravity force is so weak compared to the electromagnetic force, the rate at which stars "burn" by fusion is very slow, allowing the stars to provide a stable source of energy over a very long period of time. If this ratio of strengths had been 10^{32} instead of 10^{38} (i.e. gravity were much stronger), stars would be a billion times less massive and would burn a million times faster'[5].

3. Electromagnetism and gravity must also be carefully balanced for another reason. The types of radiation produced by the sun are dependent on the balancing of these forces so that if there were too

---

[3] Stephen Hawking, *A Brief History of Time*, Bantam, 1988, p.125

[4] Paul Davies, *Superforce: the Search for a Grand Unified Theory of Nature*, Simon and Schuster, 1984, p.242

[5] Walter J. Bradley, "The Just-So Universe", *Signs of Intelligence*, ed. William A. Dembski and James M. Kushiner, Brazos, 2001, p.164

much ultraviolet radiation, then chemical bonds on earth would be destroyed and molecules would break down, making life impossible. Overbalancing the other way, if there were too much infrared radiation, then chemical reactions on earth would be too slow for life.

4. The strong nuclear force is the third of the four fundamental forces of nature (along with gravity, electromagnetism and the weak nuclear force). The strong nuclear force holds the nuclei of atoms together, preventing the positively-charged protons repelling each other, which would naturally be the case because of the force of electromagnetism. If the strong nuclear force were even slightly weaker, the nucleus would not hold together and matter would become unstable. The result would be that atoms with more than one proton in their nucleus would not form, and the universe would consist solely of hydrogen. On the other hand, if the strong nuclear force were just a little bit greater, it would cause protons to fuse together with catastrophic results: nuclear fusion in stars would speed up, and our sun would burn through all its fuel in a very short time.

5. The mass of the proton relative to the mass of the electron is also finely-tuned: if the ratio of the mass of the proton and the mass of the electron were slightly smaller or greater, then either electrons and protons would combine to form neutrons, causing all atomic structures to collapse, or neutrons would decay into protons and electrons, leading to a universe composed only of hydrogen.

There are many other examples of fine-tuning of the physical constants, and the values of many of the physical constants are precisely calibrated to each other. Thus, gravity has to be at just the right value compared to electromagnetism and the strong nuclear force.

Paul Davies has described the situation like this: imagine a marksman hitting a bulls-eye at the far side of the observable universe, and you have the sort of accuracy with which these physical constants have to be calibrated.

Fred Hoyle summarized the situation in his 1988 book *The Intelligent Universe*: 'Such [i.e. finely-tuned] properties seem to run through the fabric of the natural world like a thread of happy coincidences. But there are so many odd coincidences essential to life that some explanation seems required to account for them'.

Here is how various other distinguished scientists have described these 'coincidences':

- Physicist Freeman Dyson: 'As we look out into the universe and identify the many accidents of physics and astronomy that have worked to our benefit, it almost seems as if the universe must in some sense have known that we were coming'[6].

- Charles Townes, winner of the Nobel Prize: 'This is a very special universe: it's remarkable that it came out just this way. If the laws of physics weren't just the way they are, we couldn't be here at all. The sun couldn't be there, the laws of gravity and nuclear laws and magnetic theory, quantum mechanics, and so on have to be just the way they are for us to be here'[7].

- Nobel Laureate Arno Penzias: 'Astronomy leads us to a unique event, a universe which was created out of nothing, one with the very delicate balance needed to provide exactly the right conditions required to permit life, and one which has an underlying (one might say, supernatural) plan'[8].

The universe appears to have been designed with us in mind, to provide a home for humanity on planet Earth. The universe is balanced on a knife-edge. Like Goldilocks' porridge, everything is 'just right' for life. The result of these cosmic 'coincidences' is that many scientists in the last half-century have come to the conclusion that the universe cannot be the result of an accident. It is just too improbable. Instead, the universe appears to be have been designed. The universe points to this fact: God really exists.

---

[6] quoted in John D. Barrow and Frank J. Tipler, *The Anthropic Cosmological Principle*, 1986, Oxford University Press, 1986, p.318

[7] "'Explore as much as we can': Nobel Prize winner Charles Townes on evolution, intelligent design, and the meaning of life", *UC Berkeley News*, June 17, 2005

[8] Arno Penzias, "Creation is Supported by All the Data So Far", in *Cosmos, Bios, and Theos*, ed. H. Margenau and R. A. Varghese, Open Court, 1992, p.86

Atheist Counter-Arguments

Atheists respond to the evidence of fine-tuning with three arguments. First, they point out that if the universe were not the way it is, we would not be here to observe it. Therefore we should not be surprised that we observe that the universe has precisely the properties that support intelligent life.

To use Stephen Hawking's analogy, it is like a teenage boy who has not cleaned up his bedroom explaining away the mess to his parents by saying that if the mess had been cleaned up it would not be there for them to see.

To see why this argument is a poor one, consider another similar example. The answer to the question, 'Why are stars bright?' is not simply, 'Because if they were not bright, we would not be able to see them'. We also need to explain what makes stars shine brightly.

Returning to Hawking's answer, and speaking as a parent of teenagers, as well as a friend of other parents of teenagers, I have to say that no parent I know of would ever be dumb enough to fall for the sort of word-game Hawking tries here. That atheists are so quick to fall for such an argument does not reflect well upon them. In the days of 'spare the rod and spoil the child', the teenage boy might have got more than a good talking-to for such an explanation for his messy room.

An analogy that helpfully clarifies the trick that is being played on us by this atheist 'explanation' comes from philosopher John Leslie: imagine a blindfolded man standing in front of a firing squad who hears the order to fire, but then survives the volley of shots. An atheist might say that the reason he lived was that if he did not survive, he would not be here to talk about it. But this answer is again dodging the issue, for the fact that the man survived must be explained in some way or other. Either the guns fired blanks, or the soldiers deliberately aimed up in the air, or the soldiers were all drunk, or were bribed. It is no real explanation to say that the man is alive because he is still alive.

Douglas Adams in his book *The Salmon of Doubt* gives another atheist analogy: 'imagine a puddle waking up one morning saying, "This is an interesting world I find myself in — an interesting hole I find myself in — fits me rather neatly, doesn't it? In fact it fits me staggeringly well, must have been made to have me in it!'" This analogy is very popular with internet atheists, probably because it makes a joke of the fine-tuning argument. However it is not a valid analogy, for a hole in the ground is remarkably easy to make (whereas a precisely-calibrated universe is inconceivably improbable) and puddles always perfectly fit holes in the ground (whereas life arises on very few planets at all, or in few possible universes). Adams' analogy would be valid if most planets in the universe had intelligent life, but they don't. The analogy is an attempt to muddy the waters and confuse the simple. The joke is again on all the atheists who have been taken in by it.

The universe demands an explanation, for the odds of things turning out 'just right' are vanishingly small. To say that the universe exists because we are here to see it does not explain why the universe is the way it is. It simply dodges the question. This first atheist answer says, in effect, that the universe exists because it exists. But this is just a tautology, like 'survivors survive'. This first atheist answer therefore fails to explain anything.

A second atheist response is to compare the situation to a lottery and say that, while the odds of one person winning are highly improbable, nevertheless there must be a winner. Someone's ticket has to be pulled out of the hat, so to speak. Just as someone must be the President of the United States, even though the chances are 1 in 300 million, the odds are irrelevant because someone always holds the office at any time. Therefore the universe exists despite the odds – because it is obviously and undeniably here. Humans have simply hit the jackpot of life.

This response involves a mathematical trick. Comparing the universe to someone winning a lottery is not really a valid analogy, because for the universe and life to exist, it would be like winning one hundred different lotteries simultaneously. Each of the odds need to be multiplied together, so that if the chance of winning the first lottery were 1 in a million, and the second also 1 in a million, the probability of winning them both would be 1 in a trillion, and so on the more lotteries are involved. After one hundred lotteries, the chances are infinitesimally small, which is why nobody ever wins one hundred lotteries in a row. Bear in mind that many of the fine-tuning variables are far more precise than 1 in a million, and to call the odds astronomically unlikely is an understatement.

In the case of the universe, the fact that we won the lottery of life, not once but hundreds of times in a row, cannot be explained by chance, nor is there any necessity that things must have turned out this way.

The third (and now most common) atheist explanation for the fine-tuning of the universe is the multi-verse. What this means is that there are an infinite number and variety of universes popping into existence all the time, and we just happen to inhabit one that is life-supporting.

The major drawback with this idea is that, because other universes are imaginary, or at least inaccessible to us, we can neither confirm or deny this idea. There is no evidence, scientific or otherwise, for the multi-verse – it is science fiction. Agnostic Paul Davies writes:

'Invoking an infinite number of other universes just to explain the apparent contrivances of the one we see is pretty drastic, and in stark conflict with Occam's razor (according to which science should prefer explanations with the least number of assumptions). I think it's much more satisfactory from a scientific point of view to try to understand why things are the way they are in this universe and not to invent imaginary universes to do the job'[9].

Furthermore, the multi-verse idea only prompts another question: how did the multi-verse come into being, or who built the machine that generates infinite varieties of universes, one of which happened to turn out just right for life?

Besides, the idea of the multi-verse does not really help the atheist. For, with the multi-verse theory, an infinite number of universes means that all possible options for universes actually exist. Not only are there universes in which the *Star Wars* movies are happening as we speak, or the *Lord of the Rings* novels, or *Winnie the Pooh*, or Zeus and his gang on Mount Olympus, but there is also a universe in which the Christian God is real – the God who is all-powerful, all-knowing, present everywhere (in all possible universes), and ruling over all – a God who can turn water

---

[9] Paul Davies, *Are We Alone?* Penguin Books, 1995, p.80

into wine and rise from the dead. If so, not only is God real, but He is the Creator and Lord of our present universe. There goes atheism!

Ironically the atheist, in running from the design argument into the multi-verse maze, is left with only one exit: there must be a God. If all universes are possible, so too is God. Whichever way we look at it, design in the universe leaves us with God as the inescapable reality.

Conclusion

Not only is the evidence we have looked at in this chapter powerful, but the atheist counter-arguments are particularly desperate, resorting to word tricks, or mathematical sleight of hand, or imaginary unscientific theories like the multi-verse. The only hope for the atheist is that some future scientific discovery somehow explains away the fine-tuning of the universe for life. I rate the fine-tuning evidence in this chapter at 9 out of 10.

Chapter 5

The Stephen King Argument: the Birds and the Bees

Popular American novelist Stephen King said this about belief in God:

'I choose to believe it. … I mean, there's no downside to that. If you say, "Well, OK, I don't believe in God. There's no evidence of God", then you're missing the stars in the sky and you're missing the sunrises and sunsets and you're missing the fact that bees pollinate all these crops and keep us alive and the way that everything seems to work together. Everything is sort of built in a way that to me suggests intelligent design'[1].

The key insight here is this: nature contains unrelated things that co-operate together, like the bees and the crops. Bees are needed to pollinate some plants and crops on which we depend for food, so which came first: the plants which produce the food for us, or the bees which keep the crops alive by pollinating their flowers, enabling the plants to reproduce? If the plants came first, how did they reproduce without the bees, and if the bees came first, what did they feed on? Both had to be present at the same time to survive off the other.

There are indeed other pollinators apart from bees: flies, beetles and moths, as well as bats, birds and some other animals. But while some plants are pollinated by wind or other means, many plants and crops depend exclusively on bees or another similar pollinator. How did the plants survive without these pollinators? And is it not amazing that two completely unrelated sets of creatures, from the plant and animal

---

[1]   https://www.npr.org/2013/05/28/184827647/stephen-king-on-growing-up-believing-in-god-and-getting-scared

kingdoms, should somehow depend upon each other so as to supply what the other needs but lacks?

Consider some amazing types of pollination. The bucket orchid is a flower that has the following features:

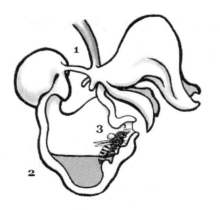

1. A gland which produces a perfume that makes a male bee attractive to a female, which the male naturally wants to acquire, drawing him to land on a slippery bridge this perfume drips onto, causing the bee to fall off into

2. a bucket with shallow fluid, with only one way for the bee to climb out, via

3. a tunnel on the side of the bucket, with a step for the bee to climb out, and as the bee passes through, it suddenly contracts, holding the bee in place while the orchid puts pollen on the bee's back, securing it there with glue, holding it in place until the glue sets, and a hook in the roof of the tunnel which picks up the pollen collected earlier at a previous orchid, allowing pollination to occur.

Seeing orchids have no brain, knowledge, intelligence or even sight or smell, they have no way of inventing such a cunning trap for bees, nor would they have any awareness of what perfume bees find attractive, nor any ability to manufacture the perfume, bridge, bucket, step, tunnel, hook and glue. How were they able, by blind trial and error, by a long succession of lucky accidents, to engineer the components for such a system for pollinating themselves as well as feeding the bees, enabling the bees to reproduce too? How many perfumes did they try before they hit on the right one? How many attempts at bridge building or tunnel construction failed before they got one to work? It seems unlikely that trial and error was the way the orchid worked out how to pollinate. The whole contraption instead appears to be designed.

Other orchids are even more astonishing. Some have flowers that so closely resemble a bee or a fly that they trick real bees and flies. These orchids also produce the exact same smell produced by the females bees or flies, so that the male is attracted to the smell of the orchid flower, and when he sees it, he thinks it is an actual female bee. When he flies into it, he picks up the pollen, which is then taken to another flower to pollinate it.

How did the orchid pollinate without insects? Here is a classic chicken-and-egg problem: which came first, the orchid or the insects? No wonder Darwin called the origin of flowering plants an 'abominable mystery'[2]. In Darwin's time, some evolutionary biologists 'solved' the problem by saying that they evolved together, but this ignores the main issue: both the bees and the flowers had to have nearly complete systems before they could help each other. Today's evolutionary explanations for the origin of flowering plants are short on details and long on imagination, like a collection of bedtime stories. One of the most common statements is simply that 'flowering plants evolved', which not only assumes what it needs to prove, but lacks the crucial hallmark of true science: evidence.

In the *Origin of Species*, Darwin wrote, 'As natural selection acts solely by accumulating slight, successive, favourable variations, it can produce no great or sudden modification; it can act only by very short and slow steps'[3]. A truly scientific account of any evolutionary origins must produce the fossil evidence of the slow and gradual acquisition, by a long and gradual process of blind tinkering, of the amazing features of the orchids from more primitive mechanisms. If the storytelling cannot be backed up with real evidence, such explanations cannot be called science. But, as E. J. H. Corner of Cambridge University wrote: 'Much evidence can be adduced in favour of the theory of evolution – from biology, biogeography, and palaeontology, but I still think that to the unprejudiced, the fossil record of plants is in favour of special creation'[4].

There are many other examples of things that co-operate in nature. Think of the way plants produce oxygen for us to breathe as a by-product

---

[2] Darwin, writing to his friend Joseph Hooker in 1879.

[3] Darwin, *Origin of Species*, 1859, p.492

[4] E. J. H. Corner, *Contemporary Botanical Thought*, ed. A. M. MacLeod and L. S. Cobley, Quadrangle Books, 1961, p.97

of their photosynthesis (which in turn recycles the carbon dioxide we breathe out). This, of course, is in addition to the fact that plants are a huge part of our food source: the hundreds of different varieties of grains, fruits, roots, herbs, nuts and other things that plants supply for us to eat. Or consider the way that the oceans supply the land with fresh water (via processes of evaporation and rainfall). Everything seems to work together for the benefit of living creatures like us, even though oceans and plants have no brains to dream up such clever co-operative schemes, nor even with all our intelligence have humans ever been able to engineer such schemes to manufacture the abundance of necessary things that nature freely provides for our benefit.

Sexual Reproduction

Reproduction is another instance of co-operation, an incredible bio-engineering fact of life, so common that we take it for granted. But it is truly astonishing to think about. We do not see automobiles or cameras producing replicas of themselves, but living creatures have the ability to give birth to another baby version of themselves.

Sexual reproduction is perhaps the most complex case of co-operation in nature. In humans, sexual reproduction requires numerous complementary male and female parts for the system to work. These include the following:

a. sex cells (sperm and ovum),
b. organs which produce and store the sex cells (ovaries and testes),
c. the tubes and ducts which transport the sex cells so they meet each other (fallopian tubes in females, various ducts in males),
d. glands which supply lubricants to help transport the sex cells (prostate in males, mucous in female fallopian tubes),
e. the matching reproductive organs (penis and vagina),
f. the different hormonal systems (producing a large number of different hormones) that each play a part in regulating the development and activity of the male and female reproductive systems, bringing them to maturity and stimulating the chemistry of sexual reproduction, and
g. the anatomical structures (bones, muscles, blood vessels, nerves) that support the reproductive organs and process of sexual reproduction.

On top of all this, there are all the complex changes in the female body which occur after the conception of the new life, to protect and nurture the fertilised egg, allowing the baby to develop, giving birth to it, and feeding it after it is born. Is it not amazing that the mother produces milk which not only provides exactly the right, balanced diet necessary for the baby's growth, but also provides the baby with built-in immunity to various diseases? Finally, we need to go right back to the beginning and mention the fact that males and females find each other attractive. What use would there be for all this anatomical equipment if the male did not find the female attractive, and the female was not drawn to the male?

How did all this complex, complementary biochemistry and anatomy develop? No one has a clue. Imagine some hypothetical ancient animal that reproduced asexually and then somehow suddenly developed all of the features of a male – with whom would this male now mate? There would have to be the simultaneous evolution of a female for the system to work. Sexual reproduction could not have arisen as a result of a gradual, unguided, evolutionary step-by-step process for the simple reason that it had to involve two different systems developing simultaneously, each unable to see where the other was heading (because evolution is blind), yet nevertheless perfectly integrating with each other. This contradicts the very heart of evolution, which happens slowly and gradually, one lucky accident, one blind unguided mutation, at a time. How would these two integrated systems originate without a purpose or plan to complement each other – in other words, without design and intelligence?

The only answer to the question of how sexual reproduction arose that atheists give is that there are a small number of animals that, in difficult environmental conditions, give birth to live young without reproducing sexually. The mother typically gives birth to a female clone of herself, reproducing asexually.

However, to suggest that this explains how sexual reproduction arose is like saying that the electrical systems in a modern house (light bulbs, wiring, switches, power points, and electrical appliances) all arose from the gradual development of candles and wood fireplaces that were used before electricity. While it is true that most houses still have candles for use in an emergency when the power fails, there is no pathway from candles and woodfires to modern electrical appliances. They are two completely different systems, separated by a vast gulf of engineering developments. Just as we do not try to explain the origin of electrical appliances in terms of the gradual development of candles and firewood, so too sexual and asexual reproduction are not simply more (or less) developed versions of one another; they are completely different bio-engineering mechanisms.

To suggest that blind, unguided evolution, by a slow and gradual, step-by-step process, without design, purpose or goal-orientation, produced the suite of perfectly matching sexual machinery is not science but speculation. However, there are not even many imaginative stories telling how sexual reproduction might have evolved.

Of course, evolutionists agree that the idea of the sudden and spontaneous arrival of the entire apparatus of sexual reproduction is not possible. But if a first male gradually developed over many hundreds of generations, what use would the partly-developed system be, until it was not only itself virtually complete, but there was also a matching female system? How would an organism gradually develop hundreds of different parts of the system without being able to reproduce until the system was functional? What would have been the advantage of these incomplete systems before their near-completion? The idea that such amazing biological engineering arose by gradual processes that blindly tinkered around until the whole system was functionally complete is not credible.

Richard Dawkins wrote in 1997, 'There are many theories of why sex exists, and none of them is knock-down convincing … Maybe one day I'll summon up the courage to tackle it in full and write a whole book on the origin of sex'[5]. Twenty years later, and despite Dawkins' fertile imagination and considerable powers of storytelling, he still hasn't plucked up the courage. Perhaps the reason is that there is no evidence (nor is there even enough imagination) to say how sexual reproduction evolved gradually. Another evolutionary scientist was more upfront and honest when he wrote, 'How sex began and why it thrived remain a mystery'[6].

---

[5] Richard Dawkins, *Climbing Mt. Improbable*, Penguin Books, 1997, p.75
[6] B. Wuethrich, "Why Sex? Putting the Theory to the Test", *Science*, 281:1980-1982, 1998

Conclusion

Let me finish this section with a few verses from two very simple poems about flowers and trees, both expressing something intuitively obvious and true. The first is called, *The Tree*, which is apparently the most quoted poem in American history, by Joyce Kilmer:

> I think that I shall never see
> A poem lovely as a tree.
>
> A tree whose hungry mouth is prest
> Against the earth's sweet flowing breast;
>
> A tree that looks at God all day,
> And lifts her leafy arms to pray;
>
> A tree that may in Summer wear
> A nest of robins in her hair;
>
> Upon whose bosom snow has lain;
> Who intimately lives with rain.
>
> Poems are made by fools like me,
> But only God can make a tree.

The second poem, *Unfolding the Rosebud*, was given to me by a car mechanic, and I will spare you some of its more sentimental verses, but its main point is clear:

> It is only a tiny rosebud, a flower of God's design
> But I cannot unfold the petals with these clumsy hands of mine.
>
> The secret of unfolding flowers is not known to such as I
> GOD opens this flower so sweetly when in my hands they fade and
> die.

I rate the Stephen King argument from co-operation in nature at about 8 out of 10. It is a mix between an intuitive argument for God's existence and a scientific argument. Intuitive arguments are lower-scoring than scientific arguments in my opinion, and therefore its rating drops.

0 (atheism)   (God exists) **10**

8

▲

Argument from Co-operation

Chapter 6

The Antony Flew Argument: the Origin of Life

A ntony Flew was one of the most influential atheist philosophers of the 20th century. However, in 2004, he renounced atheism in his book, *There is a God: How the World's Most Notorious Atheist Changed His Mind*. Flew said that he now believed in the existence of God, largely based on the amazing discoveries about the cell and what they teach us about the origin of life. Flew realized that powerful evidence now shows that chemical evolution is not even remotely likely: science has shown how truly difficult it is for chemicals to arrange themselves to become living organisms. Before we look at these arguments, we need to look at what atheists say about the origin of life.

The Origin of Life: The Atheist Narrative

The 2018 National Geographic television documentary, *One Strange Rock*, dealt with the origin of life on earth in its fourth episode, titled "Genesis". It featured the actor Will Smith, two astronauts and a number of scientists. Here is some of what was said about the origin of life:

> Will Smith: "You go back far enough, and everyone, every living thing, we all come from the same place. A moment when a dead rock came to life".
>
> Astronaut Chris Hadfield: "it's hard to imagine anywhere else where everything could have fallen into place, so magically".
>
> Will Smith: "We may never know exactly how life got started. But we do know it was a strange brew. A dash of magical liquid, a sprinkle of stardust, and a crackle of energy. Mixed together in a big bubbling cauldron to make our rock come alive".

'Magic liquid, a sprinkle of stardust and a crackle of energy' – sounds more like a story about a fairy godmother than a scientific description of the origin of life. We can excuse National Geographic for trying to make the subject interesting by getting an actor like Will Smith to ham it up a little. But the worrying thing is that this description is not very different from what leading scientists say about the origin of life. Consider the following examples:

- Professor Brian Cox: 'It's thought that in warm volcanic pools or in deep sea hydrothermal vents, conditions were right for the chemical building blocks of life to form spontaneously'[1].
- Stephen Jay Gould: 'Life presumably began in primeval oceans as a result of sequential chemical reactions based on original constituents of atmospheres and oceans, and regulated by principles of physics'[2].
- Charles Darwin imagined 'in some warm little pond, with all sorts of ammonia and phosphoric salts, light, heat, electricity, etc., present, that a proteine (sic.) compound was chemically formed ready to undergo still more complex changes'[3].
- Richard Dawkins: 'Nobody knows how it happened but, somehow, without violating the laws of physics and chemistry, a molecule arose that just happened to have the property of self-copying – a replicator'[4].

This is the story that is regularly told to the public about the origin of life. Is there any evidence for it? As we are going to see, there is zero scientific evidence for this story – no more scientific evidence today than there was in Darwin's day when he indulged in the wishful thinking quoted above. The whole thing is just a story, a narrative. Notice the way that Gould, in the quote above, uses the word 'presumably'. Just a few pages earlier Gould himself stated that he was very uncomfortable with

[1] Professor Brian Cox on the 2019 BBC-TV series, *The Planets*
[2] Stephen Jay Gould, *Life's Grandeur: The Spread of Excellence from Plato to Darwin*, Vintage, 1997, p.169.
[3] F. Darwin, *The Life and Letters of Charles Darwin*, Vol. II, D. Appleton and Co., 1911, pp.202-3
[4] Richard Dawkins, *Climbing Mount Improbable*, Viking, 1996, p.259

statements that contain words like 'presumably' but have little evidence. Such statements are no different from imaginative storytelling.

Atheists reply that they do have one piece of scientific evidence for this story. For nearly 70 years they have told the story of the famous 1953 Miller-Urey experiment, which tried to simulate lightning interacting with the atmosphere and oceans on an early Earth. Here is how one popular high-school biology textbook describes it: 'By re-creating the early atmosphere (ammonia, water, hydrogen and methane) and passing an electric spark (lightning) through the mixture, Miller and Urey proved that organic matter such as amino acids could have formed spontaneously'[5]. The Miller-Urey experiment made front-page news across the world and is still mentioned in many biology textbooks today. It was greeted in the scientific community as the first step towards creating life in the laboratory.

However, the Miller-Urey experiment got nowhere near creating life in the laboratory. It had many problems[6], and for a long time now the Miller-Urey experiment has been abandoned by serious chemists as a viable explanation of how life started. John Horgan, the American science journalist, summarizes the current situation:

[the Miller-Urey experiment at first seemed to] provide stunning evidence that life could arise from what the British chemist J.B.S. Haldane had called the "primordial soup." Pundits speculated that scientists, like Mary Shelley's Dr. Frankenstein, would shortly

---

[5] Kenneth Miller and Joseph Levine, *Biology*, Pearson Prentice Hall, 2000, pp.343-344
[6] There are five main problems with the experiment. (1) It did not replicate the situation on an early earth – it deliberately excluded oxygen, because if you spark methane gas in the presence of oxygen, like in a combustion engine, you blow everything to pieces, (2) It did not produce the right kinds of amino acids required for life – amino acids in life must be 100% 'left-handed', but the experiment produced an equal mixture of left and right-handed amino acids, (3) It only produced two or three amino acids, but all twenty amino acids are required for making proteins, the building blocks of life, (4) Life is now known to be much more complex than amino acids; a self-replicating molecule like DNA is required for life, but DNA was unknown at the time, (5) The occasional production of amino acids in the oceans would have resulted in them drifting apart instead of combining to form proteins unless there was a cell membrane holding them all together; indeed, water dissolves the bonds between amino acids in proteins.

conjure up living organisms in their laboratories and thereby demonstrate in detail how genesis unfolded. It hasn't worked out that way. In fact, almost 40 years after his original experiment, Miller told me that solving the riddle of the origin of life had turned out to be more difficult than he or anyone else had envisioned[7].

Miller told Horgan that he is:

unimpressed with any of the current proposals on the origin of life, referring to them as "nonsense" or "paper chemistry." He was so contemptuous of some hypotheses that, when I asked his opinion of them, he merely shook his head, sighed deeply, and snickered—as if overcome by the folly of humanity'[8].

The chemist Robert Shapiro criticized aspects of origin of life research, especially the Miller-Urey experiment, as follows: 'We have reached a situation where a theory has been accepted as fact by some, and possible contrary evidence is shunted aside' ... [it is] 'mythology rather than science'[9]. The *New York Times* science writer Nicholas Wade said: 'Everything about the origin of life on Earth is a mystery, and it seems the more that is known, the more acute the puzzles get'[10]. Agnostic scientist Paul Davies set out to write a book on the origin of life, 'convinced that science was close to wrapping up the mystery of life's origins', but after spending 'a year or two researching the field', he is 'now of the opinion that there remains a huge gulf in our understanding.... This gulf in understanding is not merely ignorance about certain technical details, it is a major conceptual lacuna' [i.e. a gaping big hole in the theory][11].

---

[7] John Horgan, *The End of Science: Facing the Limits of Knowledge in the Twilight of the Scientific Age*, Addison-Wesley, 1996, p.138

[8] Horgan, p.139

[9] Robert Shapiro, *Origins: a Skeptic's Guide to the Creation of Life on Earth*, Summit Books, 1986, p.112

[10] Nicholas Wade, "Life's Origins get Murkier and Messier", *The New York Times*, June 13, 2000

[11] Paul Davies, *The Fifth Miracle: The Search for the Origin and Meaning of Life*, Simon &

The atheist narrative that life self-assembled has run out of steam. Claiming the Miller-Urey experiment as evidence for the origin of life is as ridiculous as a man boasting that he has swum across the Pacific Ocean from California to China, and to 'prove' it, he takes you down to the beach where he splashes his feet at the water's edge.

The message constantly sold to the public about life arising spontaneously and effortlessly relies entirely on narrative rather than evidence. That is a polite way of saying that they are just making it all up.

The Cell: Evidence for God's Existence

The origin of life is the third major scientific headache for atheism (after the origin of the universe and its fine-tuning). The scientific evidence strongly points not only to the impossibility of life spontaneously assembling, but also to God as our Creator. These are two big claims to make, but the evidence is so powerful that even Antony Flew renounced his atheism because of them.

This chapter will again have some scientific language, but don't be put off. Believe me, the key evidence is not hard to understand. To see the evidence that convinced Flew of God's existence, we need to introduce the cell, one of the most amazing structures in the universe.

The Cell

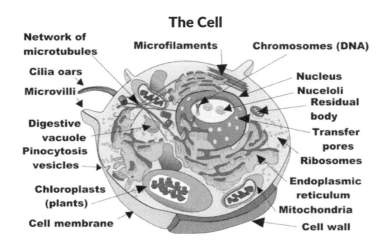

Schuster, 1999, p.17

Why do we need to learn about the cell? Because a living cell is what non-living chemicals have to organize themselves to form. The cell is the simplest form of life – the most basic, living, self-sufficient, self-replicating thing in existence. A cell is what origin of life researchers have to build from non-living chemicals. Yet, in the words of Nobel Prize winner Linus Pauling, 'just one living cell in the human body is more complex than New York City'. Here is Michael Denton's description of a living cell, a truly brilliant piece of scientific prose:

> Viewed down a light microscope at a magnification of some several hundred times, such as would have been possible in Darwin's time, a living cell is a relatively disappointing spectacle appearing only as an ever-changing and apparently disordered pattern of blobs and particles which, under the influence of unseen turbulent forces, are continually tossed haphazardly in all directions. To grasp the reality of life as it has been revealed by molecular biology, we must magnify a cell a thousand million times until it is twenty kilometres in diameter and resembles a giant airship large enough to cover a great city like London or New York. What we would then see would be an object of unparalleled complexity and adaptive design. On the surface of the cell we would see millions of openings, like the portholes of a vast space ship, opening and closing to allow a continual stream of materials to flow in and out. If we were to enter one of these openings we would find ourselves in a world of supreme technology and bewildering complexity. We would see endless highly organized corridors and conduits branching in every direction away from the perimeter of the cell, some leading to the central memory bank in the nucleus and others to assembly plants and processing units. The nucleus itself would be a vast spherical chamber more than a kilometer in diameter, resembling a geodesic dome inside of which we would see, all neatly stacked together in ordered arrays, the miles of coiled chains of the DNA molecules. A huge range of products and raw materials would shuffle along the manifold conduits in a highly ordered fashion to and from all the various assembly plants in the outer regions of the cell.... We would

66

see all around us, in every direction we looked, all sorts of robot-like machines. We would notice that the simplest of the functional components of the cell, the protein molecules, were astonishingly complex pieces of molecular machinery, each one consisting of about 3,000 atoms arranged in highly organized 3-D spatial conformation. We would wonder even more as we watched the strangely purposeful activities of these weird molecular machines, particularly when we realized that, despite all our accumulated knowledge of physics and chemistry, the task of designing one such molecular machine – that is one functional protein molecule – would be completely beyond our capacity at present and will probably not be achieved until at least the beginning of the next century. Yet the life of the cell depends on the integrated activity of thousands, certainly tens, and probably hundreds of thousands of such protein molecules … What we would be witnessing would be an object resembling an immense automated factory, a factory larger than a city and carrying out almost as many unique functions as all the manufacturing activities of man on earth. However, it would be a factory which would have one capacity not equalled in any of our own most advanced machines, for it would be capable of replicating its entire structure within a matter of a few hours. To witness such an act at a magnification of one thousand million times would be an awe-inspiring spectacle'[12].

Is Michael Denton's description just science fiction? Is he using inappropriate, exaggerated analogies when he describes the cell as a vast automated factory? Listen to Bruce Alberts, President of the US National Academy of Sciences, writing in the journal *Cell*:

We have always underestimated cells . . . . The entire cell can be viewed as a factory that contains an elaborate network of interlocking assembly lines, each of which is composed of a set of large protein machines . . . Why do we call the large protein assemblies that

---

[12] Michael Denton, *Evolution: a Theory in Crisis*, Adler and Adler, 1986, pp.328-329

underlie cell function protein machines? Precisely because, like machines invented by humans to deal efficiently with the macroscopic world these protein assemblies contain highly coordinated moving parts[13].

In our bodies, we have more than ten trillion cells, and they come in more than 200 different kinds (blood cells, nerve cells, etc.). Each is a marvel of miniature machinery. Most of the functions of the cell are carried out by proteins. When Alberts refers to 'protein machines' above, he is not using a metaphor or analogy. Protein machines are real machines. They require energy (in fact, some of them produce energy which other parts of the cell use), and as a result, they do the same sorts of work as our human-sized machines: spin, pump, open and shut, and even walk along trackways carrying loads. Motor proteins are responsible for muscle contractions, while others act as propellers, sensors, and gates. Paul Davies has written, 'the living cell contains miniscule pumps, levers, motors, rotors, turbines, propellers, scissors and many other instruments … all of them exquisite examples of nanotechnology'[14].

DNA: the Digital Code of Life

At the heart of the cell is the nucleus which contains the DNA, the spiral ladder containing the coded blueprint for life. Richard Dawkins writes that a cell nucleus 'contains a digitally coded database larger, in information content, than all 30 volumes of the *Encyclopedia Britannica* put together'[15]. Bill Gates writes, 'DNA is like a computer program but far, far more advanced than any software ever created'[16].

An anonymous molecular biologist, working on diseases caused by genetic copying mistakes in the DNA was interviewed by a newspaper journalist, George Caylor:

---

[13] Bruce Alberts, "The Cell as a Collection of Protein Machines", *Cell*, 1998, p.291
[14] Paul Davies, *The Goldilocks Enigma: Why is the Universe just right for life?* Allen Lane, 2006, p.218
[15] Richard Dawkins, *The Blind Watchmaker*, W. W. Norton, 1986, pp.17-18
[16] Bill Gates, *The Road Ahead*, Viking, 1996, p.228

Biologist: I'm a bit like an editor, trying to find a spelling mistake inside a document larger than four complete sets of *Encyclopedia Britannica.*

Newspaper: Do you believe that the information evolved?

Biologist: George, nobody I know in my profession believes it evolved. It was engineered by 'genius beyond genius' ...

Newspaper: Have you ever stated that in a public lecture, or in any public writings?

Biologist: No. I just say it evolved. To be a molecular biologist requires one to hold on to two insanities at all times. One, it would be insane to believe in evolution when you can see the truth for yourself. Two, it would be insane to say you don't believe in evolution. All government work, research grants, papers, big college lectures – everything would stop. I'd be out of a job, or relegated to the outer fringes where I couldn't earn a decent living.

Newspaper: I hate to say it, but that sounds intellectually dishonest.

Biologist: The work I do in genetic research is honorable. We will find the cures to many of mankind's worst diseases. But in the meantime, we have to live with the 'elephant in the living room'.

Newspaper: What elephant?

Biologist: Creation design. It's like an elephant in the living room. It moves around, takes up an enormous amount of space, trumpets loudly, bumps into us, knocks things over, eats a ton of hay, and smells like an elephant. And yet we have to swear it isn't there![17]

The Mathematical Impossibility of Atheism's Narrative

Is it true that the cell has been designed? How would we know this? Is there not some way that the cell could have arisen naturally? How do atheists say the cell – the first living thing – arose?

Richard Dawkins describes the origin of life as 'an initial stroke of luck'[18]. However, Antony Flew was honest enough to abandon atheism

---

[17] George Caylor, "The Biologist", *The Ledger*, Lynchburg, Virginia, Feb 17, 2000
[18] Richard Dawkins, *The God Delusion*, Bantam Press, 2006, p.135

when he understood that appealing to chance for the origin of the first living cell is the equivalent of believing in fairies at the bottom of the garden. In fact, anyone with a little knowledge of biochemistry knows that it is mathematically impossible for even the simplest parts of the first living cell to have assembled by luck.

Here is a simple analogy to help you get a basic understanding of biochemistry. In our English language, we have 26 letters (plus a few different types of punctuation). With these characters, we can write messages: sentences, paragraphs, chapters and books. Inside our cells there is something very similar. There are 20 types of amino acids – think of them like the 26 English letters. These amino acids get strung together in long chains to build proteins (which we can think of like messages, paragraphs or books). These long chains of proteins then fold into three-dimensional shapes to form moving machines inside the cell – the mini-robot work-horses inside the cell.

But where do the 20 amino acid 'letters' come from? Just like our English letters are made up of different pen strokes (e.g., circles and upright strokes make letters like b, d, p and q), so the 20 different amino acid 'letters' are made up from 'pen-strokes' that are coded on the DNA molecule. DNA is the long, spiral, ladder-like molecule with nucleic acid base-pair 'rungs'. These nucleic acids come in four types (abbreviated as C, G, A, and T) which combine in threes ('codons') to make amino acids when they are copied (technically, 'translated'), and from the amino acids, proteins are built. So, to recap, DNA bases (pen-strokes) get copied in various combinations to make amino acids (letters) that build proteins (messages, written instructions) that form molecular machines.

English	Pen-strokes	26 letters	sentences
Biochemistry	DNA bases (C, G, A, T)	20 amino acids	proteins

Here is the key point: just as sentences and messages written in English do not form by random assortments of letters – by monkeys randomly bashing away on typewriters – so proteins do not arise from randomly mixing large amounts of amino acids. Instead, amino acids must be in exactly the right sequence to form a protein. This is because amino acids must be in the right order to fold into the correct three-dimension shape. If amino acids are in the wrong order, the protein will not work. Think of it like a piece of flat-packed furniture – if we attach one piece of wood in the wrong place, it is possible to ruin the whole design. We can thus calculate the probability of a small protein consisting, say, of 100 amino acids, arising by chance. Because there are 20 types of amino acids, the probability of getting all the amino acids in the right order to form a protein comes to 1/20 x 1/20 x 1/20 (multiplied another 97 times), which equals 1 in 10^{130}, that is 1 in 10 with 130 zeros after it.

Now, 10^{130} is a big number, but here is a way to visualize it: the chance of this simple protein forming at random 'by luck' is equivalent to someone opening a combination lock safe which has 130 dials. To understand how unlikely it is to crack open this safe, there are so many combinations that if a new combination was entered every second, it would take about 13 billion years just to try 10^{18} options, which is nowhere near 10^{130}. Or, to put it another way, there are only 10^{80} atoms in the universe. 10^{130} is so huge a number – trillions of trillions – and the chance of 1 in 10^{130} is so infinitesimally small that, for all practical purposes, it is essentially equal to zero chance. Additionally, some proteins have far more than 100 amino acids and the simplest possible (hypothetical) living cell would require over 300 different proteins. The odds of randomly self-assembling just the 300 proteins in a hypothetical simplest possible living cell is mathematical nonsense[19].

But worse yet, for the origin of life, we need a self-replicating living cell, which requires DNA, which contains the code for building – not one protein – but ***all*** of the hundreds of protein machines within the cell. The DNA is the master-code for life, a vast library containing all the codes to build every single part of an organism – all combined together in one place. Human DNA is over 3.5 billion nucleic acids long, while even

---

[19] Real biochemistry is more complex than our simplistic calculation of the probability of the accidental origin of a protein with 100 amino-acids. Biochemist Dr. Douglas Axe has calculated the actual numbers by experiments: for every one functional protein sequence, there are 10^{74} (1 followed by 74 zeros) that are non-functional (Douglas Axe, *Undeniable*, HarperOne, 2016, pp.57, 180ff). Even though this number is not as small as 1 in 10^{130}, it is still an impossible hurdle for chance to clear.

simple bacteria like *E.coli* have 4 million nucleic acids (this book you are reading only has about 900,000 characters). So, even the hypothetical simplest possible living cell would have a DNA molecule consisting of hundreds of thousands of nucleic acids, many of which have to be in the precise sequence to code for the right amino acid 'letters' which in turn form the protein 'messages'. For these million-letter long chains of nucleic acids to spontaneously arrange themselves on the DNA molecule in the particular order required is astronomically harder than producing proteins which are only hundreds of amino acids long. Thus, the idea of the spontaneous, chance self-assembly of DNA is the grandmother of all mathematical non-starters. If someone tells you that life's origin was a 'stroke of luck', you can stop listening to them. They are either hopelessly ignorant, severely mathematically challenged, or just plain lying.

Sir Fred Hoyle wrote:

'Anyone with even a nodding acquaintance with the Rubik cube will concede the near impossibility of a solution being obtained by a blind person moving the cube faces at random. Now imagine 10^{50} blind persons (standing shoulder to shoulder, these would more than fill our entire planetary system) each with a scrambled Rubik cube and try to conceive of the chance of them all simultaneously arriving at the solved form. You then have the chance of arriving by random shuffling (random variation) of just one of the many biopolymers on which life depends. *The notion that not only the biopolymers [i.e. chains of amino acids that make proteins] but the operating programme of a living cell [i.e. DNA] could be arrived at by chance in a primordial soup here on earth is evidently nonsense of a high order*'[20].

Princeton professor Edward Conklin wrote, 'The probability of life originating by accident is comparable to the probability of the unabridged dictionary resulting from an explosion in a printing shop'[21].

Sir Fred Hoyle again: 'If you imagine a whirlwind sweeping through a

---

[20] Fred Hoyle, "The big bang in astronomy", *New Scientist*, 92, p.521 emphasis in the original
[21] *Readers Digest*, January 1963

junkyard, what is the chance that all the pieces of metal that it stirs up will smash themselves together and produce a brand new Boeing 747? That is the kind of situation that is supposed for the origin of life on earth, and I think that the two cases are just as absurd'[22].

Antony Flew concluded that random chance and lucky accidents in warm ponds are no longer viable explanations for the first life. They are nothing more than charming fables. As an atheist, Flew was not biased in favour of God creating life; he was simply facing up to the facts. He wrote,

'What I think the DNA material has done is that it has shown, by the almost unbelievable complexity of the arrangements which are needed to produce (life), that intelligence must have been involved in getting these extraordinarily diverse elements to work together. It's the enormous complexity of the number of elements and the enormous subtlety of the ways they work together. The meeting of these two parts at the right time *by chance* is simply minute. It is all a matter of the enormous complexity by which the results were achieved, which looked to me like the work of intelligence'[23].

The Chicken-and-Egg Problem for Atheism

Even if we overlook the mathematical impossibility of proteins or DNA self-assembling naturally, there is a second insurmountable obstacle to life originating by itself. Biochemist Michael Behe tells a story from his early days doing post-doctoral work at the National Institutes of Health about a conversation with a fellow postdoc, Joanne:

Talk turned to the origin of life. Although she and I were both happy to think life started by natural laws, we kept bumping up against problems. I pointed out that to get the first cell, you'd first need a membrane. "And proteins," she added. "And metabolism," said I. "And a genetic code," said she. After a short time we both

---

[22] *Science Today*, BBC Radio 4, 30 November 1981
[23] Antony Flew, *There is a God*, HarperOne, 2007, p.75

WHY THERE REALLY IS A GOD

looked wide-eyed at each other and simultaneously shouted, "*Naaaaahh!*" Then we laughed and went back to work, as if it didn't really matter to our views. I suppose we both thought that, even if we didn't know how undirected nature could begin life, *somebody* must know. That's the impressive power of groupthink'[24].

The second big problem with the atheist narrative of life's origin is that multiple different parts of the cell are simultaneously required and dependent upon each other for their existence. It is a classic chicken-and-egg problem.

Consider what the cell is made up of: (1) a cell membrane, which acts as a barrier wall to keep things out, with gates to let certain essential chemicals pass through, (2) DNA, thousands of 'pen-strokes' long, arranged in a precise sequence to make amino acid 'letters' which build protein 'messages'; DNA is the coded 'software' or 'blueprint' from which all the materials in the cell are manufactured, and the means by which the cell reproduces itself, (3) an energy source to fuel the various functions in the cell (ATP synthase), (4) proteins that catalyze (i.e. speed up) chemical reactions within the cell, (5) RNA, another molecule involved in digital copying processes inside the cell, and (6) ribosomes, the cell's protein-building factories, which have been called the most sophisticated machines in existence.

All of these parts need to be present from the start, for all depend upon each other. Richard Dawkins writes, 'The 'Catch-22' of the origin of life is this: DNA can replicate, but it needs [protein] enzymes in order to catalyze [speed up] the process. Proteins can catalyze DNA formation, but they need DNA to specify the correct sequence of amino acids'[25]. In other words, DNA copying processes require proteins to work, but the proteins themselves are built from the DNA. So which came first, the proteins or the DNA?

At the same time, the cell's processes require energy, but the fuel that powers the cell is built, again, from the DNA. So which came first, the

[24] Michael Behe, *Darwin Devolves: the New Science about DNA that Challenges Evolution*, HarperOne, 2019, p.7
[25] Richard Dawkins, *The Greatest Show on Earth*, Free Press, 2009, p.420

DNA or the fuel source which powers it and allows it to operate?

Think of it like a motor vehicle which requires several things if it is going to work: a driver, a working engine, wheels, and fuel. If any one of these is missing, the car will not go very far. A person who runs out of fuel in the outback of Australia, hundreds of miles from anywhere, is in big trouble. The only way the car can get more fuel is if it drives to a fuel-station hundreds of miles away, but it (obviously) cannot drive because it has no fuel. This is the situation with the first living cell – the very thing that powers its operation (fuel) is a result of its operation (driving to the fuel station). In the outback of Australia, all someone can do is wait and hope for some other vehicle to come along with fuel, or get a message to another vehicle able to tow it. But in the hypothetical first living cell, there is no other cell to come along and save the day. The cell is a huge 'chicken and egg' problem. All the parts had to be there from the start for the cell to work.

As the great medical scientist Rudolf Virchow (1821-1902, the founder of pathology) stated: *omnis cellula e cellula*, 'all cells come from cells'. The only way to get a living cell is from another living cell. Or to put it another way, *omne vivum ex vivo*: 'all life comes from life'. Atheists cannot explain the appearance of the first living cell by sheer luck, for the odds are too high, nor from natural selection, for natural selection first requires that there is a self-replicating living cell upon which it can operate. All atheists have to offer at this point are warm, fuzzy, speculative stories – a leap of blind faith – not scientific evidence.

Here is James Tour, one of the world's most accomplished synthetic organic chemists and the first to build a moving nano-car[26]. He refers to the inexplicability of the naturalistic (i.e. atheistic) origin of life as a matter of 'collective cluelessness':

'We have no idea how the basic sets of molecules, carbohydrates, nucleic acids, lipids and proteins, were made and how they could have coupled in proper sequences, and then transformed into the ordered assemblies until there was the construction of a complex biological

---

[26] James Tour is Professor of Chemistry, Professor of Materials Science, Professor of Nanoengineering and Professor of Computer Engineering at Rice University, USA

system, and eventually to that first cell. Nobody has any idea on how this was done using our commonly understood mechanisms of chemical science. Those that say they understand are generally wholly uninformed regarding chemical synthesis. From a synthetic chemical perspective, neither I nor any of my colleagues can fathom a prebiotic route to construction of a complex system. We cannot even figure out the prebiotic routes to the basic building blocks of life: carbohydrates, nucleic acids, lipids and proteins. Chemists are collectively bewildered'[27].

In other words, the world's top chemists have no idea how it would have been possible for even the most basic components of a cell to arise, let alone assemble themselves to make the amazing cell.

Sir Fred Hoyle wrote, 'The likelihood of the formation of life from inanimate matter is one to a number with 40,000 naughts after it ... It is big enough to bury Darwin and the whole theory of evolution. There was no primeval soup, neither on this planet nor any other, and if the beginnings of life were not random, they must therefore have been the product of purposeful intelligence'[28].

Hoyle, being an atheist, suggested that aliens from outer space invented life and sent it here to earth, an idea he called *panspermia*. Richard Dawkins, responding to a question by Ben Stein in the film, *Expelled: No Intelligence Allowed*, also allowed that life could have been designed by aliens:

It could be that at some earlier time, somewhere in the universe, a civilization evolved by probably some kind of Darwinian means to a very, very high level of technology, and designed a form of life that they seeded onto, perhaps, this planet. Now that is a possibility, and an intriguing possibility. And I suppose it's possible that you might find evidence for that if you look at the details of our chemistry,

---

[27] James Tour, *The Origin of Life: an Inside Story*, 2016 lecture: https://www.youtube.com/watch?v=_zQXgJ-dXM4&feature=youtu.be
[28] quoted in E. L. Major, "Big Enough to Bury Darwin", *Guardian* education supplement, 23 August 2001

molecular biology, you might find a signature of some sort of designer, and that designer could well be a higher intelligence from elsewhere in the universe[29].

For Dawkins, of course, the designer cannot be God – but aliens could have done it! But there is a big problem with the idea that highly intelligent aliens designed life on earth. We now have two huge design clues – cosmic design and biochemical design – and highly intelligent aliens are only able (hypothetically) to explain one of these clues, at the biochemical level. Intelligent aliens might have possibly designed life on earth, but they did not design the universe itself with its amazing fine-tuning (seeing they live inside the universe). Once we admit the possibility of design (as Dawkins does, in the cell), only God fits the profile of the designer. Panspermia is, in any case, just an atheist evasion – running as far away as they can from the evidence. Michael Denton wrote, 'Nothing illustrates more clearly how intractable a problem the origin of life has become than the fact that world authorities can seriously toy with the idea of panspermia'[30].

The Evidence for Design

So far, we have eliminated random chance (the odds are too great) and gradual processes (for everything needs to be present at the same time for a functional cell) as reasonable explanations for the origin of life. But is there any positive evidence that the cell is designed? There is one more piece of evidence that caused Antony Flew to abandon atheism: the digitally coded information contained within the cell's DNA. The final piece of evidence is this: information only comes from intelligence. The software contained in the DNA molecule, like any other coded communication, only comes from minds, from an intelligent programmer.

In the movie *Contact*, a scientist listens to radio signals from outer space, hoping to find communication from alien lifeforms. Why listen to

---

[29] *Expelled: No Intelligence Allowed*, 2008
[30] Michael Denton, *Evolution: a Theory in Crisis*, p.271

radio signals? Because communicated information only comes from intelligent life. That is the whole point of the SETI (Search for Extra-Terrestrial Intelligence) program, where scientists listen out for radio signals from space. In the movie, they find a repeating sequence of prime numbers (numbers divisible only by themself and 1, e.g. 2, 3, 5, 7, 11, 13, 17, 23, 29, etc.). They conclude that this unique sequence could not arise by chance, nor by some repetitive physical process, but is instead evidence of intelligent alien life. Then they find 63,000 pages of data hidden within the signal which are decoded to reveal the plans to build a special space travel machine. They rightly reason: information only comes from intelligence.

Here is the question for us: who programmed the software we find in our DNA, the coded information which contains the instructions for building all the different body plans for life on earth? Richard Dawkins writes, 'The difference between life and non-life is a matter not of substance but information. Living things contain prodigious quantities of information. Most of the information is coded in DNA'[31]. The nucleic acid 'rungs' in the DNA form a digital code, and this is again not a metaphor but a fact. Just as our computers run on a binary code, so DNA contains a four-character genetic code written in nucleic acids.

Paul Davies writes: 'Like a supercomputer, life is an information processing system ... It is the software of the living cell that is the real mystery, not the hardware'.

Davies goes on to ask the killer question:

'How did stupid atoms spontaneously write their own software? Nobody knows ... there is no known law of physics able to create information from nothing'[32].

We have already eliminated one possible explanation for the coded information in our DNA: chance. The odds are too high. But what about the laws of nature – could some natural law or force have built the DNA software?

---

[31] Richard Dawkins, *The Greatest Show on Earth*, Free Press, 2009, p.405
[32] Paul Davies, "Life Force", *New Scientist*, 163(2204), Sept 1999, pp.27-30

The software that runs our cells is written in coded chemistry, in the language of nucleic acids, millions of them that make up the 'rungs' of the twisted ladder of the DNA molecule. But these nucleic acids are not placed in exactly the right order by some law of chemistry that forces them to line up in a certain sequence. The chemical 'letters' are free to go anywhere, just as the letters that make up the words on this page are not arranged into words by the chemical properties of ink or the physical properties of paper. The letters on this page were arranged by the author in the right sequence to produce a meaningful message. So the precise sequencing of the nucleic acids are not the result of physics or chemistry.

If you were walking across a grass lawn and came across a series of rocks spelling out the words, 'Will you marry me?' no one would suggest that the latest thunderstorm had blown them into position. You would conclude that a human being had placed them there. In precisely the same way, the nucleic acids in our genetic code are neither arranged by random chance, nor are they in the precise sequence because of some law of physics or chemistry.

Antony Flew found this argument convincing, writing, 'Can the origins of a system of coded chemistry be explained in a way that makes no appeal whatever to the kinds of facts that we otherwise invoke to explain codes and languages, systems of communication, the impress of ordinary words on the world of matter?'[33].

The very first living cell already contained software, and not some primitive and simplistic kind of code. We know that just as a book cannot write itself from random inkblots, nor a computer program write itself by accidental key-strokes, so the software of life did not write itself either. Just as in the movie *Contact*, the presence of digitally coded information is the tell-tale evidence of intelligence. There is no other known explanation. Furthermore, the digital code of life is the most amazing software program ever written, far beyond any code that humans have ever written. It makes sense to believe that the intelligence which wrote the book of life, the intelligence that designed the living cell, is vastly superior to that of any human engineer.

---

[33] Flew, p.127

Conclusion

Francis Crick, atheist co-discoverer of the DNA double-helix, wrote, 'An honest man, armed with all the knowledge available to us now, could only state that in some sense, the origin of life appears at the moment to be almost a miracle, so many are the conditions which would have had to have been satisfied to get it going'[34].

The origin of life is one of the most baffling challenges for atheism. Life did not happen by chance, nor are there any physical or chemical laws that build life spontaneously, and the fact that life depends on information technology strongly points to a super-intelligence. That is why Antony Flew had the honesty and humility to abandon atheism.

I rate the argument from the origin of life at 9 out of ten. Again, the only reason I do not give it a 10 is because science in general does not give us watertight proofs. There might be future scientific discoveries that affect the argument, so we cannot rate it at 10.

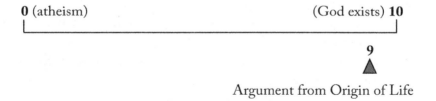

0 (atheism)   (God exists) **10**

9

Argument from Origin of Life

---

[34] Francis Crick, *Life Itself, Its Origin and Nature*, Simon and Shuster, 1981, p.88

Chapter 7

The William Paley Argument: the Eye

W illiam Paley (1743–1805) was an English clergyman and Cambridge University lecturer, whose books were not only bestsellers during the 1800s but also required reading at Cambridge University up until the 1920s. His most well-known work was the book, *Natural Theology, or, Evidences of the Existence and Attributes of the Deity* (1802).

Paley's most famous argument was about going for a walk on a heath and kicking his foot against a rock:

'Suppose I pitched my foot against a stone, and were asked how the stone came to be there; I might possibly answer, that, for any thing I knew to the contrary, it had lain there for ever'.

But if he kicked his foot against a watch on the ground, and asked how it came to be there, he would hardly say that the watch had been there for ever. Instead, he would reason that a watch had been designed by a watch-maker because of the intricate arrangement of parts fulfilling a coordinated purpose:

'its several parts are framed and put together for a purpose, e. g. that they are so formed and adjusted as to produce motion, and that motion so regulated as to point out the hour of the day'.

Paley argued that the watch would not have produced any movement at all or would not have correctly told the time if the parts were shaped different or arranged in the wrong order. He argued that the watch obviously has a maker, because of the various parts which are deliberately suited to work together with the aim of telling the time. It contains:

- a box in which there is a coiled spring (the spring being made of steel, as no other metal is so elastic),
- a series of wheels or cogs (made of brass which cannot rust) with teeth which turn other cogs as the spring relaxes,
- causing the watch hands to gradually turn, covering a given space in a given time, indicating the hour and minute
- the face being covered in transparent glass (any other material would prevent the time being told without opening the case).

Paley then extended this argument to living creatures by showing that they similarly were composed of parts that co-operated to move and thereby to fulfil purposes they could not fulfil on their own.

Paley particularly turned to another 'marvelous mechanism', the eye. He argued that, just like a watch, the eye must have been designed. Paley noted various features of the eye, comparing them with similar mechanisms used in a telescope.

The Eye

The human eye is a marvel of biology. Consider:

1. the eye is protected from injury or damage by sitting inside a bony socket, cushioned by fat,
2. it is spherical, so that it is easily able to look up and down or side to side,
3. like the pocket-watch, the eye has a transparent face, the cornea, not made of glass but of living cells, which require nutrients that cannot be supplied by blood vessels (as this would ruin the transparency); the cornea's nutrients are supplied by our tears (!) and it receives its oxygen supply direct from the air.
4. the eye automatically focuses itself by changing the shape of its lens to give us a clear picture,
5. the eye automatically contracts or dilates its aperture (light-hole), the pupil, to let the right amount of light in,
6. the eye automatically turns in the direction it wishes to look, with both eyes moving in unison, giving us binocular stereoscopic vision,

i.e. depth-perception,

7. it automatically shuts its outside cover (the eyelid) in a split-second for protection, to wipe the eye clean, and for sleep,

8. it cleans and protects itself by washing out dust and other foreign material with tears from a gland; the tears are drained by a small canal in the bone into the nose, where they are evaporated off,

9. the eye is protected from glare and perspiration by the eyebrows,

10. the eye has 130 million light-receptive cells in the retina in the back of the eye, sending 1 billion electrical impulses every second to the brain via the optic nerve.

The brain processes the signals from our two separate eyes and (to use the language of old-fashioned photography) 'develops' the picture we see. As a result, we have a 576 megapixel camera (mobile phone cameras in 2020 are between 4 and 10 megapixels) that gives us a constant high-definition, three-dimension, full-colour, instantaneous (no lag) 'livestream' video-feed of life. But that's not all: our brain is able to pull up old 'still' photo-shots of various scenes from its memory.

The Argument from Beauty

There is one other design feature of the eye we have not mentioned: beauty. In many commercial products, evidence of design is seen in the attractiveness of the product and its packaging. The same is true of the eye, with its coloured iris encircling the pupil, set against a white backdrop. Just as Apple digital products are known not just for their technology, but also for their aesthetic beauty, so too most eyes are coloured brown, blue, or green and sometimes have a shiny appearance. Humans are also unique in that the whites of our eyes are visible (whereas, for example, the whites of apes' eyes are not). The result is that our unique eyes allow us to make eye-contact from a distance, and express emotions without even speaking. Graphic design theory emphasizes the power of white space, which adds elegance, acts as a container, and focuses attention on what is important, in our case, on the beauty of the iris and the pupil. Just as BMW cars are not just well-engineered, but also have aerodynamically curved lines, our eyes also have a beautiful sleek appearance. This is the argument from beauty.

Charles Kingsley wrote, 'Never lose an opportunity of seeing anything that is beautiful, for beauty is God's handwriting'[1]. Simone Weil wrote, 'The beauty of this world is Christ's tender smile coming to us through matter'[2]. We see evidence of beauty all around us in creation, but the greatest beauty is seen in the face, and particularly in the eyes, of someone we love.

An Amazing Contraption

William Paley draws attention to an amazing contraption, a muscle called the superior oblique, which employs a pulley-system to rotate the eye. Paley writes, 'The muscle is passed through a loop formed by another muscle; and is there inflected, as if it were round a pulley'. Below is the picture from *Gray's Anatomy*, (note the word 'Pulley'):

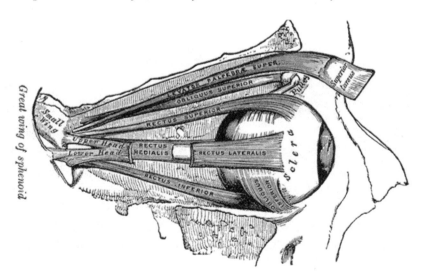

The reason for this mechanism is as follows: the pulley-system enables the muscle to pull from just above the front of the eye, yet still have

---

[1] Charles Kingsley, *Politics for the People*, 1848
[2] Simone Weil, *Waiting for God*, Harper, 1975, pp.164-5

enough length necessary for sufficient contracting power.

If Socrates' observation about the position of the eyes and nose above the mouth to prevent the consumption of what is unacceptable is a great argument for God's existence – and it is – then how much more impressive is the argument from God's existence from the masterpiece of engineering which is the eye itself.

Atheist Counter-Arguments

Richard Dawkins named one of his most popular books, *The Blind Watchmaker*, countering Paley's evidence of design by arguing that Darwin's theory of evolution, the blind tinkering watchmaker, was able to account for the appearance of design without any need for a real designer, i.e. God.

What did Darwin himself think of the eye? He wrote:

To suppose that the eye with all its inimitable contrivances for adjusting the focus to different distances, for admitting different amounts of light, and for the correction of spherical and chromatic aberration, could have been formed by natural selection, seems, I freely confess, absurd in the highest degree.

But he continued, arguing for the gradual evolution of the eye:

Yet reason tells me, that if numerous gradations from a perfect and complex eye to one very imperfect and simple, each grade being useful to its possessor, can be shown to exist; if further, the eye does vary ever so slightly, and the variations be inherited, which is certainly the case; and if any variation or modification in the organ be ever useful to an animal under changing conditions of life, then the difficulty of believing that a perfect and complex eye could be formed by natural selection, though insuperable by our imagination, can hardly be considered real[3].

---

[3] Charles Darwin, *The Origin of Species by Means of Natural Selection*, The Modern Library, 1993, p.227

Elsewhere, in a letter to Asa Gray, Professor of Natural History at Harvard, Darwin wrote, 'The eye to this day gives me a cold shudder, but when I think of the fine known gradations, my reason tells me I ought to conquer the cold shudder'[4].

Richard Dawkins similarly argues that 50% or even 5% of an eye is far better than nothing at all. The fact that we observe many different types of eyes in nature, from a primitive light-sensitive spot on some creatures all the way to the marvelously adapted eyes of humans, proves that the eye evolved gradually, step by step, removing any need for a designing Creator.

Another atheist counter-argument against the design of the vertebrate eye is that it involves flaws that no clever designer would use. One is the so-called backward wiring of the retina. Dawkins describes the problem:

'The 'wires' connecting the photocells to the brain run all over the surface of the retina, so the light rays have to pass through a carpet of massed wires before they hit the photocells. That doesn't make sense'.

We would assume that the photocells in the eye would point towards the light, with their wires behind them going to the brain. However, with our eyes, the opposite is the case: the wires are in front of the photocells. Dawkins points to another design flaw, the eye's 'blind spot':

'It gets worse. One consequence of the photocells pointing backwards is that the wires that carry their data somehow have to pass through the retina and back to the brain. What they do, in a vertebrate eye, is all converge on a particular hole in the retina, where they dive through it. The hole filled with nerves is called the blind spot, because it is blind, but 'spot' is too flattering, for it is quite large, more like a blind patch'.

The optic nerve has to travel through a hole in the retina (the 'blind-spot') to transmit its signals to the brain. By comparison, an octopus has

---

[4] Francis Darwin, ed., *The Life and Letters of Charles Darwin*, Vol. 2, D. Appleton and Co., 1899, p.67

an eye that is similar to a vertebrate eye, except that the 'wiring' is behind the layer of retinal cells and does not block the light. Dawkins concludes:

> 'it is the design of a complete idiot. Or is it? If it were, the eye would be terrible at seeing, and it is not. It is actually very good. It is good because natural selection, working as a sweeper-up of countless little details, came along after the big original error of installing the retina backwards, and restored it to a high-quality precision instrument'[5].

The atheist counter-argument against the eye's design therefore consists of two parts. First, life on earth shows that eyes developed gradually, from primitive early stages like a simple light-sensitive spot. Secondly, design flaws show that an all-knowing and almighty designer did not create eyes. Dawkins wrote, 'Paley's argument is made with passionate sincerity and is informed by the best biological scholarship of his day, but it is wrong, gloriously and utterly wrong'[6].

Four Problems with Dawkins' Arguments

Problem One: Design flaws

We shall start with the last problem first: the so-called design flaws in the eye that Dawkins says rules out the possibility of a divine designer. In a report in 2007 titled, "Müller cells are living optical fibers in the vertebrate retina", researchers found that the 'carpet of massed wires' (as Dawkins called them) in front of the retina actually contained living fibre-optic cables. Instead of blocking the light, they acted to improve vision by channeling exactly the right colour of light directly to the correct cells in the retina[7]. The science website Phys.org described the discovery as follows:

---

[5] Richard Dawkins, *The Greatest Show on Earth: the Evidence for Evolution*, Free Press, 2009, p.353-4

[6] Richard Dawkins, *The Blind Watchmaker*, W.W. Norton & Co., 1987, p.5

[7] Franze et al., "Müller cells are living optical fibers in the vertebrate retina", *Proc. National Academy of Sciences USA*, 104(20):8287–8292, 15 May 2007

Having the photoreceptors at the back of the retina is not a design constraint, it is a design feature. The idea that the vertebrate eye, like a traditional front-illuminated camera, might have been improved somehow if it had only been able to orient its wiring behind the photoreceptor layer, like a cephalopod [i.e. octopus], is folly[8].

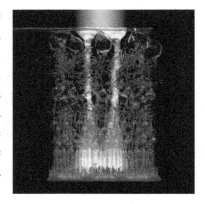

Fibre-optic cables are amongst the most advanced human engineering systems, used to transmit data over longer distances and with better results than electrical cables. The idea that our eyes contain fibre-optic cables is a staggering discovery. It turns out that the 'backward wiring of the eye' is not a design flaw at all, but a design feature.

What about the blind spot, where the optic nerve passes through the retina? Even Dawkins admits that it does not present any problem for vision. The reason is that the blind spot only takes up 0.25% of the visual field (so much for Dawkins' 'large patch') and is not in the centre but 15 degrees from the visual axis[9]. The field of vision of one eye covers the 'blind-spot' of the other eye, and vice versa, and the brain patches the picture so that we experience no loss of vision. As even William Paley knew a few centuries ago, 'no part of an object is unperceived by both eyes at the same time'. The result is that the system works perfectly. There is no 'flaw' at all.

Thus, the backward-wired eye presents no problem for vision, or for the idea that our eyes were designed. Vertebrates with this type of eye include eagles which can see objects at great distances with superb clarity. But the 'backward-wired' eye presents a big problem for Dawkins' evolutionary theory, for the vertebrate eye had to evolve from some other eye which was wired the opposite way. How did this change take place?

---

[8] https://phys.org/news/2014-07-fiber-optic-pipes-retina-simple.html

[9] Ophthalmologist Peter Gurney, "Is our 'Inverted' Retina Really 'Bad Design'?" *Journal of Creation* 13(1), 1999, pp.37-44

Did the retina detach itself from the back of the eye and flip itself over inside the eye? Did the optic nerve unplug itself from the retina during this switch, and then after the retina had flipped, poke itself through a hole in the retina and re-attach itself again to the brain? Did a carpet of fibre-optic cables lay themselves down in front of the retina? And if so, how was any creature able to see with detached retinas, unplugged optic nerves, while this carpet-laying took place (for natural selection requires sight at all times, as each step must be a slight improvement)?

As ophthalmologist Dr George Marshall writes, 'the idea that the eye is wired backward comes from a lack of knowledge of eye function and anatomy'[10]. The design flaws are nothing of the kind.

It turns out that Paley was not the one who was 'gloriously and utterly wrong' – it was Dawkins himself. The discovery of living fibre-optic cables in the eye is a stunning refutation of Dawkins' argument against biological design based on scientific ignorance. Just one year after the publication of *The God Delusion*, God took Dawkins out to the woodshed and gave him a proverbial spanking.

Problem Two: Early Eyes

A second problem for Darwin's account of the evolution of the eye is that many of the fossil creatures in the Cambrian rocks (the earliest rock layers to contain multi-cellular life) already had eyes of amazing sophistication. Many eyes found among the fossils are not the primitive light-sensitive spots of Darwin's speculation at all, but marvels of advanced technology.

For example, while our eyes have soft lenses that adjust their shape to focus, trilobites (crab-like creatures) in the Cambrian rocks had eyes with solid lenses which cannot adjust their shape. This would normally produce a blurring round the edges, called spherical aberration. However, the problem is overcome in trilobites by having their lenses specially shaped according to a mathematical formula only discovered by the scientists and mathematicians Descartes and Huygens in the 1600s, as

---

[10] George Marshall, "An Eye for Creation", *Creation* 18 (4), 1996, pp.20-21

they tried to find ways to reduce spherical aberration. How did the 'primitive' trilobites work out this mathematical formula without any intelligence, and then manufacture new lenses to this specification? If this happened by a gradual process of trial and error over millions of years, why is there no record of them evolving from earlier and more primitive eyes in Precambrian rocks in the fossil record?

For another example, fossilized prawn (i.e. shrimp) from Cambrian rocks show some of the most advanced compound eyes ever discovered, with over 3000 hexagonally-arranged lenses, 'the densest and most efficient packing pattern' (*Nature*[11]). These amazing compound eyes are virtually identical to modern prawn eyes and show no evidence of evolutionary ancestry or development before or after. There is no scientific evidence for the gradual evolution of the amazing shrimp or trilobite eyes, nor is there any direct evidence for the gradual evolution of sight in other Cambrian or pre-Cambrian fossils. These Cambrian eyes blink out at us from the fossil record fully-formed.

Thus the second problem with the atheist argument is that there is no evidence of the gradual development of sight at all – it appears perfectly formed in the first fossil-bearing rocks. Darwin's gradual evolutionary origin of sight is not so much science, but rather more like the story of a fairy godmother who waves her wand and eyes magically appear.

Problem Three: Thirty (or Sixty) Different Eyes

A third problem with the atheist argument is that, among the myriad creatures on earth with sight, eyes must have evolved in more than thirty separate ways. Ernst Mayr, one of the most prominent 20th century evolutionary biologists, wrote: 'eyes have evolved independently more than forty times in the animal kingdom'[12]. Dawkins says more than sixty times[13]. This is because there are 12 completely different major eye designs in nature and, to complicate matters more, some of the same

---

[11] Lee, M. S. Y. et al., "Modern optics in exceptionally preserved eyes of Early Cambrian arthropods from Australia", *Nature*. 474 (7353), 2011, pp.631-634.
[12] Ernst Mayr, *The Growth of Biological Thought*, Harvard University Press, 1982, p.612
[13] Richard Dawkins, *Climbing Mount Improbable*, Viking, 1996, p.127

designs are found in unrelated branches of the tree of life, meaning they had to evolve independently numerous times.

Consider some of the amazing eyes in nature:

- dragonflies have compound eyes made up of 30,000 mini-eyes,
- box jellyfish have 24 eyes of four distinct types,
- spiders can have up to eight eyes,
- chameleons have independent telephoto (i.e. zooming) eyes that also allow them to see in two different directions at once
- lobsters are unique in that they focus light by reflecting mirrors rather than bending light (refraction) as we do,
- the mantis shrimp has four times as many color receptors as the human eye and some can see ultraviolet light,
- birds use infrared sight (which we feel as heat) to see at night (police helicopters use the same 'night-vision' cameras to track people during highway chases),
- some fish have four eyes – two for seeing below the water and two for seeing above.

On the other hand, octopus eyes are similar to human eyes, i.e. they have a similar sort of design, despite being of a completely unrelated evolutionary lineage. Similarly, ants and crabs both have compound eyes, but are completely unrelated orders of animals. The 'pinhole' eye of the nautilus (a type of mollusk) is claimed as the evolutionary ancestor of our more complex vertebrate eyes, however this is falsified by the fact that the nautilus belongs to an entirely different order of creatures and is therefore not an ancestor of vertebrates at all.

This presents a problem. To put it in context, compare another wonder of nature, flight, which occurs in four completely unrelated groups: flying mammals (bats), insects, birds and reptiles (pterodactyls). For flight to have arisen once by the gradual accumulation of lucky genetic copying mistakes (i.e. mutations) would be amazing enough, but the story is harder – not easier – to believe when we find out that it evolved four times, independently. All the many billions of flying creatures in our world almost make it seem like flight is an easy feat to achieve, but we know from how long it took humans to fly planes that this is far from the case. Still today, planes crash; flight requires engineering excellence.

To see the problem, consider the illustration in Richard Dawkins' book, *Climbing Mount Improbable*. Dawkins says sight did not occur in one single leap. That would be very improbable, like a man climbing up the sheer cliff-face of a high mountain. Dawkins instead tells us that sight occurred by the man walking round the back of the mountain and climbing slowly up the gradual slope on its other side. As the man climbed up the gentle slope, step by step, his resting points on the way up marked all the different types of eyes in nature till we reach the evolutionary summit. This is a nice story – Dawkins is a good storyteller – but is there any evidence for it?

A more realistic analogy is a group of thirty deaf and blind people flying in a plane which crashes in a remote jungle canyon. The pilot and all the able-bodied passengers die in the crash, leaving all of the thirty deaf and blind people bruised and shaken, but still alive. Because they are deaf and blind, they are not sure whether there are any other survivors. After a while, they get hungry and each independently set off to try and find help, but all come up against the sides of the canyon – at different places. There is no single road out of the canyon, no gently-sloping highway that they all take. The deaf and blind survivors are all separated, so that their paths are not connected to any the others take. There is no evolutionary relationship between the thirty different varieties of sight. Instead of *Climbing Mount Improbable*, Dawkins needs to change the title of the book to *Climbing Thirty Mount Improbables*. The one gradually-ascending stairway to sight only exists in Dawkins' imagination.

If the probability of just one disabled climber making it out of the canyon is small, what are the chances of all thirty climbing their separate walls and standing atop their respective cliffs? Dawkins would say that each of the thirty climbers finds their own gradual, gently-sloping pathway out of the canyon. In fact, he would probably say that the fact that we have eyes to see means that they must have evolved this way. But that is just assuming what needs to be proved. To see what the chances are of any of the deaf and blind climbers making it out of the canyon, we need to move on to the last problem with the atheist story of how sight arose.

Problem Four: Sight Itself

The fourth problem is the most serious of all. Darwin and Dawkins start with a 'primitive' light-sensitive spot, from which all sight thereafter evolved. They contend that having 1% of an eye is better than having none, and that 5% is better than 1%, and so on all the way up to 100%.

St. George Mivart was one of the highest credentialled early scientific critics of Darwin's theory of evolution. A Professor of Zoology, he published a book in 1871 called 'On the Genesis of Species' in which he argued that Darwin's theory had a major problem: its failure to explain the 'incipient stages' of organs – in other words, the first step.

What happens if the first step in the evolution of sight does not involve a 1% increment? What happens if you don't get anything at all until you have 18% (or 68%) of sight? This is exactly what modern science has discovered, and it completely destroys Dawkins' imaginary scenario of small incremental steps.

The biggest problem with the evolution of sight is the first step. If we may continue the analogy of the canyon climbers, getting sight 'off the ground' and commencing the climb out of the canyon is the hardest part of all. The climbers are all faced with a 10 metre high sheer cliff face before the first footholds appear.

What does the 'first step' in solving the problem of sight involve? It means getting a functional light-sensitive spot or cell. As we shall see, this is the most complex bio-engineering problem to solve; by comparison with it, all the rest of the eye is child's play. It is the 'seeing' bit of sight – the truly difficult thing to produce. In Darwin's day scientists did not have the faintest clue about what biochemical reactions inside cells produced sight. It was easy for Darwin to say, 'imagine a light-sensitive' spot, without knowing how it actually worked.

Just what does the first step of sight involve? Here is the mind-boggling description by Michael Behe of the chemical reaction that produces sight in an eye:

'When light first strikes the retina a photon interacts with a molecule called 11-*cis*-retinal, which rearranges within picoseconds to *trans*-retinal. (A picosecond [10^{-12} sec] is about the time it takes light to travel the breadth of a single human hair.) The change in the shape of the retinal molecule forces a change in the shape of the protein, rhodopsin, to which the retina is tightly bound. The protein's metamorphosis alters its behavior. Now called metarhodopsin II, the protein sticks to another protein, called transducin. Before bumping into metarhodopsin II, transducin had tightly bound a small molecule called GDP. But when transducin interacts with metarhodopsin II, the GDP falls off, and a molecule called GTP binds to transducin. (GTP is closely related to, but different from, GDP.)[14]

As one other writer commented, "*Whew!*" We need not continue with the rest of the description. These are just the first few parts of the chemical chain-reaction involving eighteen different chemical players required to turn light into an electrical signal sent to the brain. Imagine eighteen different trapeze artists who must fly through the air, catching and releasing each other at just the right place and time, for the choreography to proceed. If just one of these eighteen chemical steps were missing, the chain-reaction would break down, and some (or all) of the trapeze artists would fall in a heap of jumbled, injured bodies on the ground of the circus tent. We have already seen in a previous chapter that to spontaneously self-assemble just one single specific protein by random chance involves inconceivable levels of improbability. To think that all eighteen different perfectly matching chemical players spontaneously auto-arranged themselves into existence and then collectively assembled together in the cell for no purpose, but, "Hey Presto!", sight just 'popped' into existence from their accidental interaction – this takes blind faith of the highest order.

Darwin and Dawkins conveniently assume the hardest and most important part of the explanation: how sight itself arose. Darwin wrote, 'we ought in *imagination* to take a thick layer of [light-sensitive tissue] ...

---

[14] Michael J. Behe, *Darwin's Black Box: the Biochemical Challenge to Evolution*, The Free Press, 1996, p.46

and then *suppose* [that it can vary]; we must *suppose* that there is a power [to select variants]; we must *suppose* each new state [is reproduced in great numbers]; and may we not *believe* [that this would produce the eye]?'[15]. Notice the words 'imagination', 'suppose' and 'believe' – Darwin's account is three parts imagination to one part science: a recipe for a fairy story. He starts with "assume a light-sensitive cell" and it magically appears on command.

Instead of providing a scientific account of the origin of sight, Darwin and Dawkins instead take a short-cut – imagination – and like lazy schoolboys not very keen on cross-country running, conveniently avoid the toughest section of the race, the emergence of sight itself, until breaking from the cover of the trees at just the right moment, they run forward to the finish line, claiming the prize in the scientific explanation of sight.

Just as all eighteen chemical 'trapeze-artists' are required to produce the chain-reaction of sight, so all of the main parts of the visual system had to be in place for us to see. Even if we ignore all the amazing optical machinery inside the eye, we still have three indispensable elements: light-sensitive cells, optic nerves and a brain processor. Which came first, the light-sensitive spot, or the optic nerve to transmit the signal, or the brain processing to make some sense and use of it? Sight could not have evolved step-by-step, for all three components had to be in place for it to have any functional benefit.

Conclusion

There is an old lawyer's joke about defending a man called Smith who is accused of returning a kettle with a crack. The lawyer uses the following arguments:

1. Smith never borrowed the kettle.
2. When Smith returned it the kettle was not cracked.
3. The kettle was already cracked when Smith borrowed it.
4. There is no kettle.

---

[15] *Origin*, pp.157-8, emphasis added

This is similar to the way atheists argue about the eye:

1. The eye was designed by a complete idiot
2. Even if not, the eye gradually evolved from a simple light-sensitive spot
3. Even if the fossil evidence shows no such thing, evolving a simple electro-chemical light-sensitive spot is child's play,
4. There is no God

The miracle of sight is one of the greatest wonders of nature. As we survey the arguments for and against the eye being designed by God, we conclude that all four atheist arguments are wrong:

1. The eye does not have design flaws, but amazing engineering,
2. The earliest fossil-bearing rocks show eyes of the utmost sophistication – not simplicity,
3. Instead of the atheist account of all eyes being found somewhere on the same branching path, a gradually-ascending slope, there are instead thirty (or sixty) separate paths to climb,
4. The origin of sight itself did not happen in gradual steps, but abruptly as a package, for all eighteen different chemicals in the chain-reaction of sight had to be present from the start.

The evolutionary account of sight offered by Darwin and Dawkins consists almost entirely of storytelling, not science. In the debate over the origin of the eye, God easily outpoints Dawkins and Darwin: 4 – 0. The eye is amazing evidence that we were designed – by God. It is another reason we know that God really exists. I rate it as a 9 out of 10 argument for God's existence.

0 (atheism)   (God exists) **10**

Argument from the Eye

Chapter 8

The Michael Behe Argument: Biotechnology

In 1996, the American biochemist Michael Behe published *Darwin's Black Box*. In it he argued that we can tell that something has been designed whenever we see evidence of Irreducible Complexity. By this, Behe meant that some systems need every part to be in place to work. If we take away even one part, the mechanism will not function. Behe used the ordinary old-fashioned mousetrap as an illustration of an irreducibly complex system. A mousetrap needs five parts to work: a platform, a spring, a catch, a holding bar and a hammer. All the parts must be present to catch mice: if we took away the spring, the hammer would not be loaded to catch the mouse, or if we took away the hammer, there would be nothing to catch the mouse with, and so on.

Behe argued that various biological systems are irreducibly complex. Further, he argued that such biological systems could not have been produced by natural selection, because it proceeds in a gradual, step-by-step fashion, adding one part at a time. Instead, all the parts of the system must have been present before it had any functional use.

Charles Darwin, in the *Origin of Species*, had written, 'If it could be demonstrated that any complex organ existed which could not possibly have been formed by numerous, successive, slight modifications, my theory would absolutely break down'[1]. J. B. S. Haldane, another evolutionary biologist, similarly argued that evolution could never produce 'various mechanisms, such as the wheel and the magnet, which would be useless till fairly perfect'[2]. However, as we are about to see, science has discovered examples of wheels in nature. In fact, modern

---

[1] Charles Darwin, *Origin of Species*, 1859, p.189
[2] D. Dewar, L. M. Davies and J. B. S. Haldane, *Is Evolution a Myth? A Debate*, Watts and Co. Ltd/Paternoster Press, 1949, p.90

science has discovered even more amazing biotechnology.

The Bacterial Flagellum

Perhaps the most famous biological example of irreducible complexity that Behe described in his book was the bacterial flagellum. Bacteria (like *E. coli*) move about by means of tiny whip-like tails called flagella.

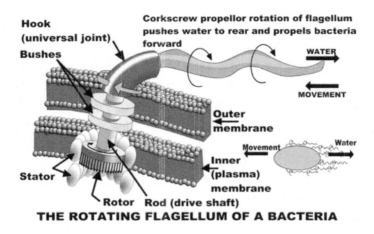

THE ROTATING FLAGELLUM OF A BACTERIA

The flagellum is a miniature version of an outboard motor with a rotating whip-like propeller, forward and reverse gears, a rotor, a stator, a drive shaft, a clutch, bushing, and a universal joint. Most modern cars 'redline' (i.e. overheat) at about 7,000rpm, but these tiny water-cooled, rotary motors operate at speeds of up to 100,000rpm. The multiple flagella on a bacteria propel it forward at a speed of 35 body-lengths per second. Compare this to the fastest human ever, Usain Bolt, whose top speed was 13.2 metres per second, or 6.7 body-lengths per second. The flagella also have hard-wired signal mechanisms, giving feedback from their environment, allowing them to stop and reverse in an instant.

Think about how amazing this technology is: these outboard motors are 1000 times smaller than a millimeter, yet more powerful and efficient than any outboard motors humans have invented. If a man landed on Mars and found an outboard motor lying on the ground more technologically advanced than anything on earth, would it not be taken as proof of alien life? Why then is an outboard motor like the bacterial flagellum not proof of an intelligence far beyond any human genius?

But back to Michael Behe's argument. This tiny outboard motor requires forty complex protein parts, and if just one of these proteins were missing, the motor would not work. This suggests that this molecular machine had to be created fully-developed. It could not have been formed bit-by-bit, in an incremental step-by-step process over a long period of time, for none of the intermediate stages would have produced anything with functional ability, giving it any advantage over a previous stage.

Objections

After Behe had claimed that the bacterial flagellum could not have developed in a gradual, step-by-step fashion, some biologists responded that it had indeed evolved, by cobbling together components from other organisms. It was claimed that the bacterial flagellum had co-opted an injection system found in *Yersinia pestis* (the bubonic plague) called the type III secretory system (TTSS). *Scientific American* magazine wrote:

> The sophisticated components of this flagellum all have precedents elsewhere in nature ... In fact, the entire flagellum assembly is extremely similar to an organelle that *Yersinia Pestis*, the bubonic plague bacterium, uses to inject toxins into cells ... The key is that the flagellum's component structures, which Behe suggests have no value apart from their role in propulsion, can serve multiple functions that would have helped favor their evolution[3].

However, there are a number of flaws in this theory. Firstly, only 10 of the 40 protein parts of the bacterial flagellum are found in the TTSS, (so the two systems are not 'extremely similar'). Despite Behe's critics claiming that the bacterial flagellum could have evolved gradually, evolutionary biologists still have not provided any account of an incremental pathway from the TTSS to the bacterial flagellum 25 years

---

[3] J. Rennie, "15 Answers to Creationist Nonsense", *Scientific American* 287 (1), 2002, pp.78-85

later, each small step providing some functional and beneficial advantage.

In fact, secondly, experts on the bacterial flagellum argue that, if anything, the TTSS has probably devolved or degenerated from one part of the bacterial flagellum: A paper in the *Journal of Molecular Microbiology and Biotechnology* states, 'We suggest that the flagellar apparatus was the evolutionary precursor of Type III protein secretion systems'[4].

A final problem with the idea that the bacterial flagellum evolved from the TTSS injection system comes from evolutionary history. Bacteria supposedly evolved before the plants and animals that they would later inhabit as parasites. But the only function of the TTSS injection mechanism in *Yersinia Pestis* (bubonic plague) was to inject its hosts (i.e. animals). Therefore, the TTSS injection system would have had no useful role for millions of years before plants and animals existed. On the other hand, before animals and plants existed, bacteria would have been swimming around, but how would this have been possible without their outboard motors, which were still evolving from the parasitic injection system? This makes no sense – everything is back to front. The idea that the bacterial flagellum evolved from the TTSS injection mechanism contradicts basic evolutionary theory.

These three problems mean that Behe's argument from irreducible complexity remains unrefuted, and seems far more reasonable than the atheist counter arguments. Our common-sense intuition is true: microscopic outboard motors look like they were designed because they were in fact designed, just like life-sized outboard motors are designed. Who would have thought that God was a mechanical engineer?

ATP synthase motor

ATP synthase is the world's tiniest motor, a marvel of nanotechnology machinery. For explaining how it works, Paul Boyer, John Walker and Jens Skou were awarded the Nobel Prize for chemistry in 1997.

Like the bacterial flagellum, ATP synthase is a rotary motor. It is a million times smaller than a millimeter, is powered by protons (i.e.

---

[4] L Nguyen et al, "Phylogenetic analyses of the constituents of Type III protein secretion systems", *J. Mol. Microbiol. Biotechnol.* 2(2), April 2000, pp.125-44

hydrogen ions) and produces ATP, which is the main fuel source of the cell, not just in humans but in all life, even the simplest bacteria. Every day, trillions of these motors inside our cells pump out ATP, which fuels every sort of activity in the body, from DNA operation to muscle contraction to electrical signals in the nerves. Each ATP synthase motor turns at up to 200 revolutions per second (12,000 rpm), producing 600 ATPs per second.

Jerry Bergman writes, 'the ATP molecule is so enormously intricate that we are just now beginning to understand how it works. ... In manufacturing terms, the ATP molecule is a machine with a level of organization on the order of a research microscope or a standard television'[5].

The biggest problem that ATP poses for atheism is the catch-22: ATP is the main energy-source for life, critical for most processes in the cell, even DNA function. But DNA is where we get ATP synthase rotary motors from in the first place. This is the ultimate chicken and egg problem: which came first, DNA or ATP synthase machines? Both had to be present in the first living cell at the same time.

If all the other machines inside the cell run on this energy source, what did cells use before ATP evolved? Before ATP evolved, were all other cellular processes different, running on a different fuel? Bergman asks, 'How did life exist before ATP? How could life survive without ATP since no form of life we know of today can do that? ... How could ATP evolve and where are the many transitional forms required to evolve the complex ATP molecule? No feasible candidates exist and none can exist because only a perfect ATP molecule can properly carry out its role in the cell'.

Michael Behe wrote about the ATP synthase motor in *Darwin's Black Box*, arguing that anything less than a complete ATP synthase motor will not work. Not only will a transitional form of ATP synthase motor not work, but without a fully-functional ATP synthase motor, neither will any the other cellular functions which rely on this critical fuel-source.

---

[5] Jerry Bergman, "The Perfect Energy Currency for the Cell", *Creation Research Society Quarterly*, 36(1), 1999, pp.2-10

The ATP synthase motor is thus irreducibly complex, and not only disproves the atheist account of the gradual self-assembly of life from non-living matter, but points to a designer who created it.

Kinesin

Kinesin is another amazing motor found inside cells, a miniature walking robot, resembling a stick-figure human being, with two feet and two arms. It is the workhorse of the cell, and literally walks along pathways inside the cell called microtubules, putting one foot in front of the other, its two arms carrying cellular cargo to various destinations. Kinesin are powered by ATP, the energy-source of the cell. Each molecule of ATP that kinesin uses triggers one step. A few fun facts about kinesin are:

- kinesin is fast, able to move at 100 steps per second. These steps are 8 nano-metres long[6] which, if scaled up to our height, would be the same as travelling at about 600 metres per second, or over 2000kph.
- kinesin is efficient, its motor operating at about 50% efficiency, which is twice as efficient as a petrol engine, and for its size produces 15 times more power than a man-made petrol engine.
- kinesin are precise, delivering loads to the correct 'address' inside the cell where the cargo is needed, just like a postman with instructions to deliver a parcel to a particular street location.

Amazing Animals

Consider some of the other amazing abilities in the animal kingdom, which if they belonged to humans, would be called super-powers.

- Geckos have 500 million suction cups on their feet, enabling them to walk up walls and crawl across ceilings upside down. If a human being had this ability, we would call him Spiderman.
- Bats use echo-location – high pitched squeaks which rebound off other objects and come back to them – to allow them to calculate where different objects are, how far away they are, and how big they

[6] A nanometer is one billionth of a metre, or one millionth of a millimetre, so that kinesin takes 125,000 steps for every millimetre.

are. Bats only come out at night and therefore have to navigate and hunt for prey in the dark. They make these calculations while they are flying at high speeds in dark caves.

- Another amazing phenomenon is called Electroreception. The Australian platypus is among a number of animals that are able to detect electrical discharges in the muscles of insects and other prey underwater, which it picks up due to electrical sensors on its bill. Because it does not use its eyes underwater and often feeds at night, it is able to use electroreception to tell the direction and distance to its prey. Electroreception is also used by some fishes to communicate with each other on a different 'channel' to any other creatures. This is called Electrocommunication and is used for species recognition, sex recognition, and in courtship and aggression.

- The fictional character Superman is said to be 'faster than a speeding bullet', and while woodpeckers do not hit trees with their beaks faster than the speed of a bullet, they do hit trees at up to twenty times per second for hours on end. The forces involved are very large – between 1000 and 6000 g-forces of deceleration. Fighter pilots black out if subjected to g-forces of about 6 for more than a few seconds (unless wearing special equipment), and 300g is large enough to give a human serious brain damage. How do woodpeckers avoid these injuries? They have shock-absorbers between their beak and skull, a beak made of elastic material, muscles supporting their neck and head, and a special skull bone containing spinal fluid. In addition, their eyes close every time they hit the tree to stop their eyeballs popping out. They also have a long sticky tongue, five times longer than other similar-sized birds, which retracts into a groove around the head. They use this tongue to eat insects and other things inside the trees.

- The Bombadier beetle mixes two dangerous chemicals in a combustion chamber so that the hot, noxious gases explode out of two tailpipes into the faces of predators. The beetle also mixes in a third inhibitor chemical so that the dangerous chemicals do not blow up while still inside his combustion chamber, and it adds in a fourth anti-inhibitor to cause the explosion. It also opens and closes the

103

inlet valves into the combustion chamber at precisely the right time to prevent itself being blown up by the chemicals.

- The Archerfish shoots a stream of water out of its mouth and up into the air for up to 3m, where it knocks out an insect, which falls into the water for the fish to eat. The most amazing thing about the Archerfish is that it hits its prey, even though, being underwater, it must compensate for the distorted position of insects out of water because of the refraction of light (when light passes through the boundary of air and water at an angle, it changes direction slightly). The archerfish forms a groove in the roof of its mouth with its tongue to enable it to fire water like a pea-shooter.

- Before lightbulbs were ever invented, fish in the deepest oceans had 'lightbulbs' on the end of long, thin projections hanging like fishing rods from their foreheads. These are twenty times more efficient than incandescent light bulbs (they do not give off heat) and more efficient than the best fluorescent and LED bulbs. These fish use bioluminescent bacteria to produce their light, while other bio-luminescent creatures (like fireflies) produce light by a chemical reaction within their own bodies. Electric eels, meanwhile, can produce up to 700 volts of electricity.

Job 12:7-9 says 'But now ask the beasts, and they will teach you; And the birds of the air, and they will tell you; or speak to the earth, and it will teach you; and the fish of the sea will explain to you. Who among all these does not know that the hand of the LORD has done this'.

Conclusion

As we consider the engineering marvels in nature, Psalm 111:2 says, 'The works of the Lord are great, studied by all those who have pleasure in them'. Albert Einstein wrote 'The scientist's religious feeling takes the form of a rapturous amazement at the harmony of Natural Law which reveals an intelligence of such superiority that, compared with it, all the systematic thinking and acting of human beings is an utterly insignificant reflection'.

What does the design we see in creation tell us about God? First, God's infinite intelligence is seen in His works – from designs one millionth of a millimeter long to galaxies millions of light-years across. Isaiah the prophet wrote, 'Have you not known? Have you not heard? The everlasting God, the LORD, the Creator of the ends of the earth, neither faints nor is weary. His understanding is unsearchable. (Isa. 40:28). Design requires intelligence, foresight and planning to achieve ends, and nature shows evidence of a designing Intelligence – God.

Secondly, one designer is simpler than the idea that there are many designers. There is a unity to the design of life – the laws of nature apply universally, and all creatures are built on the same universal genetic code, DNA.

Thirdly, this Designer is personal. Not only does intelligence require personality, but so does the act of creation itself. God created in an intentional, deliberate act. A cloud of gas cannot make decisions; only a person can.

Fourthly, the design of creation shows that the Designer was powerful, able to bring His designs into being. The design of creation therefore tells us that there is One, wise, personal and powerful Creator – God.

The evidence from the various pieces of bio-technology in this chapter argues powerfully for the existence of God. The failure of atheists to provide counter-explanations, or to document transitional forms, means that the argument from biotechnology remains unrefuted.

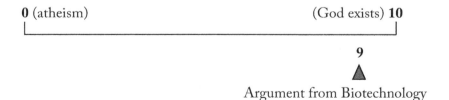

Argument from Biotechnology

Chapter 9

The Sir Isaac Newton Argument: the Human Hand

When I was nearing the end of high school, trying to improve my physics marks, I went to listen to a day of lectures in the city. The lecturer asked attendees who we thought the greatest scientist of all time was. He said, 'Many people think Einstein was the greatest scientist of all time, but Einstein only came up to Isaac Newton's kneecaps'.

Sir Isaac Newton (1643–1727) went to Cambridge University in 1661 and graduated with a bachelor's degree in 1665. The university was shut down due to the bubonic plague from 1665-67, and while he was back at home on the farm for two years, Newton made some of the greatest scientific discoveries of all time.

Observing an apple fall from a tree, he reasoned that the earth has an attractive force, which applies whatever the height from the earth's centre. He therefore argued that even the moon is attracted to the earth. Using mathematical calculus, which he himself had just discovered, and his theory of universal gravitation, Newton proved Kepler's laws of planetary motion (which said that the sun is at the focus of the orbit of the planets), explained the reason for tides, and the paths of comets. He also formulated the three laws of motion and discovered that light contains the full spectrum of colours.

Any single one of these achievements would have classed him amongst the greatest scientists of all time, but he discovered them all before the age of 25. On returning to Cambridge, he became the Lucasian Professor of Mathematics at age 26. Later, he built the first reflecting telescope in 1671. His book *Philosophiæ Naturalis Principia Mathematica* (Mathematical Principles of Natural Philosophy, 1687), has been called the greatest work of science ever written.

Stephen Hawking, like Newton, the Lucasian professor at Cambridge, wrote that 'Newton's theory will never be outmoded. Designed to predict the motions of the heavenly bodies, it does its job with unbelievable accuracy . . . it remains in daily use to predict the orbits of moons and planets, comets and spacecraft. . . . Newton is a colossus without parallel in the history of science'[1].

Evidence for God

Newton was a believer in God. Why did Newton believe in God? Newton considered the evidence of astronomy to point to a designing intelligence. He wrote, 'This most beautiful system of the sun, planets, and comets, could only proceed from the counsel and dominion of an intelligent Being'[2].

There is a story which, if not true (it's hard to track down the source), would have been endorsed by Isaac Newton. Newton had engaged a workman to build a scale model of the solar system, with the planets orbiting around the sun at the crank of a handle. An atheist friend of Newton's came to visit, and upon seeing the model, asked who made it. "Nobody", replied Newton. The visitor looked at him puzzled, and Newton continued, "What you see just happened to take the form it now has". The atheist friend became angry, "Of course somebody made it, and I would like to know who it was". Newton replied, "This is but a puny imitation of a much grander system, and I am not able to convince you that this mere toy is without a designer or maker; yet you profess to believe that the great original from which the design is taken has come into being without either designer or maker! Now tell me by what sort of reasoning do you reach such an incongruous conclusion?"

The Hand

Newton said, 'In the absence of any other proof, the thumb alone would

---

1 Stephen W. Hawking, *A Brief History of Time*, Bantam, 1988, p.199
2 Isaac Newton, *Principia*, III

convine me of God's existence'[3].

Humans are unique among mammals in being bi-pedal (that is, walking on two legs), and as a result, we are also unique in having hands that are free to perform many other tasks. We have 35 different muscles controlling the hand, as well as 27 different bones. These make the hand capable of fifty-eight distinct movements, from taking a pinch of salt, to gripping a pole or pulling on a rope, to writing with a pen or catching a ball. Apes, by contrast, have relatively simple hands and cannot perform many of the actions we can.

Essential to many movements is our unique opposable thumb, which allows us to pinch objects between our thumb and any finger. We can hold things like pens, or scalpels with great precision. No ape or other animal possesses the fine hand control that a human being has, allowing musicians to perform piano concertos and artists to paint *Mona Lisas*.

Essential to our opposable thumb is a special thumb joint. Whereas our shoulders and hips have a ball-and-socket joint, the thumb has a saddle joint. Shoulders sometimes dislocate because of the great maneuverability of the ball and socket joint, but the thumb joint 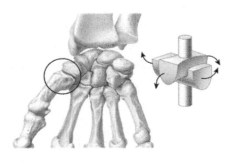 is far less likely to do so. This special joint allows the thumb to move in two planes, giving it a great range of movement, yet the interlocking system also means that the joint has great strength. The thumb has stability as well as mobility. If it were a ball and socket joint, our thumb would have much greater mobility, but less stability, and would be of much less use.

Our hands are special because they are able to perform two different functions. Anatomists describe the human hand as capable of a power grip and a precision grip. We can grab hold of things like a pole, but we can also pick up a needle and perform delicate movements with the tips

---

[3] Reported in Charles Dickens' *All the Year Round*, Vol. 10, 1864, p.346

of our fingers and thumbs.

Five things are essential for the bio-mechanics of our unique hand:

1. Humans are bi-pedal, freeing our hands for use, so they are not needed for walking (apes walk and swing on their hands, so that their middle fingers must be longer and stronger than ours)

2. We have fingers and thumbs of roughly the same length, so that the tip of our thumb can touch the tip of all our fingers (whereas apes' fingers are longer than their thumbs and do not have precision grip)

3. We have a special 'saddle' joint to enable a strong and yet mobile thumb, allowing it to be brought across the hand to touch the tip of any finger

4. We have special muscles which are just for the thumb. For example, humans have an independent muscle for flexing the last joint of the thumb (apes cannot flex their thumb independently)

5. We have a special brain centre, the motor cortex, to control the use of our hands. One quarter of the motor cortex, which controls bodily movements, is devoted to the use of our hands. (By the way, another quarter of the motor cortex is devoted to the control of facial muscles, so we can enjoy social interaction, not just survival; humans have over 50 facial muscles, allowing us to create up to 10,000 different facial expressions, while apes have only 26 facial muscles).

By the way, there are ten different features of human bi-pedalism (two-leggedness) which are all required for the system to work:

- arched feet, providing a rigid yet flexible structure enabling us to balance and spring forward (whereas apes feet are like their hands)

- strong big toes, to push off and propel the body forward (apes do not have our big toe; their big toe is like a thumb for grasping branches)

- fully extendable (i.e. straight) knee joints, which make the legs and the body straight and upright

- inwardly angled femur (upper leg) bones, which mean our feet are close together under our centre of gravity, enabling us to run with only one foot on the ground at a time (whereas apes with separated feet sway from side to side if they try to run uprightly)

- fully extendable (i.e. straight) hip joints, allowing the femur to be fully extended (unlike apes) for upright walking

- long legs, which make it easy to walk or run long distances (whereas apes have shorter legs and longer arms)
- a straight back, meaning our head and chest are directly above our hips when standing (apes have a curved back that projects forward, meaning they must lean on their hands)
- a flat face, required to see the ground at our feet to avoid tripping, which is more dangerous when we only walk on two legs,
- an upright skull, which means the face looks forward (if we walked on four legs like apes, we would have to make the effort to look up)
- and super-fine balance, via sensors in our ears which are more complex than in apes.

These factors make it very difficult for a quadruped to evolve into an upright two-legged walker, for all ten structural features must be in place at the same time for bi-pedalism to be advantageous and successful. All claimed cases of ape-like ancestors of human have either been fully quadrupedal (four-legged) or fully bi-pedal (showing they were either fully apes or fully humans, not intermediates)[4].

But back to the hand. Only humans have all of the features required for the hand's power and precision grips. The human hand will not work its wonders unless all the five features are present. If we were not bi-pedal, we would have to use our hands for walking, and our fingers would need to be different. How would our hands work without the special saddle-joint for both mobility and stability? What would the use of an opposable thumb be if it had no special muscles to move it? What use would these muscles be without nerves connecting them to the control centre in the motor cortex to co-ordinate the movements?

Dr. Paul Gentuso was not sure he believed in God until he studied the human hand in medical school. He said, 'In anatomy class we dissected a human hand. In investigating the hand, I first removed the skin, then isolated the individual tendons and muscles as I worked my

---

[4] For more detail, see Professor Stuart Burgess' book, *Hallmarks of Design*, Day One, 2004, pp.164-169

way to the bones. The tendons of the hand are aligned in tendon sheaths, like self-lubricating pulleys, allowing the hand to work in a tireless, noiseless, almost effortless, fashion. It was perfectly designed to carry out all the work it was called to do, everything from lifting a small object to lugging a tree trunk'.

Gentuso was deeply impressed with what he saw. He said, 'Seeing how each tendon was perfectly aligned along the axis of each finger and how each finger moved in a coordinated fashion when tugged by individual tendons, it became obvious to me that there was a Creator who had intelligently designed and created the human hand. This was the first time in my adult life that I could say with assurance that a Creator existed. It was really a spiritual experience for me. I went from doubt to certainty based on seeing God's creation'[5].

The Brain

The genius of the human hand is that it allows us to build civilizations. We can both hold a nail with our precision grip while holding a hammer in the other hand with our power grip. We can carry a heavy stone in our hands and then shape it with tools made by precise movements of our fingers.

However, there is one organ that is even more important to humans than our hands. We have a unique brain, not only to control the movements of our hands, but to imagine, think, calculate and design. Without the brain to invent new tools and dream up new projects, humanity would be just another animal jumping up and down in the jungle.

No other animal has made even the simplest of inventions – a cup, or a wheel. Some animals, it is true, build things – like nests or dams or webs. However, these are not true inventions. They are instincts, the hard-wired habits of their heredity, no more (or less) amazing than flight or sight or reproduction, but not true inventions of which only humans are capable. No other animal sends its children to school to learn the

---

[5] Robert J. Morgan, *Beyond Reasonable Doubt*, Evangelical Training Association, 1997, p.19

alphabet, or sends rockets to the moon to gather scientific data, or watches events in another part of the world live on television, or performs open-heart surgery. No sheep dreams of riding a motor bike like a little boy does. The animal kingdom is stuck in exactly the same place it has always been. Only the human race has a story that moves forward, with significant milestones worth writing about.

The brain is the most amazing organ in the body. Just one part of it (the cerebral cortex) contains 125 trillion synapses, which is more than the stars in 1500 galaxies. Each of these synapses are microprocessors which contain 1000 molecular switches of their own, meaning that one human brain has more switches than all the computers and internet connections on earth. The ball of grey wrinkly jelly inside a human skull, weighing only 1.5 kilograms (the weight of a medium-sized book) and running on 10 watts of electricity (the same as a dim light-bulb), is easily the most incredible computer in the universe.

Compare the human brain with a modern super-computer. As of 2020, the fastest supercomputer in the world is the IBM Summit, which is a warehouse-sized array of over 9000 connected CPUs (central processing units – i.e. ordinary computers) and is capable of 148,000 teraflops (floating-point operations per second, i.e. 148 x 10^{15} calculations per second). By comparison, the brain is thought to operate at 1,000,000 teraflops (10^{18} calculations per second), which is more than six times faster than the IBM Summit, allowing the brain to perform a billion billion calculations per second.

In 2014, researchers in Japan tried to mimic the processing power of the brain. It took the K Computer (the world's fastest supercomputer in 2011) 40 minutes to calculate what it takes just 1% of our brain to do in 1 second[6].

Further, unlike any computer, the brain is able to re-wire itself. Patients who have undergone a hemispherectomy, where half of the brain is surgically removed, are able to recover abilities that are controlled by the part of the brain that was taken out. For example, a three year old girl in Holland who had half her brain removed because of Rasmussen

---

[6]   https://www.gizmodo.com.au/2013/08/an-83000-processor-supercomputer-only-matched-one-percent-of-your-brain/

Syndrome (resulting in epileptic seizures, paralysis down one side of her body and loss of language skills) was fluent in Turkish and Dutch by age seven, her paralysis was virtually gone, and she was leading a normal life. This was even though the parts of the brain that control speech and movement were surgically removed. There is no computer on earth like our brain – able to rebuild and reprogram itself[7].

The Triple Coincidence

Socrates said, 'The gods have given man the two most precious gifts; reason for the soul and hands for the body'. What makes the evidence in this chapter compelling is not one special factor, nor even the two that Socrates mentions, but three. First we have the unique human hand; no other creature on earth possesses its dual abilities of a power grip and a precision grip. We could add the ten unique features of bi-pedalism that enable us to use our hands as well. However, these physical features on their own are not enough to suggest that humans have been given this ability by God. It is the combination of our unique hand with two other additional unique factors. The second factor is our unique brain capacity. If we only had the unique hand (and other physical features), what use would these be without the 25% extra brain capacity in the motor cortex to operate our opposable thumb and hand? On the other hand, if we had an extra-large motor cortex in the brain without any unique hand features, what use would the extra brainpower be? Presumably it would wither away with nothing to do. Both features had to be present simultaneously to be functional. It is the combination that is striking, the coincidence of the hardware in the hand and the processing power in the brain to operate it that make our unique abilities so remarkable. But as Socrates remarked, we have another third gift, a soul or mind that is able to dream and scheme, to plan and design things to build with our hands. This again is unique to human beings – no other creature on earth has the mental powers to communicate or think rationally. These mental abilities are not reducible to brain size (or elephants with their bigger brains would be talking to us and teaching us a thing or two). There are no animals who would write a book or paint a watercolour if only they

---

[7] Johannes Borgstein, Caroline Grootendorst, "Half a Brain", *The Lancet*, https://www.thelancet.com/journals/lancet/article/PIIS0140-6736(02)07676-6/fulltext

had our unique hands. Our mind – the non-physical rational component – is the third factor that enables us to put our hands to good use.

In many criminal investigations, there are three factors that must be established to prove guilt: motive, means and opportunity. 'Motive' is when someone has a reason to kill or something to gain, 'means' refers to ownership of the murder weapon, and 'opportunity' means being in the same place at the time of the murder. Without proving all three factors, prosecuting someone for murder is very difficult. But the combination of all three is powerful evidence that they committed the crime. In the same way, in geometry, it is very unlikely for three random lines anywhere on a plane to intersect at the same one point. They can intersect in an infinite number of different ways, and will only intersect at the same point if we deliberately choose to draw the three lines going through the same point. (Think of how we deliberately cut a cake or pizza through the very centre).

The fact that human beings alone, among all the creatures on earth, have not one but all three of these unique abilities, the hand, the brain and the mind, suggests something more than coincidence or accident. It suggests, as Socrates stated, that God has given us these three special abilities.

Atheist Responses

Atheists dismiss the hand as evidence for God's existence by saying that this is an argument from incredulity. Because we cannot imagine how something as functionally brilliant as the hand or technologically advanced as the brain could have come about, we give up and say that God must have done it. The reality, atheists assert, is that evolution elegantly explains the wonderful features of the human hand and brain without any need for God.

The atheist explanation for the hand is this: humans are just jumped-up apes, and the hand is simply the result of the struggle for existence in the jungle. Anything that gave an animal a survival advantage over a rival, and hence led to them producing more offspring, would naturally be selected to be passed on. The fine motor skills in the human hand must have obviously been found advantageous for survival over the millions of years of prehistory. Evolutionary scenarios for the origin of the human hand, and particularly its precision grip, include its value in using stones as tools, or for throwing stones at enemies.

However, these scenarios do not actually explain our unique precision grip, because holding or throwing stones does not require precision grip, i.e. fully-opposable thumbs. Nor are new anatomical traits acquired by use. Instead, anatomical features must exist before they can be used or improved. The idea that new anatomical features can be acquired by use is called Lamarckism, but it has long been rejected as false by evolutionary theorists. Giraffes did *not* grow long necks by stretching out to reach taller branches. Nor did the duck get his waterproof, insulated feathers by jumping into cold lakes. Lucky genetic mutations are required to produce the giraffe's long neck and the duck's thermal raincoat. Throwing lots of stones will not eventually give an ape precision grip. The only way that new anatomical features can arise is by genetic mutations just happening to grow a new muscle or bone in the right place.

But here is the problem: what use would the arrival – after hundreds of mutations – of truly opposable fingers be without the unique motor-cortex of the brain to control their use, or without bi-pedalism to free the hands for manual use? The whole package had to be present and operational for it to be functional. How would the ability to write with a pen, or play a musical instrument help an animal survive on the African savannah when lions, cheetahs, and hyenas were hunting it down, or be a benefit in the jungle when fighting to find scarce food resources?

Surely, the opposite is the case: wasting time with hobbies like painting, or scratching language symbols in the dirt, would tend to make an animal more genteel and civilized, but less fit to survive in the wild. Such skills would be of very little use except in civilized society; such abilities would be a drain on resources, not an advantage, and therefore liable to be selected against. Natural selection would be more likely to favour callous brutes than beautiful calligraphers. Power is what is required in the jungle, not fine arts.

The fine motor control of the human hand goes way beyond what we need for mere survival or the tasks of primitive jungle-dwelling hunter-gatherers. For proof, just look at all other animals; they survive very well in the wild without the amazing control of a human hand.

The idea that the struggle for survival has conferred these abilities is not very convincing – otherwise, many other animals would have these skills too. Yet all humans have these abilities, not just those who live in advanced societies. Even tribesmen fresh from the jungle, with no prior history or ability to do such things, can learn to play the piano or write with a pen.

Thus, the atheist logic is back-to-front: atheism says we got our precision grip by using it, whereas simple common sense teaches that we had to have the ability before we could use it.

The Body

Newton wrote about other wonders of the body as evidence for God, arguing that the body had not come about by accident or blind chance. Speaking of the eye, and his researches into optics, Newton wrote:

> Atheism is so senseless and odious to mankind that it never had many professors. ... Whence is it that the eyes of all sorts of living creatures are transparent to the very bottom & the only transparent members in the body, having on the outside an hard transparent skin, & within transparent juyces with a crystalline Lens in the middle & a pupil before the Lens all of them so truly shaped & fitted for vision, that no Artist can mend them? Did blind chance know that there was light & what was its refraction & fit the eys of all creatures after the most curious manner to make use of it? These & such like considerations always have & ever will prevail with man kind to believe that there is a being who made all things & has all things in his power & who is therfore to be feared (*A Short Schem of the True Religion*)

Newton also wrote about the balance and symmetry of the body as evidence of divine design. Today, our understanding of the human body is far more advanced than it was in Newton's day, and many other wonders of the human body leave us amazed at the miracle of life:

- We have 2.5 trillion red blood cells, containing the molecule haemoglobin which transports oxygen round the system via our veins and arteries. Our bodies make 2.5 million new red blood cells every second. There are 150 million red blood cells in each drop of blood; they are so small they can fit through the narrowest capillaries to reach every part of our body. There are even miniature blood vessels inside the walls of blood vessels, to supply these cells with oxygen! Every day, the red blood cells make nearly 1500 round trips from the heart and back, reloading with oxygen in the lungs (and off-loading carbon dioxide at the same time).

- Our heart beats 40 million times a year, pumping these red blood cells round our body non-stop for (on average) 70-80 years. The heart is the most efficient pump on earth.

- Our bones are four times stronger than concrete for their weight, yet light enough to run a marathon,

- our muscles can lift 100 times their own weight.

- There are 6 million olfactory (i.e. smelling) cells inside our noses, which can detect 10,000 different smells and 500,000 combinations of smells.

- Our bodies have baroreceptors (tiny barometers) that react to the outside air pressure and adjust the fluid pressure in our joints so that our joints operate efficiently[8]. People with forms of rheumatism are more sensitive to approaching storms, that is, they get joint pains, because the rheumatism disrupts the body's natural response to the dropping barometric pressure.

Conclusion

As we examine our amazing bodies, David's words in Psalm 139:14 sum up the situation: 'I will praise You, for I am fearfully and wonderfully made'. The uniqueness of the human hand, and the other marvels of the human body are yet more reasons we know that God really exists.

---

[8] Thomas Jefferson University Hospital, "People With Joint Pain Can Really Forecast Thunderstorms", *ScienceDaily*, 3 June 2008, www.sciencedaily.com/releases/2008/05/080530174619.htm

Because the hand and other mechanical parts of the body are not as amazing as sight, I rate them at an 8 out of 10 argument for God's existence.

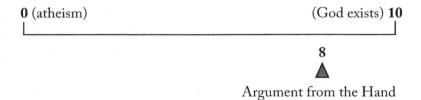

Argument from the Hand

Chapter 10

The C. S. Lewis Argument: Morality

C. S. Lewis's mother died when he was aged nine, and he became an atheist in his mid-teens. He wrote to his friend Arthur Greeves at age seventeen, 'I believe in no religion. There is absolutely no proof for any of them, and from a philosophical standpoint Christianity is not even the best'. His experiences as a soldier in World War One, seeing the senseless horrors first-hand, only served to confirm his atheism. The tragedies of youth had shattered his belief in the goodness of God.

In 1925 he began to teach medieval literature at Oxford University, but by 1929 he had abandoned atheism. One of his reasons, ironically, was the problem of suffering and evil, which Lewis came to realize also undermined atheism. He put it this way:

'My argument against God was that the universe seemed so cruel and unjust. But how had I got this idea of just and unjust? A man does not call a line crooked unless he has some idea of a straight line. What was I comparing the universe with when I called it unjust?'[1].

Atheism offered Lewis no answer or explanation for what troubled him so deeply – the reality of good or evil. Eventually, Lewis admitted that 'God was God', describing himself as the most 'dejected and reluctant convert' in all England. Later, after a long talk with two Christian friends: J. R. R. Tolkien and Hugo Dyson, and then during a motorbike ride to Whipsnade Zoo, he became a Christian: "When we set out I did not believe that Jesus is the Son of God and when we reached the zoo I did".

---

[1] C. S. Lewis, *Mere Christianity,* HarperCollins, 2001, pp.38-39.

In this chapter, we will consider what is often called the moral argument for God's existence. Here the question is not why there is something rather than nothing (creation), nor why the universe is so brilliant and beautiful (design). Here the question is why there is good and evil.

Cicero the Roman statesman said, 'It was always the conviction of all truly wise men, that the moral law was not something devised by man or introduced by the nations, but something eternal, to which the whole world must conform. Its final foundation, therefore, rests in God, who commands and forbids. And this law is as old as the spirit of God Himself. Therefore the law upon which all duty is based is in reality and above all the spirit of the supreme Deity'[2].

Atheism: There is no Good or Evil

Contrast this with what many atheists believe. Atheists not only argue that there is no such thing as conscience; they also believe there is no such thing as good and evil. Richard Dawkins writes: 'the universe we observe has precisely the properties we should expect if there is, at bottom, no design, no purpose, *no evil and no good*, nothing but blind pitiless indifference'[3].

Atheist biologist William Provine said: 'Naturalistic evolution has clear consequences that Charles Darwin understood perfectly:

1. No gods worth having exist;
2. no life after death exists;
3. *no ultimate foundation for ethics exists*;
4. no ultimate meaning in life exists; and
5. human free will is nonexistent'[4].

---

[2] Marcus Tullius Cicero, *De Legibus (On the Laws)*, Book 2

[3] Richard Dawkins, *River out of Eden, A Darwinian view of life*, Basic Books, 1995, p.133, emphasis added.

[4] William Provine, *Evolution: Free Will and Punishment and Meaning in Life*, Second Annual Darwin Day Celebration Keynote Address, University of Tennessee, Knoxville, February 12, 1998, emphasis added.

Atheists E. O. Wilson and Michael Ruse write:

> 'Ethics as we understand it is an illusion fobbed off on us by our genes to get us to cooperate... the way our biology enforces its ends is by making us think that there is an objective higher code to which we are all subject'[5].

Because there is no evil and no good, atheists like Dawkins even admit that it is hard to say that Hitler did something wrong: 'What's to prevent us from saying Hitler wasn't right? I mean, that is a genuinely difficult question'[6]. Dawkins also says that he has no problem, in principle, eating human road-kill (i.e., cannibalism), seeing we are really just another species of animal, nor does he have any problem killing children with diseases or disabilities up to one year old (i.e. extended abortion)[7].

Various atheists have argued that if there is no God, then there is no such thing as morality. Friedrich Nietzsche, the German atheist philosopher, wrote, 'Moral judgments agree with religious ones in believing in realities which are no realities.... There are altogether no

---

[5] Michael Ruse and E. O. Wilson, "The Evolution of Ethics", in *Religion and the Natural Sciences: The Range of Engagement*, ed. James E. Huchingson, Harcourt Brace, 1993, p.310-11

[6] "Richard Dawkins: the Atheist Evangelist", *By Faith*, Dec 1st, 2007, http://byfaithonline.com/richard-dawkins-the-atheist-evangelist

[7] Dawkins: 'I can think of no moral objection to eating human road kills except for the ones that you mentioned like 'what would the relatives think about it?' and 'would the person themselves have wanted it to happen?', but I do worry a bit about slippery slopes; possibly a little bit more than you do. There are barriers that we have set up in our minds and certainly the barrier between Homo sapiens and any other species is an artificial barrier in the sense that it's a kind of 'accident' that the evolutionary intermediates happen to be extinct. Nevertheless it exists and natural barriers that are there can be useful for preventing slippery slopes and therefore I think I can see an objection to breaching such a barrier because you are then in a weaker position to stop people going further. Another example might be suppose you take the argument in favour of abortion up until the baby was one year old, if a baby was one year old and turned out to have some horrible incurable disease that meant it was going to die in agony in later life, what about infanticide? Strictly morally I can see no objection to that at all, I would be in favour of infanticide but I think I would worry about/I think I would wish at least to give consideration to the person who says 'where does it end?' (Peter Singer, *The Genius of Darwin: The Uncut Interviews*, 2009).

moral facts'... [Morality] 'has truth only if God is the truth—it stands or falls with faith in God'[8]. Jean-Paul Sartre, one of the most famous atheists of the 20th century, wrote, 'It [is] very distressing that God does not exist, because all possibility of finding values in a heaven of ideas disappears along with Him'[9]. Fyodor Dostoevsky the Russian novelist argued, 'If there is no God, everything is permitted'[10].

It is important to understand that this argument is **not** saying that atheists have no morals, or cannot live in kind and generous ways. On the contrary, atheists have a conscience like everyone else – given by God. No, the argument here is that atheism undermines any *moral* basis for doing good, or from refraining from evil. (There are, of course, other legal, social or practical reasons for not doing evil, like not wanting to go to jail). Atheism renders morality meaningless.

Atheist Max Hocutt explains the logic: 'the non-existence of God ... means that there is no absolute morality, that moralities are sets of social conventions devised by humans to satisfy their need'. Hocutt also says, 'Furthermore, if there were a morality written up in the sky somewhere but no God to enforce it, I see no good reason why anybody should pay it any heed, no reason why we should obey it'[11]. Richard Rorty, an atheist philosopher, acknowledged that for people like himself, there was no answer to the question, "Why not be cruel?"[12].

Once we allow the word 'ought' (or 'ought not') into our moral vocabulary, we are affirming an external reference point, an objective moral standard to which people should measure up. This is the same as saying that there is a God whose moral laws must be obeyed. Christian philosopher Alvin Plantinga writes,

'Could there really be such a thing as horrifying wickedness [if God

---

[8] Friedrich Nietzsche, *Twilight of the Idols and the Anti-Christ*, Penguin Books, 1968, pp.55, 70

[9] Jean-Paul Sartre, *Existentialism and Human Emotions*, Philosophical Library, 1957, p.22

[10] Fyodor Dostoevsky, *The Brothers Karamazov*, 1880

[11] Max Hocutt, "Comment by Max Hocutt on Hannay Article", and "Toward an Ethic of Mutual Accommodation", *Humanist Ethics*, ed. M. B. Storer, Prometheus Books, 1980, pp.191, 137

[12] Richard Rorty, *Contingency, Irony, and Solidarity*, Cambridge University Press, 1989

does not exist]? I don't see how. There can be such a thing only if there is a way that rational creatures are *supposed* to live, *obliged* to live ... A [secular] way of looking at the world has no place for genuine moral obligations of any sort ... and thus no way to say there is such a thing as genuine and appalling wickedness. Accordingly, if you think there really *is* such a thing as horrifying wickedness (... and not just an illusion of some sort), then you have a powerful ... argument [for God's existence][13].

C. S. Lewis argued:

> 'In the very act of trying to prove that God did not exist – in other words, that the whole of reality was senseless – I found I was forced to assume that one part of reality – namely my idea of justice – was full of sense. Consequently, atheism turns out to be too simple. If the whole universe has no meaning, we should never have found out that it has no meaning: just as, if there were no light in the universe and therefore no creatures with eyes, we should never know it was dark. Dark would be a word without meaning'.

Just as the shadows prove that sunshine exists, so evil and suffering in the world proves that justice – a standard of objective good – exists. Where does this immaterial standard of right and wrong reside? The answer, as we will see, is that it cannot reside anywhere except in God Himself. Evil, paradoxically, proves the existence of God.

An Alternative Basis for Morality?

Many naïve atheists argue that it is possible to have morality without God. They ask, "Can't we all just agree that hurting other people is wrong?" From this they proceed to the fundamental law of modern morality: we all have a right to be happy!

But what happens if someone is trapped in an unhappy, down-

---

[13] Alvin Plantinga, "A Christian Life Partly Lived", *Philosophers who Believe*, ed. Kelly James Clark, IVP, 1993, p.73

trodden or abusive situation? The atheist replies that this person needs to be more assertive and stand up for their rights. This is just a polite way of saying the bullied must toughen-up and push back, the meek must become more selfish and stand up to others to get what they want. In short, we are back to the law of the jungle. The evil Voldemort from the *Harry Potter* novels put it this way, 'There is no good and evil, there is only power, there is only power, and those too weak to seek it'.

Unless there is some standard of objective morality (and even with one!), most people find it very hard to resist the idea that the ends justify the means. We have seen the way this played out in the 20th century. Whether it was a communist revolution in the cause of radical social equality or fascists fighting for their rightful national destiny, the result in the 20th century was roughly 100 million dead bodies. Eric Hobsbawm, the unrepentant Marxist historian (of the sort who argue that the only problem with communism is that it hasn't been properly tried yet), said that the millions of deaths at the hands of Soviets would have been worth it if a truly communist revolution had succeeded[14].

Other people think that society determines right and wrong, that morals are simply the collective opinion of a particular culture. Thus, because the majority opinion in society votes to make gay marriage legal, it therefore becomes acceptable. But what about strict Islamic cultures where homosexuals are thrown off roof-tops – is this okay if the majority vote for it? Or what about honour-killings (if a female is seen with a male who is not an immediate family member, both are put to death in some Islamic cultures)? Is the racial genocide of an ethnic minority okay if the majority vote for it?

Head-hunters in the jungle don't have any problem killing their enemies and eating their brains. (They have a problem with doing the same to their own tribesmen). Slavery was legal in many societies until the 19th century, and the main defence of Nazi leaders on trial at Nuremburg following World War Two was that they were just following the laws of the land. The problem here is that different societies have different laws. Any society is free to write its own laws, so which society's

---

[14] "Michael Ignatieff interviews Eric Hobsbawm", *The Late Show*, BBC, 24th October 1994.

rules shall we choose? We are left with no solid ground to stand upon.

Why do serious atheist thinkers say there is no good or evil? Simply because there is nothing in a materialistic (i.e. atheistic) universe that provides any basis for morality. Think about biology. There is no such thing as 'fair play' in nature 'red in tooth and claw'. If we are just jumped-up apes, there are no rules against murder, adultery, lying or stealing – these are just the ways animals survive and thrive.

Richard Dawkins argues that our moral values are the product of our evolutionary past. When Dawkins was interviewed by Justin Brierley on the UK radio program, *Unbelievable*, Dawkins admitted that this meant that his moral values are therefore arbitrary, that is, based on whim and fancy, rather than any solid ground.

> Richard Dawkins: My value judgement itself could come from my evolutionary past.
>
> Justin Brierley: So therefore it's just as random in a sense as any product of evolution.
>
> Richard Dawkins: You could say that, it doesn't in any case, nothing about it makes it more probable that there is anything supernatural.
>
> Justin Brierley: Ultimately, your belief that rape is wrong is as arbitrary as the fact that we've evolved five fingers rather than six.
>
> Richard Dawkins: You could say that, yeah.

The idea is that since all life is the result of Darwinian evolution, and everything we see around us arose because it was found useful in the struggle for survival, then so too did our morals. The problem with this view is that evolution is the 'dog eat dog' model of morality. It is all about survival of the fittest, and the sacrifice of the weakest.

But if all life is the result of Darwinian struggle, then rape and murder are no different to the giraffe's neck or the leopard's spots. This is the logic of two evolutionary biologists, Randy Thornhill and Craig Palmer: 'just as the leopard's spots and the giraffe's elongated neck are the result of aeons of past Darwinian selection, so also is rape'[15]. David Buss, an evolutionary psychologist, argued that even murder has evolutionary benefits: 'over the eons of human evolution murder was surprisingly beneficial in the intense game of reproductive competition'[16].

If we are just animals (as evolutionists believe), then everything is acceptable: murder, rape, theft and deception are just the ways certain animals get ahead in life. Evolutionary morality? There is no basis for morality in evolution.

Consider chemistry. If all our thoughts are merely the result of chemical reactions and electrical discharges in the brain, there is nothing 'right' or 'wrong' about any such thoughts, any more than sodium chloride dissolving in water is 'good' or 'evil'. In chemical terms, humans are little different to the mud on our shoes, and mud does not debate morality. Murder, on a materialistic analysis, is little different to spilling milk on the floor or wiping mud off our shoes.

The bottom line is that there is no such thing as good and evil in an materialist, atheist universe: there is no particle of hate or molecular weight of marital faithfulness, no forgiving hurricanes, or remorseful vultures. Instead, as C. S. Lewis put it, under atheism our moral impulses are no more true (or false) than 'than a vomit or a yawn' and thinking 'I ought' is on the same level as 'I itch'; 'my impulse to serve posterity is just the same sort of thing as my fondness for cheese'[17]. If there is no such thing as objective morality, then there are only subjective opinions, and morality is reduced to a matter of personal taste.

If all morality is relative, then it is difficult to consider anything as truly 'good' or 'evil', for it all becomes a matter of whatever we want. Peter Singer, atheist professor of Bioethics at Princeton University and an advocate for animal rights, argues that animals have more right to life than newborn human infants, because infants are not yet rational, autonomous and self-conscious. But once we have de-sensitized ourselves to killing infants, what is there to stop us thinking of clever justifications

---

[15] Randy Thornhill and Craig Palmer, *A Natural History of Rape: Biological Bases of Sexual Coercion*, Bradford Books, 2000

[16] David Buss, *The Murderer Next Door: Why the Mind is Designed to Kill*, Penguin, 2005

[17] C. S. Lewis, *Miracles*, Macmillan, 1960, pp.37-38

for killing other categories of people?

The Problem with Atheism

The problem with atheism is that morality is real, not an illusion. We may disagree over which is our favourite fruit, or our preferred flavour of ice-cream, but we all agree that what Hitler did was evil[18]. The converted atheist Michael Bird wrote that, 'I had always felt a strange unease about my disbelief. ... I "knew" that ethics were nothing more than aesthetics, a mere word game for things I liked and disliked. I felt conflicted when my heart ached over the injustice and cruelty in the world'[19].

Dawkins defines an atheist as 'somebody who believes there is nothing beyond the natural, physical world'[20]. This means that 'good' and 'evil' do not exist, because these are not physical substances. Nevertheless, Dawkins also continually complains about things he considers to be 'evil', particularly related to religion. For example, he says parents telling their children about God is 'child abuse'[21]. Dawkins struggles, it seems, to see the contradiction.

To his credit, Dawkins is troubled by things like rape and Hitler's holocaust. He thus proves the two main points being made here: firstly, he admits there is no basis for morality in an atheistic world, and secondly, he admits morality is nevertheless real – we feel it keenly. But atheists cannot have it both ways.

Humans are intensely moral; we are forever arguing about rights and wrongs. We loathe cheats and bullies, conmen and child-molesters. The airwaves of our talk-back radio stations are choked with stories of people complaining about injustices. Our newspapers and current affairs programs make millions reporting on crime and arguing over its punishment. We are positively obsessed with good and evil, rights and justice – it's virtually all we ever talk about.

---

[18] Even most holocaust-deniers do not dispute the fact that killing six million people is wrong; they just refuse to believe that Hitler killed this many Jews

[19] Michael Bird, "How God became Jesus, and How I came to Faith in Him", *Christianity Today*, April 16, 2014

[20] Richard Dawkins, *The God Delusion*, Bantam Press, 2006, p.14

[21] Chapter 9 of *The God Delusion*

As we have seen, some atheists argue that morality is just an illusion, a trick being played on us by our genes or brain chemistry. However, the same atheist (Michael Ruse) who wrote that morality is an illusion fobbed off on us by our genes also wrote that 'the man who says that it is morally acceptable to rape little children is just as mistaken as the man who says 2+2=5'[22].

There are many questions that deserve to be asked of Ruse and other atheists who believe that morality is an illusion. The most interesting question is, perhaps, now they have 'seen through' the illusion and seriously believe that there is no such thing as good and evil, whether anyone should believe anything they say any more. After all, there is nothing 'wrong' with lying or cheating so, for all we know, atheists like Ruse may just be trying to manipulate the public, motivated by a desire to sell books and get rich, or to gain cultural power, prestige, and a celebrity following. They cannot argue that their arguments are based on a love of the truth, for they themselves believe that this is an illusion.

Many politically-correct people in modern society think that morality is all relative, so that we all get to determine what's right and wrong for ourselves personally, and no one should judge anyone else. However, as William Lane Craig says, 'Just ask them, "So, do you really think that it would be alright if the government rounded up all homosexuals and threw them into concentration camps the way the Nazis did? You don't really have a problem with racial discrimination, I suppose? You think there's nothing really bad about wife-beating or child abuse?"'[23].

The Case for Conscience

Every single day, each of us is continually faced by moral choices. It is as if we are in a perpetual tug-of-war between right and wrong. Just like gravity in the physical realm, we feel the drag of selfishness, envy, revenge, cowardice, dishonesty and laziness in the moral arena, along with the voice of conscience urging us to resist these temptations. As William Sorley, professor of moral philosophy at Cambridge University

---

[22] Michael Ruse, *Darwinism Defended*, Addison-Wesley, 1982, p.275
[23] William Lane Craig, *Reasonable Faith*, Crossway, 2008, p.194

argued[24], the truth is that our moral values are as objectively real as the physical world.

Furthermore, not only is our moral sense intensely real; it is universal. The same basic moral instincts are found in all races and religions. In 1993 Hans Küng, the German liberal theologian, organized a parliament of the world's leading religions – Jews, Christians, Muslims, Hindus and Buddhists. Although they differed over their views on God, their views on morality and values were in substantial agreement. The same is true, too, of the moral teachings of the ancient Egyptians, Babylonians, Greeks, Romans and Chinese.

C. S. Lewis put it this way, 'Think of a country where people were admired for running away in battle, or where a man felt proud of double-crossing all the people who were kindest to him. You might as well imagine a country where two and two made five. ... Selfishness has never been admired. Men have differed as to whether you should have one wife or four. But they have always agreed that you must not simply have any woman you liked'[25].

We are not only intensely and universally moral. We are also instinctively moral – our passion for justice is as deep-seated as a mother's care and nurture of her newborn child. If we deny morality, we rip out our own hearts, our true humanity. C. S. Lewis wrote, 'human beings, all over the earth, have this curious idea that they ought to behave in a certain way, and cannot really get rid of it ... [but] they do not in fact behave in that way. They know the Law of Nature and they break it'[26].

I once met a homeless man called Denzel who grew up in a family which denied God's existence. His father used to say that God was just dog spelled backwards. However, Denzel remembers as a boy going to steal from a shop and being interrupted by the inaudible voice of conscience. It was almost as if someone were tapping him on the shoulder. There was no physical touch, of course, but something spoke to him telling him that what he was doing was wrong.

---

[24] Gifford Lectures, *Moral Values and the Idea of God* (1918)

[25] C. S. Lewis, *Mere Christianity*, William Collins, 2012, p.6

[26] Lewis, *Mere Christianity*, p.9

On the other hand, I once met a prisoner in jail in a Bible study who argued that there was no such thing as conscience. He said that it was just society that shaped our ideas of right and wrong. I asked him, 'So, you wouldn't have a problem if someone stole your car?' To this he gave no reply.

Augustine in his autobiographical *Confessions* argued that all men have a conscience: 'Theft is punished by Your law, O Lord, and by the law written in men's hearts, which iniquity itself cannot blot out. For what thief will suffer a thief? Even a rich thief will not suffer him who is driven to it by want'.

Theologian Erich Sauer quotes a German Professor Luthardt:

'Conscience is a majestic ruler. All bow before its authority. We may disregard its commands, but then we must hear its voice in rebuke. We can harden ourselves against this rebuke, but we cannot obliterate it. We can never reach the point where it is no longer there. Conscience does not depend upon our will. We cannot control it. We cannot command it, but it commands us. We do not stand over it, but under it … It follows therefore that it does not take its origin from our will and thought. It has not been produced by our own mind, but by a moral Spirit outside of and above us…. Thus it is the product of the highest Spirit, of the supreme Law-giver, of the absolute moral Will. The fact of conscience is a proof of the existence of God'[27].

We are more than meat machines; we have a moral and spiritual dimension that is not reducible to physics and chemistry, yet is real. This being so, there is a spiritual reality that is discerned through morality. It makes sense to believe that there is a God, who is also a Spirit, and from whom this moral sense comes.

The Euthyphro Dilemma and the Moral Cop-out

One common objection to the moral argument for God's existence is called the Euthyphro Dilemma. Plato relates a story in which Socrates

---

[27] Erich Sauer, *The King of the Earth*, Ronald N. Haynes, 1981, p.166

met a man named Euthyphro and Socrates asked him what piety was (because Socrates was on trial for impiety towards the Greek gods). Euthyphro answered that piety is whatever pleases the gods. Socrates challenged this, 'Is it loved by the gods because it is pious, or is it pious because it is loved by the gods?'

From this comes the Euthyphro dilemma: is something good just because God says so, or does God say something is good because it *is* good. In other words, is the standard of 'goodness' whatever God says, or is the standard of 'goodness' something external to God?

This presents a dilemma. If the standard of goodness were whatever God decreed this standard would seem to be arbitrary. God might say that lying was good and it would then become good. This would make God a bit like a cruel parent making up unfair rules simply to show their children who was the boss. On the other hand, if goodness existed independent of God, then He would have to submit to this standard of goodness too, and that would make God the servant of these standards.

The answer to the Euthyphro dilemma is that Socrates has set up a false dilemma, by not considering another third option, the most natural option, which is that God's decrees are a reflection of His character of perfect goodness. Jesus said, 'Out of the abundance of the heart the mouth speaks' (Matthew 12:34). People do not say things by plucking random ideas out of the air; instead our words represent and reflect what we are thinking in our hearts. The same applies to God: His decrees come from His thoughts and reflect His perfect character. Therefore, God Himself is the source of objective moral standards – His decrees are not whimsical or arbitrary, nor are good and evil standards external to Him.

The Euthyphro dilemma is worth considering because some atheists argue that 'right' and 'wrong' just exist – they don't require God. The atheist Walter Sinnott-Armstrong answers the question of why it is wrong to hurt another person: 'It simply is. Objectively. Don't you agree?'[28]

---

[28] Walter Sinnott-Armstrong, "There is no Good Reason to Believe in God", in *God?: a Debate between a Christian and an Atheist*, ed. William Lane Craig and Walter Sinnott-Armstrong, Oxford University Press, 2003, p.34.

The Euthyphro dilemma might at first seem like a trivial philosophical dispute, but it actually helps reinforce the moral argument for God's existence. Notice two points. First, if it were the case that God decreed 'good' or 'evil' in a whimsical or arbitrary way, then morality would not be objectively 'good' or 'evil'. Morality would just be 'made up', an arbitrary illusion, and not real. But we know that morality is real – we feel it keenly – there is such a thing as objective good and evil. On the other hand, good and evil cannot be independent of God either, for if God had to submit to some external standards higher than Himself, He would no longer be the Supreme Being. He would only be a servant to a higher moral authority. God, by definition as the Supreme Being, and as Creator, must be Lord over all things. If God exists, He must be the Lord of everything, including morality. If moral values exist (as we know they do), they cannot be independent of God. Morality is thus inescapably tied to, and grounded in, God. We may call this argument the Reverse-Euthyphro: it turns the tables on the Euthyphro dilemma and defeats it.

We can add that because we know that moral values are real, and objectively exist, then atheism cannot be true. The atheist who argues that good and evil could simply exist independently of God is not able to state where such objective standards of right and wrong are located or grounded. As atheist William Provine stated, there is no ultimate foundation for morality in atheism. Additionally, as we shall see in the next chapter, atheists do not believe in free will, which again undermines any foundation for morality.

Just like the cosmic cop-out we saw earlier in the book where the atheist argues that the universe 'just is', we now meet the equivalent in the realm of ethics: the moral cop-out. Just as it is irrational to say that nothing caused the physical universe, so it is irrational to say that morality 'just is', with no ultimate grounding. Moral values objectively exist, and they cannot exist independent of God. Therefore God exists.

Evidence for God

Here is the argument from morality, stated as a logical syllogism:

1.   Objective morality is real, not an illusion

2.   Objective morality has no basis in an atheistic, materialistic world

3.   Objective morality can only be explained by the existence of a moral Governor of the universe, the very source of goodness.

4.   Therefore, God exists.

Thus, not only is there evidence of God all around us in the physical creation, but morality itself is evidence for God's existence. God has even put evidence within us – a moral compass, the voice of conscience from Himself.

This is precisely what the Bible teaches. In Romans 2:14-15, Paul writes about conscience: 'for when Gentiles, who do not have the law, by nature do the things in the law, these, although not having the law, are a law to themselves, who show the work of the law written in their hearts, their conscience also bearing witness'.

Augustine wrote, 'there is no soul, however perverted ... in whose conscience God does not speak'. C. S. Lewis wrote, 'God whispers to us in our pleasures, speaks in our conscience, but shouts in our pains; it is His megaphone to rouse a deaf world'[29]. If we have been made in God's image and likeness, we would expect to find evidence of God as we examine ourselves. This is precisely what we find as we look at our inner thought lives.

The argument for God in this book is a cumulative one. With the argument from morality, we have come to its fourth stage. In the first stage, the argument from intuition (the pervasive belief in God throughout human history) suggests that God may exist. Second, the argument from creation points to the origin of the universe as powerful evidence for God's existence. The argument from design, thirdly, in addition to its own independent compelling common sense evidence for God, is reinforced by the argument from creation, for if God is our creator, then it is His design we see in the created universe. Creation makes divine design near certain.

---

[29] C. S. Lewis, *The Problem of Pain*, William Collins, 2015, p.91

Now consider the connection between the argument from design and the fourth stage of our argument, from morality. If we attribute beauty in nature to God's design (the splendour of a sunset, or a magnificent waterfall, or a tropical paradise, or the starry heavens), then we ought not be surprised that we find beauty in the moral realm. We see moral beauty in the form of kind or courageous or humble or diligent or honest acts. In this chapter, we have argued that objective moral goodness exists, and that it is inexplicable without God. The same God whose goodness and beauty is seen in creation shows His true beauty of character in morality.

It is hard to rate the evidence for God from morality on a numerical scale. However, this we can say: morality is real, and there is no basis or foundation for it in atheism. Therefore, God almost certainly exists. I personally rate this one of the most powerful arguments for God's existence, at 9 out of 10.

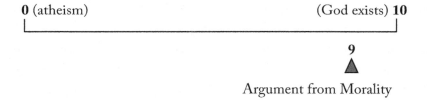

Argument from Morality

Chapter 11

The William Shakespeare Argument: Humanity

William Shakespeare (1564 – 1616) is generally regarded as the greatest playwright of all time. His thirty seven plays are still performed in countries all over the world. Shakespeare's contemporary, Ben Johnson wrote that Shakespeare 'was not of an age, but for all time'.

It seems certain that Shakespeare himself believed in God. His plays are full of biblical allusions, and his last will and testament commenced with a clear statement of Christian faith:

In the name of God, Amen. I, William Shakespeare..., in perfect health and memory, God be praised, do make and ordain this my last will and testament in manner and form following. That is to say, first, I commend my soul into the hands of God my Creator, hoping and assuredly believing, through the only merits of Jesus Christ my Saviour, to be made partaker of life everlasting, and my body to the earth whereof it is made.

However, our argument in this chapter is not about Shakespeare's personal belief in God, so much as with what Shakespeare teaches us about human beings. Shakespeare's plays largely focus on how human beings handled different, sometimes difficult, situations. He explored what makes human beings tick: their loves and fears, crimes and foibles. Shakespeare wrote:

What a piece of work is a man! How noble in reason, how infinite in faculty, in form and moving how express and admirable, in action how like an angel, in apprehension how like a god' (*Hamlet*).

The atheist view of man is the diametric opposite. Bill Nye 'the Science Guy', an American TV personality, and winner of the 2010 American Humanist of the Year award, said in his acceptance speech:

'I am insignificant. ... I am just another speck of sand. And the earth really in the cosmic scheme of things is another speck. And the sun an unremarkable star. ... and the galaxy is a speck. I'm a speck on a speck orbiting a speck among other specks among still other specks in the middle of specklessness. I suck'.

There's the uplifting message of humanism (i.e. atheism): you suck. Shakespeare counters such atheist self-loathing by showing us, from his life itself, that human beings are capable of incredible genius.

Who is right, Shakespeare or Bill Nye? Are human beings 'a little lower than the angels', as Psalm 8 says in the Bible, or are human beings just 'slime plus time'?

The Crime of the Century

In Chicago in 1924, two academically brilliant teenagers from wealthy families carried out the pre-meditated murder of Bobby Franks, the 14 year old son of a millionaire. The intention of Richard Loeb and Nathan Leopold was to commit the perfect crime, just for the thrill of it. That and the $100,000 ransom they tried to extort from their victim's parents. (The fact that they were both atheists is noteworthy, but beside our present point). However, because of certain fortuitous events and mistakes, they were identified, arrested and put on trial. Their parents hired one of the most famous lawyers in America, agnostic Clarence Darrow. As their guilt was beyond dispute, Darrow's only aim was to try and avoid the death penalty. His (successful) closing defence statement lasted twelve hours, in which he argued for clemency based on the boys' youth, abhorrence of the death penalty, and the fact that the boys themselves were victims of fate.

What Darrow meant by this last point was that in a materialistic (i.e. atheistic) universe all events, even human actions, are the inevitable result of previously existing causes, over which we have little or no control.

This is an idea called determinism: we are just cogs in the machine called the universe. As a result, human beings cannot truly be said to have free will nor can we be held responsible for our moral choices. Darrow said at the trial,

> 'Nature is strong and she is pitiless. She works in mysterious ways, and we are her victims. We have not much to do with it ourselves. Nature takes this job in hand, and we only play our parts.... What had this boy to do with it? He was not his own father; he was not his own mother.... All of this was handed to him. He did not surround himself with governesses and wealth. He did not make himself. And yet he is to be compelled to pay'.

Free Will?

We earlier quoted atheist William Provine's five consequences of atheism, the last of which was that human free will is nonexistent. At first this seems absurd. How can anyone believe there is no such thing as free will? Listen to Francis Crick, co-discoverer of DNA: '"You", your joys and your sorrows, your memories and your ambitions, your sense of personal identity and free will, are in fact no more than the behavior of a vast assembly of nerve cells and their associated molecules. Who you are is nothing but a pack of neurons'[1]. Notice the way that Crick put the word "You" in quote marks – what he means is that there is no real you. Beyond bags of chemicals, there is nothing to us.

Atheists believe that free will is an illusion, and that all our thoughts, feelings and actions are the result of physics and chemistry. Different stimuli prompt different automatic reactions in our brain. Francis Crick writes, 'It seems free to you, but it's the result of things you are not aware of'. Stephen Hawking writes, 'It is hard to see how free will can operate if our behavior is determined by physical law, so it seems we are no more than biological machines and that free will is just an illusion'[2].

Einstein, too, denied human free will: 'A human being is a part of the

---

[1] Francis Crick, *The Astonishing Hypothesis*, Charles Scribner's Sons, 1994, p.1
[2] Stephen Hawking, *The Grand Design*, p.32

whole, called by us "Universe", a part limited in time and space. He experiences himself, his thoughts and feelings as something separated from the rest – a kind of optical delusion of his consciousness. This delusion is a kind of prison for us, restricting us to our personal desires and to affection for a few persons nearest to us. Our task must be to free ourselves from this prison by widening our circle of compassion to embrace all living creatures and the whole nature in its beauty'[3].

Notice that Einstein contradicts himself here – first saying that our thoughts and feelings and free will are a delusion, but then saying that we can choose and feel and desire nonetheless. In fact, we can break free from the prison of determinism. By contradicting himself, Einstein shows his argument is false, and that free will is true after all.

Of course free will is real. If you go into a restaurant and order strawberry cheesecake for dessert instead of the chocolate mousse or apple crumble that you tried on previous visits, you have proved that you have free will, for no external physical force or internal chemical reaction compelled you to choose one over another. Now lift your arm. If you lifted your arm (or chose not to), you have again proven that you have free will, for there was no reason or necessity for raising your arm, no physical stimuli or chemical determinism at play. We display the principle of 'mind over matter' by resisting temptation all the time.

The atheist believes that free will is an illusion, because the atheist not only denies that God exists, but also that human beings have a mind, an immaterial, spiritual dimension given us by God. The atheist says that we just have a physico-chemical brain, and because we do not have a mind, we cannot make free choices.

However, if our free will is genuine (and most people intuitively believe it is real), this means that materialistic (i.e. atheistic) reductionism is false. It is really atheism that is the illusion, not our free will.

The atheist denial of free will is de-humanizing. It reduces us to robots, robbing us of our dignity. To the atheist, we are just carbon computers, machines made of meat, or overgrown germs. However,

---

[3] Albert Einstein, Condolence letter to Norman Salit, 4th March 1950

contrary to atheism, there is something very special about human beings. Wesley J. Smith writes:

What other species in known history has had the wondrous capacities of human beings? What other species has been able to (at least partially) control nature instead of being controlled by it? What other species builds civilizations, records history, creates art, makes music, thinks abstractly, communicates in language, envisions and fabricates machinery, improves life through science and engineering, or explores the deeper truths found in philosophy and religion? What other species has true freedom? Not one.

Only humans have the capacity to embrace the good and to engage in evil—a moral attribute embedded in our very natures. Moreover, we alone comprehend the grandeur, beauty, and importance of the natural world. The elephant is not awestruck at the sight of sunset. Nor can the squirrel appreciate the beauty of the blue jay and the butterfly. Yet even small children can love animals and wonder at the world.

Perhaps the most important distinction between the fauna and us is our moral agency. The sow that permits the runt of her litter to starve is not a negligent parent, but a human mother doing the same would be branded a monster. The feline that plays with a fallen baby bird before consuming it is not being sadistic; she is acting like a cat! But any human who tortures an animal is rightly seen as pathological[4].

To the atheist, the fact that we have no free will means, too, that there is no real difference between the brutality of a murderer and the tenderness of a mother, for both are simply doing what they must. Murderers and mothers are no different to machines crushing tin cans or computer printers spitting out copies of documents. However, we are not just computers; computers may be able to answer questions they are programmed to, but they do not have the power of original thought.

---

[4] Wesley J. Smith, "More than 'In God's Image'", *First Things*, 24/7/15, https://www.firstthings.com/web-exclusives/2015/07/more-than-in-gods-image

Consciousness

Bertrand Russell wrote, 'Man is the product of causes which had no prevision of the end they were achieving; his origin, his growth, his hopes and fears, his loves and his beliefs are but the outcome of the accidental collocation of atoms'[5]. However, Russell's statement presents a problem: atoms are not aware of their own existence. Humans alone possess the property of self-awareness, or consciousness. It might be difficult to prove that other human beings have consciousness – for all we know, other people might just be zombies in warmed-up corpses, all the lights on but nobody home. However, whatever other people are, we know that we ourselves are experiencing life. We not only experience the outside world around us, but we also experience ourselves subjectively, from the inside. We have access to a private screening of the movie of our lives as it is being made, inside our own heads. We talk about ourselves in the first person: 'I'. We imagine and remember. We think to ourselves all day long. This 'inner life' is the most important part of our existence; it is where we really live, 'behind the controls' of our lives. We are in the driver's seat, making the decisions as we go along.

Descartes famously said, 'I think, therefore I am'. The Scottish agnostic philosopher David Hume replied that we cannot be sure that we exist, for we cannot experience ourselves without some accompanying perception (like heat or cold, love or hate, pain or pleasure), and therefore we are just observing perceptions, not the 'self', which he held to be a fiction. The problem with this argument is that when we observe inner perceptions, who is doing the observing? 'Hume is observing sensations while ignoring the fact that he is the one who is doing the observing'[6] (Dinesh D'Souza). Hume's observer is 'the subject that forgets to take account of itself' (Schopenhauer).

The atheist philosopher Daniel Dennett argues in his book, *Consciousness Explained*, that consciousness is an illusion. However, Dennett's argument is self-refuting. Was Dennett conscious when he

---

[5] Bertrand Russell, "A Free Man's Worship", *The Independent Review* 1 (Dec 1903), pp.415-24

[6] Dinesh D'Souza, *What's so Great about Christianity?* Tyndale House, 2008, pp.247-8

wrote this book? If not, why should we believe there is any logic to it, or pay any attention to his muddled argument? The philosopher John Searle said in an interchange with Dennett on the book:

'Now what am I to do, as a reviewer, in the face of what appears to me an obvious and self-refuting falsehood? Should I pinch the author to remind him that he is conscious? ... Here is the paradox of this exchange: I am a conscious reviewer consciously answering the objections of an author who gives every indication of being consciously and puzzlingly angry. I do this for a readership that I assume is conscious. How then can I take seriously his claim that consciousness does not really exist?[7]'

The sugars that we put in our coffee are not conscious, nor are the sugars that make up part of our DNA. Nor does electricity possess self-awareness. Therefore it is hard to understand how either the chemical or electrical processes happening inside our brains produce human consciousness. Plants and animals do not possess it either; they do not reflect upon their existence. Only human beings possess consciousness. It is another indicator that we humans have a mind that is more than just our physical brain.

To the atheist, all that makes us most human – our hopes and loves, appreciation of beauty, memories and feelings – are the result of electro-chemical reactions in the brain, the products of a chain reaction going right back to the beginning of the universe. We are the product of our genes and our environment. There is no 'soul' inside us, no driver behind the wheel of life, no 'ghost in the machine'.

Rationality

Not only does atheism mean we have no free will, and no real consciousness, it also robs us of rationality. That is, atheism means that intelligence is an illusion, as well as free will and consciousness. On a

---

[7]   https://www.nybooks.com/articles/1995/12/21/the-mystery-of-consciousness-an-exchange/

materialist view of life, our thoughts are simply chemical reactions or electrical impulses in the brain. This produces a problem for the atheist, as J. B. S. Haldane describes: 'if my mental processes are determined wholly by the motions of atoms in my brain, I have no reason to suppose my beliefs are true ... and hence I have no reason for supposing my brain to be composed of atoms'.

Charles Darwin put it this way: 'But then with me the horrid doubt always arises whether the convictions of man's mind, which has been developed from the mind of the lower animals, are of any value or at all trustworthy. Would any one trust in the convictions of a monkey's mind, if there are any convictions in such a mind?'[8].

In other words, an atheistic view of rationality is self-contradictory. C. S. Lewis said: 'Supposing there was no intelligence behind the universe, no creative mind. In that case, nobody designed my brain for the purpose of thinking. It is merely that when the atoms inside my skull happen, for physical or chemical reasons, to arrange themselves in a certain way, this gives me, as a by-product, the sensation I call thought. But, if so, how can I trust my own thinking to be true? It's like upsetting a milk jug and hoping that the way it splashes itself will give you a map of London. But if I can't trust my own thinking, of course I can't trust the arguments leading to Atheism, and therefore have no reason to be an Atheist, or anything else. Unless I believe in God, I cannot believe in thought: so I can never use thought to disbelieve in God'[9].

G. K. Chesterton wrote, 'It is an act of faith to assert that our thoughts have any relation to reality at all. If you are merely a sceptic, you must sooner or later ask yourself the question, "Why should anything go right; even observation and deduction? Why should not good logic be as misleading as bad logic?" They are both movements in the brain of a bewildered ape'[10].

Atheists believe that our brains evolved due to natural selection, for the purpose of survival. However, survival value does not explain the extravagant powers of human thought. Our minds can even 'decode' the

---

[8] Charles Darwin, Letter to William Graham, 3 July 1881
[9] C. S. Lewis, *The Case for Christianity*
[10] G. K. Chesterton, *Orthodoxy*, Image Books, 1959, p.33

laws of physics and chemistry that govern the universe. Survival value does not explain why 'man is the only creature who wonders at his own existence' (Schopenhauer), nor why we ask whether there is a God or not. Einstein wrote, 'the eternal mystery of the world is its comprehensibility … The fact that it is comprehensible is a miracle'[11].

David Berlinski writes, 'Why should a limited and finite organ such as the human brain have the power to see into the heart of matter or mathematics? These are subjects which have nothing to do with the Darwinian business of scrabbling up the greasy pole of life. It is as if the liver, in addition to producing bile, were to demonstrate an unexpected ability to play the violin'[12].

It is a marvel that the universe is orderly, rather than a chaotic mess resulting from a giant explosion. It is amazing that scientific enquiry is not only possible but expressible in elegant mathematical terms. But it is even more incredible, and surely beyond co-incidence, that our inner reasoning powers, which only developed by means of meaningless accidents (according to the atheist), should correctly grasp the intelligence embedded within the universe's structures. A bowl of chicken soup does not think about anything, much less correctly formulate and communicate the laws of thermodynamics that heated it up. So why should our brains be able to do this? Christians argue that there is no co-incidence at all; man's intelligence is the gift of the Creator whose intelligence is seen in the universe, so that the intelligence seen in both man and the universe comes from the same source: God.

Meaning

Not only does atheism leave us without free will, or consciousness, or rationality, it also leaves us without meaning. If the universe is the result of meaninglessness, then we have no meaning either. Life is ultimately pointless. We are like children building sand castles on the seashore who

---

[11]   Andrew   Robinson,   "We   Just   Can't   Stop   Misquoting   Einstein",
https://primemind.com/we-just-cant-stop-misquoting-einstein-19ad4efab26e, 14 March 2016

[12] David Berlinski, *The Devil's Delusion: Atheism and its Scientific Pretensions*, Basic Books, 2009, p.17

are too busy to notice that very soon the incoming tide is going to wash it all away. All our activity will have been for no purpose.

Jean-Paul Sartre's novel *Nausea* is the story of a man who searches for the meaning of life. His conclusion, after much searching, is that life has no meaning. He discovers this terrible truth: life is nauseating – it makes you want to vomit. This is the position of a consistent atheist like Sartre. Bertrand Russell wrote: 'Unless you assume a God, the question of life's purpose is meaningless'.

Some atheists reply that we are free to make of our lives whatever we wish – we can find meaning and purpose in whatever we choose to do. However, life is better described as a pointless game that goes round and round in circles, achieving nothing.

The Russian novelist Leo Tolstoy said, 'Is there any meaning in my life that my inevitable death does not destroy?'[13] He wrote, 'What is life for? To die? To kill myself at once? No, I am afraid. To wait for death till it comes? I fear that even more. Then I must live. But what for? And I could not escape from that circle'[14]. Tolstoy turned to science for answers, but it ignored the question, and posed its own different questions. He considered philosophy, but all it could do was ask the same question more clearly, without answering it. He had already abandoned his previous pleasure-seeking ways as escapism, an attempt to ignore the absurdity of life. He finally settled on faith, the only thing that gives an answer to the question of life.

For serious and consistent atheists who do not allow themselves to be distracted from life's deeper questions by beer and football, life is pointless. The idea that we can make our own meaning is empty bravado. Mark Twain described our plight as follows:

'A myriad of men are born; they labour and struggle and sweat for bread; they squabble and scold and fight; they scramble for mean little advantages over each other. Age creeps upon them and infirmities follow; shame and humiliation bring down their pride and vanities.

---

[13] Leo Tolstoy, *A Confession and other Religious Writings*, 1879
[14] Leo Tolstoy, "The Notes of a Madman", *The Devil and Other Stories*, 1884

Those they love are taken from them, and the joy of life is turned to aching grief. The burden of pain, care, misery, grows heavier year by year. At length ambition is dead; longing for relief is in its place. It comes at last ... the only unpoisoned gift earth has for them ... and they vanish from a world where they were a mistake and a failure and a foolishness; where they left no sign that they had ever existed – a world that will lament them a day and forget them forever'.

Shakespeare said it more famously in *Macbeth* (Act 5, Scene 5):

Life's but a walking shadow, a poor player
That struts and frets his hour upon the stage
And then is heard no more: it is a tale
Told by an idiot, full of sound and fury,
Signifying nothing.

Not only is our life ultimately meaningless under atheism; it is also unsatisfying. We search in vain for something that will fill the emptiness. We try romance, adventure, fame, wealth, intellectual fulfilment, achievements, entertainment – the list is endless because we never find the satisfaction we are looking for. The result is that many people settle for a life of tedium punctuated by drunken binges.

Atheism is not so much the death of God; it is spiritual suicide for us, and we see, increasingly, the effects of this in modern secular Western society, where suicide has overtaken car accidents as the leading cause of death among young males.

Pascal and the Meaning of Life

Blaise Pascal (1623-1662) was one of the greatest intellects of all time: a brilliant French mathematician, scientist, philosopher and writer – all by his early thirties. Despite all his prodigious achievements, he understood the despair and utter darkness of life. As Pascal describes it, man is an infinitely small speck in the universe, and in eternity. He lives in a world of suffering, evil and injustice. He tries to live a happy and meaningful life, but in reality, he is full of anxiety and boredom. Despite his insignificance, man is the only thinking thing in the universe. We know we are miserable, and we know the universe will one day crush us. Here is how Pascal describes the human predicament:

'I know not who sent me into the world, nor what the world is, nor what I myself am. I am terribly ignorant of everything. I know not what my body is, nor my senses, nor my soul and that part of me which thinks what I say, which reflects upon itself as well as upon all external things, and has no more knowledge of itself than of them'.

'I see the terrifying immensity of the universe which surrounds me, and find myself limited to one corner of this vast expanse, without knowing why I am set down here rather than elsewhere, nor why the brief period appointed for my life is assigned to me at this moment rather than another in all the eternity that has gone before and will come after me. On all sides I behold nothing but infinity, in which I am a mere atom, a mere passing shadow that returns no more. All I know is that I must soon die, but what I understand least of all is this very death which I cannot escape' (*Pensées*, 11).

Where is man's hope to be found? At the age of 31, Pascal had a profound experience, an encounter with God. As a result, he abandoned his mathematical and scientific studies, and started making preparations for a book in which he would defend Christianity. Unfortunately, he died at age 39 before he was able to publish it, leaving behind only a collection of notes, called his 'thoughts' (Pensées). In the first part of his book, he planned to describe the misery of the human condition, but in the second part to write about the solution: God.

Here is Pascal's solution to the misery of life:

'What else does this longing and helplessness proclaim, but that there was once in each person a true happiness, of which all that now remains is the empty print and trace? We try to fill this in vain with everything around us, seeking in things that are not there the help we cannot find in those that are there. Yet none can change things, because this infinite abyss can only be filled with something that is infinite and unchanging—in other words, God himself. God alone is our true good. (*Pensées*, 425).

C. S. Lewis wrote about our human longing for satisfaction and true fulfilment in life:

'We remain conscious of a desire which no natural happiness will satisfy. But is there any reason to suppose that reality offers any satisfaction to it? "Nor does the being hungry prove that we have bread." But I think it may be urged that this misses the point. A man's physical hunger does not prove that that man will get any bread; he may die of starvation on a raft in the Atlantic. But surely a man's hunger does prove that he comes of a race which repairs its body by eating and inhabits a world where eatable substances exist. In the same way, though I do not believe (I wish I did) that my desire for Paradise proves that I shall enjoy it, I think it a pretty good indication that such a thing exists and that some men will. A man may love a woman and not win her; but it would be very odd if the phenomenon called "falling in love" occurred in a sexless world ("The Weight of Glory", 1962).

Where can we find true satisfaction, fulfilment and meaning in life? There is only one solution: in God. God created us and put us here so we might know Him and enjoy fellowship with Him. We were made for the highest of all fellowships, for God, not to be friends with the animals or plants, nor even to enjoy the company of our fellow-man. All the great people of the Bible had this in common:

- Adam and Eve enjoyed fellowship with God before their 'fall'.
- Enoch 'walked with God' (Genesis 5:22), as did Noah (Gen. 6:9)
- Abraham was called 'the friend of God' (James 2:23).
- Moses knew God 'face to face' (Exod. 33:11, Num. 12:8, Deut. 34:10).
- David, in Psalm 27:4, says, 'One thing I have desired of the LORD, that will I seek: that I may dwell in the house of the

LORD all the days of my life, to behold the beauty of the LORD, and to inquire in His temple'.

- Paul said in Philippians 3:10 that his life's ambition was to 'know Him', that is, Christ.
- Jesus Himself said in John 17:3 that 'this is eternal life, that they may know You, the only true God, and Jesus Christ whom You have sent'.

Life without God is ultimately meaningless and empty. God designed us, and desires us to know Him, have fellowship with Him, and glorify Him by living a life worthy of our Maker. The Westminster Larger Catechism says, 'Man's chief and highest end is to glorify God, and fully enjoy Him forever'. Augustine wrote, 'You have made us for Yourself, O Lord, and our heart is restless until it rests in You' (*Confessions*). As the popular Christian saying puts it, we have a God-shaped hole in our hearts.

In his best-selling book, *The Purpose-Driven Life*, Rick Warren tells the story of Andre Bitov who said, 'In my 27th year, while riding the metro in Leningrad, I was overcome with a despair so great that life seemed to stop at once, pre-empting the future entirely, let alone any meaning. Suddenly, all by itself, a phrase appeared: Without God life makes no sense. Repeating it in astonishment, I rode the phrase up like a moving staircase, got out of the metro and walked into God's light'.

We can know God. God waits for us to reach out to Him, to search for Him, and He promises that if we do, we will find Him. In addition, the thing that ultimately makes life meaningless, our approaching death, is defeated because God promises that all those who know and love Him will have eternal life. The most famous verse in the Bible says it like this: 'For God so loved the world that He gave His only-begotten Son, that whoever believes in Him will not perish but have everlasting life' (John 3:16). 'When all the suns and nebulae have passed away, each one of you will still be alive' (C. S. Lewis).

In summary, then, the argument for God from human dignity is this: if we were not created in the image of God, then we are robbed of all that makes us most human. Without God, there is no such thing as true freedom of will, no such thing as rationality, no meaning or purpose in life that will bring real satisfaction and true fulfilment, nor any genuine hope for the future.

But with God, all four are possible. Human beings are made in God's own likeness. We are intelligent and have free will because God made us like Himself, and we can find true meaning, satisfaction and fulfilment in knowing Him. For those who love Him, God promises the prospect of eternal life.

Although it is hard to put an exact figure on it, I rate the Argument from Humanity highly, at 8 out of 10. If we were created by God, then it makes sense for God to be at the centre of a psychologically well-balanced human life. Atheism, on the other hand, rips the heart out of human beings.

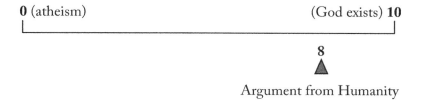

0 (atheism)   (God exists) **10**

8

Argument from Humanity

Chapter 12

The Jesus Christ Argument: Incarnation

Imagine a man who wakes up one morning in a house he has never seen before. He doesn't know where he is, and he is not sure how he got there. He gets out of bed and puts on his clothes, then starts exploring the house.

He smells something cooking, and finds his way to the kitchen. He sees a pan with bacon and eggs frying. But there is no one in the kitchen. The bacon and eggs are cooked, and ready. He calls out, but no one answers, so he turns the cooker off, finds a plate, and puts the bacon and eggs on it. He is not sure who the bacon and eggs are for, so he leaves them, sits down and waits for the cook to appear. But no one comes.

After a while, he starts looking around the rest of the house. The living room is beautifully decorated, and some music is playing. But he can't find anyone else inside the house. So he decides to look outside in the garden. The house is impressive from the outside and the gardens are beautiful, but he can't see anyone outside either. There is a shiny silver sports car in the driveway.

After some time he comes back inside and notices a set of keys on the kitchen bench. He goes outside again to see if they belong to the car. They unlock the car, and he is tempted to get in and turn it on, or even take it for a drive, but he does not dare. Looking more closely, he notices that the key fob has his initials on them: A.D. He is unnerved by this discovery. He walks down the driveway to the street, and looks at the sign at the front of the house. It reads, Dunn. "That's my name", he says. "Do I live here? Does all this belong to me? How did I get here? What is going on?"

This is the human predicament. Is there a God who has put us here and gave us all the things we need: the house we live in – planet Earth, the food we enjoy, the comforts we take for granted? Sometimes these questions cross our minds, but instead of trying to work out how we got here, most of us just get on with eating the bacon and eggs and driving the sports car.

But imagine if, one morning the door-bell rang, and a man stood there who introduced himself as the owner of the house and car, the one who cooked the bacon and eggs that morning. This is what Christianity claims has happened. To a world that asks where God is, and why we never get to see Him, God's reply is this: He Himself has stepped into our world, and came to earth as one of us, in the person of Jesus Christ.

D. James Kennedy, an American preacher, told of an occasion when he visited a man's house and asked the man who he thought Jesus was. He said, 'Oh, Jesus was a wonderful man, the greatest man who ever lived, the most loving and kind person who ever walked upon this earth'. Kennedy said, 'Let me tell you something I believe will startle you. According to the Bible, Jesus of Nazareth, the carpenter of Galilee, was and is the eternal Creator of the Universe, the omnipotent, omniscient and Almighty God'. Instantly, the eyes of this fifty-five or sixty year old man filled with tears and he said, 'I've been in church all my life and I have never heard that before. But I have always thought that is the way it ought to be – that God ought to be like Jesus'.

When Neil Armstrong walked on the moon, he said, "One small step for man, one giant leap for mankind". While it was a great step for man to walk on the moon, a more amazing event has happened: God has walked on Earth. No astronaut has died on the moon, but when God came to Earth we crucified Him.

Jesus Christ is the most important man who ever lived. His death is the most famous in history. 'It is from his birth that most of the human race dates its calendars, it is by his name that millions curse and in his name that millions pray' (Jaroslav Pelikan[1]).

Is Jesus Christ God Almighty, who came to earth, suffered and died just like one of us, as a real human being? If true, Jesus is the ultimate evidence for God's existence. If God has come, died and risen again, this is the most important event in the universe. If false, it is the most

---

[1] Jaroslav Pelikan, *Jesus through the Centuries*, 1985

monstrous hoax ever foisted upon the human race. How do we tell which it is?

Was Jesus Merely a Legend?

C. S. Lewis famously posed a question, sometimes called the Trilemma: if Jesus claimed to be God, we must either consider him a lunatic, or put him down for a liar, or acknowledge that He is Lord. If He is not God, then he must be mad, or bad:

'I am trying here to prevent anyone saying the really foolish thing that people often say about Him: I'm ready to accept Jesus as a great moral teacher, but I don't accept his claim to be God. That is the one thing we must not say. A man who was merely a man and said the sort of things Jesus said would not be a great moral teacher. He would either be a lunatic — on the level with the man who says he is a poached egg — or else he would be the Devil of Hell. You must make your choice. Either this man was, and is, the Son of God, or else a madman or something worse. You can shut him up for a fool, you can spit at him and kill him as a demon or you can fall at his feet and call him Lord and God, but let us not come with any patronizing nonsense about his being a great human teacher. He has not left that open to us. He did not intend to'[2].

Nowadays, atheists argue that Lewis merely overlooked a fourth option: Jesus is a legend. One Russian communist dictionary apparently defined Jesus as 'a mythical figure who never existed'. Others accept that there is probably a kernel of historical truth to the stories about Jesus but, just like Robin Hood, they suspect the tale has 'grown in the telling'. Richard Dawkins writes, 'Nobody knows who the four evangelists [gospel writers] were, but they almost certainly never met Jesus personally … It is even possible to mount a serious, though not widely supported, historical case that Jesus never lived at all …' (*The God Delusion*, p96, 97).

By the way, Dawkins also responded in his book to Lewis' trilemma

---

[2] C. S. Lewis, *Mere Christianity*, William Collins, 2016, p.52

by saying that Jesus was simply mistaken when He said He was God. But someone who says they are God cannot simply be mistaken. John Stott tells a story about a young man who sent him a letter in which he told Stott he had made a great discovery. 'Almighty God had two sons: Jesus Christ was the first, I am the second'. Stott glanced at the address at the top of the letter, and sure enough, the young man was writing from a well-known psychiatric hospital[3]. Anyone who says they are God cannot be just mistaken – they are either mentally ill, or telling the truth.

The historical evidence that Jesus lived is very strong. There are about ten non-Christian historical sources within 150 years of Jesus that mention Him and confirm the basic details of His life that we find in the gospels:

- **Cornelius Tacitus** (AD 56-120), considered the greatest of Roman historians wrote: 'Consequently, to get rid of the report [i.e. that he had started the fire of Rome], Nero fastened the guilt and inflicted the most exquisite tortures on a class hated for their abominations, called Christians by the populace. Christus, from whom the name had its origin, suffered the extreme penalty during the reign of Tiberius at the hands of one of our procurators, Pontius Pilatus, and a most mischievous superstition, thus checked for the moment, again broke out not only in Judea, the first source of the evil, but even in Rome, where all things hideous and shameful from every part of the world find their centre and become popular' (*Annals* 15.44).

- **Flavius Josephus** (AD 37-100), the great Jewish historian, wrote: 'Now there was about this time Jesus, a wise man, if it be lawful to call him a man, for he was a doer of wonderful works, a teacher of such men as receive the truth with pleasure. He drew over to him both many of the Jews, and many of the Gentiles. He was the Christ, and when Pilate, at the suggestion of the principal men among us, had condemned him to the cross, those that loved him at the first did not forsake him; for he appeared to them alive again the third day, as the divine prophets had foretold these and ten thousand other wonderful things concerning him. And the tribe of Christians so

---

[3] John Stott, *Basic Christianity*, IVP, 2008, p.48

named from him are not extinct at this day' (*Antiquities of the Jews*, xviii.33). Josephus also mentioned in other places two other related biblical characters: John the Baptist who was executed by Herod Antipas, and James the brother of Jesus who was put to death by the Jewish Council in about AD 66.

- **Mara bar Serapion** (c. AD 70), a Syrian philosopher, writing to his son: 'What advantage did the Athenians gain from putting Socrates to death? Famine and plague came upon them as a judgment for their crime. What advantage did the men of Samos gain from burning Pythagoras? In a moment their land was covered with sand. What advantage did the Jews gain from executing their wise king? It was just after that that their kingdom was abolished. God justly avenged these wise men: the Athenians died from hunger; the Samians were overwhelmed by the sea; the Jews, ruined and driven from the land, live in complete dispersion. But Socrates did not die for good; he lived on in the teaching of Plato. Pythagoras did not die for good; he lived on in the statue of Hera. Nor did the wise king die for good; He lived on in the teaching which he had given'.

- **Lucian of Samosata**, a second-century satirist, who wrote of Christ as 'the man who was crucified in Palestine because he introduced this new cult into the world ... Furthermore, their first lawgiver persuaded them that they were all brothers one of another after they have transgressed once for all by denying the Greek gods and by worshipping that crucified sophist himself and living under his laws' (*The Passing Peregrinus*).

- **Pliny the Younger**, Roman Governor of Bithynia (AD 112), wrote to the Emperor Trajan. He had been killing so many Christians, men and women, boys and girls, that he wondered whether he should only kill certain ones. He writes of the Christians: 'They affirmed, however, that the whole of their guilt, or their error, was, that they were in the habit of meeting on a certain fixed day before it was light, when they sang in alternate verse a hymn to Christ as to a god, and bound themselves to a solemn oath, not to do any wicked deeds, but never to commit any fraud, theft, adultery, never to falsify their word, not to deny a trust when they should be called upon to deliver it up' (*Epistles*, X. 96)

These non-Christian historical sources confirm that Jesus was a real historical person, that he lived in Judea, was famous for his wise teachings and amazing deeds, was crucified under Pontius Pilate during the reign of Tiberius, and that his followers said that he had risen again. Also, we see that Jesus was being worshiped as God by the early Christians soon after his death. In fact, Christianity spread so quickly that the fire of Rome was blamed on them little more than 30 years after Jesus' death. What caused this obscure Jewish sect to grow so quickly, as to be seen as a threat to the Roman empire? Other non-Christian historical sources that confirm parts of the historical facts about Jesus include Thallus (AD 52), Phlegon (AD 80-140), Suetonius (AD 69-140), Celsus (AD 175), and the Jewish Talmud (AD 400-700, but based on early traditions). The Talmud is vehemently anti-Christian, but still confirms that Jesus was accused by the Jews of being born out of wedlock, that he did miracles (these were said to be acts of sorcery), and that he was executed at Passover (i.e. Easter) time.

Professor F. F. Bruce rejects the idea that Christ was merely a legend, saying, 'Some writers may toy with the fancy of a 'Christ-myth', but they do not do so on the ground of historical evidence. The historicity of Christ is as axiomatic for an unbiased historian as the historicity of Julius Caesar. It is not historians who propagate the 'Christ-myth' theories'[4].

Professor Gary Habermas writes, 'We can perceive all the more how groundless the speculations are which deny His existence or which postulate only a minimal amount of facts concerning Him. Much of ancient history is based on many fewer sources which are much later than the events which they record ... While some believe that we know almost nothing about Jesus from ancient non-New Testament sources, this is plainly not the case. Not only are there many such sources, but Jesus is one of the persons of ancient history concerning whom we have a significant amount of quality data. His is one of the most-mentioned and

---

[4] F. F. Bruce, *The New Testament Documents: Are they Reliable?* 5th rev. ed. IVP, 1972, p.119

most-substantiated lives in ancient times'[5].

While atheists like Dawkins insist that we cannot believe anything that the gospels say because they are supposedly biased, it is clear that non-Christian (i.e. unbiased) historical sources confirm the historicity of Jesus and the main facts of his life. The suggestion that Jesus never existed is simply a measure of how ignorant and biased modern atheists are.

Even more significant than the non-Christian historical sources is the information we find about Jesus in the New Testament letters of Paul. These were written (historians of all stripes agree) in the 50s and 60s of the first century, and confirm that the earliest Christian churches worshipped Jesus as God, practised his teachings, and preached that Jesus rose again on the third day after his death, being seen alive by many witnesses. These ideas were not myths that developed centuries after Jesus, but were held (on pain of death by the mid-60s during Nero's persecution) by people who belonged to the same generation as Jesus himself.

This evidence locks down another important fact: the stories about Jesus did not 'grow with the telling' over a few hundred years. They are found right from the earliest years after Jesus. The New Testament letters do not fit the category of legendary literature. These letters deal with the struggles of the early Christian communities as they faced external persecution, internal problems, and false-teachings from other contemporary religions. Their references to Jesus are mentioned incidentally amongst other advice on how to deal with these difficulties.

The fact that we have these early Christian church communities in the first place is strong evidence for the historical reality of Jesus. Why would people all over the Roman world be worshipping a crucified Jewish peasant? Not unless it was true that He had risen from the dead and was who He claimed to be, i.e. God. Otherwise, these churches had no reason to exist.

Most significantly of all, we have the evidence for Jesus' life in the gospels. The gospels give us four different biographies of Jesus' life. They

---

[5] Gary Habermas, *Ancient Evidence for the Life of Jesus*, Thomas Nelson, 1984, p.169

are all dated (except John's gospel), even by non-Christian historians, before the Jewish-Roman War of AD 67-70. The gospels again confirm the historical facts about Jesus.

The Personality of Jesus

In 1929, Albert Einstein was interviewed by journalist George Viereck, and they discussed the person of Jesus Christ.

Einstein: 'I am enthralled by the luminous figure of the Nazarene'

Viereck: 'You accept the historical existence of Jesus?'

Einstein: 'Unquestionably! No one can read the gospels without feeling the actual presence of Jesus. His personality pulsates in every word. No myth is filled with such life'[6].

Einstein says something that any open-minded reader of the gospels notices: how powerful and genuine the personality of Jesus is, and how inadequate any theory is that argues that the gospels are fictional accounts.

The gospels are the most popular and powerful books that have ever been written. The reason they are so amazing is not because of any literary brilliance, but because of the personality of the central character. If, in the early New Testament letters we find incidental evidence of Jesus, the gospels give us an up-close and in-depth look at His personality and life.

Writer Beverley Nichols was not a Christian, but responded to a professor who argued that Jesus was a legend as follows:

If you have ever done any writing you may have a faint idea of the immense difficulty of making a character *live* even for a single publishing season, in a single language. And if you have ever done any reading, the remotest acquaintance with European literature will inform you that there are no "characters", not even Don Quixote (the most lifelike evocation of an individual in literature) which are more than tiny shadows against the immense reality of the character of Jesus.

---

[6] Interview recorded in *Einstein, his Life and Universe*, Simon and Shuster, UK, p.386

You cannot deny the reality of this character, *in whatever body it resided*. Even if we were to grant the Professor's theory that it is all a hotch-potch of legend, *somebody* said "The Sabbath was made for man, and not man for the Sabbath"; *somebody* said "For what shall it profit a man if he shall gain the whole world and lose his own soul"; *somebody* said "Suffer the little children to come unto me, and forbid them not: for of such is the Kingdom of God"; *somebody* said "How hardly shall they that have riches enter into the Kingdom of God"; *somebody* said "All they that take the sword shall perish with the sword".

Somebody said these things, because they are staring me in the face at this moment from the Bible. And whoever said them was *gigantic*. And whoever said them was *living*, because we are in the year 1936 and I am "modern" and you are "modern", and we both of us like going to the cinema and we can both drive a car and all that sort of thing, and yet we cannot find in any contemporary literature any phrases which have a shadow of the beauty, the truth, the individuality, nor the *indestructibility* of those phrases. And remember, I have only quoted five sentences at random'[7].

C. S. Lewis argued that if the authors of the gospels invented Jesus, they themselves must have been literary geniuses of the first magnitude. He said, 'The historical difficulty of giving for the life, sayings and influence of Jesus any explanation that is not harder than the Christian explanation is very great'[8]. What Lewis meant is that to capture in writing such a perfect and yet compellingly realistic personality who is worshipped on every continent of the world twenty centuries later is an incredible achievement. If someone invented the person of Jesus, we would almost have to worship whoever it was that made him up. How did first century peasant-fishermen manage to write the gospels, unless the story they are telling is true?

Nor was the person of Jesus Christ invented by the Church to cement

---

[7] Beverley Nichols, *The Fool Hath Said*, Messrs. Jonathan Cape Ltd., 1936, p.126ff.
[8] C. S. Lewis, *Miracles*, Geoffrey Bles, 1947, p.132

its power over the masses. As atheist Matthew Parris put it,

'One of the reasons we can be pretty sure Jesus actually existed is that if He had not, the Church would never have invented Him. He stands so passionately, resolutely and inconveniently against everything an established church stands for. Continuity? Tradition? Christ had nothing to do with stability. He came to break up families, to smash routines, to cast aside the human superstructures, to teach abandonment of earthly concerns and a throwing of ourselves upon God's mercy'[9].

Further, it is not one literary genius who gave us Jesus; it was four different authors whose central character is undeniably, identifiably the same astonishing, real person. The French writer Rousseau wrote, 'It is more inconceivable that several men should have united to forge the Gospel, than that a single person should have furnished the subject of it'.

How did four different authors manage to dream up the same (supposedly imaginary) portrait, despite their different perspectives? The answer, again, is that the unity of the four gospels derives from the fact that they are portraying the life of the same, real, person – not an imaginary creation.

It is ironic that atheists accuse C. S. Lewis of overlooking the option of Jesus being a legend. Lewis was not only an atheist for many years, but also a professor of Medieval Literature at Oxford and Cambridge, and thus very familiar with legends – it was his area of expertise. In his essay, *Modern Theology and Biblical Criticism*, he wrote,

'I have been reading poems, romances, vision-literature, legends, and myths all my life, and I know what they're like. I know none of them are like this. Of the gospel texts there are only two possible views. Either this is reportage, or else, some unknown ancient writer, without known predecessors or successors, suddenly anticipated the whole technique of modern novelistic, realistic narrative. The reader

---

[9] https://www.spectator.co.uk/2012/02/beware-i-would-say-to-believers-the-patronage-of-unbelievers/ 25th Feb, 2012

who doesn't see this has simply not learned how to read'.

Let us take two little examples to see the sort of realistic reporting that Lewis is talking about. The first relates to Pontius Pilate, the Roman governor who condemned Jesus to death. When Jesus stood on trial before him, Pilate realized he was innocent of any political crime, and wanted nothing to do with a Jewish religious dispute. Yet he was caught in a trap by the Jewish leaders. They threatened him, "if you let this man go, you are not Caesar's friend". Pilate, already in trouble with Caesar for his harsh government of the Jewish people, had to keep their leaders onside.

Speaking to Jesus amid this political pressure, Pilate famously said, 'What is truth?' The cynicism, frustration and sarcasm of a politician is perfectly captured. The brevity of the words breathes authenticity.

Later, after Jesus had been hung on the cross, Pilate himself wrote the accusation that was nailed above His head: 'Jesus of Nazareth, the King of the Jews'. Pilate worded it this way, in part, to mock the Jews. In their typically pedantic way, the Jews argued that it should be re-written: "Write, '*He said*, I am the King of the Jews'". Pilate replied, 'What I have written, I have written'. Again, the gospels capture the exasperation and contempt that Pilate felt for the Jews. This is not the stuff of legend. It is the reporting of the raw reactions of real people.

For a second example, when the women came back from the empty tomb early on the morning of Jesus' resurrection, they told the disciples they had seen some angels who said Jesus was risen. Here is the reaction of Jesus' disciples, as recorded by Luke (24:11): 'their words seemed to them as idle tales, and they did not believe them'. The Greek word behind our English translation 'idle tales' here is *leros*, which means 'silly talk' or 'nonsense'. We might even translate it 'old wives fables'. The disciples' reaction went way beyond mere skepticism; it has been described as 'lofty masculine scorn'. It carries sexist overtones, something along the lines of 'stupid women with their silly tales'.

Whether we like their language or not, what we have here are raw emotions being exposed. For Jesus' closest friends, His death was still an open wound, and with their normal emotional defences shattered by grief, we see what is really in their heart. It is a snapshot of the realism with which the gospels describe what is happening.

Jesus' disciples do not come out well from the gospels: by turns sectarian, squabbling, afraid, unbelieving, slow to understand, sarcastic, self-important, without any nobility or great wisdom. If this is fiction, it is as realistic a description of ordinary humanity as we will find anywhere in world literature. They are exactly like most real men. Jesus, on the other hand, is someone in a different category altogether.

General Bertrand, surprised by Napoleon's religious convictions in exile on St. Helena, suggested that Christ was just a great man. Napoleon replied: "I know men and I tell you that Jesus was not a man". Napoleon said:

'Superficial minds see a resemblance between Christ and the founders of empires, the conquerors and the gods of other religions. This similarity does not exist: between Christianity and other religions, there is the distance from infinity... Everything about Christ amazes me; his spirit exceeds me and his will confuses me. Between him and anything in the world, there is no possible term of comparison... Whether he speaks or acts, Jesus is luminous, immutable, impassive. The sublime, it is said, is a trait of divinity ... Those who examine the Gospels find nothing to criticize in his life. If the title of impostor is easily added to the name of Muhammad, it is repugnant with that of Christ... And yet there is no middle ground: Christ is an impostor or he is God[10].

If the disciples were the authors of a legend – and they certainly claim to be the authors of the gospels and letters that tell us about Jesus – why did they not present themselves in more favourable light? Why do they describe themselves with such realism? Why tell about all their mistakes and faults? No one today treats the disciples as heroes or aspires to imitate them, let alone worships them. What do the disciples stand to gain from inventing a story like this? The answer is, nothing. All of the

[10] Napoleon Bonaparte, *Conversations sur le Christianisme*, preface by Jean Tulard , ed. du Rocher, 2014, pp.109, 27, 38, 41.

disciples, with the exception of John, died gruesome deaths – because they would not keep quiet about who Jesus was. Why die for a lie, if the whole thing was an invention?

Charles Colson, President Nixon's 'hatchet man', who went to jail for his part in the Watergate cover-up, and later became a Christian, said:

'I know the resurrection is a fact, and Watergate proved it to me. How? Because twelve men testified they had seen Jesus raised from the dead, then they proclaimed that truth for forty years, never once denying it. Every one was beaten, tortured, stoned and put in prison. They would not have endured that if it weren't true. Watergate embroiled twelve of the most powerful men in the world-and they couldn't keep a lie for three weeks. You're telling me twelve apostles could keep a lie for forty years? Absolutely impossible'[11].

Why, moreover, were the Gospels written without the least literary ornament? The power of the stories does not lie in the choice of clever words. There is nothing poetic or polished about the writing, nor is there any lofty imagery or powerful metaphor. The Gospels are written in the plainest language ever put to paper – the simple, direct language of ordinary, unlettered men, like Jesus' disciples. Yet they are the best-selling books of all time. The attraction is the towering presence of the person of Christ.

Lunatic, Liar or Lord?

If Jesus is not a legend, we are back to Lewis' trilemma: lunatic, liar or Lord. There are many routes we could take to try to think about who Jesus really is, but the best way is, with Einstein, to go straight to the gospels themselves.

As we shall see, Lewis' alternatives of liar or lunatic do not make sense, which is why nobody ever makes the case for them. We will look at three reasons why Jesus is neither a lunatic or a liar. For sake of simple alliteration, we will look at Jesus' words, His walk and His works.

---

[11] Charles Colson, "An Unholy Hoax?", *Breakpoint Commentaries*, Mar 29, 2002

Jesus' Words

Lewis' trilemma – liar, lunatic or Lord – actually comes straight from the gospels themselves. Mark's Gospel chapter 3 tells us how at one point certain members of Jesus' extended family thought that He was going mad. The crowds of followers pressing about him, preventing him from even getting time to eat meals, had given Jesus delusions of grandeur, thought his relatives. He had developed a Messiah-complex.

Jesus did not make any reply to this accusation. Instead, straight after this, Mark tells us how some of the religious leaders from Jerusalem had started saying that Jesus was 'Beelzebub', that is, Satan, the ruler of the demons, and that it was by the Devil's power that Jesus did His miracles. Jesus' replied to this accusation in words still proverbial today: 'a house divided against itself cannot stand ... if Satan has risen up against himself, and is divided, he cannot stand, but has an end' (Mark 3:26). Without dignifying the earlier accusation of lunacy with a direct reply, He refutes the outrageous accusation that He is Satan with a speech of calm and powerful logic, clinically dismantling both accusations, that he is mad or bad.

Further, Jesus goes on to turn the argument against his critics. If He is casting out Satan in His miracles of exorcism, He must be stronger than Satan himself: 'no one can enter a strong man's house and plunder his goods unless he first binds the strong man'. And if Jesus is more powerful than Satan, then who is He? Logically, there is only one Being more powerful than Satan, and that is God Himself.

The first piece of evidence, then, that argues against Jesus being either a lunatic or a liar is His words and teachings. Jesus' wisdom is conveyed in words of brilliance and beauty unparalleled in world literature. Even His enemies said, 'No man ever spoke like this man' (John 7:46). Whether it is the sustained moral depth of His Sermon on the Mount, or the pathos of his parables like the Prodigal Son, or brilliant one-liners like, 'He that is without sin among you, let him cast the first stone' (John 8:7), the reactions were always astonishment. Still today, Jesus' words catch us by surprise and work their way into our hearts.

It might perhaps be easy to invent a perfect character if he never had to say much, but the gospels record large quantities of Jesus' words and teachings: his longer speeches (or sermons), his stories (or parables), his debates with critics, and his conversations with individuals. Yet there is nothing in them that is banal, bland, stale, or silly, let alone blameworthy. Instead, Jesus' words show evidence, not only of a most original mind, but also of a consistently brilliant communicator. G. Campbell-Morgan wrote:

'Jesus said things which reveal the consciousness of a Being both superior to His own age, and subsisting in all ages; and therefore, ageless, timeless, age-abiding, eternal. But Jesus also spoke of things like poverty, suffering, sorrow and weakness – all of the things of one age, its limitations and its human experiences'[12].

Another incident where we see the 'trilemma' is the famous story of Jesus and the Samaritan woman by the well, but here we have another option introduced. Maybe Jesus was a prophet; not God but a man sent by God.

Jesus was returning from Jerusalem to Galilee, a distance of about 100km, a three day walk. As part of this journey, Jesus and His disciples travelled through the territory of Samaritans – people who were of a different race and religion to the Jews. The Jews and Samaritans were virtual enemies; they did not get on with each other. Jesus and His disciples came to a Samaritan town and the disciples went to buy some food while Jesus, weary from the journey, sat beside a well.

A woman came out from the town to fill up her water pot, and Jesus asked her for a drink. This request broke two generally-accepted social rules. Firstly, Jews had no dealings with Samaritans, and secondly men did not speak with women in public.

The woman was taken aback at this stranger. She said, "How is it that you are speaking with me, a Samaritan woman?"

"If you knew what the gift of God was, and if you knew who I am", Jesus replied, "you would be asking me for living water".

The woman now thought she was dealing with someone with mental

---

[12] Campbell-Morgan, *The Teaching of Christ*, Pickering and Inglis, 1946, p.36

problems. Not only was he offering her 'living water' (whatever that was), but he also seemed to think he was someone very special.

She pushed back, pointing out the absurdity of his words: "Sir, the well is deep, and you have no bucket to draw water. Where are you going to get this living water? Are you greater than our father Jacob who dug this well?"

Jesus replied, "Whoever drinks from this well will thirst again, but whoever drinks of the water that I will give him will never thirst again, but will have everlasting life".

Now the woman was certain that Jesus had psychological problems; he had just said his imaginary water was able to give people eternal life.

The woman decided to put an end to the man's pretensions by asking him to produce the goods: "Give me some of this water, so I don't have to come and draw from this well", she said.

"Go and call your husband", Jesus said.

"I have no husband", she replied.

"You're right about having no husband", Jesus said, "because you have had five husbands, and the man you now have is not your husband. In this, you are telling the truth!". In addition to telling her sorry life-story, Jesus was almost insinuating that it was not her habit to be totally honest all the time.

The woman was stunned. Jesus had instantly gone, in her estimation, from a surprising Jew, or someone with a few screws loose, to exposing her deepest, most embarrassing secrets. Who on earth was this?

"I see that you are a prophet", she said in suddenly respectful tones, and then tried to change the subject from her embarrassing personal life to the long-standing religious dispute between Jews and Samaritans.

Jesus shut down this religious diversion pretty quickly, telling her that the Samaritan religion did not know or worship the true God.

The woman backed out: "I know that when the Messiah comes, he will explain it all"

"*I am* the Messiah", said Jesus.

At this point, Jesus' disciples returned from the town, surprised that Jesus was talking with a woman. She left her water pot by the well, and ran back into town. "Come and see a man who has told me everything I ever did – is not this the Messiah?"

The Samaritan townsfolk came out to see Jesus and, after hearing the woman's tale, invited Jesus and his disciples to stay in their village for the night – a rare privilege and honour for a Jew.

When Jesus and His disciples left two days later, the Samaritans said to the woman, "Now we believe, not because of what you told us, for we have heard him ourselves, and we know that this is truly the Messiah, the Saviour of the world".

Jesus' words here give us two more reasons to reject the lunatic or liar options. First, Jesus's words were supernatural: He 'knew all things', in this case, even though He had never met her before. 'Knowing everything' is how theologians define 'omniscience', an attribute of God's.

But, Jesus' words were special in a second way too. Jesus' words demonstrated a supernatural care for other people. He had a revolutionary way of reaching across racial, cultural, moral and religious divides to people like this sinful Samaritan woman. Here was a woman who many people in her own community would have been reluctant to talk to, a woman with a reputation. How much more shocking for a Jew to talk to her, all the more so (in Jesus' case) knowing the worst about her lifestyle and history. If this woman lived today, she would probably be a chain-smoking single-mother missing a few teeth, with children from three or four different men, living with a new boyfriend in a council house. Yet Jesus did not choose to ignore her as an awkward personality, nor simply to make polite conversation, but to speak words of genuine friendship and interest.

On another occasion, a Jewish prostitute came and washed Jesus' feet with her tears as He sat at dinner in a religious Jews' house. To the disgust of those present, Jesus did not recoil, or even rebuke her interruption, but forgave her sins, sending her away in peace, just like He offered the Samaritan woman eternal life. In this ultra-religious, morally-strict society, Jesus gained the reputation of a radical.

By the way, we see here a second reason Jesus' words defy the lunatic or liar explanations. Jesus' words refute the 'Devil of Hell' or liar explanation because instead of being an evil genius taking advantage of people and turning them into demons, Jesus is famous for the exact opposite, a superhuman love and grace to sinful people that transforms them into wholesome people. Jesus was mocked and criticized bitterly by religious Jews for being an associate of prostitutes and swindling Roman tax-collectors. They called Him 'the friend of sinners'.

At a more general level, Jesus' amazing words call for an explanation. How is it possible that a young carpenter, with no public speaking experience, should suddenly start drawing crowds of thousands to listen to his teachings? The country-folk of His hometown heard him speak in the synagogue for the first time, and 'marveled at the gracious words that proceeded out of his mouth' (Luke 4:22). They asked, 'Where did this fellow get this wisdom?' (Matthew 14:54). One thing we can say for certain is that He did not get His public-speaking ability from Nazareth!

Whereas the Jewish religious teachers of the time quoted the various opinions of the famous rabbis on disputed theological questions and difficult Bible verses, leaving their listeners none the wiser, Jesus cut straight to the truth, clearing up their understanding of Scripture, despite having no formal theological training or advanced education.. We read, 'they were astonished at his teaching, for he taught them as one having authority and not as the scribes' (Matthew 7:28-29). There was no ambiguity, no 'maybe this means ...', or 'perhaps' or 'I guess ....'. G. Campbell Morgan writes:

'The greatest human teachers have always been reticent as to the ultimate authority of their teaching. They have always admitted that there is room for interpretation, for question, for further investigation. That note is entirely absent from the teaching of Christ'[13].

Whereas the Jewish prophets of the Old Testament began by saying, 'Thus says the Lord', claiming to be merely the messenger, Jesus never used such words. Instead He said, 'Truly, *I say* to you', basing His teachings on His own personal authority. In Jesus' famous Sermon on

---

[13] Campbell-Morgan, *The Teaching of Christ*, p.9

the Mount, for example, He says, 'You have heard that it was said to those of old, You shall not commit adultery. ***But I say to you*** that whoever looks at a woman to lust for her has already committed adultery with her in his heart' (Matthew 5:27-28). It is no co-incidence that Jesus delivered this sermon on a mountain – it was, in part, a commentary on the Ten Commandments which were given to Moses on Mt. Sinai. Jesus was advertising himself as the new Moses. Jesus' trademark statement, 'Truly, I say to you', occurs over 100 times in the gospels. In the Sermon on the Mount, Jesus was deliberately re-interpreting the Ten Commandments on his own say-so. He was thus claiming to have greater authority than Moses, in effect asserting that he is God.

Jesus' amazing teaching ability is not easily accounted for. Jesus' words are not like those of today's literary try-hards: the polished orators, or learned lecturers, or studied wordsmiths. Nor is he like Shakespeare: full of obscure metaphors, padded verbiage, weird vocabulary and jumbled sentence constructions, amongst which the odd diamond shines through. With Jesus, the simple, effortless but sustained brilliance is easily understood still today. Two thousand years later, his are still the best-selling and most-read words ever spoken. The question of where Jesus got his ability from remains unanswered: like a root out of dry ground, Jesus' words cannot be explained by his society, family, upbringing, education or training.

Jesus' Walk

By Jesus' 'walk', I am using the common biblical metaphor for 'lifestyle' or 'character'. The gospels tell the story of a perfect man – not a very easy literary invention to pull off. Fyodor Dostoevsky, the great Russian novelist, put it this way:

'All writers, not ours alone but foreigners also, who have sought to represent Absolute Beauty, were unequal to the task, for it is an infinitely difficult one. The beautiful is the ideal; but ideals, with us as in civilized Europe, have long been wavering. There is in the world only one figure of absolute beauty: Christ. That infinitely lovely figure is, as a matter of course, an infinite marvel'[14].

Consider the beauty and perfection of Christ's character. Jesus lived in humble poverty yet never showed any evidence of bitterness or jealousy towards others. Coming from a backward country village with a bad reputation, He was subject to discrimination and prejudice yet we never read about Him speaking one sarcastic word of resentment at how others treat Him. The last three years of His life were busy with constant travel, teaching and helping others, yet not one word of self-pity escapes His lips. His life is considered the noblest ever lived, yet we never hear Him speak in pride or boasting. He is famous for His ethic of non-retaliation and forgiveness, even towards the Roman oppressors and overlords of His people. He reached out to the outcasts of His hyper-religious society with an inclusiveness that was scandalous. He frequently showed great courage, which the Romans considered the principal virtue, standing up to religious hypocrisy and taboos. Yet He also displayed incredible patience and gentleness toward his students, the disciples.

Dostoevsky elsewhere wrote:

'I believe that there is nothing lovelier, deeper, more sympathetic, more rational, more manly, and more perfect than the Saviour; I say to myself with jealous love that not only is there no one else like Him, but that there could be no one. I would even say more: If anyone could prove to me that Christ is outside the truth, and if the truth really did exclude Christ, I should prefer to stay with Christ and not with truth'[15].

To see something more of Christ's perfection, look at His interactions with other people. We have mentioned a few cases of Jesus interacting with women already, but it is worth listening to some comments of

---

[14] Fyodor Dostoevsky, in a letter to his Niece Sofia Alexandrovna, Geneva, January 1, 1868. Ethel Golburn Mayne (1879), *Letters of Fyodor Michailovitch Dostoyevsky to His Family and Friends*, Dostoevsky's Letters XXXIX, p.136

[15] Letter To Mme. N. D. Fonvisin (1854), from *Letters of Fyodor Michailovitch Dostoevsky to his Family and Friends* (1914), translated by Ethel Golburn Mayne, Letter XXI, p.71

Dorothy Sayers on this subject:

'Perhaps it is no wonder that the women were first at the Cradle and last at the Cross. They had never known a man like this Man – there never has been such another. A prophet and teacher who never nagged at them, never flattered or coaxed or patronised; who never made arch jokes about them, never treated them either as "The women, God help us!" or "The ladies, God bless them!"; who rebuked without querulousness and praised without condescension; who took their questions and arguments seriously; who never mapped out their sphere for them, never urged them to be feminine or jeered at them for being female; who had no axe to grind and no uneasy male dignity to defend; who took them as he found them and was completely unself-conscious. There is no act, no sermon, no parable in the whole Gospel that borrows its pungency from female perversity; nobody could possibly guess from the words and deeds of Jesus that there was anything "funny" about woman's nature'[16].

H. G. Wells describes Jesus' relationship with the religious and political leaders of the day:

'[Jesus] was dragging out all the little private reservations they [the Priests, rulers and rich] had made from social service into the light of a universal religious life. He was like some terrible moral huntsman digging mankind out of the smug burrows in which they had lived hitherto … Is it any wonder that men were dazzled and blinded and cried out against him? Even his disciples cried out when he would not spare them the light. Is it any wonder that the priests realized that between this man and themselves there was no choice but that he or the priestcraft should perish?'[17]

---

[16] Dorothy L. Sayers, *Are Women Human? Astute and Witty Essays on the Role of Women in Society,* Eerdmans, 1971

[17] H. G. Wells, *Outline of History,* Garden City, Garden City Publishing Co., 1931, p.535

It isn't just his public persona and popular speeches that impress us. His private life was inspected at close quarters by his disciples during three years of busy travelling. Yet they all report nothing silly, clumsy, vindictive or shameful about him. Instead, they testify that He never had to retract a word, or ask for pardon from others, or humble himself penitently before God. Strauss the German sceptic said, 'Jesus had a conscience unclouded by the memory of any sins'.

There have been other men in history famous for their virtue, but they all had various faults and blemishes. The greatest of all the Romans was the noble Seneca, Nero's tutor, who taught the ideal of poverty but lived as a millionaire. He apologized, saying, 'I am not perfect nor ever will be. I am deep in all sorts of vices. I only hope to be better than the wicked and to improve daily'[18].

Confucius said, 'In letters I am perhaps equal to other men; but the character of the perfect man, carrying out in his conduct what he professes, is what I have not yet attained to'[19].

Mohammed asked for God's forgiveness: 'Oh God, I acknowledge and confess before You, all my sins, please forgive them, as no one can forgive sins except You. Forgive my mistakes, those done intentionally, or out of my ignorance, with or without excuses'[20].

Mohandas Karamchand Gandhi, also known as Mahatma ('great soul') Gandhi, who led India to independence by a policy of non-violent resistance, is an enlightened hero to many, a saintly symbol of peace, love and harmony. Yet while asserting the rights of Indians, he was scathingly racist towards blacks in South Africa, arguing constantly that Indians were superior, and calling black people 'raw kaffir whose occupation is hunting, and whose sole ambition is to collect a certain number of cattle to buy a wife with, and then, pass his life in indolence and nakedness'[21].

---

[18] Quoted in Edwin Yamauchi, *The World of the First Christians*, Lion, 1981, p.51

[19] *Holy Confucian Analects*, Chapter 7

[20] A synthesis of Mohammed's personal prayers found in Sahih Bukhari Vol. 8, #s 335, 379, 407, 408, translated by Dr. Muhammad Muhsin Khan, Islamic University of Medina, published by Kitab Bhavan, New Delhi, India

[21]   https://www.washingtonpost.com/news/worldviews/wp/2015/09/03/what-did-mahatma-gandhi-think-of-black-people/

His eccentricities are also embarrassing; he was obsessed with bodily functions. Gandhi's first question every morning to the women in his commune who waited on him was about their bowel movements and he even slept naked with young women to prove his imperviousness to sexual desire[22].

Nelson Mandela is another modern example of high-minded ideals, of forgiveness and reconciliation. But he was also responsible for the deaths of many people, including women and children, in the terrorist campaigns of the African National Congress, and his personal life included a string of adulterous affairs. Mandela's own admission was, 'I am not a saint, unless you think of a saint as a sinner who keeps on trying'.

The contrast with Jesus is stark. For someone famous for his hatred of hypocrisy, Jesus never confesses to any faults, or apologizes, or says anything about trying harder to be good. Instead, he says, 'I always do those things which please the Father' and, 'Which of you convinces me of sin?'[23]. Peter, His chosen leader of the disciples, could say that Jesus 'did no sin, nor was deceit found in His mouth, who when He was reviled, did not revile in return; when He suffered, He did not threaten, but committed Himself to Him who judges righteously' (1 Peter 2:22-23).

Jesus' life was certainly the most influential ever lived. Although he was an agnostic, H. G. Wells nevertheless said, 'Christ is the most unique person of history. No man can write a history of the human race, without giving first and foremost place to the penniless teacher of Nazareth'[24]. Phillip Brooks wrote, 'All the armies that ever marched, and all the navies that ever were built, and all the parliaments that ever sat, and all the kings that ever reigned, put together, have not affected the life of man upon this earth as powerfully as has this one solitary life – the life of Jesus Christ'.

---

[22] Paul Johnson, *Modern Times*, Phoenix, 1992, p.471
[23] John 8:29, 46
[24] H. G. Wells, *A Short History of the World*, 1922

Jesus' Works

Any liar or lunatic may claim to be God, but to demonstrate it is another matter. The gospels present Jesus' miracles as the proof of His claims to Deity. Most Westerners today are quite ignorant of the gospels, and so before we look at whether this claim of Jesus' supernatural power is credible, it is worthwhile recounting one of these miracle stories, and considering some of the important observations we gain from it.

A paralyzed man heard that Jesus had come to his town, and so he asked four of his friends to carry him on his bed to the house where Jesus was. When they arrived they found a crowd listening to Jesus' teachings who would not make way, even for the crippled man. Undeterred, the paralyzed man got his friends to carry him up onto the flat roof, presumably via some steps, break open a large hole in the roof, and lower him down into the room where Jesus was sitting teaching.

Jesus' response was not, at first, to heal the man, but to assure him that his sins were forgiven. The religious Jews who were present were scandalized by Jesus' claim to forgive sins, saying 'This fellow is a blasphemer; who can forgive sins but God alone?" But Jesus turned round and asked them a question: "Which is easier: to say to the paralyzed man that his sins are forgiven or to say, Get up and walk?" Having said this, Jesus told the paralyzed man to get up, pick up his mat and go home. Immediately, the man got up, picked up his bed and walked out, to the astonishment of everybody present (Mark 2:1-12).

Notice a few things about this story. First, it is obvious that many people in Jesus' time, including the paralyzed man, actually believed He could heal them. This is why the paralyzed went to so much trouble (calling four friends, ripping open a gaping hole in someone's roof, being lowered down on ropes) to get to Jesus. It is not simply Christian historical sources which claim that Jesus performed miracles – non-Christian historical sources refer prominently to Jesus's miracles too. In the gospels, Jesus' enemies try to explain away Jesus' miracles by accusing him of being Satan himself. But extra-biblical documents (both Jewish and non-Jewish) also acknowledge that Jesus performed miraculous healings. There are about forty different miracles reported, and some of

173

them tell of large numbers of people healed. They are not a peripheral part of the story, and it was largely because of His miracles that the crowds gathered to hear His teachings. Jesus' public ministry in the gospels is shot through with the supernatural. It wasn't just his teachings that drew the crowds, or his personality – it was his miracles. Just as there is 'no smoke without fire', it would seem that the miracles must have some basis in reality.

Thomas Jefferson used scissors to cut out all of the miracle stories in the gospels, leaving just Jesus' teachings, whose sublime moral wisdom Jefferson admired. Jefferson's rejection of the miracles was not because he had access to any evidence casting doubt on their historicity, but simply due to his own anti-theistic bias. However, as we have seen in this story of Jesus' forgiving sins, Jesus' miracles are inextricably linked with His words. Jesus' miracles substantiate Jesus' claim to be God Himself. This cuts the legs from under the argument of Jefferson who is willing to accept Jesus as merely a great human teacher. As C. S. Lewis said, Jesus' own words have not left this option open to us.

Secondly, sometimes it almost seems as if people today think that the men and women of Jesus' time were easily duped by reports of miracles, or that living in pre-scientific times, they had no idea of how the world worked. However, this is easily disproven by the astonished reaction of the crowds to the healing of the paralyzed man, rather than polite applause as if this was to be normally expected. Jesus Himself asked, "Which is easier, to say to the paralyzed man, 'Get up and walk', or to say, 'Your sins are forgiven'?" Everyone knew that it is no easy thing to tell a paralyzed man to get up and walk, or at least, to make it happen by saying so.

People in Jesus' day lived with death and disease as constant threats, and knew that there was little that could naturally be done in many cases. They did not superstitiously believe in an enchanted world of magic. The early Christians did not accept the virgin birth because they did not understand the mechanics of child birth. They knew what was impossible just as well as we do today. Their amazement at Jesus' miracles testifies to the historicity and factuality of Jesus' supernatural works.

Thirdly, there was nothing special or mysterious about the way that

Jesus performed His miracles; no lights or curtains or mirrors. There was nothing hidden, nor any mysterious ritual or spooky mumbo-jumbo. In full view of everybody present in the house, and simply by saying the words, Jesus healed the man, instantly and completely.

Jesus' miracles do not have the feel of legendary narratives about them. British biblical scholar Anthony Harvey, in his "Jesus and the Constraints of History," the 1982 Bampton Lecture, argued that Jesus' miracles are described in a matter-of-fact way that supports their authenticity:

'In general one can say that the miracle stories in the gospels are unlike anything else in ancient literature. ... They do not exaggerate the miracle or add sensational details, like the authors of early Christian hagiography [biographies of saints]; but nor do they show the kind of detachment, amounting at times to skepticism, which is found in [Greek historians] Herodotus or Lucian. ... To a degree that is rare in the writings of antiquity, we can say, to use a modern phrase, that they tell the story straight'.

Fourthly, Jesus' miracles were given as proof of the fact that He is God, and linked with Jesus' claim, as God, to heal a paralyzed man as well as forgiving his sins. Only God can do either of these things. The gospels tell us of Jesus' power over sickness of various kinds, rescuing people with disabilities like blindness, deliverance of people from demonic spirits, power over nature (turning water into wine, stilling a storm on the lake, walking on water), and even raising the dead. Just as God is the Ruler of all things, so Jesus demonstrated His authority over all realms: natural, physical, mental, and spiritual. He is the Governor of all domains.

Fifthly, it is important to notice that Jesus not only forgave people of their sins; the reason he did so is revealing too. Jesus forgave the sins of people when he saw that they believed in Jesus Himself. It was not the man's good deeds, human decency, giving to charity, or good citizenship that prompted Jesus' forgiveness. Nor, significantly, was it because of the paralytic's belief in God. Instead, the signal fact that Jesus publicly applauded faith in Himself again points to the fact that Jesus is God.

Atheists dismiss Jesus' miracles out of hand as violations of the laws of nature, and therefore impossible. This is a point at which I genuinely feel some sympathy for the atheist, not because I think the argument is logical (why should it be impossible for God to do miracles if He created the world from nothing?), but rather because anti-supernaturalism is so ingrained in our culture.

However, I want to sincerely ask those who do not believe in miracles one question: what evidence would they possibly accept for the existence of God? What sort of evidence would they accept for Jesus being God, if they refuse to consider miracles?

If the answer is something non-supernatural, like a lightning strike, then how could it ever convince anyone that a supernatural God exists? Lightning strikes occur thousands of times every day on earth. We require supernatural evidence as proof of a supernatural Being, but how then can miracles be ruled out of court as evidence? Supernatural evidence is the only real evidence that will prove God's existence. Above all, to show that He is God, the invincible and all-powerful Source of all life, Jesus had to show that He has power over death itself. What greater supernatural act could He do than to come back to life from the dead?

In other words, if God was to come to earth and offer us evidence that He really exists, He would have to do precisely the sorts of supernatural things that Jesus did. If we are honest and fair-minded seekers after the truth, we have to investigate Jesus' miracles, evaluate the evidence presented for them, and try to weigh up whether they really happened or not.

If a person is not open to the possibility that God can do the supernatural, it is obvious that they do not really have an open mind about the question of God's existence at all. C. S. Lewis coined a phrase that I like to apply to the person who asks God for evidence but refuses to countenance the supernatural: 'they bid the gelding be fruitful'. They are not open to evidence at all.

Jesus is God

Richard Dawkins argues: 'the historical evidence that Jesus claimed any sort of divine status is minimal. ... there is no good historical evidence that he ever thought he was divine'[25]. Muslims would agree. They accept virtually all the evidence we have mentioned so far – about Jesus' character, teachings and miracles. Yet they believe He was a prophet, not God. New Age religion (which teaches we are all gods) would likewise have no quibble with most of the arguments we have presented so far, and yet would reject the idea that Jesus was the One True God come to earth.

However, the evidence that Jesus claimed to be divine is abundant. The reason the Jews wanted to kill such a good man was not simply because He argued against some of their religious traditions. It was because He continually claimed, in subtle and less than subtle ways, to be God.

Take a famous case. In John's Gospel, at the end of a lengthy debate with the Jews, Jesus said, 'Truly, truly, I say to you, before Abraham was, I am' (John 8:58). This at first sounds like a grammatical mistake; as if Jesus should have said, 'before Abraham was, I *was*'. But Jesus was not only claiming to be older than Abraham who lived two thousand years before. By saying 'I am', Jesus was taking one of the most sacred names of God from the Old Testament, the I AM, and applying it to himself. This was the name that God used when He spoke to Moses when He appeared to him in the burning bush. It means God the self-existent, eternal Being. The Jews did not miss Jesus' meaning. We read that they took up stones to throw at Him – the way the Jews put someone to death for blasphemy (John 8:58-59).

Or take another instance a few chapters later. In John 10:30, Jesus says, "I and My Father are one". The Jews took up stones again to kill him, saying, 'For a good work we do not stone you, but for blasphemy, and because you, being a man, make yourself God'.

Some people argue that Jesus' words here fall short of a claim to deity. Jesus was claiming to be one in will or purpose, or in partnership, with God. But Jesus removes these options when he says, just a few verses later, 'the Father is in me, and I in Him'. Jesus was one in person with the Father. The Jews reacted by trying to seize him and kill him. Again

---

[25] Richard Dawkins, *The God Delusion*, p.92

he again escaped out of their hand (John 10:38-39).

Just a few chapters further on in John, we read of Jesus' conversation with some of his skeptical disciples. Jesus said, 'If you had known Me, you would have known My Father also; and from now on you know Him and have seen Him'.

Philip (one of Jesus' disciples) responded, "Lord, show us the Father, and it is sufficient for us".

Jesus said to him, "Have I been with you so long, and yet you have not known Me, Philip? He who has seen Me has seen the Father; so how can you say, 'Show us the Father?' Do you not believe that I am in the Father, and the Father in Me? The words that I speak to you I do not speak on My own; but the Father who dwells in Me does the works. Believe Me that I am in the Father and the Father in Me, or else believe Me for the sake of the works themselves' (John 14:7-11).

To take another example from John's Gospel, consider the words of 'doubting' Thomas' when he saw Jesus risen from the dead: 'My Lord and My God'. Remember that Jews like Thomas insisted that we must not worship idols, natural or manmade objects. To worship the sun, or to bow before a human being, were equally blasphemous, because there was only one true God. Yet here Thomas falls down and confesses Jesus to be God.

Jesus' reaction to Thomas' confession is equally important. If Jesus was not truly God, he should have rebuked Thomas for saying such words. Instead Jesus said, 'Thomas, because you have seen me, you have believed. Blessed are those who have not seen and yet have believed' (John 20:28-29).

We have just scratched the surface of Jesus' claims to be divine – there are many more. John's gospel records how Jesus claimed to have pre-existed his life on earth (and to have pre-existed earth itself), to have come from heaven, to be without sin, and to be the Judge before whom all people will one day stand[26].

Matthew's Gospel tells how Jesus claimed to be greater than the temple, the most sacred place on earth to a Jew. (The only thing more

[26] John 17:5, 6:51, 8:46, 5:22

holy to a Jew was the God of the temple). He also claimed to be greater than the Sabbath, the Jewish holy day, and indeed, to be the Lord of the Sabbath. In other words, he claimed to be the Creator who made the world and rested on the seventh day, the first Sabbath. We have already seen how He claimed to be more powerful than Satan – and demonstrated it by casting demons out of people. Only God is more powerful than Satan. He also claimed to be the Messiah, David's Lord, worthy of being seated alongside God and therefore equal to God[27].

Above all, Jesus claimed to be God by promising to rise from the dead after his enemies had put him to death. The sheer audacity of the promise is interesting. It is impossible to conceive of a greater test by which anybody claiming to be God could be evaluated.

It is thus very hard to understand how Richard Dawkins can say that Jesus never claimed to be divine. Dawkins might have been a professor for the public understanding of science, but he is astonishingly ignorant about the basics of Christianity.

The very fact that Jesus presents Himself as God, in subtle but undeniable ways, provides yet another piece of evidence for the historicity of the gospel narratives. This might not seem surprising to us, accustomed as we are to hear talk of Jesus being the Son of God, but to religious Jews of Christ's time, the idea that a man should claim to be God was the height of blasphemy, and (normally) a one-way ticket to execution. Jewish society at the time of Christ was the most fiercely monotheistic culture the world has ever known. Such an idea was totally unthinkable for any Jew – it belonged to a completely different universe. Yet this is what Jesus claimed and His disciples later wrote about in the gospels. This is what resulted in Jesus' death and it was for refusing to deny Jesus' Deity that His disciples eventually lost their lives too. The Jesus of the gospels is the most dangerous and counter-cultural idea that first century Jews could have ever imagined or invented, and what did Jesus' disciples gain from it?

Atheists and others deny that Jesus ever claimed to be God, but the evidence is so abundant that the denial is almost comical.

---

[27] Matthew 12:6, 8, 29, 22:41-45

Conclusion

Christianity, said Dorothy Sayers, is not about 'comforting sentiments, nor vague aspirations to loving kindness and uplift, nor the promise of something nice after death – but the terrifying assertion that the same God who made the world lived in the world and passed through the grave and the gate of death' (*The Whimsical Christian*).

Lee Strobel was a graduate of Yale Law School and an investigative journalist working for the *Chicago Tribune*. He was also an atheist. In 1979 he was stunned by the announcement of his wife that she had become a Christian. Expecting the worst, he was pleasantly surprised by the changes he saw in her. Intrigued, he launched an all-out investigation into Christianity, trying his best to set aside his prejudices. Here was his conclusion:

> I'll admit it: I was ambushed by the amount and quality of the evidence that Jesus is the unique Son of God. As I sat at my desk that Sunday afternoon, I shook my head in amazement. I had seen defendants carted off to the death chamber on much less convincing proof! The cumulative facts and data pointed unmistakably toward a conclusion that I wasn't entirely comfortable in reaching.
>
> Frankly, I had wanted to believe that the deification of Jesus was the result of legendary development in which well-meaning but misguided people slowly turned a wise sage into the mythological Son of God. That seemed safe and reassuring; after all, a roving apocalyptic preacher from the first century could make no demands on me. But while I went into my investigation thinking that this legendary explanation was intuitively obvious, I emerged convinced it was totally without basis[28].

Jesus was not a legend. Nor was He a lunatic with delusions of grandeur. Nor was He a liar, a religious conman or cult-leader. Nor was Jesus simply a great prophet, a wise human teacher, for He continually claimed to be God, in direct and in more subtle ways. This leaves us with the last

---

[28] Lee Strobel, *The Case for Christ*, Zondervan, 1998, p.264

option. Jesus was indeed Almighty God, come to earth, to provide us with the ultimate revelation of Himself.

If this is so, then none of the other arguments for God's existence are as important as this one. Christ is not simply a messenger from God, with important truths to tell us. He is God Himself, come to earth in person. Jesus Christ is the ultimate evidence for God's existence.

Here is an argument that almost seems irreverent to put a rating on. Here we can only bow in worship like Thomas and say, 'My Lord and my God'. But this argument gets as close to a rating of 10 as it is possible to score. Ultimately, though, evidence is not enough: readers themselves have to take the last step of believing in God because of Jesus Christ.

0 (atheism)   (God exists) 10

9

Argument from Jesus Christ

Chapter 13

The King George VI Argument: Providence

Imagine that you went out to the front of your house to the letterbox to collect the mail, and there was a letter with your name on it. When you opened it up, you found $100 inside, but no clue as to who sent it to you. Then, the next day, the same thing happened – another letter with your name on it and $100 inside, but nothing to say who sent it. The same thing happened every day for three weeks. At this point you would have $1500 (the mail arrives five days in the week). What would you do with the money?

When I ask this question of children in school, they all start to talk about the toys and gadgets they would buy with such a large amount of money. I stop them after a little while and tell them that this is not what they should do. Instead of spending the money, they should find out who posted the money and send a thank-you.

This situation is precisely where we find ourselves in the real world. Year after year, the seasons produce a harvest of food for us to eat, growing up out of the ground and hanging from the trees. The earth is full of the right nutrients that the plants need, the sunshine falls upon them until they are ripe, while water is evaporated off the oceans, transported onto the land and falls as rain.

Yet despite all the good things we enjoy, month after month, we are like little children who greedily spend all the gifts upon ourselves and ignore the Giver and His kindness.

Providence is an old-fashioned theological term meaning God's care for His creation. It means that not only is God the cause of our existence, but He also keeps us in existence. God is our Provider and Preserver as well as our Maker. God is not an absentee landlord, a divine watch-maker who wound the Universe up, and then left it to run on its own. Instead, God is actively and intimately involved in ruling over His creation.

God keeps creation going: night and day, summer and winter, seedtime and harvest. Jesus said that God 'makes His sun rise on the evil and on the good, and sends rain on the just and on the unjust' (Matthew 5:45). The Bible says that this is evidence for God's existence. In fact, it says that God is speaking to us to us though His faithful care for creation: God 'did not leave Himself without witness, in that He did good, gave us rain from heaven and fruitful seasons, filling our hearts with food and gladness' (Acts 14:17).

Providence also means that God, as the controller of creation, is able to intervene in it. God hears and answers prayer.

King George VI and Prayer

King George VI, the father of the present Queen of England, was a man who not only believed in God, but also believed that God answers prayer. I personally knew of Christians who told how, during World War Two, the King would come down from Windsor Castle to a little Gospel Hall on a midweek evening to kneel on the floor and pray alongside the other Christians.

Prince Albert Frederick Arthur George, the second son of King George V, became King in 1938 when his older brother King Edward VIII abdicated to marry his mistress. During World War One, Prince Albert had served in the Royal Navy, and fought at the Battle of Jutland. As a young man, Prince Albert was embarrassed by his stutter, which he overcame through the help of Lionel Logue, an Australian-born speech therapist, as pictured in the 2010 film "The King's Speech".

King George VI was a humble man of faith in God. During his coronation ceremony, the King reportedly told his friend the Archbishop of Canterbury "that [I] felt throughout that Some One Else was with [me]"[1].

In the foreword to *The Servant Queen And The King She Serves*, the present Queen writes about the poem quoted by her father as he addressed his people in his Christmas broadcast in 1939: 'I said to the

---

[1] Sarah Bradford, *The Reluctant King*, St. Martin's, 1990, p.212

man who stood at the Gate of the Year, "Give me a light that I may tread safely into the unknown". And he replied, "Go out into the darkness, and put your hand into the hand of God. That shall be to you better than light, and safer than a known way"' (from *The Gate Of The Year*, by Minnie Louise Haskins).

In his speech at the outbreak of World War Two, King George said: 'The task will be hard. There may be dark days ahead, and war can no longer be confined to the battlefield, but we can only do the right as we see the right, and reverently commit our cause to God. If one and all we keep resolutely faithful to it, ready for whatever service or sacrifice it may demand, then with God's help, we shall prevail. May He bless and keep us all'. In another speech, he said, "Let us then put our trust, as I do, in God and in the unconquerable spirit of the British people"[2].

The most amazing, and without doubt the most important, instance of answered prayer in King George's life came in the darkest hour of World War Two. The German army had overrun Holland, Belgium and northern France in 1940, and the British Expeditionary Force which had been sent to France had retreated to Dunkirk where they were trapped by the sea. Over 400,000 men were facing imminent destruction. King George VI called for a national day of prayer on the 26th of May, urging the people of Britain to commit their cause to God. Initial plans estimated that only 45,000 men could be rescued from the beaches of Dunkirk in the two days before the German tanks cut off this escape route. On the 27th of May the German High Command boasted that 'The British army is encircled and our troops are proceeding to its annihilation'. British General Alan Brooke said, 'Nothing but a miracle can save the BEF now'. Instead, nearly 340,000 men were evacuated over the next nine days. Winston Churchill called it a miracle of deliverance.

There were no less than five amazing turns of events. First, Hitler ordered his tanks to halt when they were only 10 miles from Dunkirk, perhaps wanting to spare them for the continuing invasion of France, but also believing that the Luftwaffe's air superiority would be able to finish off the job. By the time the halt order was lifted three days later, most of

---

[2] Bradford, *The Reluctant King*, p.325

the British army had made it to Dunkirk behind new defensive positions. Secondly, on the 28th of May, a storm broke over Flanders grounding the Luftwaffe, allowing the remnants of the British army to make it to the coast. Thirdly, unnaturally calm seas which were essential to evacuation lasted for nine days, allowing men to stand for hours shoulder deep in the water to be picked up. The day after the evacuation, the North Sea, which is usually rough, returned to normal as the wind shifted and large waves broke on the empty beaches. Fourthly, clouds and fog seemed to come at just the right moment to cover the army waiting on the beaches and prevent the Luftwaffe from finishing it off. Three times the Luftwaffe mounted all-out assaults on Dunkirk, but smoke and low cloud cover prevented them from doing as much damage as they might have done. Fifthly, an armada of small boats – fishing boats, yachts, lifeboats – were able to pick the soldiers up from the shallow waters of the beaches and bring them to safety.

Sunday the 9th of June was appointed as a day of national thanksgiving, and Psalm 124 was read, 'If it had not been the LORD who was on our side, when men rose up against us, then they would have swallowed us alive … Our help is in the name of the LORD, who made heaven and earth' (Psalm 124:2, 3, 8).

Brain Surgeon Dr. Ben Carson

Atheists mock the idea of a God who hears and answers prayer. But consider another amazing story. Dr. Ben Carson was already a world-famous brain surgeon, before retiring to enter politics as a Republican Presidential candidate. He is currently U.S. Secretary of Housing and Urban Development under President Donald Trump. As a neurosurgeon, he was in charge of a medical team of seventy that performed the first successful operation separating conjoined twins joined at the back of the head, as well as a number of other 'firsts' in neurosurgery.

On another occasion, he was in the middle of operating on ten-month old baby girl Shannon with a condition called craniosynostosis, in which the brain had grown abnormally fast, leading to a build-up of pressure, requiring a cranial expansion. During the operation, her blood pressure started falling, and then she went into cardiac arrest. Carson pulled back the scalp over the gaping wound in her skull and closed it with clips so that the girl could be placed on her side and CPR (cardiopulmonary resuscitation) could commence. But after twenty minutes of CPR her heart had not re-started. Carson was asked by a member of his team, 'Do you want to call it off?' Knowing that after twenty minutes of no brain activity, the child would now be severely brain damaged even if she were able to be revived, Carson (a believer) refused to give up hope, and started praying to God to intervene while continuing with CPR. After 24 minutes of CPR, Shannon's heart responded, and a few moments later she started breathing again.

Shannon was rushed to the intensive care unit, but when the anaesthesia wore of, she showed all the signs of being brain-dead: her pupils were fixed and dilated. Carson continued praying for the girl, and just under 24 hours later, her pupils began reacting, astonishing everyone on the intensive care team. However, the next day, Shannon's breathing became difficult, and it was discovered that sections of her lungs were ruptured and bleeding. Carson was told that the child had a five percent chance of surviving until morning. Then at 3.00am, Carson was phoned by the intensive care staff who told him that the last functioning segments of Shannon's lungs had ruptured and she would die in the next few minutes.

However Carson continued praying, and when he later contacted the hospital to talk to the parents, he found that Shannon had not only not died, but her lungs had actually improved, and over the next five days they improved so much she was taken off the ventilator. Nevertheless, Shannon's parents were told that she was still so badly brain damaged that she would not see or hear or be able to do enough for herself to justify rehabilitation.

However, prayers for Shannon continued and after three days, she was able to see and hear again. Eventually she recovered and grew to become a perfectly normal child[3].

---

[3] For a fuller account, see B. Carson and G. Lewis, *The Big Picture: Getting Perspective on What's Really Important in Life*, Zondervan, 1999, pp.259-63

George Müller

For an even more amazing account of answered prayer, consider the case of George Müller. In 1836, one year before Charles Dickens wrote *Oliver Twist*, George Müller, a German who had come to England to preach the gospel, set up an orphanage in Bristol, England, not just to help orphans, but also to demonstrate to Christians and unbelievers that God answers prayer and can be trusted. He wrote, 'Now, if I, a poor man, simply by prayer and faith, obtained, without asking any individual the means for establishing and carrying on an Orphan-House: there would be something which with the Lord's blessing, might be instrumental in strengthening the faith of the children of God, besides being a testimony to the consciences of the unconverted of the reality of the things of God'.

Müller was a Christian minister who drew no salary, but instead trusted in God alone to provide for his needs. He never spoke directly or indirectly to Christians about his needs and often came close to running out of food or money. Nevertheless, God supplied his needs through the gifts of his fellow-believers. This was the same basis upon which he started to take in and care for orphans. Over a period of sixty years, he fed, clothed, housed, and educated ten thousand children. In addition, he had staff to pay. He still had no salary of his own, nor did he ask for money, nor did he advertise the needs of the orphan-work, nor did he ever go into debt to pay for any of these expenses. Instead, he simply looked to God in childlike faith and believing prayer for the support of these children. Müller said, 'My trust has been in God alone; He has many ways of moving hearts of men to help us all over the world. While I am praying He speaks to this one and another, on this continent and on that to send us help'.

Charles Dickens wrote about Müller's orphanage in his weekly journal, *Household Words*, on November 7, 1857. Dickens had heard a rumour that Müller's orphans were shoddy and starving, and decided to investigate. Müller gave his keys to an employee with instructions that Dickens be allowed to look over any of the orphan houses. Here is some of the report from Dickens' journal:

He [Müller] believes, with a liveliness of faith perhaps unequalled in our time, that all things fitting for His children will be supplied by our Father in heaven in direct answer to trustful prayer. He points to the Orphan-house on Ashley Down, near Bristol, for the justification of his faith. He has now been labouring in Bristol for a quarter of a century. He has undertaken large works of benevolence. He has established that asylum for destitute orphans, which for some time maintained three hundred inmates, and to which a new wing has just been added for the reception of four hundred more. He expects to add another wing and find room for a thousand. For the prosecution of this orphan-work, as he calls it, he has received ninety thousand pounds, without once asking for a penny. When he wants money he prays for it, and in his annual reports, which are summed up in the publication we have named, shows how it comes. His reports make no appeal. The spirit and intention of them is to bear testimony to the truth of which he is convinced, that "the Lord will provide" (*Household Words*, November 7, 1857)

The remarkable thing about Müller's story is the way that God repeatedly answered prayer. Here is one of Müller's journal accounts from October 9, 1838: 'Today we were brought lower than ever. The money for milk in one of the houses was provided by a labourer selling one of his books. The matrons in the Boys' Orphan House had two shillings left this morning. We were wondering whether to buy bread with it or more meat for dinner when the baker left seventy-five loaves of bread as a gift'.

Then again, on November 21, Müller writes, 'Not even a single halfpenny was left, in the three houses. Nevertheless, we had a good dinner, and by sharing our bread, we made it through this day also. When I left the brothers and sisters after prayer, I told them we must wait for help and see how the Lord would deliver us this time. I was sure of help, but we were indeed in another serious situation. When I left the meeting, I felt that I needed more exercise so I walked home a longer way. About twenty yards from my house, I met a brother who walked back with me. After a little conversation, he gave me ten pounds ... The brother had come to see me twice while I was away at the Orphan House. Had I been one half minute later, I would have missed him. But the Lord knew our need, and therefore allowed me to meet him'.

In 1845, Müller moved the orphans out of rented accommodation into the first of five huge Orphanages he built, eventually housing over two thousand orphans on Ashley Down. The first house cost £10,000 – equivalent to £1.25 million in today's money – all coming in donations for which he had not appealed. Müller eventually built four more Orphan Houses at a cost of over £100,000, equivalent to over £12 million today. The running costs for these orphanages came to about £30,000 every year (nearly £4m). In total, during his life, Müller received donations worth more than 100 million US dollars at today's rates.

Müller died in 1898, aged 92. For 62 years he had operated his orphanage on these principles, and the orphans had never missed a meal. He always had just enough. Just before he died, Müller was interviewed, and asked if he had ever thought of saving money for himself. Müller drew from his pocket an old purse and said, 'All I am possessed of is in that purse – every penny! Save for myself? Never! … I dare not save; it would be dishonouring to my loving, gracious, all-bountiful Father'[4].

Biographer W. H. Harding wrote that the story of Muller's life presents 'one of the most striking testimonies to the faithfulness of God that the world has ever seen'. Another biographer, A. T. Pierson, wrote, 'George Müller's life was one long witness to the prayer-hearing God'.

Another biographer tells the story: 'a man living in Horfield, in sight of Ashley Down, said that, "whenever he felt doubts about the Living God creeping into his mind he used to get up and look through the night at the many windows lit up on Ashley Down, gleaming out through the darkness as stars in the sky"[5].

On his death, the city of Bristol (once the second-largest city in the country) shut down and stopped as thousands attended his funeral. All the national newspapers carried reports on his death, and the *Bristol*

[4] Roger Steer, *Admiring God: The Best of George Müller*, Hodder and Stoughton, 1986, p.190
[5] Roger Steer, *Delighted in God: a Biography of George Muller*, Christian Focus Publications, Fearn, 1997

Times wrote, 'He was raised up for the purpose of showing that the age of miracles is not past, and rebuking the sceptical tendencies of the time'.

Atheist Objections

The obvious objection to the idea that God answers prayer is the fact that He often does not! Many people have given up faith in God when their prayers went unanswered. However, prayer does not work the same way as a coin-operated washing machine at the launderette.

When I was a small boy, four or five years old, I wanted a bike for Christmas. Rather than asking my parents for a bike, or appealing to Santa, I went straight to the top, and prayed to God directly. On Christmas morning, without telling anyone, I ran out the front door, down the side of the house, and opened the garage door, fully expecting God to have answered my prayers, and to have put my new bike in the garage. Much to my surprise, there was no bike.

This dented my boyhood faith in prayer, I'm sure, and maybe even in God, but time passed and I forgot about it. During that next year we moved house. Previously we had lived on a busy street on a hill. But our new house was on a quiet, flat, dead-end street. The next Christmas, even though I had forgotten all about my previous year's prayer, I (along with my brother and sister) was given a bike for Christmas.

It was actually a good thing that I didn't get a bike for Christmas the first year. The house on the busy street on the hill was no place for a little boy to learn to ride a bike. My brother and sister were also too young to be given bikes at that time. God did answer my prayer – not in the way that I wanted – but in a better way.

Many people think of prayer like a magic spell, or finding a genie in a bottle and making a wish. When we fail to get what we ask for, we throw the bottle away. However, God is not a puppet on a string who jumps at our command. God is the All-Mighty Lord of heaven and earth. We would not expect the President of any earthly country to instantly drop everything and attend to our every wish, so why should we expect the High and Lofty One who inhabits eternity? Our world is (largely) in active rebellion against God's authority; God owes us nothing.

This is not the place for an in-depth explanation of prayer. However, in the Bible, God promises to hear and answer prayer, although there are a number of conditions attached. One condition is that our prayer is according to God's will, another is that we should forgive others before God forgives us and hears our prayers, another is that we should believe when we pray. There are other conditions too, and we should not get upset about them. In 1 John 3:22 we read, 'And whatever we ask we receive from Him, because we keep His commandments and do those things that are pleasing in His sight'. What parent on earth would give whatever their teenager selfishly asked for, regardless of their behavior, regardless of how they were treating their parents and siblings, and regardless of what they would do with the gifts once they received them? What parent thinks it is unreasonable to tie conditions to requests their children ask of them? The idea that prayer is either *carte blanche* or a delusion is a false-dilemma.

Some of the greatest people in the Bible had their prayers turned down, like the apostle Paul who asked for a physical ailment he described cryptically as a 'thorn in the flesh' to be removed, and even Jesus who asked for the 'cup' of suffering facing Him to be taken away. In Paul's case, the reason for God's refusal was that the physical problem was designed to keep him humble, while in Jesus' case the reason was that it was God's will for Him to suffer and die for our salvation. The famous English preacher Charles Haddon Spurgeon said, 'It is not God's will that every mountain should be levelled, but that we should be the stronger for climbing the hill Difficulty'.

Prayer is not primarily a matter of asking for what we desire, although God indeed tells us to bring our needs (not our selfish wants) to Him and He will answer us. Instead, prayer is about changing our hearts and desires to be more in line with God's. God is more interested in changing us than changing our situation. Christians sometimes teach their children that prayer is a bit like the traffic lights: sometimes God says yes, sometimes God says no, and sometimes God says wait. Just as in the case of the bike for Christmas, sometimes God's "no" is for our best, sometimes God's "no" is not final, sometimes God waits for our growth, and sometimes God says "yes".

Conclusion

God's ongoing care for His world is seen in many ways besides answered prayer, but we have focused on prayer here because of its evidential value. Here is an experiment for those who do not believe in God. Put prayer to the test. Not just any prayer. I encourage you to pray to God, maybe for the first time in your life, praying about the most important thing in your life. What is that?

Pray to God, asking Him, if He really exists, to reveal Himself to You in an unmistakable way, offering in return to lay down your arms and cease your rebellion against Him. God doesn't do party tricks. He is only interested in sincere seekers. Other peoples' answered prayers will not convince you that God exists. The only sort of answered prayer that will show you that God truly exists is one from your own experience. God promises that those who seek Him with all their heart will find Him. For this reason, we will leave the rating evenly-balanced for this argument. After you have accepted this challenge, you may set your own rating for the evidence of God from prayer.

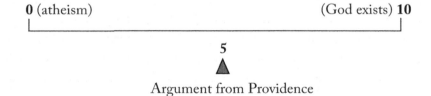

0 (atheism)   (God exists) **10**

5

Argument from Providence

Chapter 14

The Rosalind Picard Argument: Scripture

Rosalind Picard is Professor of Media Arts and Sciences at the Massachusetts Institute of Technology, a multi-award winning scientist and inventor, named by CNN as one of seven Tech Superheroes to watch in 2015[1]. Brought up as an atheist in a loving and happy family, Picard had no need for religion and didn't think much of people who did. Religion was something for people who were emotionally crippled, or who weren't very intelligent or who were taught some myth and never thought to question it. In her teens she became friends with some Christians and they invited her to church, but because she didn't want to go (or to dress up in special clothes), she made excuses. However, her friends said it didn't really matter whether she went to church or not – what matters is what we believe.

They asked her whether she had ever read the Bible. Picard says, 'I just believed the Bible was wrong without having read it, and it occurred to me that that was actually an inconsistent intellectual position – to think that I was so well educated and knew about the Bible, but actually hadn't read it'[2]. So she got herself a Bible and read it through in a year, as a result of which she became a Christian. She said, 'I started reading the Bible not because I believed in Christianity, but because it was the best-selling book of all time. To my surprise, it started to change me'[3].

Is Scripture another way that God speaks to us? It is difficult to believe that, if God created us, He would be unable to communicate with us using language. After all, why would God, having created people who can talk, not be able to do the same Himself? Why would God bother to

---

[1]   http://edition.cnn.com/2015/01/20/business/7-tech-superheroes-watch-2015/index.html
[2] See the 'www.testoffaith.com' video at youtube.com/watch?v=jnS2ovwtx-g
[3] See the graphic from Veritas Forum: twitter.com/Veritas/status/679450688481406976/photo/1

create human beings with the unique ability to communicate, and then stay totally silent Himself? Further, having communicated in a variety of other ways (revealing His power in creation, His wisdom in design, His sense of morality in conscience, His care in providence), why would God never go one step further and use the most direct, clear, precise, permanent and information-rich means of communication, written language? After all, humans do not settle for anything less than written documents in our acts of parliament or legal contracts. Why would God adopt a lower standard than written communication in His dealings with us?

Many religions believe that God has revealed Himself to us through the medium of language, and that these words have been preserved in written documents: Scripture. Christians believe that God has spoken to us in the Bible, using men's words inspired by His Spirit. Because God is so far greater than we are, and so different from us, it would be impossible for us to know anything about God without revelation, that is, God's self-disclosure. God is unknowable, except He chooses to reveal Himself to us.

David Suchet

David Suchet, the actor famous for portraying Agatha Christie's detective Hercule Poirot, was born into a non-religious Jewish family. He describes himself as 'always looking for something beyond', and in his twenties and early thirties he explored Zen Buddhism. After the death of a grandfather he was close to, he still strangely felt that his grandfather was with him.

One day, lying in a bath in a hotel in Seattle, asked himself, 'Why do I believe that my grandfather is with me, and not believe in life after death?' He said, 'that got me thinking about the most famous person who they say had a life after death, Jesus'. He decided to investigate Christianity, but his hotel room didn't have the usual Gideon's Bible, so he went out and bought himself one. Believing that a lot of what was written about Jesus in the New Testament was probably mythical, he decided instead to read about someone he considered more historical – Paul.

He said, 'I read Paul's Letter to the Romans. By the end of that letter, I had seen and read about a way of life to which I wanted to aspire. I thought: 'This is what I have been looking for all my life'. As a result of reading the Bible, Suchet became a believer in the Lord Jesus Christ, a Christian. In 2012 he became a vice-president of the British Bible Society and in 2014 he made an audio recording of the entire Bible.

The Bible

Is there any reason to believe the Bible might be God's Word? I have written at length about this subject in a previous book: *Is the Bible Really the Word of God?* and there is no point going over all the ground again. Here are four simple facts – all beginning with the letter P – that show there is something very special about the Bible.

Its Prophecies

Peter Orasuk was a drug addict by the age of 18. Despite coming from a good home, the emptiness of life led to him dabbling in drugs. He was expelled from university in his third year, and went from a drug user to a drug mule (a distributor) to a drug lord. He saw many of his friends die in drug turf wars, and was sent to jail four times. His life had reached rock bottom when his young wife decided to leave him for the sake of their children.

One day two Christian men visited him. Peter handled their arguments with ease; he either had a theory to counter them or he made up a lie on the spot. Having completely refuted them, he finished off with this: "You know, you and I are like people stranded on a desert island who have no hope. We're stuck here till we die. We have told ourselves that a big ship is going to come and take us off the island. That is what keeps us going from day to day, so we don't go insane – we have our big ship. This syringe is my big ship. It gets me by from day to day. Your Jesus and your being saved are your big ship, but really we are just in the same boat. They are just a crutch to help cripples through life".

Rather than trying to argue, one of the Christian men pulled out a Bible and said, "Can I read something from the Bible to you?" For some reason, Peter was afraid of the Bible, he didn't know why, and he didn't want the man to read from it. He said, "Go ahead, read, but make it quick". The man read these words:

> He was wounded for our transgressions,
> he was bruised for our iniquities:
> the chastisement of our peace was upon him;
> and with his stripes we are healed.
> All we like sheep have gone astray;
> we have turned every one to his own way;
> and the LORD hath laid on him the iniquity of us all[4].

Peter later said, "That touched me the first time I heard it. I can't tell you what it was, but in the dark tunnel of my hopeless experience, there was just the faintest glimmer of hope". He had a lump in his throat and a tear in his eye. But turning away to cover it, he said, "Oh, anybody could have written about Jesus. I know all about Jesus".

"Who told you it was talking about Jesus?" the Christian responded. "It was written 700 years before Christ came into the world".

Peter said, "You know, it dawned on me right then, here is something written about Christ 700 years before he came, and even a drug addict in the gutter could see who it was talking about. That's how clear a prophecy it was. How could a person dispute this and say that the Bible is not the Word of God? At that moment, I realised that this is real".

There are over 300 different prophecies relating to the coming Messiah fulfilled in the life of Jesus Christ. Professor Peter Stoner studied eight of these prophecies – the Messiah would: be born in Bethlehem (Micah 5:2); be preceded by a messenger (Isa. 40:3); ride into Jerusalem on a donkey (Zech. 9:9); be betrayed by one of his friends (Psalm 41:9, 55:12-14); be sold for thirty pieces of silver (Zech. 11:12), the money being thrown down in the temple (Zech. 11:13); be silent before accusers (Isa. 53:7); and be pierced in his hands and feet (Psalm 22:16). Stoner estimated the probability of someone fulfilling just eight of the prophecies at one in one hundred million billion[5]. That's the number 1 followed by 17 zeros.

---

[4] Isaiah 53:5-6, KJV
[5] Peter W. Stoner, *Science Speaks*, Moody Press, 1963, pp.109-10

Stoner used an illustration to help people understand the probability: if someone dumped one hundred million billion silver coins into the state of Texas (or France, or New South Wales), the coins would cover the ground two feet deep. If a special mark were placed on one of those coins, and a blindfolded man was sent out to find this one special coin, the chances of him finding the one special coin out of the other 100,000,000,000,000,000 coins would be the same as the chances of one person fulfilling just eight of the prophecies about Christ. The fact that all three hundred of these prophecies were fulfilled by one person, Jesus of Nazareth, is beyond the possibility of human manipulation or coincidence. It points to a divine author behind the Bible's prophecies. In Isaiah 46:9-10, God said, 'I am God, and there is none like Me, declaring the end from the beginning, and from ancient times things that are not yet done'.

Its Permanence

Despite being an ancient book (some parts are over 3,500 years old), the Bible has survived to this day. No other book in the history of the world has been attacked, banned or burned like the Bible. The Bible has survived all attempts to destroy it, and has outlived the mightiest empires on earth (from the Caesars of ancient Rome to Russian communists) committed to its destruction. 'A thousand times over, the death knell of the Bible has been sounded, the funeral procession formed, the inscriptions cut on the tombstone, and the committal read. But somehow the corpse never stays put' (Bernard Ramm[6]). The Bible says that it is 'the word of God which lives and abides forever' (1 Peter 1:23).

Its Popularity

Despite being written thousands of years ago, the Bible has universal appeal. It is read and loved by millions of people of all countries, cultures, ages and classes. According to the *Guinness Book of Records*, it remains the world's best-selling book, and it is specifically excluded from best-seller

---

[6] Bernard Ramm, *Protestant Christian Evidences*, Moody Press, 1957, p.232

lists (like the *New York Times Bestsellers List*) because it would always win.

Its Power

When I was in my late teens, I was challenged to read the Bible through in a year. I gave a dismissive answer, but afterwards, I decided to try to follow the advice, and I managed to read the Bible through in a year. At the end of the year, even though there were lots of things I did not understand, there were many things that I had learned and enjoyed greatly. However, the most amazing thing was that I realised I was a different person to what I had been one year before. The Bible had changed me.

Still today, I find the Bible not only a source of peace and joy in my life, but life-transforming. Paul wrote to the new Thessalonian Christians about how the Word of God works powerfully in peoples' lives: 'For this reason we also thank God without ceasing, because when you received the word of God which you heard from us, you welcomed it not as the word of men, but as it is in truth, the word of God, which also effectively works in you who believe' (1 Thessalonians 2:13). Napoleon said about the Bible: 'The Gospel is not a book, it is a living being, with an action, a power, which invades all that is opposed to its extension. Here it is on this table, this book par excellence (and here the emperor touched it with respect). I never tire of reading it, and every day with the same pleasure. ... Nowhere do we find this series of beautiful ideas, beautiful moral maxims, which parade like battalions of the celestial militia, and which produce in our soul the same feeling that we experience when considering the infinite extent of Sky shining on a beautiful summer night, with all the radiance of the stars. Not only is our mind preoccupied, but it is dominated by this reading, and the soul never runs the risk of getting lost with this book ... What proof of the divinity of Christ! With such absolute power, he has only one goal, the spiritual improvement of individuals, the purity of consciousness, union with what is true, the sanctity of the soul'[7].

---

[7] Napoleon Bonaparte, *Conversations sur le Christianisme*, preface by Jean Tulard, ed. du

Missionaries in China were translating the Bible using the help of a local Chinese man. At first the work of translating the Bible did not seem to have any effect upon him, but later he said, 'What a wonderful book this is'. When the missionary asked why, the Chinese man said, 'Because it tells me so much about myself. It knows all that is in me. The one who made this book must be the one who made me'.

Five Atheist Objections

Atheists object to these evidences by arguing that the Bible has five big problems that prevent us from accepting it as the Word of God.

Contradictions

Many modern people think that the Bible cannot be the Word of God because it is full of 'contradictions'. For example, *Encyclopedia Britannica* argues that 'despite the many points of agreement among the Gospels, there also are considerable discrepancies'[8] in the accounts of the death of Jesus. As an example, *Encyclopedia Britannica* mentions that the four gospels do not all tell us the same words that Christ spoke on the cross. This is, of course, quite true. Matthew and Mark give us only one saying ('My God, my God, why have You forsaken me?'), Luke gives us three different ones ('Father, forgive them, they do not know what they are doing', 'Truly I say to you, today you will be with me in paradise', and 'Father, into Your hands I commit my spirit'), and John gives us another three different ones ('Woman, behold your son ... son, behold your mother', 'I thirst', and 'It is finished').

However, to say these are 'contradictions' is to misunderstand the way that ancient historians recorded events. Professor David Gooding in his commentary on Luke's Gospel writes:

... as modern people we are used to the ways of modern historians. The modern historian is expected not merely to collect and record the

---

Rocher, 2014, p.50; see https://fr.wikipedia.org/wiki/Robert-Augustin_Antoine_de_Beauterne

[8] "Jesus: The Christ and Christology", *Encyclopedia Britannica*, 1994-1999

facts of a case, but to point out the significance of the facts, to offer interpretations and to pass judgments … [However, Luke] … has features in common with some of the classical historians and notably with that great pioneer of scientific history, Thucydides[9] … [who] has a way of juxtaposing two incidents or two speeches containing such clear similarities and/or contrasts that the reader is led to reflect on these similarities and contrasts. From there, without Thucydides having to intrude any comment of his own, the reader is led to see for himself the irony, the tragedy, or whatever it is in human affairs that becomes apparent when one holds the two stories or the two speeches together in one's mind and thoughtfully compares and contrasts them. Luke may have different lessons to teach, but he uses a similar method'[10].

The approach of Thucydides and the gospel writers requires that the historian is selective in what he records, sometimes only reporting one event or saying out of a string of many available. There is no contradiction when different gospel writers mention different sayings of Christ on the cross, for there is no reason why they must all report everything that was said. In fact, strange as it might seem to us, the gospel writers are much less interested in the chronological order of events than they are in the logical connections between events.

John's Gospel explicitly tells us that 'truly Jesus did many other signs in the presence of His disciples, which are not written in this book; but these are written that you might believe that Jesus is the Christ, the Son of God' (John 20:30-31). It is the same with the other gospels; they do not us everything it is possible to know about Jesus, nor do all tell the same stories; some are unique to just one gospel.

Take another example of a 'contradiction'. At the very beginning of the Bible, we have the story of how Cain, the older son of Adam and Eve, killed his brother Abel. Soon after we read about Cain's wife giving birth (Gen. 4:17). Many people have wondered where Cain got his wife

---

[9] Thucydides (c.460 – c.400 BC) is said to have written the first 'scientific' history, concerning the Peloponnesian wars between Athens and Sparta.
[10] David W. Gooding, *According to Luke*, IVP, 1987, Myrtlefield House, 2013, pp.4-5

from. Apart from his mother Eve, the only other women Cain could have married were his sisters, who (if we keep on reading in the very next chapter) are mentioned in Genesis 5:4 (Adam had 'sons and daughters'). Since Cain cannot marry his mother, (or monkeys or Martians), he must have married one of his sisters. This seems the only sensible answer, but notice: the Bible does not give us this detail. To expect the Bible to give exhaustive information, explain all minor events, tell who every character married, and tie off all the loose ends of history is unreasonable.

Biblical narratives will also sometimes give a shorter version of an incident, on the principle that 'a little simplification saves tons of explanation'. Some people accuse the different gospels of disagreeing with each other but this accusation fails to allow the Gospel writers the editorial freedom that we would gladly grant any modern historian.

J. Warner Wallace was an atheist until the age of thirty-five, when he started to look at the gospels. As a police detective, it was his job to investigate real-life murders and other crimes. As a specialist in the examination of witness statements, he describes his approach to discrepancies in his book, *Cold-Case Christianity*:

> 'If there's one thing my experience as a detective has revealed, however, it's that witnesses often make conflicting and inconsistent statements when describing what they saw at a crime scene . . . but that is the natural result of a witness's past experience, perspective, and worldview. I can deal with inconsistencies; I expect them. . . . The apparent contradictions are usually easy to explain once I learn something about the witnesses and their perspectives (both visually and personally) at the time of the crime'[11].

The very fact that the Bible contains apparent discrepancies is, strangely enough, a reason for us to trust it. This is because real life is complex. If everything in the Bible was as neat and straightforward as some fictional storylines we would have every reason to suspect a fabrication. As Gregory Boyd has written:

---

[11] J. Warner Wallace, *Cold-Case Christianity: a Homicide Detective Investigates the Claims of the Gospels*, David C. Cook, 2013, pp.74-75.

'The Gospels present a consistent portrait of who Jesus is and what He did, as well as of the events which surrounded His life. If the four accounts were individually fabricated, where did this consistency come from? But there are also significant differences in each account, showing the relative differences of their perspectives. If they were all fabricated together, the consistency would be greater than we find'[12].

For *Encyclopedia Britannica* to call the differences between the gospels discrepancies or contradictions is a clumsy category error, misunderstanding the normal way that ancient literature worked.

Historical Inaccuracy

A second argument against the Bible is the frequent claim that the Bible is full of historical errors and inaccuracies. The Bible is a book set in time and space, telling us about real people in real places, and this enables us to test whether its history is true or not. What many people do not realise is the way that fresh discoveries have repeatedly proven the Bible right and the sceptics wrong.

For example, in the March/April 2014 issue of *Biblical Archaeological Review*, Professor Lawrence Mykytiuk of Purdue University wrote an article entitled, *Archaeology Confirms Fifty Real People in the Bible*. He listed people like Shishak king of Egypt, Tiglath-Pileser king of Assyria, Nebuchadnezzar king of Babylon, Mesha king of Moab, Ben-Hadad king of Syria, Hezekiah king of Judah, Ahab, Jehu and David kings of Israel. In addition, hundreds of biblical locations, some of which had been dismissed as mythical, have been identified and excavated by archaeologists. In 1845, Nineveh was discovered, the capital of the mighty Assyrian empire where Jonah was sent. In the royal archives of King Ashurbanipal were found 22,000 cuneiform texts, confirming many biblical people and events, like Sargon's conquest of Israel (found in 2 Kings 17:6). William Albright, the greatest authority on biblical archaeology of his day, wrote: 'There can be no doubt that archaeology has confirmed the substantial historicity of Old Testament tradition'[13].

Sir William Ramsay is considered one of the greatest archaeologists to have lived. At one point in his life he was a sceptic, convinced that the Book of Acts in the New Testament was written in the 2nd Century, long after the events it relates. He set out with a mind prejudiced against the historical reliability of the New Testament, but after his excavations in Asia Minor (modern day Turkey), he was forced to reverse his opinion of Luke (who wrote the book of Acts concerning the travels of Paul). He said:

'I may fairly claim to have entered on this investigation without prejudice in favour of the conclusion which I shall now try to justify to the reader. On the contrary, I began with a mind unfavourable to it ... but more recently, I found myself brought in contact with the book of Acts as an authority for the topography, antiquities, and society of Asia Minor. It was gradually borne upon me that in various details the narrative showed marvellous truth. In fact, beginning with a fixed idea that the work was essentially a second century composition, and never relying on its evidence as trustworthy for first century conditions, I gradually came to find it a useful ally in some obscure and difficult investigations'[14].

Ramsay later wrote, 'Luke is a historian of the first rank; not merely are his statements of fact trustworthy; he is possessed of the true historic sense ... In short, this author should be placed among the very greatest of historians'[15].

[13] William F. Albright, *Archaeology and the Religions of Israel*, The Johns Hopkins University Press, 1968, p.176
[14] Sir William Ramsay, *St. Paul the Traveller and the Roman Citizen*, Hodder and Stoughton, 3rd Ed., 1898, pp.7-8
[15] Sir William Ramsay, *The Bearing of Recent Discovery on the Trustworthiness of the New Testament*, Baker, 1953, p.222

Scientific Unreliability

Sceptics claim that the Bible is full of myths and scientific absurdities. However, the Bible is not a science textbook – it is written to tell us about God not nature. Sometimes the Bible will use 'phenomenological language', everyday terms rather than using technical jargon. For example, 'the sun rises' (Psalm 104:22) is not strictly true in a scientific sense (the earth spins on its axis). Yet it is true in terms of what we see and even scientifically-trained meteorologists and weather reporters speak this way. The Bible also often uses figures of speech that are not meant to be taken literally. Psalm 19:5 speaks of the sun, 'which is like a bridegroom coming out of his chamber, and rejoices like a strong man to run his race'. This is simply figurative language – psalms are songs, i.e. poetry – the Bible is not teaching that the sun is actually a bridegroom or a runner.

Further, the Bible has often proved the scientists wrong. For example, the Bible teaches that the universe had a beginning (Gen. 1:1), whereas many scientists believed it was eternal up until the 20th century. The Bible teaches that the earth hangs upon nothing (Job 26:7), whereas many ancient cultures and religions taught that it rested on the back on various giant creatures. Nor does the Bible teach that the earth is flat; rather, it tells us that the shape of the earth is spherical (Isaiah 40:22, Proverbs 8:27, and Job 26:10). The Bible teaches that the centre of the earth is molten and moving: 'As for the earth, from it comes bread, but underneath it is turned up as by fire' (Job 28:5). Ancient astronomers were only able to see a very limited number of stars with the naked eye, less than 5000, yet the Bible said in its first book that the number of the stars of heaven was comparable with the number of grains of sand on the seashore (Gen. 22:17, see also Jer. 33:22) and Hebrews 11:12 says that the stars are 'innumerable'. Scientists today tell us that in our Milky Way galaxy alone there are 400 billion stars and that there are about 170 billion other galaxies in the universe. These are estimates, of course, and the actual number of the stars is truly beyond the ability to definitively count, just as the Bible said long ago. How did the Bible manage to get these scientific facts correct without our modern scientific equipment and discoveries?

The biggest problem sceptics have with the Bible is that it records supernatural miracles. But why should God not be able to do miracles? Why should the One who made the Universe not be able to tweak anything in it? This objection is just an *a priori* rejection of the existence of God.

Dan Brown and 'The Greatest Cover-Up in History'

The Da Vinci Code, Dan Brown's bestselling 2003 novel is premised on the claim that the Bible was 'forged' in the fourth century. Church authorities tried to suppress the true story of Jesus by holding a council in which they decided which books would be allowed in the Bible. Those they approved made it into the Bible and those they disliked were burned. As one of the characters in the book puts it: 'Behold the greatest cover-up in human history'.

Dan Brown claims that the Roman emperor Constantine decided which books went into the New Testament when he convened a church council in Nicaea in AD 325. He also claims that at this council the church decided in favour of the divinity of Jesus: 'until that moment in history, Jesus was viewed by his followers as a mortal prophet . . . Jesus' establishment as the 'Son of God' was officially proposed and voted on by the Council of Nicea . . . a relatively close vote at that'[16].

In actual fact, however, the council of Nicaea had nothing to do with deciding what books were included in Scripture. It was called to deal with Arianism, the teaching which denied that the Son was of the 'same substance' as the Father. Only two of the three hundred bishops failed to sign the Nicene Creed which affirmed the Son's equality with the Father. The emperor Constantine had nothing to do with deciding on what books went into Scripture, neither did the Council of Nicaea, and the 'vote' on Christ's Deity was hardly 'close'. So much for Christianity being the Big Lie – Dan Brown's book is a better contender for that title.

What of claims that Scripture was decided upon by a church council –

---

[16] Dan Brown, *The Da Vinci Code*, Doubleday, 2003, p.233

some say the council of Hippo in AD 393, or the council of Carthage in AD 397? There is no more truth to this claim than the idea that a fourth-century council decided upon the deity of Christ. The belief in the divine inspiration of certain books pre-dated any fourth-century council, and went right back to the earliest era of Christianity. The church councils that made declarations about Scripture were remote (North African), local affairs of limited authority. They did not create the Bible; all they did was restate what was already a 'fact on the ground'. They merely affirmed the already-existing position of the churches. Professor F. F. Bruce writes, 'The first ecclesiastical councils to classify the canonical books were both held in North Africa – at Hippo Regius in 393 and at Carthage in 397 – but what those councils did was not to impose something new upon the Christian communities but to codify what was already the general practice of those communities'[17]. Professor B. F. Westcott, commenting on the various councils, wrote that the canon was 'fixed by usage rather than by law'[18].

For those wanting to further explore the subject of other 'gospels' besides those in our New Testament, my book, *Is the Bible Really the Word of God?* provides an accessible summary of the reasons why these are not considered authentic records of the life of Christ.

Craig Evans, an expert on the extra-canonical Gnostic gospels, reviewing Dan Brown's *The Da Vinci Code* claims writes, 'Most of these assertions are either false or grossly misleading, as all trained historians know. Constantine apparently did commission the production of 50 copies of Scripture (as Christian historian Eusebius reports), but he did not decide which Gospels to include and which to omit. Furthermore, the claim that the Dead Sea Scrolls preserve the truth regarding Jesus is ludicrous, for the scrolls mostly date from the first century BC and do not refer to Jesus or to anyone in His following. Many of the Gnostic books found in Egypt (at Nag Hammadi) do refer to Jesus and His disciples, but all of these books are later not earlier than the Gospels in the New Testament. The "true" story of Jesus is not preserved in these

---

[17] F. F. Bruce, *The New Testament Documents: Are they Reliable?* p.27

[18] B. F. Westcott, *A General Survey of the History of the Canon of the New Testament*, Macmillan and Co., 1896, p.449.

writings. Indeed, the Gospels of the New Testament present Jesus as truly human, while the Gnostic Gospels exalt Jesus' heavenly status and often deny the reality of His humanity. And, of course, there is not a shred of credible evidence that Jesus had a wife and children'[19].

Playing Telephone with the Word of God?

Bart Ehrman's surprising 2005 bestseller, *Misquoting Jesus: The Story Behind Who Changed the Bible and Why*, made him a media celebrity, and elevated him alongside other atheist heroes like Richard Dawkins. Ehrman argues that the Bible was hopelessly corrupted in the process of its copying. To quote from its blurb on amazon.com, he believes that 'many of our widely held beliefs concerning the divinity of Jesus, the Trinity, and the divine origins of the Bible itself are the results of both intentional and accidental alterations by scribes'.

Ehrman argues that not only do we lack the original manuscripts of the New Testament, but the copies we possess are riddled with scribal mistakes and, even more seriously, deliberate alterations. We have no certain way of knowing what the original New Testament said, but if we did, Ehrman is sure that it would teach a very different message to what modern Christians believe.

The same criticism was made by Kurt Eichenwald on 23 December 2014 in a remarkable *Newsweek* magazine article entitled, 'The Bible: so Misunderstood it's a Sin'. Under a sub-heading reading 'Playing Telephone with the Word of God', Eichenwald wrote, 'No television preacher has ever read the Bible. Neither has any evangelical politician. Neither has the pope. Neither have I. And neither have you. At best, we've all read a bad translation—a translation of translations of translations of hand-copied copies of copies of copies of copies, and on and on, hundreds of times'.

Bible sceptics make three claims about the text of Scripture. The first is that we no longer possess the original 'autographs', hand-written by the authors, of Bible books. Secondly, the Bible was copied many times

---

[19] Craig A. Evans, "How Scholars Fabricate Jesus", in *Contending with Christianity's Critics*, eds. Paul Copan and William Lane Craig, B&H Publishing, 2009, p.126-7

by scribes down through time, who made many copying mistakes, until the invention of the printing press in the 15th Century. Just like a message gets mixed up in the 'telephone game' as people whisper a sentence round a circle, so the original words of the Bible may have been lost in transmission.

Thirdly, in addition to accidental mistakes, some scribes deliberately changed the wording and corrupted the message of the Bible. Ehrman argues that it was not heretics who tried to change the Bible, but early Christians who changed certain parts of the New Testament to make Jesus divine. To summarise, the case against the text of Scripture alleges:

1. We do not possess the original manuscripts of the Bible
2. There are many copying mistakes in the surviving manuscripts.
3. Scribes have also made deliberate alterations to the Bible.

Contrary to what the critics argue, however, we have a huge amount of evidence that confirms the text of our Bibles. There are three very good reasons for believing that the text of our New Testament is reliable:

1. We have over 5,800 manuscript copies of the New Testament in Greek, in part or whole, dating from the second century onwards. In addition to this, the New Testament was very early translated into other languages, and we possess about 20,000 manuscript copies of parts of the New Testament in other languages like Latin, Syriac, Coptic and Armenian. On top of all this, we have over a million catalogued quotations from the New Testament in the writings of early church theologians, commentators, apologists and preachers.

2. We can have confidence in our New Testament because of how early some of this textual evidence is. We have about 65 papyrus manuscripts of parts of the New Testament dating from the 2nd century to AD 300. Sir Frederick Kenyon of the British Museum wrote, 'The interval then between the dates of original composition and the earliest extant evidence becomes so small as to be in fact negligible, and the last foundation for any doubt that the Scriptures have come down to us substantially as they were written has now been removed. Both the authenticity and the general integrity of the

books of the New Testament may be regarded as finally established'[20].

3. We can trust our New Testament because of the high levels of agreement among these manuscript copies. Apart from spelling differences and accidental blunders, the manuscripts are all telling the same story in the same words.

New Testament textual criticism has an 'embarrassment of riches' when it comes to manuscript evidence for its text. The New Testament's manuscript evidence is far more reliable than any other works of literature from classical antiquity, which typically have far fewer surviving manuscript copies, which are far removed in date from their original copies.

For anyone interested in the issue of the textual reliability of the New Testament, or Ehrman's claim that scribes deliberately changed its wording, see my book, *Is the Bible Really the Word of God?*

Professor F. F. Bruce wrote, 'Fortunately, if the great number of manuscripts increases the number of scribal errors, it increases proportionately the means of correcting such errors, so that the margin of doubt left in the process of recovering the exact original wording is not so large as might be feared; it is in truth remarkably small. The variant readings about which any doubt remains among textual critics of the New Testament affect no material question of historic fact or of Christian faith and practice'[21]. We can be confident that the New Testament we possess today is authentic.

Rosaria Butterfield

Rosaria Butterfield was an atheist English literature and women's studies professor in a long-term relationship with her lesbian partner. Engaged in a variety of causes including LGBT activism and AIDS charity work, she had a deep-seated dislike of anything to do with Christianity – it condemned her lifestyle and community as sinful. The Bible was a book

---

[20] F. G. Kenyon, *The Bible and Archaeology*, Harper and Row, 1940, p.288
[21] F. F. Bruce, *The New Testament Documents: Are They Reliable?* IVP, 1987 reprint, pp.19-20

she loved to tear down as irrational and dangerous. But as part of her research into the religious right and their politics of hate, she decided she needed to read it. In 1997, she wrote an article for a local newspaper, attacking Christianity, right-wing politics and the patriarchy.

Her article engendered many responses, for and against, but she found one Christian pastor's response hard to pigeon-hole. Ken's letter was neither rude nor defensive, but rather encouraged Rosaria to explore the sorts of questions she normally asked as a postmodern literature professor. Ken's letter also invited Rosaria to dinner, which she accepted for research purposes. So started a two-year friendship with Ken and his wife Floy.

During this time, Rosaria started seriously reading the Bible. She describes what happened: 'I continued reading the Bible, all the while fighting the idea that it was inspired. But the Bible got to be bigger inside me than I. It overflowed into my world. I fought against it with all my might'. One day, at a dinner gathering Rosaria and her partner were hosting, her transgendered friend J cornered her in the kitchen. "This Bible reading is changing you, Rosaria," she warned. With tremors, I whispered, "J, what if it is true? What if Jesus is a real and risen Lord? What if we are all in trouble?"

Eventually, Rosaria came to Christ. She described her conversion as a 'train wreck'. It meant losing everything she loved. Many of her former friends felt betrayed; not all accepted her decision, and friendships were destroyed. But she figured that if Jesus could conquer death, he could fix her world again. Today she is a married mother of a Christian family.

Conclusion

The Bible is the most powerful book in the world. It changes lives. It is the best-selling book of all time. It is the book no regime has been able to get rid of. It claims to be the Word of God. Importantly, Jesus Himself said the Bible is God's Word[22]. Many people claim to have found God Himself through reading it.

I am going to rate this argument at 7 our of 10, based on the objective

---

[22] Matthew 4:4, 5:17-18, 22:43, Mark 7:9-13, John 10:35

evidence of its popularity, permanence, power to change lives, prophecies and most importantly, Jesus Christ's pronouncement as the Word of God.

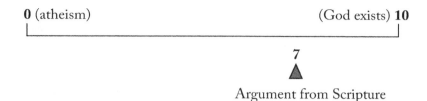

Argument from Scripture

But ultimately, the only way to test whether the Bible is God's Word is to experience it for yourself. Read it with an open heart and mind. The Bible is self-authenticating. Put it to the test and ask God to speak to you through it.

Chapter 15

The General von Zieten Argument: History

W here in the world are we heading? Atheists do not believe that there is any plan or purpose to human history. André Maurois wrote, 'The universe is indifferent. Who created it? Why are we here on this puny mud heap spinning in infinite space? I have not the slightest idea and I am convinced nobody has'. G. N. Clarke wrote, 'There is no secret and no plan in history to be discovered'[1]. Henry Ford famously said that 'History is more or less bunk'[2].

But if God is the creator of life on earth, then it stands to reason that He also has a plan for human history. C. S. Lewis wrote, 'History is a story written by the finger of God'[3]. This chapter will explore four evidences of God's involvement in history.

General von Zieten's Argument

King Frederick the Great of Prussia (1712-1786) is one of the most important figures of German history. Becoming King at age 28, he greatly enlarged Prussia by a series of military conquests and diplomatic maneuvers, taking Prussia from a small principality to the position of dominant power in all Germany. This trajectory ultimately led, in the following century, to the unification of all Germany under the Kings of Prussia. Frederick the Great became the prototype, the ideal leader, for future militaristic German rulers to follow, from Bismarck to Kaiser Wilhelm II to Hitler (who placed a golden wreath on his tomb). Frederick the Great's militaristic bent was balanced by a love of the arts

---

[1] Both Maurois and Clark quotes come from William Barclay in *Great Themes of the New Testament*, Westminster John Knox Press, 2001, p.77
[2] Chicago Tribune, 2016
[3] C. S. Lewis, *Christian Reflections*, Wm. B. Eerdmans, 1967, p.130

and philosophy, but his militaristic model of leadership produced a harvest of misery for the world in the twentieth century.

Frederick the Great was an irreligious sceptic, a friend of Voltaire, the noted French critic of Christianity. Frederick the Great is quoted as saying, 'Christianity is an old metaphysical fiction, stuffed with fables, contradictions and absurdities: it was spawned in the fevered imagination of the Orientals, and then spread to our Europe, where some fanatics espoused it, where some intriguers pretended to be convinced by it and where some imbeciles actually believed it'.

General Hans Joachim von Zieten (1699-1786) was a cavalry officer whose brilliance in battle saved Frederick's armies on more than one occasion. He was a man of great bravery: he fought seventy-four duels in his life, as well as four wars, but died in his sleep aged 86. General von Zieten not only saved Frederick's army in battle, he also rescued the King himself. During a period of depression towards the end of the Seven Years War, Frederick actively sought death in battle, but was saved by von Zieten. He was a hero in the army and among the general population (his statue stands in Berlin today), and he was a favourite of the Frederick the Great's. However, von Zieten was very different from the King in one respect: he was a Christian.

Von Zieten was once invited to dinner with the King but declined because he wished to go instead to the Lord's Supper at church. The King and his friends mocked both him and the Lord's Supper, but von Zieten stood up and replied, "My lord, there is a greater King than you, a King to whom I have sworn allegiance even unto death. I am a Christian man, and I cannot sit quietly as the Lord's name is dishonored, His character belittled, and His cause subjected to ridicule. With your permission I shall withdraw". The other guests trembled at von Zieten's answer, fearing he might be put to death. But to their surprise, Frederick took his hand, asked his forgiveness for mocking Christian things, and requested that he remain.

On another occasion, King Frederick asked General von Zieten to defend his Christianity in just one word, if he could. The General bowed, and replied, "Sire, Israel". This is the argument we now turn to.

Israel

What is so special about Israel? For a start, we need to remind ourselves that it was Israel that introduced the idea of monotheism – of one true God – to the world. Or, to put it the right way round, it was through Israel that God introduced Himself to the world. God placed Israel at the very centre of the world – at the intersection of the European, Asian and African continents. God's name, character and cause is intimately connected with the nation of Israel.

Next we need to remind ourselves that the nation of Israel is an anomaly and enigma on the page of history. For example, while the Jewish people only make up 0.2% of the world's population, nearly one quarter of all Nobel Prizes have been awarded to Jews (203 Jewish winners of Nobel Prize out of 902 awarded, 22.5%, as of 2017). The Jewish people rule the intellectual world.

Of the greatest significance, however, is the story of Jewish survival. David Ben Gurion, the first Prime Minister of the State of Israel, said: 'A Jew who does not believe in miracles is not a realist'. What else explains the existence and accomplishments of the Jewish people? Mark Twain wrote:

'If the statistics are right the Jews constitute but one per cent of the human race. It suggests a nebulous dim puff of stardust lost in the blaze of the Milky way. Properly, the Jew ought hardly to be heard of, but he is heard of, has always been heard of. He is as prominent on the planet as any other people, and his commercial importance is extravagantly out of proportion to the smallness of his bulk. His contributions to the world's list of great names in literature, science, art, music, finance, medicine, and abstruse learning are also away out of proportion to the weakness of his numbers. He has made a marvellous fight in this world, in all the ages; and had done it with his hands tied behind him. He could be vain of himself, and be excused for it. The Egyptian, the Babylonian, and the Persian rose, filled the planet with sound and splendor, then faded to dream-stuff and passed away; the Greek and the Roman followed; and made a vast noise, and they are gone; other people have sprung up and held their torch high for a time, but it burned out, and they sit in twilight now, or have vanished. The Jew saw them all, beat them all, and is now what he always was, exhibiting no decadence, no infirmities of age, no weakening of his parts, no slowing of his energies, no dulling of his alert and aggressive mind. All things are mortal but the Jew; all other forces pass, but he remains. What is the secret of his immortality?"[4]

Mark Twain wrote before the twentieth century, which witnessed the liberation of Israel's ancient homeland from the Ottoman Empire in 1917, the re-establishment of the state of Israel in 1948, and the defence of Israel from three attacks mounted by numerically superior enemies on all sides in 1948, 1967, 1973.

Josh McDowell relates the story of being in Israel and asking a high official in the Israeli government how Israel had managed to survive two exiles from their homeland, the second almost 1900 years long, the holocaust and the attacks from the Arab world in both 1967 and 1973. Was this the result of a divine hand watching over them? The government official replied, 'Although most of the people in my country today would claim to be atheists, don't you believe it. I think that all of us know deep down inside that some force greater than us has been protecting this nation'[5].

David Baron, the 19th century Jewish Christian wrote, 'The most eloquent monument to the faithfulness of God and to the everlasting truth of His holy Word is the JEW; and there is an inscription more striking and legible than any which can be found written on papyrus or graven on rock – and inscription nearly twenty centuries long, consisting of the history of the Jewish nation since their dispersion, written for the most part in their own blood, and which supplies more light upon, and confirmation of, God's living oracles, than can be obtained from any other source except the Bible itself'[6].

Three times God says to the nation of Israel through the prophet

---

[4] Mark Twain, "Concerning The Jews", *Harper's Magazine*, 1899
[5] Josh McDowell, *Answers to Tough Questions Skeptics Ask about the Faith*, Here's Life Publishers, 1983, p.33
[6] David Baron, *The Shepherd of Israel*, Morgan and Scott, n.d., pp.v-vi

Isaiah, 'You are My witnesses' (Isaiah 43:10, 12, 44:8). God has protected this nation as a witness to the truths about Himself that He has taught the world through them.

It could be argued that the nation of Israel is as much proof of the Devil's existence as God's, in view of the hatred that in each generation rears its ugly head against the Jews. It is the only nation continually faced with genocidal enemies threatening to wipe it from the face of the earth.

The Bible speaks of the Jews as God's chosen people, His vehicle for revealing Himself to the world. Through the Jewish nation, God gave the Law containing the Ten Commandments, as well as the Scriptures telling of His self-revelation down through time, and the prophecies explaining where the world's history is headed.

But why would God decide to reveal Himself through a 'chosen nation'? The most important reason, the Bible says, is because God's ultimate plan was to reveal Himself to the world through a person born into that nation: the Messiah, Jesus Christ. The Messiah is the centrepiece of God's plans for history, the One through whom God's purposes will be fulfilled.

In most detective stories, it is the inconsistency – the thing out of place – that cracks open the case. The same is true in the field of science; it was the unusual orbit of Mercury that could not be explained by Newton's theory of gravity that confirmed Einstein's theory of relativity. Is the same true of history? Israel is the anomaly in world history, the wrinkle on the page of time. When we look at ancient history, at Egypt or the Babylonian and Persian empires, or the 'glory that was Greece' and Rome, we see the nation of Israel there in the background too. The same is true of the twentieth century too: Israel is at the centre of 20th century history, and Israel is the open wound in the Middle East still.

The Resurrection

Christianity is not a philosophy or a system of morality. Christianity is history. It concerns certain events that happened to real people in time and space, in particular, the events surrounding Jesus' life and death.

All historical events have continuing consequences. The fact that most people in Australia have white skin and speak the English language is a result of English explorer Captain James Cook's discovery of the east coast of Australia in 1770 and the resulting British colonization in 1788. Similarly, the existence of the Christian church for the last 2000 years calls for an explanation.

Cambridge Professor C. F. D. Moule said, 'The birth and rapid rise of the Christian Church … remain an unsolved enigma for any historian who refuses to take seriously the only explanation offered by the Church itself'[7]. Moule wrote that the emergence of the Church 'rips a great hole in history, a hole the size and shape of Resurrection'. The best explanation for the Christian church is that Jesus Christ rose from the dead on the third day, showing that he was truly the Son of God.

Lee Strobel, the journalist and atheist we met in a previous chapter, investigated Christianity and cited five key pieces of evidence for the historicity of the resurrection:

1. The disciples sincerely believed that Jesus rose from the dead, even being prepared to die for this belief. Why would they suffer and die for a lie? What did they gain?
2. Early enemies and opponents like Paul and James (the brother of Jesus) converted to Christianity and also died for their faith. What caused them to change and give up their lives?
3. Very soon after Jesus' death, many Jews abandoned long-standing cultural and religious practices. Why did they desert Judaism?
4. Christian baptism and the Lord's Supper were very early symbols of the central Christian claim of Jesus' resurrection and deity.
5. The emergence of the church in the face of Roman persecution, which reached for the sword for 250 years, until Rome surrendered, and Christianity became the religion of the Empire.

Three other theories have been suggested to explain the disciples' belief that Jesus rose from the dead. All three fail to account for the data[8].

---

[7] C. F. D. Moule, *The Phenomenon of the New Testament*, SCM Press, 1967, p.13

[8] More details of these problems may be found in Andrew W. Wilson, *Believers Bible Doctrine Handbook*, Believers Publications, 2018, p.63

1. **The Swoon Theory:** Christ did not die on the cross, but merely swooned, or was drugged, and later revived in the tomb. But apart from the fact that Romans were brutally efficient at making sure crucifixion killed a man, the German sceptic David Strauss himself argued that even if Christ was still alive after being taken down from the cross, 'One who had thus crept forth half dead from the grave and crawled about a sickly patient in need of medical and surgical assistance ... but notwithstanding finally succumbed to His suffering, could never have given the disciples the impression that He was the conqueror over the grave and death, and the Prince of life'[9].

2. **The Stolen Body Theory:** Someone took Jesus' dead body, either the disciples (as the chief priests bribed the guards to say, Matthew 28:11-15), or the Jews (as the disciples first thought, John 20:2). This gave the appearance that Jesus' body had disappeared. However, against this theory are the guards posted to prevent this very thing, the undisturbed grave-clothes (nobody would ever have stolen a mutilated and bloodied body of a crucified man without his grave-clothes, but these were left intact and unwound in the tomb), and the fact that if the disciples had stolen the body, why would they later die for a lie, as martyrs?

3. **The Hallucination Theory:** The disciples, under the strain of the events of Christ's crucifixion, imagined that they had seen the Lord risen. However, the disciples not only claimed to have seen the risen Lord, but also to have walked with Him, held His feet, and ate and drank with Him. The theory also runs aground on the fact that Jesus appeared to multiple people at once (hallucinations are individual events). C. S. Lewis wrote, 'any theory of hallucination breaks down on the fact ... that on three separate occasions this hallucination was not immediately recognized as Jesus'[10].

Christ's resurrection was not a case of Christ living on in the hearts of

---

[9] David Strauss, *Life of Jesus*, 1835, p.298
[10] C. S. Lewis, *Miracles*, Collins, 2016, p.241

those who loved him, a 'recollection of the personality of Jesus himself'[11], 'by which a memory has been projected into the idea of a living presence'[12]. It was not 'the rise of faith' among the early disciples[13] (as opposed to the rise of Christ). The disciples' faith had collapsed at His death, and it was only Christ's resurrection that revived it.

The suggestion that the resurrection was a 'cunningly devised' lie concocted by the disciples years later (when it was impossible for people to disprove) simply does not stack up. The disciples were preaching the resurrection in Jerusalem at the major Jewish religious festival of Pentecost fifty days after His death. It was not a late or legendary development, but the heart of their missionary message through the Roman world in the 40s and 50s. Christ's resurrection is mentioned in very early letters written to Christian churches. Words like 1 Corinthians 15:3-4 ('Christ died for our sins ... was buried ... He rose again the third day'), written in the early 50s, were a well-established statement of faith among early Christians. Paul says he received this creed from the early disciples (v3), and most historians agree that this belief-statement originated within 10 years of Christ's death – from the AD 30s.

The Resurrection is based on eye-witness evidence, the same way we verify any historical event today – from a car crash to a murder. We cannot perform scientific experiments to prove historical events like, say, Julius Caesar's assassination, or that Captain Cook sailed to Australia. In the New Testament, the apostles constantly claim to have witnessed the risen Christ. Paul describes a list of eyewitnesses in 1 Corinthians 15:3-8.

Even more tellingly, the gospel accounts of the resurrection do not try to set out a legal case or even a logical argument. Instead, they tell us about the emotional reactions of the disciples: Mary weeping (John 20:11), the confusion of the two on the road to Emmaus (Luke 24:13-27), and the startled reaction of the disciples when Jesus appeared, unbelieving and joyful at the same time (Luke 24:41).

When real people recount an incident – when a TV reporter puts a microphone in front of them – ordinary people tell of their feelings. The

---

[11] David Strauss, *The Life of Jesus*

[12] Alister McGrath, *Christian Theology: An Introduction*, 3rd Ed., Blackwell, 2001, p.399

[13] Rudolf Bultmann, "NT and Mythology", in *Kerygma and Myth*, SPCK, 1964, p.42

disciples show some extremely raw emotional responses, dismissing the women's report of the empty tomb (with sexist undertones) as 'silly nonsense' (Luke 24:11), and Thomas' gross-out language – refusing to believe unless he stuck his finger into Jesus's nail-wounds and spear-pierced side. Real men say extreme and unguarded things like this when they are stressed and overwhelmed. The gospels are giving the sort of raw reporting that accompanies real historical events.

Professor B. F. Westcott of Cambridge wrote, 'Taking all the evidence together, there is no single historic incident better or more variously supported than the resurrection of Christ'[14]. Josh McDowell, a party-going university student who was challenged to examine the resurrection, said: 'After more than 700 hours of studying this subject and thoroughly investigating its foundation, I have come to the conclusion that the resurrection of Jesus Christ is one of the most wicked, vicious, heartless hoaxes ever foisted upon the minds of men, or it is the most fantastic fact of history'[15].

The History of Christian Civilization

Even those who do not accept the historical foundation of Christianity are forced to accept the historical reality of its consequences. Historians are increasingly recognizing that it was only in Christian societies that it was possible for modern civilization to arise. This is too big a subject to adequately cover here, but only Christianity provided an adequate basis for human dignity, freedom, compassion, equality and reason. These, in turn led to education, democracy, science and human rights.

Take democracy. According to Sanford Lakoff, Emeritus Professor of political theory at the University of California, San Diego:

'The Christian teaching with the greatest implications for democracy is the belief that because humanity is created in the image of God, all human beings are of equal worth in the sight of God ... As Alexis de Tocqueville noted when he observed in the introduction to his study

---

[14] B. F. Westcott, *The Gospel of the Resurrection*, London: Macmillan, 1891, p.137
[15] Josh McDowell, *Evidence that Demands a Verdict*, Nashville: Nelson, 1972, p.179

of democracy in America ... Christianity, which has declared all men equal in the sight of God, cannot hesitate to acknowledge all citizens equal before the law'[16].

This leads directly to universal human rights. G. K. Chesterton wrote, 'The [American] Declaration of Independence dogmatically bases all rights on the fact that God created all men equal; and it is right, for it they were not created equal, they were certainly evolved unequal. There is no basis for democracy except in a dogma about the divine origin of man' (*What I saw in America*).

The history of social Darwinism proves this. In the century following Darwin's publication of *The Origin of Species* and *The Descent of Man* (denying God's role in the creation of man), the world witnessed an upsurge in attempts to justify ruthless competition and struggle. These included:

- **robber-baron capitalism**, whose advocates argued against social welfare or relief for poor workers,
- **imperialistic militarism**, which resulted in the conquest and colonisation by Western powers of African and Asian countries (contributing directly to World War One),
- **eugenics**, which applied the science of breeding to human beings, resulting in the forced sterilisation of about 60,000 people in the U.S. with diseases and disabilities deemed a hindrance to human evolution, and
- **racism**, seen at its worst in Nazi Germany with the holocaust and the attempt to conquer the Slavic races on the basis of the so-called superiority of the Aryan people.

Not all of these evils can be blamed directly on Charles Darwin (although he did believe non-white races were less evolved and Africans

---

[16] Sanford Lakoff, *Democracy: History, Theory and Practice*, Westview Press, 1996, p.90. It is true that democracy originated in Athens in ancient Greece, however only about 10-20% of the population could vote (only adult males, and not if they were foreigners, or slaves, which made up 30-40% of the population).

were closer to the apes), but the denial of God as our Creator pulls the rug out from any idea of universal equality.

Or consider another consequence of Christianity: the debt of modern science to Christianity. Many people today live under the mistaken impression that religion and science are irreconcilable enemies. But those who know their history are aware that the great founders of modern science were godly Christians: Galileo, Kepler, Pascal, Boyle, Newton, Faraday, Mendel, Pasteur, Kelvin and Clerk-Maxwell. Christianity was the soil in which science sprung up for one simple reason: Christians believed the universe was orderly and rational, the product of a divine mind, and therefore its secrets could be decoded by human minds.

Many secular Western people think that we owe such concepts as liberty, equality and fraternity to the French and American revolutions. However, the truth is that the Christian doctrines of all people made in the image of God, endowed with reason and free will, are the ultimate foundation of the values Westerners treasure, as various recent histories have argued.

Tom Holland's book *Dominion: How the Christian Revolution Remade the World*[17] was born out of the author's realization that, although an agnostic, his morals were profoundly Christian, and very unlike those of the people he wrote about in earlier works of history dealing with ancient Rome, Greece and Persia. These ancient cultures exalted brutality and exploitation whereas Christianity brought human dignity and care for the vulnerable. Rather than ushering in an age of superstition and ignorance, Christianity's missionary message that salvation was available to all nations (not just the chosen Jewish race), to male and female, slave and free (Galatians 3:28), meant the equality and value of all people everywhere. This message laid the foundations for our modern Western world with its concern for human rights, democracy, equality before the law, humility as a virtue, help for the needy and the pre-eminence of the virtue of love towards others. Holland argues that even when atheists attack various abominable acts in Christian history, their conception of what is immoral is itself based on the standards of Christian morality.

---

[17] The U.S. title; the British title was *Dominion: The Making of the Western Mind*, 2019

Like the fish in the poem who cried, "Oh, where is the sea" as they swam the Atlantic's blue waters, Christianity is the atmosphere we all unknowingly breathe today, even atheists.

Similarly, Oxford scholar Sir Larry Siedentop in *Inventing the Individual: the Origins of Western Liberalism* argued that 'the Christian conception of God provided the foundation for what became an unprecedented form of human society. Christian moral beliefs emerge as the ultimate source of the social revolution that has made the West the way it is'[18].

It is not just the Western world that Christianity has impacted. Matthew Parris is an English journalist, atheist, homosexual and former Member of Parliament. He grew up in Africa, and in 2008 returned on a visit. He wrote an article in the London *Times* titled: "As an Atheist, I truly Believe Africa needs God", sub-titled, "Missionaries, not aid money, are the solution to Africa's biggest problem – the crushing passivity of the people's mindset". Parris wrote about how Africa's need for God is a belief he has 'been trying to banish all my life, but an observation I've been unable to avoid since my African childhood. It confounds my ideological beliefs, stubbornly refuses to fit my world view, and has embarrassed my growing belief that there is no God'.

Now a confirmed atheist, I've become convinced of the enormous contribution that Christian evangelism makes in Africa: sharply distinct from the work of secular NGOs, government projects and international aid efforts. These alone will not do. Education and training alone will not do. In Africa Christianity changes people's hearts. It brings a spiritual transformation. The rebirth is real. The change is good … The Christians were always different. Far from having cowed or confined its converts, their faith appeared to have liberated and relaxed them. There was a liveliness, a curiosity, an engagement with the world – a directness in their dealings with others – that seemed to be missing in traditional African life. They

---

[18] Larry Siedentop, *Inventing the Individual: the Origins of Western Liberalism*, Penguin, 2014, p.353

stood tall.

Parris talked about the traditional problems of Africa: the tribalism, the 'big mama and gangster politics of the African city', the deep-seated fear of spirits, ancestors and nature, the lack of initiative, and lack of responsibility. Then he talked about how Christianity with its direct link between the individual and God breaks through the barriers that these African problems raise, liberating people from the 'crushing tribal group-think'. He concluded by saying:

> Those who want Africa to walk tall amid 21st-century global competition must not kid themselves that providing the material means or even the know-how that accompanies what we call development will make the change. A whole belief system must first be supplanted.
>
> And I'm afraid it has to be supplanted by another. Removing Christian evangelism from the African equation may leave the continent at the mercy of a malign fusion of Nike, the witch doctor, the mobile phone and the machete'[19].

Kenneth Scott Latourette, the Yale historian and theologian, wrote about Christianity's civilizing effects as follows:

> We have much to say about the effects of Christianity upon the collective life of communities, nations and mankind as a whole. Here has been the most potent force which mankind has known for the dispelling of illiteracy, for the creation of schools, for the emergence of new types of education. From Christianity have issued impulses for daring intellectual and geographic adventure. The universities, centres for pushing forward the boundaries of human knowledge, were at the outset largely Christian creations. Many of the most courageous of the explorers of the earth's surface were to no small degree impelled by the Christian faith. Music, architecture, painting, poetry and philosophy have owed some of their greatest achievements to

---

[19]   https://www.thetimes.co.uk/article/as-an-atheist-i-truly-believe-africa-needs-god-3xj9bm80h8m, December 27 2008

Christianity. Democracy, as it was known in the nineteenth and twentieth centuries, was in large part the outgrowth of Christian teaching. The abolition of Negro slavery was due chiefly to Christianity. So, too, were the measures taken to protect the Indians against the exploitation of the whites. The most hopeful movements for the regulation of war, the mitigation of the sufferings entailed by war and for the eventual abolition of war owed their inception chiefly to the Christian faith. The nursing profession of the nineteenth century had the same origin and the extension of Western methods of surgery and medicine to much of the non-Occidental world in that and the twentieth century was chiefly through the Christian missionary enterprise. The elevation of the status of women owed an incalculable debt to Christianity. Christian ideals made for monogamy and for a special kind of family life. No other single force has been so widely potent for the relief of suffering brought on by famine and for the creation of hospitals and orphanages'[20].

Many atheists argue that Western society has made its greatest progress since it repudiated religion in favour of science. Everything is on the up: health, wealth, peace and pleasure. Our ancestors could not have dreamt of what we enjoy. But just taking everyday crimes into account (that is, leaving aside the great atheist atrocities of the 20th century), our world is getting worse, not better. In England and Wales, the total recorded number of cases of violence against the person in 1898 were just 2,144, whereas in 1998 they were 256,070, while robberies went from 354 to 62,652 over the same period[21]. The one-hundred to two-hundred fold increases are the effect, in part, of going from a Christian society to a post-Christian one.

For another comparison, consider a very different part of the world. When cruise ships visit islands in the South Pacific, affluent Westerners are often surprised at how religious the native people are. One man overheard complaining about all the religion on the island was pointed

[20] Kenneth Scott Latourette, *A History of the Expansion of Christianity*, Harper & Brothers, 1945, vol. 7, pp.490-91.
[21] https://www.gov.uk/government/statistics/historical-crime-data

towards a large rock and told that he ought to be thankful for the coming of Christianity. If he had arrived a little over one hundred years before, his head would have been smashed open on the rock and his brains eaten.

The historian Rodney Stark's book, *The Victory of Reason: How Christianity Led to Freedom, Capitalism and Western Success*, commences its last chapter with these words:

> Christianity created Western civilisation. … Without a theology committed to reason, progress, and moral equality, today the entire world would be about where non-European societies were in, say, 1800: A world with many astrologers and alchemists but no scientists. A world of despots, lacking universities, banks, factories, eyeglasses, chimneys, and pianos. A world where most infants do not live to the age of five and many women die in childbirth – a world truly living in "dark ages"[22].

Stark concludes his chapter with a quote from TIME magazine's David Aikman, who reported the summary of a member of one of China's premier academic research organizations—the Chinese Academy of Social Sciences (CASS):

> 'One of the things we were asked to look into was what accounted for the success, in fact, the pre-eminence of the West all over the world," he said. "We studied everything we could from the historical, political, economic, and cultural perspective. At first, we thought it was because you had more powerful guns than we had. Then we thought it was because you had the best political system. Next we focused on your economic system. But in the past twenty years, we have realized that the heart of your culture is your religion: Christianity. That is why the West has been so powerful. The Christian moral foundation of social and cultural life was what made possible the emergence of capitalism and then the successful

---

[22] Rodney Stark, *The Victory of Reason: How Christianity Led to Freedom, Capitalism and Western Success*, Random House, 2005, p.235

transition to democratic politics. We don't have any doubt about this'[23].

Douglas Murray, another British atheist homosexual, argues that 'for centuries in Europe one of the great – if not the greatest – sources of such energy came from the spirit of the continent's religion. It drove people to war and stirred them to defence. It also drove Europe to the greatest heights of human creativity. It drove Europeans to build St. Peter's in Rome, the Cathedral at Chartres, the Duomo of Florence and the Basilica of St. Mark in Venice. It inspired the works of Bach, Beethoven and Messiaen, Gruenwald's altarpiece at Isenheim and Leonardo's *Madonna of the Rocks*'[24].

However, in the 19th century, this cultural foundation was dealt two blows: biblical criticism in Germany and Darwinian evolution in England. These undermined belief in the Bible, resulting in the decline and eclipse of Christianity and its values; Murray writes, 'Europe had lost its foundational story' (p212). He comments:

The result was the slow death of Europe. 'The fact that all of our utopias failed so terribly did not only destroy our faith in them. It destroyed our faith in any and all ideologies. It does seem, living in any Western European society today, that this particular world-view has caught on. Not only the entertainment industries but also the information industries speak to populations intent only on a fairly shallow kind of personal pleasure' (p222). 'We sometimes behave as though we had the certainties of our ancestors, yet we have none of them, and none of their consolations' (p223).

There have been atheist cultures, but far from being the paradises their citizens were promised, the fruits of atheism were poisoned, and such

[23] David Aikman, *Jesus in Beijing: How Christianity Is Transforming China and Changing the Global Balance of Power*, Regnery, 2003, p.5.
[24] Douglas Murray, *The Strange Death of Europe: Immigration, Identity, Islam*, Bloomsbury Continuum, 2017, pp.209-210

societies were short-lived. With the atheistic regimes[25] of the 20th century came also the gulags, the purges, the suppression of human freedom and a slaughter of millions unparalleled in the history of the world. Before these 20th century experiments, the 'enlightenment' of the 18th century led to the French Revolution with its worship of the Goddess of Reason in the Notre Dame, but the terrors, the guillotine and the Napoleonic wars that ravaged Europe were not far behind. Getting rid of God has not been good for human flourishing.

There are few atheist countries still left in the world, most having collapsed of their own dysfunctional accord. Communist Albania under Enver Hoxha declared itself the first atheist state, but visitors in the 1990s (after the fall of communism) described it as the most backward country in Europe, still stuck in the 1940s. Nor are there many people queuing up to move to the few remaining atheist countries in the world, like North Korea. Who wants to live in a huge concentration camp?

The evidence from history shows that God is good for the world, or at least for societies that honour Him and follow His ways. Atheism not only destroys human dignity, but the lesson of history is that atheism is societal suicide, while Christianity results in human flourishing.

Where History is Heading

The poet T. S. Eliot wrote, 'This is the way the world ends. Not with a bang but a whimper'. Nothing could be further from the truth. One of the evidences that the Bible is truly God's Word is what it says about where human history is heading. There are four main features of the Bible's picture of the future. The first three prophecies align with what we see happening in the world today. The fourth is the longing of human hearts.

One-World Government

The first thing the Bible says about the future is that the world is going

---

[25] Virtually all communist regimes were explicitly and ruthlessly atheistic, in line with Marxism's doctrine of dialectical materialism (rough translation: violent atheism).

to eventually come under the control of a one-world government. At the head of this government will be a man that the Bible calls by various names: the man of sin, the beast, the antichrist. Not only will he govern the world politically, and control the world economically, but he will also demand world-wide religious worship. Revelation 13:7-8 says: 'authority was given him over every tribe, tongue, and nation. All who dwell on the earth will worship him'. His lieutenant, called the false prophet, 'causes all, both small and great, rich and poor, free and slave, to receive a mark on their right hand or on their foreheads, and that no one may buy or sell except one who has the mark or the name of the beast, or the number of his name'. The apostle Paul says that the antichrist 'opposes and exalts himself above all that is called God or that is worshipped, so that he sits as God in the temple of God, showing himself that he is God' (2 Thessalonians 2:4).

This is exactly where our world is heading – towards a one-world government. The modern process of world unification arguably began with German unification in the 19th century (inspired by the militaristic methods of Frederick the Great), and is being carried forward with projects like the European Union today. The process of economic globalization is increasing at pace, technological advances mean that the world is more connected than ever, and amidst all this, the United Nations is increasingly binding national governments into global treaties for environmental and economic purposes. It will only take one big global crisis and we will have a One-World government, just as the Bible has long predicted, hastily convened to deal with the problem.

The 'Great Tribulation'

The second prophecy the Bible makes is that this future world-ruler is going to come to power after a series of terrible events often referred to as the Four Horsemen of the Apocalypse. World war, and the resulting anarchy, famine and disease will bring about the death of one quarter of the world's population (Revelation 6). Following this, a series of further plagues and devastating catastrophes will kill another one third of people living on earth (Revelation 8-9). This is when the Antichrist, the man indwelt by Satan himself, will take control.

Albert Einstein once quipped, 'I know not with what weapons World War III will be fought, but World War IV will be fought with sticks and stones'. What he meant is that World War III will see nuclear weapons which wipe out human civilization. The book of Revelation predicts that one-quarter and then a further one-third of the world's population will be destroyed (at present rates, over 3 billion people) in the future. The Bible's prediction aligns with what we know about a future world war scenario, and based on human nature there is little to stop it. This future devastation will give rise to the most terrifying ruler the world has ever known, just like World War One gave rise to Hitler in Germany, Stalin in Russia, and Mao Tse-tung in China. The Antichrist will dwarf all three for pure evil genius.

The remarkable fact that there has been no nuclear war for 75 years is a testament to God's providential care and protection. But the Bible teaches that in the days of the Antichrist, God's restraining hand holding back human evil will be withdrawn, nor will He any longer counteract the Satanically-deceptive lies of the Antichrist (2 Thessalonians 2:6-12). Some contrarians today think that too many people are given to gullibly following the latest intellectual and social fads, but even the cynics will be singing the praises of Satan's man in a day to come.

Israel and Armageddon

The third main feature of Bible prophecy is that Israel will be the centre and focus of future events. Israel will be the site the Antichrist's future world religion, and it will also be the site of the future Battle of Armageddon. Israel remains the key to world peace, the thorny problem that no politician seems able to solve, with the Middle East in perpetual meltdown all around it. The Antichrist will solve this Jewish problem by enforcing a seven year treaty (Daniel 9:27), guaranteeing Israel protection and freedom to worship in a rebuilt Temple. At the mid-point of this seven year treaty, however, Antichrist will set up his own religion in the temple in Jerusalem, and enforce this world-wide worship. This will usher in a period that Jesus called 'the great tribulation' (Matthew 24:21).

Anyone who will not worship the Antichrist, or carry the 'mark of the beast' (666) on their body, will be put to death.

The battle of Armageddon will occur at the end of 'the great tribulation'. The nation of Israel will be attacked by Muslim nations from its south, headed by Egypt (Daniel 11:40-45). This attack will provoke a counter-attack by the Antichrist's forces from the north (Ezekiel 38-39), trying to re-establish control over the Holy Land. The city of Jerusalem will be besieged (Zechariah 12) as other nations from the east also get involved. Finally, Jesus Christ Himself will return, destroying the massed armies of the world encircling the Jewish nation. The Jews will finally believe in their Messiah when they see His visible return.

Today, more than ever, we see the truth of the Bible's prophecies. Israel is the open wound on the earth's surface that refuses to be healed. Israel is the epicentre of the world's troubles, the flashpoint, where the world's races, religions and politics collide. Bear in mind, too, that it is only within the last 70 years that Israel has returned to their ancient homeland and been re-established as a nation. Critics mocked the Bible's prediction, and even some Christians doubted that the Jewish people would ever return home. But these Bible prophecies have come true before our very own eyes. Little did General von Zieten know how right he was when he said that Israel is evidence that God exists.

The Kingdom of God

There is one final, fourth, feature of Bible prophecy that will fulfil the deepest longings of human hearts. Christ is not simply returning to defeat the Antichrist. He is coming to reign over the world as King of Kings and Lord of Lords. We read of Christ's coming kingdom in many places in the Old Testament prophets, but Isaiah's prophecy gives us the most details. Christ's kingdom will put an end to wars on earth: 'They shall beat their swords into plowshares, and their spears into pruning hooks; nation shall not lift up sword against nation, neither shall they learn war anymore' (Isa. 2:4). Social justice will replace unfairness and criminality (Isa. 11:1-4), nature will no longer be under the curse ('the wolf also shall dwell with the lamb, the leopard shall lie down with the young goat, the calf and the young lion and the fatling together; and a little child shall lead them'), and everyone on earth will know God, 'for the earth shall be full of the knowledge of the LORD as the waters cover the sea' (Isa. 11:6-9). Environmental problems will be solved and disease done away with (Isa. 35:1-7), and with its rightful King upon the throne, earth will finally be the paradise God created it to be.

This is God's plan and purpose – that the Messiah, Jesus Christ, should be the King over the world, reigning in peace, plenty, justice and joy with those who love Him. Finally, after one thousand years of Christ's reign, the great Judgment Day will come (Revelation 20). God will then bring in new heavens and a new earth, and eternity will begin, with things so wonderful that we cannot even imagine what awaits.

Conclusion

This is the argument from history: the nation of Israel is indeed unique. They are God's people chosen to introduce the world to Himself. The Christian church, another historically undeniable fact, is not only best explained by the resurrection of Christ, but its effects on the world stage have been, for the most part, elevating and beneficial. This is exactly what we would expect if it represents (however imperfectly) a God who is both true and good. But God has even better plans ahead, a kingdom paradise for all who love Him. The world today, in continuing rebellion against God, thinks that mankind alone will solve its own problems. Under the Satanically-inspired Antichrist and his world-government, these attempts will usher in the most terrible days of earth's history. Time alone will tell how true the argument of this chapter is, but from where we are today, the world is on track to fulfil the prophesied future.

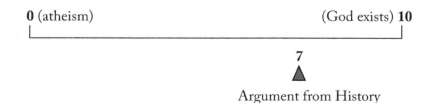

0 (atheism)   (God exists) **10**

7

Argument from History

Chapter 16

The Blaise Pascal Argument: Personal Experience

Blaise Pascal (1623-1662) was a brilliant French mathematician, scientist, inventor, philosopher and writer who was born six years after Shakespeare died. Despite being educated at home by his father, he invented the first computer (a mechanical calculator: *la machine arithmétique*) at age 16, performed experiments on vacuums and hydraulics, and in his twenties his mathematical papers astonished the leading mathematicians of the day. His satirical *Provincial Letters* (1656-57), attacking the moral hypocrisy of the Jesuits, established him as one of the greatest of all French prose writers, and his 'Thoughts' (*Pensées*) is considered one of the great literary masterpieces of all time, despite being unfinished.

Pascal grew up in a Roman Catholic family, but his religious interest was largely nominal until an experience that occurred on the night of November 23rd, 1654. It is possible, but far from certain, that this experience was the result of a brush with death in a carriage accident. From 10.30 pm to 12.30 am, he had an encounter with God that was to radically change his life. Here is how he described it:

FIRE.
GOD of Abraham, GOD of Isaac, GOD of Jacob
not of the philosophers and of the learned.
Certitude. Certitude. Feeling. Joy. Peace.
GOD of Jesus Christ.
My God and your God.
Your GOD will be my God.
Forgetfulness of the world and of everything, except GOD.
He is only found by the ways taught in the Gospel.

Grandeur of the human soul.

Righteous Father, the world has not known you, but I have known
 you.

Joy, joy, joy, tears of joy.

I have departed from him:

They have forsaken me, the fount of living water.

My God, will you leave me?

Let me not be separated from him forever.

This is eternal life, that they know you, the one true God, and the
 one that you sent, Jesus Christ.

Jesus Christ.

Jesus Christ.

I left him; I fled him, renounced, crucified.

Let me never be separated from him.

He is only kept securely by the ways taught in the Gospel:

Renunciation, total and sweet.

Complete submission to Jesus Christ and to my director.

Eternally in joy for a day's exercise on the earth.

May I not forget your words. Amen.

Pascal's experience is considered one of the most notable and genuine conversions of Christian history, partly because Pascal never shared the experience with anyone. He wrote an account of this event and sewed the paper inside his coat lining, where it was only found after his death. Even atheist Sam Harris admitted the following about Pascal's experience: 'It is true that Pascal had what was for him an astonishing contemplative experience on the night of Nov. 23, 1654—one that converted him entirely to Jesus Christ. I do not doubt the power of such experiences'[1].

As a result, Pascal abandoned his mathematical and scientific pursuits and devoted himself to God. In particular, he started preparing to write a book defending Christian belief. Pascal died before this book was written or published, but he left behind many notes (pensées) he was making in preparation for this work. These were later collected and published as

---

[1] Sam Harris, *The End of Faith: Religion, Terror, and the Future of Reason*, W.W. Norton & Company, 2004, p.257 fn.35.

Pascal's *Pensées*.

Here is our final argument for God's existence, and some would suggest, the ultimate argument for God's existence: a personal experience of God Himself. When a man or woman personally encounters God, like Paul on the road to Damascus, it may be difficult to prove this event to others, but for the individual concerned it is the most life-changing and convincing reason for God's existence possible.

Pascal did not come to know God through a clever philosophical argument or through scientific research. Instead, God met with him in a personal encounter. From then on, nothing else in life mattered any more.

Pascal's conversion teaches us that there is something more important than believing in God. Many people claim to believe in God, but this is not enough: if God exists, we must personally experience Him for ourselves, and come to know Him. How does this happen? How does someone come to know God? There are four important factors.

Seeking God

Charles Marsh was a 20th century Christian missionary to Algeria in North Africa. When civil war came to Algeria, he was forced to leave the country. As a result, he started travelling further south in Africa, to the land-locked country of Chad on the edge of the Sahara desert. Not only were there many Muslim people in Chad, there were also many animists. But even amongst the most primitive animists, Marsh found a thirst for God, and told the story in his book, *Streams in the Sahara*.

One case is unforgettable. Marsh tells about a leper named Dubarri who, despite his deformities, started to climb to the top of the tallest tree in the bush every day. The other Africans heard a voice which seemed to come out of the sky. It was Dubarri calling out to God from the tree-tops. "Oh God, can you hear me? Oh God, the living God, if you can hear me, please send someone to tell me about You. I want to know. Give me some proof that You exist. Oh God, send someone to tell me about You".

The other Africans laughed; it was a great joke. But to Dubarri it was serious. The next day he climbed the tree again and called out to God with the same words. He believed that God was somewhere up there. He wanted to know for certain, to find Him, to satisfy the deep longing he had for God. So he kept climbing the tree and calling out to God, day after day.

One day, people came to the bottom of the tree and called out to him, "Dubarri, they have come. God must exist. He has answered your prayer. Come and listen". Dubarri climbed down and hobbled painfully to where the white-skinned strangers were speaking. They told the people about the God who had created the world, and everything in it. They said that God loved the world so much that He gave His only Son. Dubarri listened, drinking in the words of the message. God had heard his prayers and answered him. Dubarri believed the message, and started telling others. He led over one hundred men and women of his village to Christ.

The story of Dubarri teaches us that we are never going to find God until we start looking for Him, calling out to Him, seeking Him with all our heart. Like an adopted child who wants to find their birth parent, we need to start searching for our True Father. This is the first step in coming to know God. If we are not serious about finding God, we have no right to think that we ever will.

Often it is the case that we do not seek for God until we are desperate, like Dubarri the leper. But whatever the reason, we must seek God. Paul preaching on Mars Hill in Athens said that God has created human beings, 'so that they would seek him and perhaps reach out for him and find him, though He is not far from any one of us'. Isaiah said, 'Seek the LORD while He may be found, call upon Him while He is near'. God said through Jeremiah, 'And you will seek Me and find Me, when you search for Me with all your heart'. The Psalm says, 'The LORD is near to all who call upon Him, To all who call upon Him in truth'[2]. This is God's promise: seek Him and you will find Him.

Surrendering to God

The act of seeking God also involves a surrender. Take the case of C. S.

---

[2] Acts 17:27 NIV, Isaiah 55:6, Jeremiah 29:13, Psalm 145:18.

Lewis. He described his abandonment of atheism in the book, *Surprised by Joy*, as follows:

'You must picture me alone in that room at Magdalen, night after night, feeling, whenever my mind lifted even for a second from my work, the steady, unrelenting approach of Him whom I so earnestly desired not to meet. That which I greatly feared had at last come upon me. In the Trinity Term of 1929 I gave in, and admitted that God was God, and knelt and prayed: perhaps, that night, the most dejected and reluctant convert in all England'[3].

The opening lines of the poem, *The Hound of Heaven*, by Francis Thompson (1857 - 1907) express this well:

I fled Him, down the nights and down the days;
I fled Him, down the arches of the years;
I fled Him, down the labyrinthine ways
Of my own mind; and in the mist of tears
I hid from Him, and under running laughter.
    Up vistaed hopes I sped;
    And shot, precipitated,
    Adown Titanic glooms of chasmed fears,
    From those strong Feet that followed, followed after.
But with unhurrying chase,
And unperturbèd pace,
Deliberate speed, majestic instancy,
They beat – and a Voice beat
More instant than the Feet –
"All things betray thee, who betrayest Me".

Even so, Lewis had not yet found God. He had only taken the first step by acknowledging His existence. His conversion to Christianity came a few years later when Lewis along with J. R. R. Tolkien and their friend

---

[3] C. S. Lewis, *Surprised By Joy*, Geoffrey Bles, 1955, p.266

Hugo Dyson went for a walk in the grounds of Magdalen College, Cambridge. They talked about the myths of various cultures, and the glimpses of the Truth in them. Then they talked till three o'clock in the morning about Christ. A few days later Lewis wrote to his old friend Arthur Greeves, saying: "I have just passed on from believing in God to definitely believing in Christ, in Christianity.... My long night talk with Dyson and Tolkien had a great deal to do with it".

What does surrendering to God mean? Lewis explains:

'What was the sort of 'hole' man had got himself into? He had tried to set up on his own, to behave as if he belonged to himself. In other words, fallen man is not simply an imperfect creature who needs improvement: he is a rebel who must lay down his arms. Laying down your arms, surrendering, saying you are sorry, realizing that you have been on the wrong track and getting ready to start life over again from the ground floor – that is the only way out of our 'hole'. This process of surrender – this movement full speed astern – is what Christians call repentance'[4].

The reason we are cut off from God, why we don't know Him, estranged and lost, alone in the universe, is because of our sin. Just as no doctor will treat a patient before diagnosing the illness, so we need to understand our problem. Our sins have to be faced up to, and dealt with, before we can know God. This is why Jesus Christ went to the cross. However, we must ourselves make a decision about our sins, choosing between them and God. The word the Bible uses for this decision is repentance.

Lee Strobel, the journalist we met in earlier chapters on Jesus and History, concluded at the end of his investigation into Christianity that Jesus really was the Son of God who died as his substitute to pay the penalty for his wrongdoing. He said this:

'And there was plenty of wrongdoing. I'll spare myself the embarrassment of going into details, but the truth is that I had been

---

[4] C. S. Lewis, *Mere Christianity*, p.56

living a profane, drunken, self-absorbed, and immoral lifestyle. In my career, I had backstabbed my colleagues to gain a personal advantage and had routinely violated legal and ethical standards in pursuit of stories. In my personal life, I was sacrificing my wife and children on the altar of success. I was a liar, a cheater, and a deceiver.

My heart had shrunk to the point where it was rock hard toward anyone else. My main motivator was personal pleasure – and ironically, the more hungrily I sought after it, the more elusive and self-destructive it became.

When I read in the Bible that these sins separated me from God, who is holy and morally pure, this resonated as being true. Certainly God, whose existence I had denied for years, seemed extremely distant, and it became obvious to me that I needed the cross of Jesus to bridge that gulf. Said the apostle Peter, "For Christ died for sins once for all, the righteous for the unrighteous, to bring you to God" (1 Peter 3:18).

All this I now believed. The evidence of history and of my own experience was too strong to ignore'[5].

Saving Grace

There is a third facet to knowing God, in addition to seeking and surrendering to God. It involves a realization that we do not come to God by trying to improve ourselves. There is only one way to return to God – just as we are: prodigal sons and daughters – dirty, broken, sinful rebels. We do not try to clean ourselves up so that God will take us in. We have nothing to offer to God that will impress Him – no good deeds to curry His favour, no church membership to earn His acceptance, no good neighbourliness to get us over the line. We can never measure up to God's standard.

Lewis put it like this in *Surprised By Joy*: 'I did not then see what is now the most shining and obvious thing; the Divine humility which will accept a convert even on such [reluctant] terms. The Prodigal Son at least walked home on his own feet. But who can duly adore that Love

---

[5] Lee Strobel, *The Case for Christ*, Zondervan, 1998, pp.267-8

which will open the high gates to a prodigal who is brought in kicking, struggling, resentful, and darting his eyes in every direction for a chance of escape?'

The Bible's term for this 'divine humility' is grace. It is sheer grace, pure kindness, that God should take any interest in such insignificant yet arrogant and rebellious creatures, let alone accept us when we turn back to Him.

God welcomes and accepts the seeking, surrendering sinner on one condition only: because of His grace in Christ. What do we mean by that? In God's amazing grace He sent His Son to die for us. Death is what sin deserves; by our sin we forfeit the right to live, not only on God's green earth, but in any relationship with Him. So in His great love, He sent His own Son to die our death. We come to God via the cross of Christ, putting our trust in it alone. Only in Christ is there forgiveness and acceptance with God. This is why Jesus said, 'I am the way, the truth and life; no one comes to the Father except by Me' (John 14:6).

Here is where many people make a great mistake. Instead of coming to God and trusting in His grace, we try to placate God with good deeds or earn His acceptance by observing religious rituals, or even (ridiculously!) try to bribe Him by offering money to buy His pardon. Others depend upon community spirit or common decency. But we can never come to God with our works. The apostle Paul wrote, 'By grace you have been saved through faith, and that not of yourselves, it is the gift of God, not of works, lest anyone should boast (Eph. 2:8-9). The only payment for our rebellion and wickedness that satisfies God has already been made. By His death on the cross, Jesus has made it possible for us to be forgiven and restored to God. By His resurrection, Jesus the only Mediator between God and man makes it possible for us to come to God. If we are looking for God in any other direction than through God's grace in Jesus Christ, we are not going to find Him.

The hymn writer Augustus Toplady described how it is only in the death of Christ (the Rock of Ages split asunder) that we can find shelter:

Rock of Ages, cleft for me,
Let me hide myself in Thee;
Let the water and the blood,
From Thy riven side which flowed,
Be of sin the double cure,
Save me from its guilt and power.

Not the labor of my hands
Can fulfill Thy law's demands;
Could my zeal no respite know,
Could my tears forever flow,
All could never sin erase,
Thou must save, and save by grace.

Nothing in my hands I bring,
Simply to Thy cross I cling;
Naked, come to Thee for dress,
Helpless, look to Thee for grace:
Foul, I to the fountain fly,
Wash me, Savior, or I die.

Simple Faith

Personally coming to know God also involves simple faith. Here is how Peter Orasuk, the heroin dealer we met in a previous chapter, was converted and came to know God:

> One of the men kept coming back. I would tell him what a righteous drug addict I was and what he would say, "You know, it is a wonderful thing that God loves you and sent His Son to die for you." He told me that Christ was the Savior no matter how vile you were …But one day tears were in his eyes as he said, "Oh Peter, salvation is not only the joy of receiving Christ, it is being delivered from a real hell. Unless you get serious about this matter you are going to die in your sin and go to hell."
>
> That night I went to a party. I used as much as I could in order to

forget his words, but I could still hear and see him. I said to a man I knew, "Billy, I have to go. I can't stay here. I am going to hell." Billy said, "We are all going to hell." "But," I replied, "someone told me there was a way out, I have to find it." Billy said, "You go. I'll cover for you. But if you ever get it, let me know".

The next night I was invited to a Bible reading. No matter what portion they were reading they would say, "Isn't it wonderful that there is no limit to the mercy of God?" After the meeting a man asked me I was saved. "No," I replied, "but I really want to be saved. I don't want to go to hell".

He started reading Bible verses, but I couldn't understand how I could know my sins forgiven. Finally he said, "The Word of God tells you that the work that can take you to heaven has been perfectly done. If that is not enough, you will just have to go to hell." I thought, "I can never live knowing that I am going to hell with all the sins I will have to account for. I can't live that way and I certainly can't die that way". I started to cry and said, "I don't want to go to hell. Please help me".

"The Bible tells us that the very worst sinner is in heaven tonight because of the power of the blood of Christ," he replied. "It's too bad it isn't enough for you".

It just dawned on me that the God who told me that I was going to hell was also telling me that the worst sinner could be in heaven. At that moment I couldn't think of one reason why it wasn't enough. Not one. As low as I was, I realized that I could go to heaven because of the power that was in the blood of Christ. I accepted by faith the truth that, "the blood of Jesus Christ His Son cleanses us from all sin".

I bowed my head and prayed. "It seems so obvious and yet so simple that the Lord Jesus did it all and because of Him I can go to heaven. Lord, is that it, is that salvation?" I looked down at the Bible and saw three words, "It is finished." It seemed as if God was saying, "Peter that is it". I cried, "Oh God, it is not fair! It is not fair that I should do all the sinning and He should do all the suffering".

God saved me that night over twenty years ago. This is a faithful saying, and worthy of all acceptance, that Christ Jesus came into the world to save sinners; of whom I am chief (1 Timothy 1:15).

Salvation is simple. Most Christians do not have a dramatic story to tell. I came to Christ as a boy of nine years age. I knew I was a sinner who needed to be saved, and I knew God had sent His Son to die for me. I knew the experience of the 'hound of heaven' tracking my steps, and I wanted to surrender. My problem was that I was not sure how. I wanted to become a Christian, but I was not clear about how to do this. When an old Christian evangelist told me how to take that simple step, I embraced the opportunity. I prayed to God in simple words, acknowledging I was a sinner, telling God I believed in His Son and thanking Him for giving Him to die for me, and asking God to forgive me and save me. It was a simple bedside prayer, a surrender of childlike faith. I went to sleep at peace and woke up the next day knowing that I was saved.

It does not end with conversion, of course. This is just the beginning to a new life, knowing God and growing in that relationship. This is what the New Testament letters are about, and the best way to understand how to grow in your knowledge of God is to read them. But, briefly, we can distill their teachings down to three things.

1. We grow by reading God's Word, the Bible, through which God speaks to us.
2. We grow by prayer, by which we speak to God.
3. We grow by spending time with other Christians, enjoying the common fellowship we have with each other and with God.

It is just like any other relationship – it all comes down to communication and time spent together.

Conclusion

Here is the final argument for God, the argument from experience, when a person encounters God, coming to know Him personally. For many people, the experience is nowhere near as dramatic as Blaise Pascal's. It is a simple surrender, a cry from the heart to God, and then a quiet trust in the person of Christ and the promises of God.

If it is true that God exists because of the evidence of Creation, Design, Morality, Humanity, Jesus Christ, Providence, History, and Scripture – if any of these are true – then the final argument from Personal Experience is also true. It teaches us that God exists and may be known.

0 (atheism)   (God exists) **10**

9

Argument from Personal Experience

We have now come to the end of Part One of the book, and the combined ratings at the end of each chapter total 125 out of 160 (or 78.125%). For those who want to put a figure on it, the probability of God's existence is nearly 8 out of 10. But remember: even if only one of the sixteen arguments we have made is true, then God definitely exists. For atheism to be true, all sixteen arguments must be proven wrong. Further, if one of the arguments is true, then God really exists, and this makes the other arguments exponentially more likely to be true. In fact, it means it is highly likely that all of the arguments are true, and that God really does exist. God is as real as this book you are reading.

But this raises our next question. If God exists – if there is some spiritual reality beyond our physical world – what is it (or He) like? There are many ideas about God in our world. Which one is correct? What is the true religion? Who is the true God and what can we learn about Him? This is what Part Two of the book is all about.

PART TWO:

What You Need

to Know

about God

Chapter 17

God is Spirit

Mary Slessor was a 19th century Scottish missionary to Calabar, in modern-day Nigeria on the west coast of Africa. The native people were animists, living in fear of spirits, which they believed indwelt everything in their jungle world. They had no concept of accidents. For example, if someone was injured or died, they thought it must be a spirit's fault. The witchdoctor would be called to find out who had been invaded by an evil spirit and had caused the injury, and this person would be put to death. When twins were born, they believed that the father of one of the twins must be an evil spirit. As a result they would leave both twins out in the jungle to die (because they couldn't tell which twin's father was an evil spirit). In addition, the mother would also be banished to the bush, usually to starve to death or to be killed by wild animals. When a chief died, many other people were put to death (and eaten) in order to go with him into the spirit world as his servants. People lived under the power of the witchdoctors; to test whether someone was guilty of a crime, they would be given deadly poison to drink, or have their hands dipped in boiling oil which, of course, killed or burnt them, thus confirming (so it was thought) their guilt.

This was West African animism with its belief that everything is spirit-possessed. Mary Slessor went alone into the jungle to reach the inland tribes where previous male missionaries had been killed. She succeeded in not only bringing the Christian gospel to the people, but changing their customs. On one occasion, the son of the chief died from a falling tree, and the witchdoctor blamed the death on the people of another village. Soldiers were sent to attack the village and carried off a dozen men and women captive, who were sentenced to death. Mary Slessor challenged the chief and pleaded with him until he spared the lives of the human sacrifices. Other animist practices, like the killing of twins, were also eventually stopped. Only the Christian message was able to break through the terrible traditions of centuries of savagery.

West Africa one hundred years ago was not the only place where such practices happened. At the same time in India, millions of gods were worshipped, and in scenes similar to West Africa, wives were burnt alive on the funeral pyres of their husbands ('sati') to accompany them in the afterlife (until Christian missionaries campaigned against the practice and it was banned by the British government). Further east, Buddhists practised spiritual disciplines to try to achieve enlightenment, and prayed to enlightened souls like Buddha, believing (like Hindus) in the reincarnation of the soul in another body after death. While Chinese followers of Confucius did not believe in God, they nevertheless prayed to the spirits of their ancestors who they believed had control over the fortunes of their descendants. In northern Africa, right through the Middle East and down into Indonesia, millions of Muslims prayed five times every day to Allah and submitted to the rules of their religion in hope of entering paradise after death. In Europe and the Americas, the vast majority of people in the 1800s were Christians, even if only nominally so, and believed in life after death in either heaven or hell.

All these cultures were deeply spiritual. They believed there is more to life (and death) than just the material world. The question for us in this chapter is not whether such a spiritual realm exists. We already know the answer to that question. Because God really exists, then there is a spiritual realm beyond the physical. That is what Part One of this book was about. Atheism – with its denial of God and the spiritual realm – is wrong. But what sort of spiritual being is God? Which spiritual reality – for there are many different religions in the world – is true?

When Yuri Gagarin, the Soviet cosmonaut and first man in space, said that he hadn't seen God, C. S. Lewis responded by saying that this was like Hamlet going up into the attic of his castle and reporting that he could not find Shakespeare. Lewis's point was that God is the author of the human story – He is not a character in the play.

God is not part of the physical, created Universe at all. Another way of saying this is that God is Spirit. This is part of what Jesus meant by

His famous words in John 4:19-24: 'God is Spirit and those who worship Him must worship in spirit and in truth'.

What does it mean for God to be Spirit? By spirit, we mean that God does not have a body. He is not made of matter or energy. He does not have size or measurements. He does not take up space. God is not part of the fabric of Creation. He is different to anything in the physical universe.

This is one of the hardest things for us to understand about God. As we will see, even many of the world's religions struggle with the concept that God is a spirit. What does it mean for God to be Spirit? For God to be Spirit means three things: He is immaterial, omnipresent and invisible.

Immaterial

God is immaterial – He is not made of matter. God is not part of Creation at all. He is the Creator of all things, the One who is High over all, the Transcendent Lord. He is 'the High and Lofty One who inhabits eternity, whose name is holy', yet 'He dwells in the high and holy place, with him who is of a contrite and humble spirit' (Isaiah 57:15).

Mormons deny that God is immaterial. They teach that God has a body. God the Father is not a Spirit, but has a body of flesh and today lives on a planet orbiting the star Kolob (wherever that is). To Mormons, God is an ascended, exalted human being who once lived on earth. In fact, they teach that all people have the potential to become gods – just like Satan said to Eve in the garden. Joseph Smith, the founder of the Mormons, wrote, 'The Father has a body of flesh and bones as tangible as man's'[1].

To prove that God has a body, Mormons point to Bible verses which speak of God's eyes or hands:

- 'The eyes of the LORD are toward the righteous, and His ears are open to their cry. The face of the LORD is against evildoers, to cut off the memory of them from the earth' (Psalm 34:15-16)
- 'I have stretched out My hands all day long to a rebellious people'

---

[1] Joseph Smith, *Doctrine and Covenants*, 130:22

(Isaiah 65:2)

- 'For the eyes of the LORD run to and fro throughout the whole earth, to show Himself strong on behalf of those whose heart is loyal to Him' (2 Chronicles 16:9).

However, these verses do not prove that God has a body, any more than verses which speak of God covering us with his wings and feathers (Psalm 91:4) prove that God is a bird, or verses calling God our rock (e.g. 2 Samuel 22:32) mean that He is made of minerals, or verses calling God a sun and shield (e.g. Psalm 84:11) mean that God is a blazing ball of gas. These are all word-pictures that the Bible uses to help us understand God's characteristics. God cares and protects like a bird covers it chicks with its feathers. God is an unchanging, upright, strong place of safety – just like a rocky fortress. God is the source of all life, light and love, just like the sun, and He is our protective shield. But these are only poetic metaphors, not statements about what God actually is. When we ask what God actually is, the answer is, as Jesus taught, that 'God is Spirit', and as such, He is immaterial.

Omnipresent

Being spirit also means God is omnipresent, that is, everywhere. Psalm 139:7-10 expresses this most beautifully:

'Where can I go from Your Spirit?
Or where can I flee from Your presence?
If I ascend into heaven, You are there;
If I make my bed in hell, behold, You are there.
If I take the wings of the morning,
And dwell in the uttermost parts of the sea,
Even there Your hand shall lead me,
And Your right hand shall hold me'.

God is everywhere. We could not escape from Him were we to try, nor will God forsake us no matter how far we travel. Because God is a spirit, He is not located in a particular place nor is His presence confined to a particular material object. Wherever we are, we can call out to God. The apostle Paul, preaching on Mars Hill in Athens to the idol-worshippers there, said:

> 'He has made from one blood every nation of men to dwell on all the face of the earth … so that they should seek the Lord, in the hope that they might reach out to Him and find Him, though He is not far from each one of us; for in Him we live and move and have our being (Acts 17:26-28)

This is again where some religions make mistakes. Followers of 'New Age' religious ideas believe that everything is God – the sun, the sand, the sky, the sea, the rivers, the trees. This is pantheism: the belief that everything is God. While it is true that God is everywhere, it is not true to say that everything is God. God is separate and distinct from His material creation.

Animists believe that the world is full of spirits – in the rocks, the trees, the rivers and everything else. Everything is divine. A. W. Tozer tells of Hindu worshippers tapping on trees and stones and whispering, "Are you there?" to the gods they hoped resided inside[2]. However, while God is everywhere, He is not limited to any one place.

Some religions make the mistake of thinking that God dwells in a special temple or sacred site. Judaism at various stages fell into the trap of placing too much emphasis upon their temple at Jerusalem. This led to an over-emphasis upon external religion, at the expense of the spiritual essence of true worship. Even King Solomon at the dedication of this temple acknowledged that the temple he had built was not really God's house:

> 'But will God indeed dwell with me on the earth? Behold, heaven and the heaven of heavens cannot contain You. How much less this temple which I have built' (2 Chronicles 6:18).

---

[2] A. W. Tozer, *The Knowledge of the Holy*, OM, 1987, p.102

God is both transcendent, the sovereign Lord far above all things, yet also immanent, pervading the universe, 'a very present help in trouble' (Psalm 46:1). He is a 'God near at hand' (Jeremiah 23:23), 'near to all who call upon Him' (Psalm 145:18).

Invisible

Because God is a Spirit, He is also invisible. Paul could write, 'unto the King, eternal, immortal, invisible' (1 Tim. 1:17). However, amazingly, Christ is the 'image of the invisible God' (Col. 1:15). Christ is God made visible. John 1:18 says that 'no one has seen God at any time, the only begotten Son who is in the bosom of the Father, He has declared Him'.

Augustus Strong the theologian tells the story of how the French scientist Laplace looked through his telescope at the starry universe, but said that he could not find God. Another astronomer, Dr. Sawyer, replied that he might as well as have swept his kitchen with a broom and said that he could not find God there.

Some people find it hard to believe in a God they cannot see. However, there are plenty of invisible things we believe in: electricity, radio waves, gravity, love, thoughts, democracy. How do we know they exist? We see their effects. Similarly, God's effects are clearly seen by the world He created. 'From the creation of the world His invisible attributes are clearly seen, being understood by the things that are made, even His eternal power and Godhead, so that they are without excuse' (Romans 1:20).

There was once an atheist who said, "Where is God, I want to see Him". He was taken outside and told to look at the sun. When he turned his eyes away, he was asked, "If you can't look at the sun, how could you bear the sight of the One who made it?" If God were physical or visible, He would be no different to nature, but simply part of creation, and therefore He would not be God at all.

Ken Ham was once asked, "Why doesn't your God come and physically show Himself to us?" Ham replied, "He did, and they nailed Him on a cross".

Idolatry

God being spirit means that He is immaterial, omnipresent and invisible. This leads us on to the one special mistake many people have made about God: idolatry. Because God is invisible and immaterial, He is completely different to idols, that is visible images or representations of a deity. Athens in Paul's day was 'given over to idols'. The second of the ten commandment forbids the worshipping of carved images. The Bible records people who worshipped 'the sun, moon and stars', or 'birds, beasts and creeping things', in effect, worshipping 'creation rather than the Creator'[3].

Perhaps the most beautiful passage in the Bible that contrasts God with the idols is Jeremiah 10:1-16. The prophet Jeremiah lived in a day when Israel had turned to idols. In Jeremiah 2:5, God says, 'What injustice have your fathers found in me, that they have gone far from me, have followed idols and have become idolaters?' In verse 11, we read, 'Has a nation changed its gods, which are not gods? But My people have changed their glory for what does not profit'.

When we come to Jeremiah chapter 10, we find a contrast drawn between God and the idols. In verses 3-5, the idols are made from trees cut down in the forest, decorated with silver and gold, fastened with hammers and nails so they do not topple, and they have to be carried around and cannot speak. Do not be afraid of them, Jeremiah says, for they cannot do anything, good or bad. By contrast, God is described as:

- The great God ('You are great, and Your name is great in might', v6)
- The unique God ('there is none like You', v7)
- The true God ('But the Lord is the true God', v10)
- The Living God ('He is the living God', v10)
- The eternal God ('and the everlasting King', v10)
- He is the God of wrath ('At His wrath the earth shall tremble, and the nations will not be able to endure his indignation', v10)

---

[3] Acts 17:16, Exodus 20: 4, Deuteronomy 4:19, 2 Kings 23:5, Jeremiah 8:2, Romans 1:23, 25

- He is the God of power ('He has made the earth by His power', v12)

- He is the God of wisdom ('He has established the world by His wisdom, and has stretched out the heavens at his discretion', v12)

- He upholds and cares for Creation ('when he utters His voice, there is a multitude of waters in the heavens, and He causes the vapours to ascend from the ends of the earth, He makes lightnings for the rain, He brings the wind out of His treasuries', v13)

- He is the Portion of His people – He belongs to us ('The Portion of Jacob is not like them [the idols], for He is the maker of all things', v16a) and we belong to Him ('Israel is the tribe of His inheritance', v16b).

God is the opposite of idols and visible images, of animism and pantheism, and of atheism that denies spiritual reality. God says:

'Let not the wise man glory in his wisdom, nor the mighty man in his might, or the rich man in his riches, but let him who glories glory in this, that he understands and knows me, that I am the Lord, exercising lovingkindness, judgment and righteousness in the earth' (Jeremiah 9:23-24).

Sadhu Sundar Singh

Sadhu Sundar Singh was born into a noble Sikh family, and as a boy was very religious. Taught at his mother's knee, his religion consisted in pleasing God by obeying the laws their fathers had taught them and seeking spiritual peace. This was considered to be the greatest treasure in the world, far more desirable than money, power, worldly success, or earthly enjoyment. His father sent him to be educated at a Christian missionary school, but Sundar Singh hated Christianity and argued against it in class. He even burnt a Bible, and threw stones at Christian preachers. But when he was fourteen years old his mother died, and all his joy died with her.

Sundar Singh decided that if the unknown God he was seeking for did not reveal Himself and show the true way of peace, he would commit suicide by throwing himself under the train that passed the family estate every day at 5am. So he woke at 3am to pray to God to reveal Himself. Nothing happened, but as it got closer to 5am, he kept praying. Then in the darkness, Singh said he saw a light, a vision – not of Buddha or of Krishna or some other Hindu god, but of Christ whom he hated. Like the apostle Paul, Singh went from being an enemy of Christ, and gave up everything to preach the gospel at age fifteen. Rejected by his father, he walked around the country with only his robe and sandals.

We should not expect Christ to appear visibly to us, much less threaten to commit suicide if He does not do so. But we must seek for Him. 'Those who come to God must believe that He exists and that He is a rewarder of those who diligently seek for Him' (Hebrews 11:6).

If God is real and is a Spirit, then spiritual things are more important than material things. Paul writes, 'we do not look at the things which are seen, but at the things which are not seen, for the things which are seen are temporary, but the things which are not seen are eternal' (2 Corinthians 4:18). We should live for the things of the Spirit rather than physical things like money, clothing, houses. It is so easy for us today to be consumed by material possessions and status symbols, by distractions like politics and sport. But the result is spiritual poverty and emptiness. Paul says, 'For those who live according to the flesh set their minds on the things of the flesh, but those who live according to the Spirit, the things of the Spirit' (Romans 8:5). The next verse says, 'For to be carnally minded is death, but to be spiritually minded is life and peace'.

When Sadhu Sundar Singh visited England after the first World War, he was shocked at the difference with India. In India, there was an awareness of spiritual things, a seeking after what would bring peace to the soul. But in England there was a preoccupation with material satisfaction. He was asked at a dinner table what he thought of Christianity in England, and he didn't want to be rude, but he said that too little was made of religion: more time should be given to prayer and meditation on the Word of God.

Worshipping God in Spirit and in Truth

If God is Spirit, then we ought 'to worship God in spirit and in truth' (John 4:24). What does this mean? When Christ said these words, He was speaking to the Samaritan woman. What he meant was this: the Samaritan religion was not the truth – Christ said, 'you worship you know not what' whereas 'salvation is of the Jews'. But Jewish religion had a problem too. It was an outward, external religion, with its grand temple in Jerusalem, beautiful music, priestly garments, smells and bells, sacrifices and offerings.

But all these external religious expressions are not what God desires; He insists on inward religion – those who worship Him must worship in Spirit and in truth. We can go through the outward motions of religion and impress or fool others, but not God. He wants to see true and sincere religion of the heart. Micah the prophet wrote: 'With what shall I come before the LORD, and bow myself before the High God? Shall I come before Him with burnt offerings, with calves a year old? Will the LORD be pleased with thousands of rams, ten thousand rivers of oil? Shall I give my firstborn for my transgression, the fruit of my body for the sin of my soul? He has shown you, O man, what is good; and what does the LORD require of you but to do justly, to love mercy, and to walk humbly with your God' (Micah 6:6-8).

We should not only worship God in spirit, but we also need to realise that we can only really serve God in Spirit. Paul said, 'the weapons of our warfare are not carnal (fleshly, physical), but mighty in God for pulling down strongholds' (2 Corinthians 10:4). The Christian's weapons are prayer and the Word of God. That is how God works, and nothing else will do the job – not great buildings, or talented musicians. Paul elsewhere tells us that the gospel message is foolishness to the unbeliever, and it is only through the work of the Holy Spirit that people receive spiritual truth (1 Cor. 1:18-31). It is not by the great oratory or cleverness of the preacher, or through any other external or outward means that people are brought to know God. It is instead the work of God's Spirit in the heart.

Chapter 18

God is Personal

Wayne Baird was born and grew up in New Zealand. When he was a boy his parents divorced and he went to live with his father. But in his teens he started drinking and getting in trouble with the police. Although he was a bright student, he was worried about bringing more shame and trouble on his father. So at eighteen he decided that instead of going to university, he would take several years out to visit Australia and save money for tuition.

Rather than turning his life around, however, he found himself in Kings Cross, at the heart of Sydney's red-light district. He worked by night as a bouncer at a nightclub and as a personal trainer by day. During twelve years in Sydney, Wayne became an alcoholic, got addicted to cocaine, and was involved in crime, not only associating with many criminals but profiting from the proceeds.

After twelve years of this lifestyle, Wayne moved out of the big city to the north coast of New South Wales. He started doing triathlons, and for training would often ride 100km on his bike in a day. One evening as he was returning home he was dazzled by a car's headlights. He was thrown over the handlebars and landed in a ditch on the side of the road. He had broken his neck, and was unable to move. He lay in the water, listening to the sound of mosquitos buzzing around him. The next morning, he woke up in his own bed. To this day, he does not know how he got home.

He went to the chiropractors after five days of pain, and was referred to the doctors. After x-rays, they told him he had broken one of the vertebrae in his neck. He was put in a neck brace to prevent movement, in the hope that the bones would fuse together again. A month or so later, he went back to the doctors and after further x-rays, he was told that the bones had not fused. Without the bones joining up, they would not heal. There was nothing more the doctors could do, besides keeping the brace on for another six weeks.

Wayne was devastated. He was now in his early thirties, with no university qualifications, having wasted the best years of his life. He also had a broken neck that the doctors were unable to do much for besides waiting. His life seemed over. He started thinking of committing suicide. In his distress, he called out to God: "I know You are there, God, I need help".

Because he was now unable to ride his bike, he had to walk everywhere. The next day, as he was hitch-hiking home, a car pulled over and offered him a lift. The driver was a Christian pastor, and they got talking. As he was getting out of the car, the pastor offered to pray for Wayne. It was a short, simple prayer for God's healing.

Later the same day, Wayne wanted to have a shave and took off his neck brace. As he was shaving, he noticed that he was able to move his neck without any pain or problems. He was so excited that he phoned up the pastor and told him what had happened: his neck was better! The pastor was as surprised as Wayne, who asked where the pastor's church was so he could come that Sunday.

That evening he went to the pub to celebrate, and started telling everyone how God had healed his broken neck. He even rebuked some Christians for being at the pub drinking! From that Sunday onwards, Wayne started going to church. After a few weeks, the pastor invited any people who wanted the Lord to come into their lives to walk out the front. Wayne went out and prayed a prayer, not really knowing what he was saying or doing. Afterwards, to his surprise, all the other people gathered round him congratulating him on becoming a Christian. Wayne wasn't really sure what all the fuss was about.

A few days later, he was down at the beach by himself, and he broke down in tears. For a few hours, Wayne cried out all of the bitterness and pain from his life. In its place came a peace from God.

Not long after, God brought Wayne's future wife into his life. Later, he studied theology, then ancient history at university, and became involved in leading a church himself for twelve years. He now leads the men's ministry at his local church and lives with his large family on a small farm, where they homeschool their children, look after their animals and grow vegetables.

God versus Pantheism

Is there a God who hears and answers prayer, a God who dramatically intervenes in and changes the lives of people like Wayne? Is there a God who is interested in us, and interacts with us? Is it true, as the Bible teaches, that we will find God if we sincerely seek for Him with all our hearts?

Many people believe there is a God, but not a personal God who is interested in our lives. Many people believe in a form of religion called Pantheism that accepts that there is a spiritual reality underlying the universe. Pantheism says that everything in the universe is god. All trees and plants, mountains and rocks, oceans and rivers are part of god. This 'god' is unconscious and aloof, without emotions or desires, as lifeless as an inert gas, as cold and uncaring as a corpse. 'It' might as well be a block of granite for all 'It' knows or cares; after all, every block of granite is god. Consider four modern examples of belief in impersonal, pantheistic gods.

In the *Star Wars* movies, the characters say, 'May the Force be with you'. 'The Force' is a mysterious power that Jedi knights use to enhance their own abilities. However, we never meet 'the Force', for the simple reason that 'the Force' is not a person. 'The Force' is more like gravity, electricity or the wind than anything personal. In the 2001 census in some countries, many people stated their religion as Jedi; it was the fourth largest religion in England and Wales[1]. The Jedi Church's website says, 'The Jedi Church believes that there is one all powerful force that binds all things in the universe together. The Jedi religion is something innate inside everyone of us, the Jedi Church believes that our sense of morality is innate'[2]. In other words, there is no 'god' out there; this 'god' is within everyone and everything.

For a second example of pantheism, consider Mahatma Gandhi. He said, "My religion is based on truth and non-violence. Truth is my God.

---

[1] https://en.wikipedia.org/wiki/Jedi_census_phenomenon

[2] www.jedichurch.org

Non-violence is the means of realising Him'. It is clear that Gandhi believed in some sort of spirituality, but not in a personal God. When he says that 'truth is my God', he is appealing to the abstract qualities of truth, honesty, fairness and equality, and an ethic of peace and non-violence. Gandhi believed in moral and spiritual values, but these values were disembodied and impersonal.

A third example comes from Thomas Nagel, the prominent atheist philosopher. In his 2012 book, *Mind and Cosmos: why the Materialist Neo-Darwinian Conception of Nature is Almost Certainly False*, he argued from the starting-point of human consciousness (i.e. self-awareness), rationality and morality. He insisted that atheistic materialism cannot explain these most precious human possessions (they are mere illusions to materialists). But Nagel also rejects God as an explanation for the universe and humanity, insisting that there must be a third way between atheistic Darwinism and theism. His answer is that the universe has some sort of in-built teleology, which means a plan or purpose. The universe saw us coming, so to speak. More than that, rather like an acorn programmed to produce a tree, so the universe came into being with the goal of spawning thinking, moral, conscious beings. In this scheme, the universe itself is a God-substitute, possessing all His attributes.

For a fourth example, hear Albert Einstein. While he was not an atheist, Einstein rejected the idea of a personal God[3], saying it was a naïve and childish idea. His worship of God amounted to little more than an admiration of the intelligence behind the natural laws that governed the universe. He said, 'Scientific research can reduce superstition by encouraging people to think and view things in terms of cause and effect. Certain it is that a conviction, akin to religious feeling, of the rationality and intelligibility of the world lies behind all scientific work of a higher order. [...] This firm belief, a belief bound up with a deep feeling, in a superior mind that reveals itself in the world of experience, represents my conception of God. In common parlance this may be described as "pantheistic"[4].

---

[3] Einstein said, 'I do not believe in a personal God' (Helen Dukas, *Albert Einstein the Human Side*, Princeton University Press, 1981, p.43)

[4] Albert Einstein, *Ideas And Opinions*, Three Rivers Press, 2010, p.262

The problem with all these impersonal gods quickly becomes apparent under cross-examination. Think about Einstein's idea. How is it possible to have an intelligent universe without an intelligent mind to design it? Stars and space-dust have no minds or brains, so what generated the intelligence that Einstein reverences? William Hoste writes, 'To assert that Infinite Intelligence must be unconscious is to deny that Intelligence, for, if it cannot know itself it cannot be infinite'[5].

Einstein's denial of the personality of God is matched by his determinism (humans have no free will, morality is an illusion, we are just cogs in a cosmic machine). He said, 'Everything is determined, the beginning as well as the end, by forces over which we have no control. It is determined for the insect, as well as for the star. Human beings, vegetables, or cosmic dust, we all dance to a mysterious tune, intoned in the distance by an invisible piper'[6]. Thus, Einstein not only denied the personality of God, he also denied human personality too. This is a miserable and mistaken view of existence: our personalities are real.

How is it possible to worship a system of ethics like Gandhi, without believing in the highest ethic of love? And if we believe in love, how do we get love from the great "It" of pantheism, that emotionless, expressionless, and indifferent vacuity? Love cannot be impersonal. We cannot find love in a cubic metre of wind. Nor do impersonal objects like atoms, stars, or rocks love or treat others kindly. So where do love, fairness and morality come from? Pantheists, particularly of the Indian variety, hold that both good and evil (as much as everything else) are part of God. This accounts for their resigned and complacent attitude to the terrible poverty of the lowest classes in their country, who they believe are suffering for sins of a past life. People with disabilities or diseases are likewise treated without compassion, love or fairness. The denial of the personality of God leads again directly to the denial of the value of human beings, the denial of human decency, and to the denial of love itself.

Thomas Nagel's view is also absurd. How did the Great Nothing before the universe existed plan ahead and design human beings? Once

---

[5] William Hoste, *Studies in Bible Doctrine*, Pickering and Inglis, 1932, p.12
[6] Ronald W. Clark, *Einstein: The Life and Times*, Thomas Y. Crowell, 1971, p.422

the universe came into existence, how did illiterate atoms in empty space peer into the future and program the shape of things to come? Can the wind decide where it will go, or dirt choose what it will grow? Atoms have no brains to think ahead, nor do carbon molecules have degrees in design and technology. Even more ridiculous is the idea that the universe conjured itself into being, creating itself from nothing, and in a form that would unfold in a certain way. How can a mindless universe decide anything? There cannot be a planned universe without an intentional, thinking, Mind possessing the creative power to bring it all into being.

Lastly, how is it possible to believe in a 'Force', as in *Star Wars*, which is the 'collective consciousness' but does not have consciousness itself, so that it is aware of itself, i.e. personal? How can the 'Force' have a light and dark side – good and evil – if the 'Force' is not itself moral in nature? Or if the 'Force' is moral, how does morality arise from uncaring matter and energy? Where does a universal and supernatural Force itself come from, and what force brought the Force into existence? Of course, some will remind us that the Force is a fictional construct that few people really believe in, but even so, it helpfully serves the purpose of helping us face up to this reality: it is virtually impossible to even *imagine* fictional ways in which there can be an impersonal god-substitute that is able to create a universe and impart to it life, morality, intelligence, design and consciousness.

C. S. Lewis wrote, 'A good many people nowadays say, 'I believe in a God, but not in a personal God'. They feel that the mysterious something which is behind all other things must be more than a person. Now the Christians quite agree. But the Christians are the only people who offer any idea of what a being that is beyond personality could be like. All the other people, though they say that God is beyond personality, really think of Him as something impersonal: that is, as something less than personal. If you are looking for something super-personal, something more than a person, then it is not a question of choosing between the Christian idea and the other ideas. The Christian idea is the only one on the market'[7].

---

[7] Lewis, *Mere Christianity*, p.160

Of course, when we say that God is personal, we do not mean that God is a human being. We do not mean that God is some sort of 'super-sized chap' (Terry Eagleton). There is also some truth in Pantheism, as Hoste writes:

> 'The idea of the unity of all being, of the connection of our life with all life is true. The error is in stopping short there, and not recognizing Him Who is the Author of that unity, as the Cause and Object of all. Pantheism recognizes too that the Universe in its origin and continuance cannot be severed from God, seeing He must be omnipresent and everywhere active'[8].

All these ideas of impersonal gods with characteristics of intelligence, morality and consciousness (each characteristic essentially personal) are self-contradictions. Each of Gandhi, Einstein, Nagel and *Star Wars* fans resemble the blind men in the parable who reach out and touch the different parts of an elephant, one saying the leg is a tree, another the tail is a rope, another the side is a wall, another the tusk is a spear. Each of Einstein, Ghandi, Nagel and *Star Wars* describe one aspect of the True and Living God who is not an impersonal wall, rope, spear or tree, but a conscious, intelligent, living, moral, powerful Being.

The German writer Goethe mocked the sophisticated pantheists of his day and their impersonal God with this line: 'The professor is a person, but God is not'. Those who deny God's personality are, in effect, arguing that we are greater than God which, it hardly needs stating, is obviously not true. How can God, the Supreme Being, be inferior to human beings who possess personality? We derive our personality from Him, for we were made in His image (Genesis 1:26-27). How can all the highest personal qualities we possess as human beings like intelligence, love, and consciousness spring from impersonal forces? Something cannot impart what it does not itself possess. The only real alternative to the Christian view of a personal God is to deny the reality of personal qualities, not only in God, but in humanity as well. This is the hardcore

---

[8] Hoste, *Studies*, pp.12-13

(i.e. consistent) atheist response: morality, free-will, design, and consciousness are illusions. No wonder then that the great atheist leaders of the twentieth century murdered so many million people, seeing they devalued them to the status of non-persons.

The theologian Erich Sauer writes, 'if one asserts that God and the world are the same, finally this comes to the same as saying, "There is only one world, but there is no God"'[9]. He quotes Schopenhauer, 'The statement of pantheism, "God and the world are one", is only a polite way of sending the Lord God about His business'. In the end, then, pantheism is just a polite but confused form of atheism.

God is Personal

God is not a force, nor a philosophical idea, nor a law of Nature. He is the Creator of the laws of nature, the Mind behind the Universe's brilliant design and beauty, the Prime Mover from whom all forces flow. God is not a cloud of gas, or 'the soul of the Universe'. Sir Isaac Newton denied pantheism, writing, 'This most beautiful system of the sun, planets, and comets, could only proceed from the counsel and dominion of an intelligent Being. [...] This Being governs all things, not as the soul of the world, but as Lord over all; and on account of his dominion he is wont to be called "Lord God" *pantokrator*[10], or "Universal Ruler". [...] The Supreme God is a Being eternal, infinite, [and] absolutely perfect'[11].

God is not like electricity – lots of power but no personality. God is not simply 'the Ground of Being', a phrase once popular among a breed of theologian thankfully now dying out. God is not 'an Infinite and Eternal Energy, from which all things proceed' (Herbert Spencer, the 19th Century evolutionary philosopher). God is not an 'It' at all – He is a Person. Proof that God is personal is seen in three ways:

1. **In Creation**. Because the universe had a beginning, and seeing it did

---

[9] Erich Sauer, *The King of the Earth: The High Calling of Man according to the Bible and Science*, Ronald N. Haynes, 1981, p.157

[10] *Pantokrator* is the Greek word for 'all-mighty'

[11] Isaac Newton, *Principia*, Book III; cited in *Newton's Philosophy of Nature: Selections from his writings*, ed. H.S. Thayer, Hafner Library of Classics, 1953, p.42.

not create itself, but rather God called it into being, then God must possess will and intentionality. Unless it was an accident on God's part (which it was not), then God must have chosen to create the universe. For His power and intelligence to be deployed in creation, He had to will the Universe into being. Revelation. 4:11 teaches this: 'You are worthy, O Lord, to receive glory and honor and power; for You created all things, and by Your *will* they exist and were created' (emphasis added). It was God's will and decision to create. Such free will is only possible if God is personal.

2. **In Communication**. We see that God is personal by His communication with His creature. Many sceptics refuse to admit the possibility that God has communicated with mankind, however as William Hoste puts it, 'those who deny that God can communicate are denying to the Almighty what even man possesses: the power of self-communication'[12]. If there is a God, He must be greater than man, and therefore capable of communication. Similarly, the fact that God is able to hear and answer prayer is a logical necessity, for as the Psalmist put it centuries ago, 'He who planted the ear, shall He not hear? He who formed the eye, shall He not see? (Psalm 94:9). If there is a God, He must be able to see and hear, seeing He was the One who invented the abilities in His creatures. Relationships with others are what make personality so precious, and this necessitates the ability to communicate. The Bible says that God has clearly communicated in a number of different ways to mankind. He has communicated wordlessly in creation, which proclaims His eternal power, wisdom, and glory. He communicates with us in conscience's still, small voice, and also through human prophets, protesting humanity's crimes and calling for us to turn back to His ways. He has communicated with us through Scripture, putting His message in writing, the clearest form of communication, leaving on record His truth as a testament to His love for us.

---

[12] Hoste, *Bible Doctrine*, p.16

3. **In Christ**. Above all, we see that God is personal in Jesus Christ. In Christ, we see the very face of God, as the apostle Paul puts it: we see 'the glory of God in the face of Jesus Christ' (2 Corinthians 4:6). The invisible God has been revealed in the flesh, and we see what He is really like, up close and personal. The apostle John wrote: 'that which was from the beginning, which we have heard, which we have seen with our eyes, which we have looked upon, and our hands have handled, concerning the Word of life – the life was manifested, and we have seen, and bear witness, and declare to you that eternal life which was with the Father and was manifested to us' (1 John 1:1-2). Christ taught us to call God 'our Father in heaven'. What more tender and personal description could possibly help us understand God? We see that God's personality is loving by Jesus' acts of kindness and justice for those oppressed; as Peter said, 'He went about doing good' (Acts 10:38). Jesus Christ shows us that God is real; more than that, Jesus has shown that God is personal.

Knowing God

Just as it is possible to know *about* some people (for example, the Queen of England) without truly knowing them, in the sense of knowing them as a close personal acquaintance, so too it is possible to believe in God without having any personal knowledge of God. This is hardly any different to a pantheist or a deist, who believes in a 'God away out there, who doesn't care', a God who exists, but is irrelevant to our lives.

In one sense, whether you believe in God or not does not matter. If, after reading this book, you believe in the idea of God, this intellectual stance on its own will probably not make much difference to your life. But if you come to know God personally, it will make all the difference in the world. We must encounter God and meet Him.

Furthermore, coming to know God is a personal thing. It is between you and God. Your parents might know God, but this does not mean, nor will it ensure, that you know God. You might attend church, but this is not the same thing as knowing God, nor can your church substitute for personally knowing God yourself. You have to take the step of coming to know God on your own, for yourself.

God is Personal

The fact that God is personal makes all the difference in the world. It means that we can encounter Him ourselves, personally. Whereas no one in the *Star Wars* movies ever met 'The Force', we can know God personally, the Almighty Creator of the heavens and the earth. We can be friends with God, like Abraham and many other people down through history.

This might sound ridiculous to some. After all, why would God take any personal interest in an insignificant speck of dust like me? The answer is this: as your Creator, He cares for you as much as any earthly father cares for his own daughter. This is why Jesus constantly referred to God as 'our Father in heaven'. Moreover, because God knows all things, you are not a statistic to Him. God knows you better than anybody else on earth knows you. It is true that we are insignificant, but it is false to suggest that God is incapable of knowing who we are, uninterested in our lives, or unable to reach across the distance to us. God calls us to seek Him with all our hearts, and promises that if we do so, we will find Him.

Chapter 19

The Trinity

A lthough it was not widely known at the time, Sir Isaac Newton did not believe in the Christian doctrine of the Trinity, even though ironically, he was a member of Trinity College, Cambridge. He argued that the Trinity was not found in Scripture, nor was it found in the writings of Church 'Fathers' before Athanasius (AD 293 – 378) in the 4th century.

Newton also held that the doctrine was illogical, writing about the Athanasian Creed: 'let them make good sense of it who are able; for my part, I can make none'[1]. (The Athanasian Creed states that the Father, Son and Spirit are all uncreated, immeasurable, eternal, almighty; all are God, co-eternal and co-equal, yet there is One God, not three Gods, so that Christians worship Unity in Trinity and Trinity in Unity).

Newton's preference for simplicity in scientific explanations may also have influenced him against the doctrine of the Trinity. Newton believed that the true, early, Christian position was that Christ was 'god', but in an inferior sense, a view which is open to charges of polytheism (i.e., there are many gods).

Richard Dawkins once wrote on his Twitter account, 'God is simultaneously himself and his son (and a ghost). Makes sense'. Others have similarly ridiculed the Christian belief in the Trinity. Thomas Jefferson wrote 'no man ever had a distinct idea of the trinity. It is mere abracadabra of the mountebanks calling themselves the priests of Jesus'[2]. In another letter, Jefferson wrote about the Trinity as 'The hocus-pocus phantasm of a God like another Cerberus, with one body and three heads'[3].

---

[1] Isaac Newton, *An Historical Account of Two Notable Corruptions of the Scriptures*, 1690
[2] Thomas Jefferson, Letter to Francis Adrian Van der Kemp on 30 July 1810
[3] Jefferson, Letter to James Smith, December 8 1822; Cerberus was the three-headed

Ravi Zacharias wrote about the Trinity: 'it is either the most farcical doctrine invented by the early disciples or the most profound and thrilling mystery revealed by the Creator Himself'[4].

The doctrine of the Trinity means that God is one and yet He is three. It is not surprising that many irreligious people find the idea laughable, while many religious people (particularly Jews and Muslims) consider it blasphemous. It seems either incomprehensible mumbo-jumbo or new-fangled religious chicanery.

Professor John Lennox tells about how he was speaking to an audience of scientists about God and afterwards, a scientist asked how it was possible for an intelligent Christian like Lennox to believe in the obvious absurdity of the Trinity. Lennox replied by asking him if he, as a physicist, could explain what energy was. The scientist replied that he could measure energy and use it. Lennox pointed out that this was avoiding the question, and pressed him on what energy was. The scientist had to admit that nobody knows what energy *actually* is. Lennox asked him what consciousness is, and again the scientist was unable to answer.

"Now then", Lennox asked, "if there are mysterious things in nature that we do not understand (like energy, or light, or gravity, or consciousness), why should we be surprised that there are things about God – the Creator of all these things – that are also mysterious?"

Lennox asked the scientist if he believed in energy and consciousness. The scientist replied that of course he believed in energy and consciousness, and Lennox asked him why he believed in these things. Not being sure how to answer, Lennox helped him out: because of the explanatory power of these concepts. In a similar way, Lennox replied, Christians believe in the Trinity because it is the best explanation that makes sense of the facts concerning God and Jesus Christ[5].

How strange it would be, indeed, if our three-pound brains could comprehend God. If we could understand God, God would not be God, and He would hardly be worth knowing.

---

hound that guarded Hades in Greek mythology
[4] Ravi Zacharias, *Can Man Live Without God*, Thomas Nelson, 1994, p.149
[5] See *'Who Created God?'*, www.youtube.com/watch?v=UlknACeeSOg

Athanasius, Arius and Sabellius

Athanasius was born some time before AD 300 in Alexandria, Egypt, where he was appointed a deacon and became secretary to the bishop. In this capacity he attended the Council of Nicaea in AD 325, a gathering of bishops from all over the Christian world called by the Emperor Constantine. The Council of Nicaea met to decide upon the question of who exactly Jesus Christ was. This question had been prompted by the teaching of an elder from Alexandria called Arius, who said that only the Father was God. Christ, said Arius, was the first and greatest of God's creatures, an inferior 'god'.

The Council of Nicaea came down decisively against Arius' teachings. Of the approximately three hundred delegates, only two disagreed with the ruling. The Council condemned Arius' teachings as heretical, and affirmed that Christ was not created by the Father, but was of 'one being with the Father'. The Greek word for 'of the same being or substance' is *homoousios*. Arius, by contrast, taught that Christ was 'of similar being' (*homoiousios*). Some people made fun of this ruling, joking about Christians fighting over an iota (the smallest Greek letter). However, there was a great deal at stake.

Athanasius probably did not play too much part in the debates at the Council, being only the secretary to the bishop. Soon after this council, however, Athanasius was elected the bishop of Alexandria in AD 328, and spent the rest of his life battling against the teachings of Arius. Despite the ruling of the Council of Nicaea, the followers of Arius gained political power in many places, and Athanasius was exiled five times from Alexandria. Four of these exiles were for his stance on the full equality and deity of Christ. Athanasius never buckled, although at times it seemed as if the whole world was against him ('Athanasius contra mundum'). In his greatest writing, *The Incarnation of the Word*, Athanasius argued that if Christ was not fully God there could be no salvation, for no one other than God become man could fully bear the sin of the world and redeem us.

It is important to understand that the controversy over the person of Christ in Athanasius' day was not the first time the question had arisen. One hundred years before Athanasius, Sabellius (who lived around AD

215), taught that there was only one God, but that He revealed Himself in three different ways – as the Father in creation, as the Son in redemption, and as the Spirit in the work of new birth and sanctification. This teaching was called 'modalism' – God takes different modes at different times in revealing Himself to us.

Sabellius obviously believed in the full Godhood of Jesus Christ. Jesus' deity was not a new idea invented at the Council of Nicaea. The fact that Jesus is fully God is found numerous times in the New Testament and this truth was taken for granted by people like Sabellius. In fact, it is reported that Sabellius had even used the term '*homoousios*' – of the same substance – to describe the Father and the Son. The obvious problem with Sabellius' thinking was that we have numerous places in the New Testament where the Father, Son and Holy Spirit are spoken of as separate persons. For example, at Jesus' baptism, the Father spoke from heaven as the Spirit descended as a dove upon the Son. Sabellius was condemned as a heretic in AD 220 and Tertullian (AD 155-240), who first coined the term 'trinity', wrote against his teachings.

It was against this background that both Arius and Athanasius wrestled with the question of who Jesus is. If Jesus is fully God – but not the same person as the Father – how can they both be God? Arius denied the Son's full deity to maintain the idea that there is one God, Sabellius denied the Son's distinct personality to maintain the unity of God, while Athanasius asserted three truths: Jesus is God, God is One, and there are three distinct persons in the Godhead. This is what the Trinity means.

Jesus is the Key to Understanding God

Why do Christians believe in the Trinity? For one simple reason: Jesus. Christians did not come up with the concept of the Trinity because they were fond of philosophical speculation or religious mumbo-jumbo. The reason that the earliest Christians believed in the doctrine of the Trinity (without using the word) is this: the repeated claim of Jesus Christ that He was God, and His resurrection as the proof of this claim. These two facts call for a revolution in our understanding of God. If Jesus Christ was God manifest in the flesh, we must expand our idea of God.

Recall that Jesus' disciples were monotheists of the strictest sect the world has ever known: Judaism. To worship anything in heaven or earth – sun, moon, man or beast – other than the Creator was to break the first and greatest of the Ten Commandments. For someone like doubting Thomas to fall down at the feet of the resurrected Jesus and say, "My Lord and my God" was unspeakable blasphemy to a Jew. Yet Jesus neither rebuked the words, nor diluted their force. Instead he congratulated Thomas for finally believing: "Thomas, because you have seen Me, you have believed; blessed are those who have not seen and yet have believed" (John 20:29).

Where did the early Christians get the idea of the trinity? Klaas Runia answers:

'The basic issue was: Is Jesus Christ God, is He really and fully God? If so, what does this tell us about the being of God? At a later stage the same question was asked about the Holy Spirit... The controversy about the divinity and personality of the Holy Spirit was more in the nature of a consequence. The core of the doctrine of the Trinity was and is the divinity of Christ... How then can we describe the New Testament picture of God? On the one hand God is one, truly and absolutely one. On the other hand this one God exists as Father, Son, and Holy Spirit. This threefoldness is present throughout the whole New Testament not as a formal statement but as a pattern to be seen everywhere'[6].

The Doctrine of the Trinity

Dorothy Sayers wrote, "'Why do you want a letter from me? Why don't you take the trouble to find out for yourselves what Christianity is? You take time to learn technical terms about electricity. Why don't you do as much for theology? ... 'Why do you balk at the doctrine of the Trinity – God the three in One – yet meekly acquiesce when Einstein tells you $E=mc^2$? What makes you suppose that the expression "God ordains" is narrow and bigoted, while your own expression, "Science demands" is

---

[6] Klaas Runia, "The Trinity," *Eerdman's Handbook to Christian Belief*, ed. Robin Keeley, Eerdmans, 1982, pp.165, 169

taken as an objective statement of fact?'

'You would be ashamed to know as little about internal combustion as you know about Christian beliefs. I admit, you can practice Christianity without knowing much theology, just as you can drive a car without knowing much about internal combustion. But when something breaks down in the car, you go humbly to the man who understands the works; whereas if something goes wrong with religion, you merely throw the works away and tell the theologian he is a liar'.

'Why do you want a letter from me telling you about God? You will never bother to check on it or find out whether I'm giving you personal opinions or Christian doctrines. Don't bother. Go away and do some work and let me get on with mine."

Following Dorothy Sayers' sparky advice, we are going to do a little bit of biblical spade work. No doubt this will bore some readers but (as Sayers remarked) the sorts of people who reject the Trinity without examining the biblical case first-hand are not serious inquirers.

The truth of the Trinity rests on three facts we learn from the Bible:

1. The Father, the Son and the Spirit are all fully God
2. They are Three Distinct Persons
3. Yet God is One

If these three statements can all be shown to be true, then Christians are forced to the fact that God is a Trinity. However counterintuitive and confusing the idea may at first seem, it is agreed across virtually all Christian denominations as the correct answer.

The Father is God

It is not particularly difficult to demonstrate that the Father is God. Jesus prayed to God in the gospels, addressing Him as 'Father', spoke of God as the Creator (Mark 10:6), and of Himself as the Son of God (John 5:25, 11:4), who 'came from God' (John 8:42). In all these ways, Jesus spoke of God as someone distinct from Himself. In various verses, He is referred to as 'God the Father' (John 6:27, Galatians 1:1, Philippians

2:11, and other verses). We could add more evidence to this list, but it is unnecessary: virtually everyone accepts that Jesus spoke of His Father God.

The Son is God

The crucial point is that Jesus also Himself claimed to be God. We have already seen how Jesus said that He was I AM in John 8:58 ('Most assuredly I say to you, before Abraham was, I AM'), taking the name of God from Exodus 3:14 to himself. In John 14:8-9, Jesus told His disciples that whoever has seen Him has seen the Father: 'Have I been with you so long, and yet you have not known Me, Philip? He who has seen Me has seen the Father; so how can you say, "Show us the Father?"'.

He claimed to have been seated alongside God before the foundation of the world, and to be worthy of sitting alongside God after His death and resurrection in John 17:5 ('And now, O Father, glorify Me together with [literally, 'alongside'] Yourself, with the glory which I had with [lit. 'alongside'] You before the world was'). But how can God have a co-equal, worthy of sitting alongside Him on the throne of the Universe?

In the last book of the Bible, Jesus says that He is the Alpha and Omega, the Beginning and the End, the First and the Last (Revelation 22:13). These are divine titles; in Revelation 1:8, God Almighty is said to be the Alpha and Omega, and in Isa. 41:4, 44:6, 48:12, God says that He is the First and the Last. By claiming these titles, Jesus was saying that He was the creator of all things, and the One who would bring history to completion, as we see in the book of Revelation. In other words, Jesus is God.

In addition, the New Testament writings credit Jesus with things only God can do. He is described as:

* **Creator**: 'For by Him (Christ) all things were created that are in heaven and that are on earth ... All things were created through Him and for Him'. (Colossians 1:16). 'All things were made through Him (the Word, i.e. Jesus), and without Him nothing was made that was made' (John 1:3). 'He was in the world, and the world was made through Him, and the world did not know Him' (John 1:10).

- **Eternal** (i.e. without beginning): 'That which was from the beginning, which we have heard, which we have seen with our eyes, which we have looked upon, and our hands have handled, concerning the Word of life -- the life was manifested, and we have seen, and bear witness, and declare to you that eternal life which was with the Father and was manifested to us' (1 John 1:1-2).
- **Forgiving Sin**: 'Jesus said, "Son, your sins are forgiven you". And some of the scribes were sitting there and reasoning in their hearts, "Why does this Man speak blasphemies like this? Who can forgive sins but God alone?"' (Mark 2:5-7).
- **Worshipped**: Only God is to be worshipped (see Matt. 4:10). Yet we read, 'When He again brings the firstborn into the world, He says, "Let all the angels of God worship Him' (Hebrews 1:6).

The conclusion we draw from these claims is that Jesus was, and is, God. Jesus is referred to as God numerous times in the New Testament:

- John 1:1 – In the beginning was the Word, and the Word was with God, and the Word was God.
- Romans 9:5 – [Israelites], of whom are the fathers and from whom, according to the flesh, Christ came, who is over all, the eternally blessed God. Amen.
- Matthew 1:23 – Behold, the virgin shall be with child, and bear a Son, and they shall call His name Immanuel, which is translated, "God with us".
- Titus 2:13 - looking for the blessed hope and glorious appearing of our great God and Savior Jesus Christ
- Hebrews 1:8 But to the Son He says: "Your throne, O God, is forever and ever; A sceptre of righteousness is the sceptre of Your Kingdom".

Even in the Old Testament writings, the prophesied Messiah is stated to be God Himself:

- Isaiah 9:6 – For unto us a Child is born, unto us a Son is given; and the government will be upon His shoulder. And His name will be called Wonderful, Counselor, Mighty God, Everlasting Father (or

Father of Eternity), Prince of Peace.

- Micah 5:2 – But you, Bethlehem Ephrathah, though you are little among the thousands of Judah, yet out of you shall come forth to Me the One to be Ruler in Israel, whose goings forth are from of old, from everlasting.
- In Psalm 102:24-27, 'the LORD' (Hebrew: Yahweh) is praised, but in Hebrews 1:10-12 the same verses are attributed to the Son. This New Testament passage ascribes to Jesus the praise given to Yahweh in the Psalm, in effect saying that this is who Jesus is.
- Psalm 110:1 says, 'The LORD said to my Lord, "Sit at My right hand, till I make Your enemies Your footstool"'. In this Psalm, David (the writer) sees someone else sitting at God's right hand as co-equal. Jesus quotes this Psalm and refers it to the Messiah, Himself (Matthew 22:41-45).

The Holy Spirit is God

The Holy Spirit is also God. The Holy Spirit is called the 'Spirit of God' twenty-six times in the Bible, starting in Gen. 1:2.

In the New Testament, the Holy Spirit is said to be God. 'Peter said, Ananias, why has Satan filled your heart to lie to the Holy Spirit ... you have not lied to men but to God' (Acts 5:3-4). In Romans 8:9, the Holy Spirit is called both the 'Spirit of God' and the 'Spirit of Christ'. If Christ is God, this means that the Spirit is God too.

The Holy Spirit also has all the attributes of God. That is, all the characteristics of God also belong to the Holy Spirit:

- **Omnipresent**: 'Where can I go from Your Spirit, or where can I flee from Your presence?' (Psalm 139:7)
- **Omniscient**: 'no one knows the things of God except the Spirit of God' (1 Corinthians 2:10-11)
- **Eternal**: 'How much more shall the blood of Christ, who through the eternal Spirit offered Himself without spot to God ...' (Hebrews 9:14).

The Holy Spirit is a Person, not a Force

The Holy spirit is also a Person, not just an influence. He uses 'I' to speak of Himself: 'the Spirit said to Peter, Go with them ... for I have sent them' (Acts 10:20). Later we read the Holy Spirit saying, 'Separate to me Barnabus and Saul for the work to which I have called them' (Acts 13:2).

The Holy Spirit is described as 'He'. Thus, although the Greek word for 'spirit' is neuter ('it') yet the Holy Spirit is also given the masculine pronoun: 'but the Comforter, the Holy Spirit (neut.), which (neut.) the Father will send in My name, He (masc.) will teach you all things' (John 14:26)

The Holy Spirit is seen to be a Person, not just a force or influence, by the things we learn of Him:

- He can be grieved (Isaiah 63:10, Ephesians 4:30)
- He can be jealous (James 4:5)
- He has a will: 'dividing to each one individually as He wills' (1 Corinthians 12:11)
- He prays (Romans 8:26)
- He can be sinned against (Matthew 12:31)

There are Three Distinct Persons

The second step in our proof is a less-contested claim: that all three persons (Father, Son and Spirit) are distinct. This is seen at Christ's baptism, where the Father spoke from heaven and the Spirit descended as a dove upon Christ. We see three distinct persons interacting with each other. In John 14:16, Christ said, 'I will pray the Father, and He will give you another Helper, that He may abide with you forever'. Here Christ prays to the Father (a distinct person, for one cannot pray to oneself), and asks for the Spirit to be sent, a third person. Other verses which show the three persons are distinct include John 14:26, 15:26, 16:13-14, Romans 8:26 and 1 John 4:14.

See also the many verses which present the Father, Son and Spirit in triplets, showing their essential unity, equality and also distinctiveness. These verses include Matthew 28:19, 1 Corinthians 12:4-6, 2

Corinthians 13:14, Ephesians 2:18, 4:4-6, Hebrews 9:14, 1 Peter 1:2 and Revelation 1:4-5. In relation to this last reference, J. I. Packer writes, 'When the Father is put first and the Son third and the Spirit between them, as here, no room remains for doubt as to the Spirit's co-equality with them'[7].

There is One God

The third element of our proof is that the Bible teaches there is one God. The Bible does not teach that there are three Gods. Deuteronomy 6:4 says, 'Hear, O Israel: The LORD our God, the LORD is one!' 1 Corinthians 8:4 says, 'we know that an idol is nothing in the world, and that there is no other God but one'. Many other verses in the Bible attest to the fact that the LORD (Yahweh) is God and there is no other (Deuteronomy 4:35, 32:39, Isaiah 44:8, 45:5, 22).

Indirect References to the Trinity in the Bible

While the word 'Trinity' is not itself found in the Bible, there are references to the idea of the Trinity. In the very first verse of the Bible, Genesis 1:1, we read, 'In the beginning God (Hebrew: Elohim – a plural noun) created (a singular verb) the heavens and the earth'. The word 'God' here is not in the singular form, nor even in the Hebrew dual form (which is used for things that come in pairs, like 'eyes'), but in the plural form (literally, 'gods'), yet the verb form that follows is in the singular, indicating that it was only one God who created the heavens and the earth.

Genesis 1:26 tells us, 'Then God said, "Let Us make man in Our image, according to Our likeness"'. Some anti-trinitarians argue that God was speaking here to the angels, but man was not made in the image of angels, nor did angels have any part in the work of creation, either of the world or, here, mankind. Who is God talking to, and who is the 'Us' in whose image mankind was made?

In Matthew 28:19-20 Jesus says, 'baptising them in the name of the

---

[7] J. I. Packer, *Keep in Step with the Spirit*, Baker Books, 2005, p.54

Father and of the Son and of the Holy Spirit'. This is one of the best known 'proof-texts' for the Trinity in the Bible. This verse lists three names (Father, Son and Holy Spirit), yet it says that people are to be baptized in the 'name', singular.

Mark's Gospel commences with these words (Mark 1:1-3):

'The beginning of the gospel of Jesus Christ, the Son of God. As it is written in the prophets, "Behold I send My messenger before Your face, who will prepare Your way before You". The voice of one crying in the wilderness: "Prepare the way of the LORD; Make His paths straight"'.

Mark commences his gospel by quoting two Old Testament prophecies, one from Malachi and one from Isaiah. In the first, God is speaking ('I send My messenger') about the coming of someone (John the Baptist). But to whom is God speaking in this verse when He says 'before Your face'? It is obvious that John the Baptist prepared the way before Jesus, so here God is speaking to Jesus about the preparations for Jesus' coming. However, the next quotation tells us that the One who John is preparing the way before is none other than the LORD Himself: 'prepare the way of the LORD' (i.e. Yahweh). Thus, we have God expressing His thoughts to the LORD, an inter-trinitarian conversation. Mark commences his gospel with verses which immediately raise the question of the deity of Christ and the trinitarian nature of God.

A number of times in Paul's letters he prays for his readers, addressing his prayer to both the Father and the Son, but he puts the verb which follows in the singular form. Thus, in 1 Thessalonians 3:11, we read, 'Now may our God and Father Himself, and our Lord Jesus Christ, direct (singular) our way to you'. Similarly, in 2 Thessalonians 2:16, he prays, 'Now may our Lord Jesus Christ Himself, and our God and Father, who has loved (sing.) us and given us everlasting consolation and good hope by grace, comfort your hearts and establish you in every good word and work'.

Summary

These are just some of the many references to the truth of the Trinity that we find in the Bible. They show three things: (1) God is One, yet (2) all three of the Father, Son and Spirit are equally and fully God, and (3) they are distinct persons. If these things are true, then we are left with the Trinity as the only possible resolution. Although the word 'Trinity' itself is not found in the Bible, the truths that make up the doctrine are found everywhere throughout it.

B. B. Warfield writes, 'It is not in a text here and there that the New Testament bears its testimony to the doctrine of the Trinity. The whole book is Trinitarian to the core; all its teaching is built on the assumption of the Trinity; and its allusions to the Trinity are frequent, cursory, easy and confident ... it has been remarked that "the doctrine of the Trinity is not so much heard as overheard in the statements of Scripture" ... The doctrine of the Trinity does not appear in the New Testament in the making, but as already made'[8].

Pictures of the Trinity

Because it is difficult to make the case for the Trinity without listing lots of Bible verses and explaining their logic, many Christians instead try to justify the Trinity by using illustrations from nature. However, these illustrations all have problems and faults. No illustration or analogy perfectly captures the Trinity.

The Egg, the Three-Leafed Clover, and Coffee

One of the most common illustrations is the egg. An egg has three parts: the shell, the yolk and the egg-white. It is therefore three-in-one. The problem with this illustration is that while an egg has three parts, God does not. This illustration would make the Father one-third of God, the Son one-third of God and the Spirit one-third of God.

The same problem applies to some other illustrations, like the three-

---

[8] B. B. Warfield, "The Biblical Doctrine of the Trinity" in *Biblical Doctrines*, Baker, 1981, p.143

leafed clover that Patrick used to explain the Trinity to the Irish, or the triangle with its three angles and three sides. The problem is that the three lines of the triangle are different parts of the triangle, while the Father, Son and the Spirit are not parts of the Trinity. I had a friend once who tried to explain the Trinity by likening it to instant coffee, which requires coffee powder, milk and sugar: three-in-one.

However, the trinity does not mean that God is tri-partite, or that Jesus is 1/3 of God. Christ is fully God. Colossians 2:9 says, 'For in Him dwells all the fullness of the Godhead bodily'. Each of the Father, Son and Spirit are fully God. The Father, Son and Holy Spirit are not part of God, or lower or less than fully God.

Water, Father-Son-Husband

Another common illustration of the Trinity is water, which can be liquid, solid (ice) or gas (steam), depending on the temperature. However, this illustration makes out that the Holy Spirit and the Son are merely different forms that God takes. God becomes a bit like Clark Kent who takes off his glasses, goes into a phone booth, and changes into Superman. Others use the illustration of the man who can play the roles of father, son and husband all at the same time.

This is the error of Modalism or Sabellianism, named after Sabellius who taught that there is only one God, who revealed Himself in the Old Testament as Yahweh, in the Gospels as Jesus, and in the Acts as the Holy Spirit. However, the Trinity is not to be understood as one God who takes on three different 'faces' when He reveals Himself. Rather, there is one God in three distinct persons.

1 x 1 x 1 = 1

Another illustration sometimes used is mathematical: $1 \times 1 \times 1 = 1$. However, this is really an illusion rather than an illustration. Multiplication is really just repeated addition. Thus, 2×4 is really $2 + 2 + 2 + 2$. But $1 \times 1 \times 1$ does not involve any repeated addition at all. It does not matter how many times we multiply 1 by itself, we are not really doing any adding. $1 \times 1 \times 1$ is nothing different to $1 \times 1 \times 1 \times 1 \times 1 \times 1 \times$

1. Thus, this illustration is more appropriate for a Unitarian God than for the Trinity, for no matter how many times you try to multiply this Unity, all you ever have is the same Unity. Another mathematical way of looking at 1 x 1 x 1 = 1 is to think of a cube, with each side (length, breadth, height) of one unit. However a cube is not a good illustration of the Trinity for the simple reason that it is Modalistic – each face of the cube reveals a different 'side' to God, which is not what we mean by the Trinity. A better mathematical illustration of the Trinity would be this: 1 + 1 + 1 = 1. This is a more accurate depiction of the Trinity but it is not a very helpful illustration. Although it expresses the mystery it does nothing to help explain it (which is the main purpose of an illustration).

The Trinity Diagram

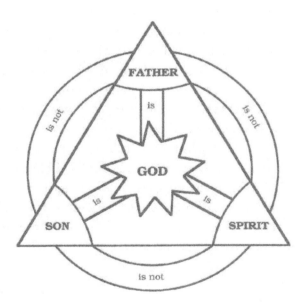

One common illustration of the Trinity is a geometric diagram. This illustration shows that that the Father, Son and Spirit are all God, and yet the Son is not the Father, the Father is not the Spirit and the Spirit is not the Son. Thus, the three persons of the Trinity are distinct, yet they are all God, and there is one God.

However, there are problems with this diagram too. It is more correct to say that the Son and Spirit are distinct and yet, at the same time, One. In John 14:16-18, Christ said: 'I will pray the Father, and He will give you another Helper ... the Spirit of truth ...; but you know Him, for He dwells with you and will be in you. I will not leave you orphans; I will come to you'. In these verses we see that the three persons of the Trinity are distinct. The Son prayed to the Father, asking Him to send the Spirit, another comforter (John 14:16) – the word 'another' implies that the Spirit is distinct from the Son. However, just two verses later, Christ says: 'I will not leave you orphans; I will come to you' (John 14:18). Thus, while verse 16 shows that the Son and Spirit are distinct persons, verse 18 teaches that the Son and Spirit are the one and the same. It is not quite true to say (as the diagram does) that the Son is not the Spirit. It is better to say that the Son is not the Spirit, and yet He is.

There are other similar verses that speak of the Spirit dwelling in us in one verse, and then Christ dwelling in us in the next. It is almost as if the Son and the Spirit are interchangeable. Romans 8:9-10 tell us: 'But you are not in the flesh but in the Spirit, if indeed the Spirit of God dwells in you. Now if anyone does not have the Spirit of Christ, he is not His. And if Christ is in you, the body is dead because of sin, but the Spirit is life because of righteousness'. This verse speaks of 'the Spirit', 'the Spirit of God', 'the Spirit of Christ', and of 'Christ' being 'in you' – these almost seem to be the one and the same descriptions of the indwelling presence within the believer.

The same is true of the unity of the Father and the Son. Christ said, 'I and My Father are one' (John 10:30). Anti-trinitarians argue that this verse simply means that the Father and the Son are one in purpose, or in partnership. However, this is disproven by what follows. The Jews take up stones to stone Christ (v31), and accuse Him of blasphemy, 'because You, being a man, make Yourself God' (v33). In verse 38, Christ does not explain away His unity with the Father in terms of purpose or partnership. Instead He says, 'though you do not believe Me, believe the works, that you may know and believe that the Father is in Me, and I in Him'. Christ states that His unity with the Father is a unity of person and identity. The result is that the Jews again try to seize Him (v39).

Similarly, the Father and the Spirit are both distinct, and yet they are

One. We see this even in the Old Testament, where we might be forgiven for thinking that the 'Spirit of God' is just another name for God Himself. In Isaiah 48:16 we read these amazing words:

'Come near to Me, hear this: I have not spoken in secret from the beginning; from the time that it was, I was there. And now the Lord GOD and His Spirit have sent Me'.

Here we have what, at first, seems to be the prophet Isaiah speaking, saying that the LORD God and His Spirit have sent him. From this, we learn that God and His Spirit are separate and distinct. But notice further that this verse cannot be referring to Isaiah, for the speaker says 'from the beginning, from the time that it was, I was there'. The speaker is God Himself. It is God Himself who has been sent. Just a few verses prior we read that He is the First and the Last who foretells events from the beginning (Isaiah 48:12). These words are quoted by Jesus, referring to Himself, in Revelation 22:13: 'I am the Alpha and the Omega, the First and the Last, the beginning and the end'. This person can only be the Servant-King mentioned in Isaiah 42, 45, 49, 50, and 53, sent by God into this world for our salvation. Notice further that both the Father and the Spirit here send the Son, showing their unity in sending Him. From this we see the essential identity, yet distinction, between the Father and the Spirit. Thus, Old Testament glimpses of the Trinity show that the Father and the Spirit are distinct, while also speaking of them as identical with each other.

Here we are confronted with the true mystery of the Trinity: the Father, Son and Spirit are all God, as well as being distinct persons, but they are also one in the fullest sense. The modalist who says the Father, Son and Spirit are interchangeable revelations of the One God is partly correct, but also incorrect at the same time, in that he does not also acknowledge that the Father, Son and Spirit are distinct as well as identical. But how can the members of the Trinity be distinct yet one? Here is the fathomless mystery.

Quantum Physics

One final illustration of the Trinity comes from modern physics, and particularly the world of quantum physics. In quantum physics, light is described as having the properties of particles, but also the properties of waves. But particle and wave properties are very different things – matter cannot ordinarily have both. There are other paradoxes in quantum physics too: a particle's position and momentum cannot both be measured at the same time. These paradoxes have been compared to the paradox at the heart of the Trinity – God is one and yet God is three.

However, this appears yet again to be a form of modalism – God sometimes reveals Himself as One, and sometimes as three, just as some particles show certain properties at one time and others properties later. Another problem with quantum physics is that (in the words of a famous scientist) 'if you think you understand quantum physics, you don't understand quantum physics'. In other words, no one really understands what is going on. It is a bit hard to make a powerful illustration from something that we do not understand very well.

The Problem with Illustrations of the Trinity

The truth of the Trinity is this: there is no illustration that accurately and adequately pictures it. The reason is simple: 'God is not like anything. That is, He is not exactly like anything' (A. W. Tozer[9]). God transcends anything and everything in this created world.

There are many things about God that we cannot understand. How can God have no beginning? How can He create from nothing? How can He hear all the prayers of people all over the world at the same time, or read all the minds of everybody at once? How can God be sovereign and in control of all events, yet humans have genuine free will?

The truth of the Trinity falls into the same category of things about God that we cannot understand, because He is God and we are not.

---

[9] A. W. Tozer, *The Knowledge of the Holy*, OM, 1987, p.17

Logical, Theological and Practical Considerations

The doctrine of the Trinity is the best explanation we can draw from the biblical evidence. But it also has profound logical, theological and practical results.

Firstly, we learn that God is beyond the grasp of our puny human minds. This is why the Athanasian Creed spoke of God as immeasurable, that is, incomprehensible, a quality that is true of the Son as much as it is of the Father (see Matthew 11:27), again proving the doctrine of the Trinity. It is a strange and puzzling thing to see highly intelligent people who admit that they cannot comprehend some of creation's mysteries (like quantum physics, or light) demanding that the Creator of all things must be as easy to understand as infant school arithmetic. Maybe this was Newton's problem: a refusal to admit that our human intellect cannot fathom something like God's nature. This is a blow to the pride of a scientist who likes to get to the bottom of everything, to understand how everything works, to reduce everything to a simple formula. Some people make fun of the idea of the Trinity as 'irrational' or 'hocus-pocus', as if God should be so simple that a Sunday School student could understand Him. But as John Wesley said, 'Bring me a worm that can comprehend a man and then I will show you a man who can comprehend God'.

Secondly, the Trinity shows us the true nature of God. Consider the contrast between Christianity and the other two monotheistic religions, Judaism and Islam. Hoste writes, 'The Jewish and Moslem conception of the unity of God leaves Him before creation in solitary, awful loneliness; the Christian belief that unity means union, not One alone, but Three in One, makes that abyss of antecedent Eternity glow with a glory of life and love'[10].

C. S. Lewis wrote: 'All sorts of people are fond of repeating the Christian statement that 'God is love'. But they seem not to notice that the words 'God is love' have no real meaning unless God contains at least two Persons. Love is something that one person has for another person. If God was a single person, then before the world was made, He was not

---

[10] quoted by W. Hoste, in *Studies in Bible Doctrine*, p.39

love. Of course, what these people mean when they say that God is love is often something quite different: they really mean ' Love is God'. They really mean that our feelings of love, however and wherever they arise, and whatever results they produce, are to be treated with great respect. Perhaps they are: but that is something quite different from what Christians mean by the statement 'God is love'. They believe that the living, dynamic activity of love has been going on in God forever and has created everything else'[11].

The Trinity shows us that God is Himself a fellowship of love. Theologian W. H. Griffith-Thomas put it this way: 'Love must imply relationships, and as He is eternally perfect in Himself, He can realise Himself as Love only through relationships within His own Being ... Belief in Theism postulates a self-existent God, and yet it is impossible to think of a God without relationships. These relationships must be eternal and prior to His temporal relationships to the universe of His own creation. He must have relationships eternally adequate and worthy...'[12].

Thirdly, the Trinity is at the very centre of the divine plan of salvation enacted in human history and recorded in Scripture. God did not create a being, angelic or human, to 'do His dirty work for Him', to fix His broken creation, to heal the rift between God and man, to reconcile us back to Himself. If God had done that, how would this angelic or created being have been able to truly represent and reveal God to us? How would we know that an angelic being was without sin? Angels can sin, and many rebelled with Satan. So how could an angel be a perfect sinless sacrifice? Further, how could God claim to truly and perfectly love us if He was prepared to sacrifice someone other than Himself to save us? What was displayed in Christ would not have been the love of an infinite God. A non-Trinitarian salvation would have been a display of cheap, cut-price love, and the revelation of something less than God to humanity. God would thus remain a remote and unknowable Creator, and our ability to love and worship Him in return would be undermined. Everything in the plan of God falls apart and breaks down unless Jesus is

[11] Lewis, *Mere Christianity*, pp.174-5
[12] W. H. Griffith Thomas, *The Principles of Theology*, Church Book Room, 1956, p.25

truly God, and therefore God is a Trinity.

Fourthly, God as Three-in-One raises questions of how the three persons relate to each other. What a contrast their inter-relationships present with the juvenile bickering of Zeus and his crew in the Greek pantheon. In one sense we have seen that the Father, Son and Holy Spirit are all equal, yet they relate to each other in different ways. The Son perfectly submits to the Father, and the Holy Spirit takes an almost 'backstage' role, invisibly working for the glory of the Son. Theologians use the terms 'ontological equality' and 'functional diversity' to speak of the Trinity. In their 'being' (the meaning of 'ontology') they are equal, yet in their work they have different complementary roles. J. I. Packer writes: 'God is Triune; there are within the Godhead three Persons; the Father, the Son and the Holy Ghost; and the work of salvation is one in which all three act together, the Father purposing redemption, the Son securing it, and the Spirit applying it'[13]. Prayer is similarly trinitarian: we pray to the Father through the Son in the energy of the Holy Spirit (see Ephesians 2:18). Some theologians have argued that the Trinity is the model for human relationships, particularly in marriage, showing that equality of dignity and worth can exist alongside different functional roles.

---

[13] J.I. Packer, *Knowing God,* Inter-Varsity Press, 1973, p.70

Chapter 20

God is All-Knowing

Deism was a form of watered-down belief in God that flourished in the 1700 and 1800s. In the United States of America it was held by celebrities like Thomas Jefferson and Benjamin Franklin, while in France its effect was so great that it was made the religion of the French Revolution. Voltaire was a deist, as were Rousseau and Robespierre, and in Germany, Frederick the Great. Voltaire wrote, 'It is perfectly evident to my mind that there exists a necessary, eternal, supreme, and intelligent being. This is no matter of faith, but of reason'[1]. These people believed in God, but they rejected the Bible as God's Word, and the idea of miracles, or scriptural prophecies, or a God who answered prayer. Instead of relying on revelation, they trusted human reason and the evidence of nature as guideposts to God, and were highly skeptical of anything that they could not understand, like the Trinity. In short, they believed in God, but not one who intervened in our world's affairs. God was conceived of as a Cosmic Clockmaker, who after designing and creating the world, stepped back and let it run itself. He was 'a God away out there, who doesn't care'.

However, the facts of modern scientific discovery, particularly at the microbiological level, disprove the idea of a distant, uncaring, uninvolved God. God is the creator of the nanotechnology we can see through our most powerful microscopes, of the molecular machines that perform all the work inside the cell, of the coded information in the DNA, of the very small as much as the very large. J. B. S. Haldane, the British scientist (and atheist), when asked what he thought of God from His works in creation, said sarcastically, 'An inordinate fondness for beetles'. The fact that there are over 400,000 species of beetles, however, hardly

---

[1] W. Dugdale, "Voltaire", *A Philosophical Dictionary*, 1843, p.473

disproves God's existence; it simply means that He takes a great interest, and maybe even fondness, in the smallest details of His creation.

Dr. A. McCaig writes, 'He numbers the hairs of our head; counts and cares for the sparrows; clothes the grass of the field [with wildflowers]; feeds the ravens; provides His children with all the necessities of life. He is ever with His people, ever near them, ever in them. Deism, with its coldness and abstractions and mechanicalness, and Pantheism with its vagueness, its impersonalness, its mingling of human and Divine, both die in the presence of the Life and Teaching of Jesus Christ'[2].

We live in an information age. Not only can we find (almost) any information we want on the internet, but the worrying thing is that the internet knows a lot of information about us. We are almost at the stage of George Orwell's novel *1984*, where 'Big Brother' is watching us. Our credit card purchases disclose our spending habits, and the ways that we use our smart phones capture more information about us, like where we are at any moment, while social media use shows our likes and dislikes, or our political and religious views. In China, the government monitors each citizen and gives them a social credit score that rates everyone on their economic and social reputation. People can be prevented from getting a job or using certain forms of transport if they have a bad reputation with the government.

The Bible teaches us that God knows everything. He is not only watching us, but He knows our very thoughts. Is this is something good, or something worrying?

God's Omniscience

Psalm 139 teaches us about God's omniscience: God knows all things. The Psalm is divided into four sections of six verses each. The first six verses tell us about how God knows everything. The second set of six verses tell us that God is everywhere. The third section teaches us that God knows all our days – from beginning to end. The final six verses talk about what our attitude should be to this God who knows all.

Look at what the first six verses tell us about God's omniscience.

[2] Dr. A. McCaig, *Doctrinal Brevities*, Marshall, Morgan and Scott, 1933, p.90

O LORD, You have searched me and known me.
You know my sitting down and my rising up;
You understand my thought afar off.
You comprehend my path and my lying down,
And are acquainted with all my ways.
For there is not a word on my tongue,
But behold, O LORD, You know it altogether.
You have hedged me behind and before,
And laid Your hand upon me.
Such knowledge is too wonderful for me;
It is high, I cannot attain it.

Verse 1 says that God is actively looking into our lives, searching and scrutinising us. Verse 2 says that He knows all our movements, our sitting down and rising up, as well as our motives. We sometimes do or say things that seem harmless to others, but our motives are selfish. God sees it all. There is no hiding our hypocrisy from God. Verse 3 says that God knows our habits and He weighs up our ways. Verse 4 says that God hears all our words and knows all our thoughts.

God's knowledge is amazing. Job asked, 'Does He not see my ways and count all my steps?' (Job 31:4). Psalm 56:8 says that God knows all about our sorrows and difficulties: 'You number my wanderings; put my tears into Your bottle; are they not in Your book?' Solomon, when he was praying at the dedication of the temple said to God, 'You alone know the hearts of all the sons of men' (1 Kings 8:39). 1 John 3:20 comforts Christians by reminding us that 'He knows our hearts', even when we have doubts and anxieties. But Hebrews 4:13 should cause us to fear God, when it reminds us that 'there is no creature hidden from His sight, but all things are naked and open to the eyes of Him to whom we must give account'.

When we consider God's omniscience, we are overwhelmed. Psalm 139:6 says, 'Such knowledge is too wonderful for me; it is high, I cannot attain it'. God's omniscience is truly mind-boggling. If we stop and think, it is hard to understand how God is able to hear the prayers of people all over the world all praying at the same time (not to mention all the words that everybody on earth is saying at the same time).

A. W. Tozer writes, 'God knows instantly and effortlessly all matter and all matters ... all relations, all causes, all thoughts, all mysteries, all enigmas, all feeling, all desires, every unuttered secret, all thrones and dominions, all personalities, all things visible and invisible in heaven and in earth, motion, space, time, life, death, good, evil, heaven and hell'[3].

Three Amazing Things God Knows

Consider three amazing things the Bible tells us God knows in the natural world. Firstly, Psalm 147:4 says: 'He counts the number of the stars; He calls them all by name'. Roughly how many stars are there? With the naked eye, it is possible to see a few thousand stars in the night sky, but with telescopes, we can see many more. Scientists tell us that in our galaxy, the Milky Way, there are over 100 billion stars. But there are estimated to be over 100 billion galaxies in the universe, so that the total number of stars is about 10^{24} (that is 1 followed by 24 zeros). God alone knows the true number, and the Bible says that He calls all of these stars by name. Isaiah, speaking about the stars, says 'Lift up your eyes on high, and see who has created these things, who brings out their host by number; He calls them all by name, by the greatness of His might and the strength of His power; not one is missing' (Isaiah 40:26).

By the way, Isaiah goes on to say that the God who knows the number of the stars knows all about us too. He says, 'Why do you say, O Jacob, and speak, O Israel: "My way is hidden from the LORD, and my just claim is passed over by my God?" Have you not known? Have you not heard? The everlasting God, the LORD, the Creator of the ends of the earth, neither faints nor is weary. His understanding is unsearchable' (Isaiah 40:27-28).

Secondly, the Lord Jesus Christ tells us in Matthew 10:29 that not one sparrow falls to the ground without God's notice. The hymwriter wrote, 'His eye is on the sparrow'. There are nearly 7 billion human beings on earth, which is a lot of people, but there are estimated to be up

---

[3] A. W. Tozer, *The Knowledge of the Holy*, OM, 1987, p.78

to 400 billion birds alive on earth. Furthermore, human beings tend to spend a lot of time sitting around or sleeping, while birds are constantly on the move. But God keeps track of the whereabouts of the smallest of these 400 billion birds. He knows where they all are, and (Jesus says) God cares about them.

Thirdly, Matthew 10:30 tells us that God knows how many hairs there are on our heads: 'the very hairs of your head are numbered'. Scientists tell us there are between 90,000 and 140,000 hairs on the ordinary person's head – even those people who are bald have the same number of hairs, their hairs have just become very small and almost invisible – but God knows the exact number of hairs on each person's head.

God's Knowledge and Ours

Compare God's knowledge with our human knowledge. Think of all the different courses of study at all the schools and universities in the world. Then think of this: God knows all the languages that are being learned there, God knows all about the mysteries of mathematics and physics and chemistry and biology and every other science that we do not yet perfectly grasp. God knows all about medicine and the human body.

When my daughter was a little girl she started having fainting episodes. After a few years of investigations that never seemed to uncover the problem, the doctors finally worked out that her heart was stopping. This got them so worried that they flew her straight away in a helicopter to the main children's hospital in the capital city in our state. We went to see the top pediatric cardiologist and he recommended that she have a pace-maker fitted to make sure her heart didn't stop, because they didn't know if her heart would start again when she had one of these heart stoppages – it could be fatal. However, we still did not know what was causing her heart to stop, so I asked the doctor what was the root cause of the problem. It seemed to me like they were applying a band-aid to the problem, rather than discovering the root cause. While I was happy that they were putting in a pace-maker to prevent the problem being fatal, I still wanted them to get to the bottom of it.

The top heart doctors said that they were not too worried about trying to work out the root cause of the problem, as long as they made sure it didn't cause any harm. I was surprised by his attitude and pressed my question again. In reply the top children's heart-doctor said, 'there is more about the heart that we don't know than what we do know'. I had assumed that the heart was just a simple pump; turns out it is far more complicated. It has its own elaborate electrical circuitry that causes the muscles to contract at just the right time, and in turn pump blood through the different chambers of the heart, and this circuitry is also connected to the brain and controlled from there. The heart is an amazing piece of engineering, and our top scientists don't know the half of what goes on in it. But God who made the heart knows how it works.

God also knows the future. When we pray, we need to remember that God already knows our needs, for Jesus said, 'your Father knows the things you have need of before you ask Him' (Matthew 6:8). Job could likewise comfort himself in his difficulties by remembering that 'He knows the way that I take; when He has tested me, I shall come forth as gold' (Job 23:10). He not only knows the end from the beginning, He has written it for us in His Word. He is the One 'declaring the end from the beginning, and from ancient times things that are not yet done, saying, My counsel shall stand, and I will do all My pleasure' (Isaiah 46:10). Jesus, speaking about the day of His coming, could say 'But of that day and hour no one knows, not even the angels of heaven, but My Father only' (Matthew 24:36).

God's omniscience is truly mind-boggling. Once, when our family were renting a house, we joked about the possibility of our landlord 'bugging' the house with an eavesdropping device so that they could hear every word we said about him. Then someone mentioned that this is precisely how we should think about God: he hears all the words we say, and even knows our thoughts.

God's Knowledge, Intelligence, Wisdom and Care

The Bible speaks of three main types of mental faculty: knowledge, understanding and wisdom. Knowledge is the most basic: we learn facts and information. The second type, understanding, involves thinking; it has to do with intelligence and perception. Wisdom is the highest of the three, and refers to the practical application of knowledge and the prudent use of intelligence. Someone has said that knowledge is knowing what to say, but wisdom is knowing when to say it. Someone else has joked that knowledge is being aware that tomato is a fruit, but wisdom is not putting it in fruit salad.

God possesses all three: knowledge, understanding and wisdom. God is not only all-knowing, He is also supremely intelligent and perfectly wise[4].

Creation shows God's intelligence and wisdom in innumerable ways. For example, just like we rub sunscreen on our skin to protect against sunburn and skin cancer, so too plants produce special molecules (sinapate esters) and send them to the outer layers of leaves to block UV rays, so that they do not penetrate deeper into leaves where they might disrupt normal development. Our human bones have a built-in lubricant (citrate) which acts as a shock-absorber. Without this lubricant, the crystals in bone mineral would collapse and shatter, but with the lubricant, the bone plates slide over each other.

God not only possesses all three of these mental faculties in perfection, He is also, unlike us humans, perfectly balanced in His mental faculties. Scientists tell us that we lose 0.1% of our brain capacity or mental ability every year, but the eternal God is unchanging in His perfect knowledge, understanding and wisdom.

It might sound strange to us that God thinks, but the fact that *we* are able to think is probably more remarkable – none of the animals in creation are able to do this – they are called 'brute (Greek: *alogos*, i.e. unthinking, non-rational) beasts' in 2 Peter 2:12 and Jude 10. The reason why we have mental faculties and can think is because we are made in God's image.

Atheistic scientists today argue that matter came first in the universe, and then only at the end of a long process of evolution did mind arise. However, the Bible teaches the opposite – it was mind first, God's mind, then matter. John 1:1 says, 'In the beginning was the Word (Greek: *logos*), and the Word was with God, and the Word was God'. The Greek

---

[4] See Psalm 147:5, Isaiah 40:28, Romans 16:27, Psalm 104:24, and Proverbs 3:19.

word *logos* refers to rationality, the faculty behind speech as well as its output.

God not only has a mind (1 Corinthians 2:16) and thinks (Isaiah 55:8-9). Even more wonderful is the fact that God thinks about us. This is a great comfort. The psalmist could say, 'I am poor and needy; yet the Lord thinks upon me (Psalm 40:17). Earlier in the same psalm, he said, 'Many, O LORD my God, are Your wonderful works which You have done; and Your thoughts toward us cannot be recounted to You in order; if I would declare and speak of them, they are more than can be numbered' (Psalm 40:5). Psalm 139:17 says, 'How precious also are Your thoughts to me, O God! How great is the sum of them!'

Deism is false: God knows about us, and cares about our situation. Peter said we are to cast all our care upon Him, 'for He cares for you' (1 Peter 5:7). God is not an absentee landlord, but a God who is intimately concerned with His creatures.

Practical Implications

Here are three lessons we can learn from God's omniscience. First, God's omniscience should make us fear Him. The book of Genesis tells us how God promised to give Abraham and Sarah a baby even though they were very old. God came to Abraham's tent one day in the form of a man along with two angels, and Abraham ran to greet these three visitors. He made some lunch for them, and then God repeated His promise that Abraham and Sarah were going to have a son in a year's time. Sarah was inside the tent listening to the conversation, and she laughed within herself at the thought of a ninety year old woman having a baby. But God said, 'Why did Sarah laugh ... Is anything too hard for the Lord?'. Sarah denied it, saying, 'I did not laugh'; the Bible says that she was afraid. But God replied, 'No, you did laugh'. Sarah was not only behind a tent curtain, but she was speaking in the quietness of her own heart, yet God saw and heard it all instantly. This sort of knowledge should make us fear God, for He sees and hears us too.

Secondly, while God knows the worst about us, He still loves us. We have already recounted the story in John's Gospel of Jesus with the woman at the well. Jesus asked this Samaritan woman for a drink of water, and she responded with surprise that a Jew should be talking with a Samaritan, and that a man should be talking in public with a woman. Jesus in turn offered her living water that would give her everlasting life. She thought that Jesus was slightly mad – he neither had any bucket to draw water, nor did she believe his talk of drinking something that gave you eternal life. So she said, "Alright, give me some of your water". In reply, Jesus said, "Go, call your husband". She said, "I have no husband". Jesus said, "You have rightly said that you have no husband, for you have had five husbands, and the man you are now with is not your husband. In this you spoke truly".

Jesus, a stranger sitting on the well, had just told the woman the story of her entire life. All her failures and sins were exposed before Him. Yet, even more amazing was the fact that Jesus was sitting there offering this sinful woman everlasting life. Knowing the very worst about the most sinful people, Jesus still loved them. He came to save the very worst of us, and gave His life for our sins. God knows us, and yet He still chooses to love us. If we knew the worst about others, we would find it very hard to love them. But God loves us despite knowing all about us.

Thirdly, we should trust God. Proverbs 3:5-6 says, 'Trust in the Lord with all your heart and lean not on your own understanding. In all your ways acknowledge Him and He shall direct your paths'. God knows everything, therefore we can trust Him completely.

Conclusion

Paul writes, 'Oh, the depth of the riches both of the wisdom and knowledge of God! How unsearchable are His judgments and His ways past finding out!' (Romans 11:33). God's amazing knowledge, understanding and wisdom should cause us to praise and worship Him.

Chapter 21

God is All-Powerful

Jonathan Edwards (1703-1758) is generally regarded as America's greatest theologian. He was not only one of America's greatest philosophers, the President of Princeton University, but he was also a powerful preacher. He saw a revival break out in which 300 people from his small town of Northampton, Massachusetts, were converted in 1734 over a period of a few months as he preached on the subject of justification by faith. Then, in the First Great Evangelical Awakening in 1740-42, many more people were converted up and down the east coast of the United States through the preaching of Edwards, George Whitefield and others.

Jonathan Edwards grew up in a Christian family, but he knew he was not a Christian, even though during his youth he had periods of emotional enjoyment of Christian things. He understood certain doctrines of the Bible intellectually, and even tried to find God in religious observances (like praying five times a day). Edwards was finally converted one Sunday when, for some reason, he was unable to go to church and he went to the library. Out of curiosity, he pulled down a leather-bound volume with no title on its cover. It was a Bible, and he opened it at random, and the verse in 1 Timothy 1:17 caught his eye: 'Now to the King eternal, immortal, invisible, the only wise God, be honour and glory for ever and ever amen'.

In his *Personal Narrative*, Edwards gives an account of what took place that day in 1721: 'The first instance that I remember of that sort of inward, sweet delight in God and divine things that I have lived much in since, was on reading those words, "Now unto the King eternal, immortal, invisible, the only wise God, be honor and glory for ever and ever, Amen" (1 Timothy 1:17). As I read the words, there came into my soul, and was as it were diffused through it, a sense of the glory of the

Divine Being; a new sense, quite different from any thing I ever experienced before. Never any words of scripture seemed to me as these words did. I thought with myself, how excellent a Being that was, and how happy I should be, if I might enjoy that God, and be rapt up in him in heaven, and be as it were swallowed up in him for ever!' This 'new sort of affection' overwhelmed him with an inward, sweet sense of the things of God.

Edwards was spiritually awakened by the realisation that God is the majestic and awesome Ruler of the universe. He realised his own sinfulness at resisting such a great God for so long, and for neglecting to worship, thank and serve Him.

Here we turn to another aspect of God, His attribute of omnipotence. Omnipotence means all-powerful and refers to God's almighty power.

Objections to an All-Powerful God

When I was still a teenager I heard an objection from a high school friend to the idea of an all-powerful God. It went like this: can God create a rock so big that He cannot lift it? The atheist philosopher A. C. Grayling makes another similar objection: can God eat Himself for breakfast?

Both of these objections are actually quite easy to answer once you understand the trick that is being played here. C. S. Lewis wrote, 'Can a mortal man ask questions which God finds unanswerable? Quite easily, I should think. All nonsense questions are unanswerable' (*A Grief Observed*).

To see what Lewis means, consider the following questions: Can God make a non-reflective mirror? Can God make a square circle? Can God make a woman to be pregnant and not pregnant at the same time? Can God make a fish that lives only on land? We could go on indefinitely in this fashion, thinking up things that are logical contradictions. These questions do not make any sense because, because it is a logical contradiction to be the something and not something simultaneously. When one of our children was very little, they would ask, "When are we there yet?" on long car journeys. The question was technically unanswerable because it was a mashed up version of two different questions in one.

Questions with inbuilt logical contradictions are not very different from thinking up three random words (like in some computer spam emails) and putting them in a question. For example, Can God quantum breast Richmond? Or, Can God cord financial vest? (these are both examples from actual email spam I have received). We might equally have asked, Can God osjr ktnpsodf ginartg? These questions have no meaningful content to reply to, therefore they are unanswerable; God cannot do these things. The same is true of the two questions posed earlier by atheists. They are just riddles, word-games, logically contradictory combinations of words.

Another atheist objection to the omnipotence of God is this: God cannot be all-powerful because even the Bible says that God cannot do certain things, like lie (Numbers 23:19, Titus 1:2), or be tempted by evil (James 1:13), or remember forgiven sins (Isaiah 43:25). Therefore (says the atheist) God is not infinite or perfect in His power – there are limitations to what He can do.

However, these questions simply misunderstand evil. Evil is a deficiency in something; for example, lying is not telling the whole truth. Therefore, when we say that God cannot lie, what we are really saying is that God always tells the truth. He is infinite in His power to speak the truth. Similarly, God cannot do evil simply means that God is perfect in His goodness and holiness – He has the power to always do what is right. Similarly, God cannot make Himself cease to exist because He has eternal life; He is infinite in His power to exist. God's attributes are not in conflict at all, as the atheist alleges. God is positively perfect in every way.

Isaiah and the Greatness of God

Isaiah 40 is the start of the second half of Isaiah's prophecy, where God promises to provide salvation for Israel through the coming of the Messiah. In verses 1-2, God announces to sinful Israel His pardon and comfort. In verses 3-5, we have the promise of the one who is going to prepare the way for the Messiah, who heralds the news that God Himself is coming. All flesh is going to see the glory of God, says verse

5. Verse 9 says, 'Behold your God'.

The stage is set for what Isaiah 40 is all about. This chapter gives us a glimpse of the majesty and greatness of God, the One who is coming. But how is it possible to describe the greatness of God? The way Isaiah does it is to compare God with things that we know.

Twice in the chapter God asks the question: 'To whom will you liken Me?' (vs 18 and 25). To help us understand how great God is, He is compared to four other things.

Firstly, God is compared to humans. 'All flesh is grass, and all its loveliness is like the flower of the field; the grass withers, the flower fades because the breath of the Lord blows upon it' (v6-7). Humans are compared to the flower that fades and the grass that withers once it is cut down. All it takes is for God to blow upon us, and we perish. Again, in verse 22, we read 'It is He who sits above the circle of the earth, and its inhabitants are like grasshoppers'. Out in the garden we sometimes see a small grasshopper sitting on the leaf of a tree, and maybe flick it off onto the grass rather than letting it eat the leaves of trees. Compared to God, we are like grasshoppers, or small insects.

Jonathan Edwards answered the question, What is a man? He said, 'Man is a leaf, a leaf driven by the wind, poor dust, a shadow, a nothing'. Of himself, Edwards said he was an empty helpless creature of small account and needing God's help in everything.

Secondly, God is compared to the nations. Verse 17 says, 'Behold the nations are as a drop in a bucket, and are counted as the small dust on the scales. Look, He lifts up the isles as a very little thing ... all nations before Him are as nothing, and they are counted by him less than nothing and worthless'. The most powerful nations and empires on earth, even when all put together, still amount to nothing compared to God.

Thirdly, God is compared to the idols in verses 18-20. The nations in Isaiah's day had their various gods, made of gold or silver or a tree that would not rot, an image bolted down so it would not totter. But God says that we cannot compare empty idols to Him.

Fourthly, God is compared to creation. In Isaiah 40, verse 12, the largest things in creation (the starry heavens, the oceans, the mountains and hills) are compared to God: 'Who has measured the waters in the hollow of His hand, measured heaven with a span, and calculated the dust of the earth in a measure, weighed the mountains in scales and the hills in a balance?' All these large structures are shown up as small things besides God.

Isaiah 40:12 says God measures the size and weight of various things. He measured the waters in His hand: the ocean trenches are twice as deep as the highest mountains, so that if all the earth's crust were evened out flat, the oceans would cover the land to a depth of 3km. There is a terrible lot of water on earth, but this verse says that God measured the waters in His hand. To him these great oceans are just a small thing held in the cup of His hand.

We read that God measured the universe by a span (that is, the distance from the wrist to the tips of the fingers). The universe is massive beyond our ability to understand. The nearest star to our Sun (Proxima Centauri) is 40 trillion kilometres away, and there are many other stars much further away. It takes the fastest thing in the creation, light travelling at 300,000 km/sec, billions of years to travel across the Universe, so vast are the distances. This universe is massive, but to God it is small enough to fit in His hand.

In verse 26, God's greatness is seen in the stars: 'Lift up your eyes on high, and see who has created these things, who brings out their host by number; He calls them all by name, By the greatness of His might and the strength of His power; not one is missing'. God not only knows how many billions of stars there are – He also knows all their names. More than that, He holds all the stars in place; by His great power, not one is missing.

Isaiah's message is that God's greatness, power and wisdom is seen in His Creation. Verse 28 puts it this way, 'have you not known? Have you not heard? The everlasting God, the LORD, the Creator of the ends of the earth, neither faints nor is weary, His understanding is unsearchable'.

Twice in the chapter God asks, 'Have you not known? Have you not heard?' God asks, 'Don't you realise how great I am? Don't you know how majestic and powerful the God who created all these things is?' The question is slightly sarcastic. Well, yes, of course, Israel knew that God was the Creator, but somehow Israel has allowed itself to forget these facts and had started to think small thoughts of God. It is possible for us, too, to become spiritually jaded and blind, distracted or self-centred, so that we lose sight of God's power and greatness.

God's Power in Upholding all things

God's power is seen in another way: upholding the universe. Hebrews 1:3 says that Christ upholds all things by his powerful word (Hebrews 1:3), and that all things are held together by Him (Colossians 1:16). God not only created all things by His power, but He keeps it all going.

We get a little glimpse of this by thinking about our solar system and the movement of the earth around the sun. Those who are mathematicians can work out the speed of the earth as it orbits the sun. We are 150 million kilometres (or 90 million miles) from the sun, so we know the distance our planet travels around the sun each year, because basic maths teaches us that the circumference of a circle equals *pi* multiplied by the diameter of the earth's orbit. This gives us a figure for the distance of our journey around the sun every year: a trip of nearly a billion kilometres. This means that the Earth journeys more than 2 million kilometres every day, travelling through space at over 100,000 kilometres per hour. When we go up in an airplane, we travel at nearly 1000 kilometres per hour, but the slightest bit of wind or turbulence seems to make the whole plane shake. Yet, God keeps our earth on its orbit, and we don't even need seatbelts. In fact, we do not even notice that we are hurtling through space at such great speeds. In addition, the earth is also spinning on its own axis once a day, yet we don't even feel the slightest wobble. Only our minds reel to think of it all.

The force that keeps us going round the sun is gravity, but another one of the four fundamental forces of physics is seen in Colossians 1:16. When that verse says that in Him all things consist, or stand together, some argue that this refers to the strong nuclear force. It is an amazing fact, but in the centre of every atom we have a nucleus made up of protons and neutrons. The protons are positively charged, while the neutrons are neutral, and around this nucleus we have the negatively charged electrons. Positives and negatives attract each other, but the positively charged protons in the nucleus repel other positively charged protons, so how is it possible that the nucleus holds together, instead of exploding apart? Scientists call the force that holds the nucleus together the strong nuclear force. It is 10^{38} times stronger than gravity.

Another way of getting an idea of God's power is to compare it against other natural forces. In 2013, a meteor exploded over Chelyabinsk in Russia, damaging buildings and resulting in 1200 people being hospitalized. It was about 30 times more powerful than the Hiroshima nuclear bomb. The energy released by an average hurricane in one second is about twice as powerful as Hiroshima, while a severe thunderstorm is about 10 times more powerful than Hiroshima. The volcanic explosion of Mt. St. Helens in the USA in 1980 was about 1000 times greater than the atomic bomb dropped on Hiroshima, and the eruption of the volcano Krakatoa in 1883 was 10,000 times greater than Hiroshima. The Sun is basically one big non-stop nuclear explosion, and its power output per second is about 6 trillion times that of the atomic bomb dropped on Hiroshima. But the sun is only a small to medium sized star; there are stars which are thousands of times more powerful than the sun.

In 1906, the day after the great earthquake in San Francisco, a newsboy was showing a dazed man the way through the city. The boy said: "It took a long time to put all this stuff up, but God tumbled it over in a minute. Say Mister, it ain't no use for a feller to think he can lick God".

God is the creator of all things, the source of all these natural forces. God's power is far greater than the sum of all the forces of nature. Even the most powerful angels in heaven cover their faces before the Almighty Creator.

How Great Thou Art

In the summer of 1885, Carl Boberg (1859 – 1940) was returning home from church one Sunday afternoon in Sweden when he was caught in a thunderstorm. After the rain and lightning cleared, he looked across a bay and could hear church bells ringing. He was so caught up in the beauty of the scene that he wrote the first few verses of what was to become the most popular hymn in the English language:

O Lord my God, when I in awesome wonder,
consider all the works Thy hands have made,
I see the stars, I hear the mighty thunder,
Thy pow'r throughout the universe displayed.

Then sings my soul, my Saviour God to Thee,
How great Thou art, How great Thou art.

We ought to marvel and wonder at God's greatness, and worship Him. Psalm 95 says this: 'the LORD is the great God, and the great King above all gods. In His hand are the deep places of the earth; the heights of the hills are His also. The sea is His, for He made it; and His hands formed the dry land. Oh come, let us worship and bow down; let us kneel before the LORD our Maker'.

Years after Boberg wrote his hymn, Stuart Hine, an English missionary to eastern Europe, was visiting a village in Ukraine with his wife and asked if there were any Christians there. He was directed to the house of a man named Dmitri and his wife Lyudmila. Dmitri's wife knew how to read, having taught herself from a Bible left by a Russian soldier. When the Hines approached Dmitri's house, they heard a strange yet wonderful sound: Dmitri's wife was reading from the Gospel of John about the crucifixion of Christ, and the guests in the house were in the very act of repenting, loudly calling out to God, saying how unbelievable it was that Christ would die for their own sins, and praising Him for His love and mercy. The Hines did not want to interrupt, so they stayed outside listening, and Stuart wrote down the words he heard the people using as they repented. These words became the third verse that we know today:

And when I think that God, His Son not sparing,
Sent Him to die, I scarce can take it in,
That on the cross, my burden gladly bearing,
He bled and died to take away my sin.

What a wonder that God, so great and mighty, should take any notice of us. David in the Bible wrote a psalm about this: 'When I consider Your heavens, the work of Your fingers, the moon and the stars, which You have ordained, what is man that You are mindful of him, and the son of man that You visit him?' (Psalm 8:3-4). Even more amazing is the thought that God should come in the likeness of men, humbling Himself to become one of His creatures, and even submit to death upon a cross. That is what Isaiah is telling us: the great God has come and died for us in the person of our Lord Jesus Christ.

Another amazing thing about God's power is that, in the words of the book of Job, 'how small a whisper we hear of Him' (Job 26:14). For One so powerful, He is very longsuffering and patient with a rebellious and corrupt world. He is gentle and holds off showing His tremendous power. But there is a day coming when this same God will show Himself, coming on the clouds of heaven with power and great glory (Matthew 24:30). Paul is 'looking for the blessed hope and glorious appearing of our great God and Saviour Jesus Christ' (Titus 2:13). But he also says that those 'who do not know God and ... do not obey the gospel of our Lord Jesus Christ ... shall be punished with everlasting destruction from the presence of the Lord and from the glory of His power' (2 Thessalonians 1:8-9).

Chapter 22

God is Eternal

Arthur Stace grew up in poverty in Sydney, Australia, his parents both being alcoholics. As a child, he had to steal bread and milk and search in bins for food to survive. In his teens he worked in a coal mine, went to jail at age 15, and became an alcoholic. He signed up as a soldier in World War One but was later discharged on health grounds. In 1930, during the Great Depression, a drunkard and a down-and-out, he went to a church in downtown Sydney for a cup of tea and piece of cake, and while there heard Anglican Archdeacon R. B. S. Hammond preach. He went out of the building, crossed the road into a park and, kneeling under a tree, turned to God and became a Christian.

In 1932, he heard a sermon on Isaiah 57:15, 'For thus says the High and Lofty One who inhabits eternity, whose name is Holy: "I dwell in the high and holy place, with him who has a contrite and humble spirit"'. The preacher, Reverend John Ridley, said, "Eternity, eternity, I wish that I could sound or shout that word to everyone in the streets of Sydney. You've got to meet it, where will you spend Eternity?"

Stace later said, 'Eternity went ringing through my brain and suddenly I began crying and felt a powerful call from the Lord to write Eternity'. Despite the fact that he was illiterate, hardly able to write his own name, he started writing the word 'Eternity' on the footpaths of the city of Sydney. For 35 years, he would leave home at 5am most mornings in the week, and write the  word Eternity in beautiful copperplate handwriting. It is estimated that he wrote the word nearly half a million times. No one knew who 'Mr. Eternity' was until he was caught in the act and identified in 1956. On New Year's Eve in the year 2000, the Sydney Harbour Bridge was lit up with Stace's word "Eternity" for the start of the new millennium.

The Eternal God and the Brevity of our Lives

Psalm 90, written by Moses, makes a sobering point. God is eternal; He is 'from everlasting to everlasting', the One who existed before the mountains were born or the earth formed. One thousand years with God are like a watch in the night – a soldier's turn to keep guard for a few hours.

But while God is eternal, we live only a few short years. We are like people swept away in flood waters – the stream of time carries us quickly away. Or, like we wake after a sleep and think, "Where did all that time go?" We are like the grass which grows up and flourishes in the morning, but in the evening it is cut down and withers. We are reminded that 'The days of our lives are seventy years; and if by reason of strength they are eighty years, yet their boast is only labour and sorrow; for it is soon cut off, and we fly away' (v10)'.

Isaac Watts, in his hymn, *O God our Help in Ages Past*, a paraphrase of Psalm 90, puts it like this:

Before the hills in order stood,
Or earth received her frame,
From everlasting Thou art God,
To endless years the same.

Time, like an ever rolling stream,
Bears all its sons away;
They fly, forgotten, as a dream
Dies at the opening day.

Psalm 90 shows us the human predicament, the brevity and emptiness of life, but while the first two stanzas of Moses' psalm are somewhat depressing, the third is more hopeful and positive. Here Moses prays for:

- God to have compassion on us (v13),
- to 'satisfy us early with Your mercy that we may rejoice and be glad all our days' (v14),

- to make up for the difficult days, by giving us gladness (v15),
- that we may see His work and His glory (v16),
- that the beauty of our God may be upon us (v17),
- and that He might establish the work of our hands (v18).

Even in this short life, we can experience God and He can give us joy, fulfilment and purpose.

Arthur Stace was the living embodiment of Psalm 90. Despite growing up in poverty, turning to alcohol, and ending up a down-and-out, God showed compassion upon him, and 'made up for the difficult days', giving him a task, purpose and gladness, so that something beautiful was done by the 'work of his hands'. Stace died at the age of 83, well beyond the allotted span, and through his life-work, God's glory was seen.

The Eternal God

The Bible repeatedly affirms that God is eternal. He was not created, nor had a beginning, nor will He ever cease to exist. Listen to some of the ways this truth is stated.

- He is called 'the LORD, the Everlasting God' (Genesis 21:33).
- The prophet Habakkuk asks, 'Are you not from everlasting, O LORD my God, my Holy One?' (Habakkuk 1:13).
- God is pictured as the eternal God who carries His people in His arms: 'the eternal God is your refuge and underneath are the everlasting arms' (Deuteronomy 33:27).
- Isaiah says, 'Have you not known? Have you not heard? The everlasting God, the LORD, the Creator of the ends of the earth, neither faints nor is weary. His understanding is unsearchable' (Isaiah 40:28).

The eternal God is trinitarian. That is, the Son and the Spirit are eternal as well as God the Father. Consider two verses about the Son from the Old Testament. Firstly, Isaiah 9:6 says, 'For unto us a child is born, unto us a son is given: and the government shall be upon his shoulder: and his name shall be called Wonderful, Counsellor, the mighty God, the everlasting Father, the Prince of Peace'. Micah 5:2 says, 'But you, Bethlehem Ephrathah, though you are little among the thousands of Judah, yet out of you shall come forth to Me the One to be Ruler in Israel, whose goings forth are from of old, from everlasting'. In the New Testament, 1 John 1:2 speaks of our Lord Jesus as 'that eternal life, which was with the Father, and was manifested to us'. John's Gospel opens with a glimpse of the eternal fellowship between the Father and the Son: 'In the beginning was the Word, and the Word was with God, and the Word was God' (John 1:1).

The Holy Spirit is described as eternal also. In Hebrews 9:14 we read of 'the blood of Christ, who through the eternal Spirit offered himself without spot to God'.

The fact that the Son and the Spirit are eternal means that they are truly and fully God, for only God is eternal. The Bible therefore teaches an eternal Trinity – Father, Son and Holy Spirit, uncreated, equally God because equally eternal.

God is Beyond our Comprehension

We are creatures of time and find it impossible to understand how God can be 'from everlasting', without beginning. Our minds go into meltdown when we try to think about it. But this is true generally about God. We cannot understand how He can be Three in One, or how He can hear all the prayers of people all over the world at the same time. God is beyond our ability to fathom or understand. That is why we worship Him – He is far greater than us.

The old pagan gods all had beginnings. The gods of Greece and Rome were all the offspring of earlier gods. The Greek pantheon, for example, were the children of the Titans, whom the Greek gods overthrew. The pagans could not conceive of their gods being eternal – everything had to have a beginning. It is the same with the modern day Mormons, who believe that God the Father is an exalted human being, who himself had a Father, setting up an infinite regression of fathers.

Although we find it hard to understand how God could be eternal, we understand what eternal means. The Bible says that God 'has made everything beautiful in its time', and 'also He has put eternity in their hearts' (Ecclesiastes 3:11). We see things in their prime, like a beautiful flower, and wish this beauty would not decay, but last forever. God has put this idea of eternity in our hearts. Our dismay at the transience of life causes us to long for something lasting, something called eternity.

We wish that we wouldn't grow old: we try to eat the right food and get enough exercise. Some people get cosmetic surgery, or have their dead bodies frozen, hoping they will one day be revived to live on. We would all like to be twenty-one years old – for ever. We have a longing for eternity.

God is Self-Existent

Because God is eternal, He does not owe His existence to anyone or anything else. He has always existed and will always exist. He was not created or caused by anything else. He is life itself (John 5:26, Psalm 36:9).

Because God is self-existent, He is also self-sufficient. God does not need food or drink like we do, or sleep to refresh Him, nor is there anything else that He needs supplied to Him. Acts 17:24-25 says, 'God, who made the world and everything in it, since He is Lord of heaven and earth, does not dwell in temples made with hands. Nor is He worshiped with men's hands, as though He needed anything, since He gives to all life, breath, and all things' (see also Romans 11:35-36, and Psalm 50:7-12).

This raises a question. If God is self-sufficient and content in Himself, why did He create the Universe? Why did He create man? Does this suggest that God needed something?

God is a Trinity, eternally existing in a relationship of perfect fellowship between the Father, the Son and the Spirit before the creation of the world (see John 1:1, 17:5, 24). God did not create us because He lacked something which only we could supply. On the contrary, He created us out of the overflow and abundance of His great love, so that by His grace we would be added to that divine fellowship of the Father, Son and Holy Spirit.

God is Unchanging

David Livingstone the great African missionary explorer was in extreme physical danger. In the territory of a hostile tribal chief, alone in his tent, Livingstone wrote in his journal the following words:

> January 14, 1856. Evening. Felt much turmoil of spirit in prospect of having all my plans for the welfare of this great region and this teeming population knocked on the head by savages to-morrow. But I read that Jesus said: "All power is given unto Me in heaven and in earth. Go ye therefore, and teach all nations, and lo, I am with you alway, even unto the end of the world". It is the word of a gentleman of the most strict and sacred honour, so there's an end of it! I will not cross furtively to-night as I intended. Should such a man as I flee? Nay, verily, I shall take observations for latitude and longitude to-night, though they may be the last. I feel quite calm now, thank God!'

Livingstone underlined the words: *It is the word of a gentleman of the most strict and sacred honour, so there's an end of it*!

Because God is eternal, He is unchanging. 'I am the LORD, I do not change' (Malachi 3:6, see also Psalm 102:25-27). The fact that God is unchanging is reassuring. If God could change, our confidence in Him would be shattered. We could no longer be sure that God still exists, or that He loves us and cares for His children. We could not trust His promise of eternal life through faith in Christ or that He answers prayer, or that Christ will return. Because God is the same yesterday, today and forever we can fully put our faith in Him. Consider three ways that God's unchanging nature gives us hope.

Firstly, while human love can grow stronger or cooler, God's love for us is an 'everlasting love' (Jeremiah 31:3). 'His love is a constant force, not a fitful emotion' (T. C. Hammond). At various places in the New Testament, we are told – not that God loved us – but that God loves us, in the present tense. Revelation 1:5 says that 'Jesus Christ' is the One who 'loves [not loved[1]] us and washed us from our sins in His own

---

[1] 'Loved' is the reading of the KJV, but virtually all Greek manuscripts read the present

blood'. Romans 8:39 assures us that nothing 'shall be able to separate us from the love of God which is in Christ Jesus our Lord'.

Secondly, because God is unchanging, He is faithful. We can trust what God has promised in His Word because 'He who promised is faithful' (Hebrews 10:23). As the children's song says:

'Faith is just believing what God says He will do.
He will never fail us, His promises are true'.

Just as Livingstone realised alone in Africa, God's promises can be trusted. Jeremiah wrote that the Lord's compassions 'are new every morning; great is Your faithfulness' (Lam. 3:22-23). Psalm 100:5 says, 'For the LORD is good; His mercy is everlasting, and His truth [or faithfulness, ESV] endures to all generations'.

Thirdly, God's truth does not change. His Word is 'settled forever in heaven' (Ps. 119:89); it 'stands forever' (Isaiah 40:8). We live in an age when the moral and ethical foundations of society are collapsing, and some Christians are desperate to follow the trends. Dean Inge of St. Paul's cathedral warned: 'He who marries the spirit of the age will be a widower in the next'. We must hold fast to the God's Word and what it teaches. Isaiah 40:6, 8 says, 'All flesh is grass... The grass withers, the flower fades: but the word of our God shall stand for ever'.

We can trust God because 'this God is our God forever and ever' (Psalm 48:14, KJV). His is an 'everlasting kingdom' (Psalm 145:13), an 'everlasting salvation' (Isaiah 45:17), and an 'everlasting covenant' (Hebrews 13:20).

The fact that God is unchanging is sometimes suggested as the meaning of the name Jehovah, or more properly, Yahweh, which is itself a shortened form of the words I AM who I AM (Exodus 3:14) in Hebrew. God often says, 'I am the LORD', or 'I am Yahweh'. In effect, He is saying, I am the always existing One. I am the One who will always be. Therefore, I will be faithful to keep My covenant. Yahweh is therefore spoken of as the covenant-keeping God.

---

tense: 'loves'

How do we reconcile the fact that God is unchanging with evidence that God changes His mind in the Bible? For example, in Genesis 6, God was sorry He had made man and decided to flood the world, while in Exodus 32, Moses interceded for Israel not to be destroyed and God promised not to destroy them, and in Jonah's day, God spared Nineveh after they repented (Jonah 3).

The answer is that God is unchanging in His character. He always remains true to His principles of justice and mercy. When people sin, God must judge, but when someone intercedes or people repent, God in mercy spares them. God's warnings are conditional – if people sin, God will judge, and if people repent, God will spare them (Jeremiah 18:1-10, Ezekiel 33:11).

While God is eternal and unchanging, He is also personal and relational. God interacts with people throughout the changing circumstances of history. God is also sovereign and free, and able to respond when people change (for good or ill).

Eternity is Real

People today mock the idea of life after death: 'life is short, play hard' is their motto. In other words, enjoy life while you can. But God says the opposite: eternity is long, and we are wise to prepare for it. This world is passing away. Eternity is real and coming soon.

When I was a boy at school, I remember a religion class where a boy interrupted the teacher to say that he did not want to live forever. In one sense, who would want to live forever in this present broken world? But what God has planned is beyond our wildest imagination: 'Eye has not seen, nor ear heard, nor have entered into the heart of man, the things which God has prepared for those who love Him' (1 Corinthians 2:9).

The good news is that God offers us the gift of eternal life through Christ. The apostle Paul speaks of 'eternal life, which God, who cannot lie, promised before the world began' (Titus 1:2). John writes, 'this is the promise that He has promised us – eternal life' (1 John 2:25). Romans 6:23 says, 'The wages of sin is death, but the gift of God is eternal life through Jesus Christ our Lord'. John 3:16 says that 'whoever believes on the Son shall not perish but have everlasting life'.

On the other hand, the Bible warns that those who do not know God will not have eternal life. Jesus says to those whose sins are not forgiven, 'where I am you cannot come' (John 7:34), for 'if you do not believe that I am He, you will die in your sins' (John 8:24). Instead, those who are not saved will stand before God as their Judge: 'It is appointed for men to die once, but after this the judgment' (Heb. 9:27). This great Judgment Day is described in Revelation 20, where we read that 'the dead were judged, each one according to his works' and 'anyone not found written in the Book of Life was cast into the lake of fire (Revelation 20:13, 15). The Judge will say, 'Depart from me, into everlasting punishment, prepared for the Devil and His angels' (Matthew 25:46). Those who are not saved will go to hell, separated from God and all that is good for eternity.

George Whitefield, the eighteenth century English preacher, was a great dramatist. He once preached a sermon before Lord Chesterfield, in which he told a story about a blind man who left his house with his dog and his cane, and made his way through a forest to the home of his daughter. He had made the trip many times before and knew the way by heart.

A rabbit suddenly darted out of the grass and disappeared into the forest. The dog ran after it, ignoring the pleas of his master to come back. By the time he had given up trying to get his dog back, the man could no longer feel the path beneath his feet. He tried to retrace his steps and finally came to what he thought was familiar ground. He started out for his daughter's house again. However, he was not on the path at all, but making his way ever closer to a cliff-edge with a two thousand foot drop to rocks below. The blind man drew closer and closer to the edge, tapping with his cane, until finally the cane fell out of his hand over the edge.

Supposing he had dropped the cane on the grass, the man bent down and felt for it. However, there was no ground in front of him, only the drop-off. Thinking there must be a slight depression in the ground, he leaned forward until his whole head and shoulders were over the edge. He continued feeling for his cane, reaching further forward. His heels left the ground, and his body rocked back and forth. He reached for the

315

ground to brace his fall, but there was nothing in front of him. Suddenly, with a scream of terror, the blind man fell headlong over the cliff. Lord Chesterfield, engrossed in the story, cried out, "Great God, he's gone".

Like the blind man, we stand on the brink of a never-ending eternity, which we are going to spend in endless joy with God, or in endless hell. Time is short; be saved today.

Pascal's Wager

Blaise Pascal famously stated that if the evidence for God and atheism were evenly balanced (50/50), it would be worth choosing God. He reasoned that if God exists and we choose to follow Him, we might lose out in this life from denying ourselves some of the passing pleasures of sin, but we would in the end obtain eternal life which far outweighs these limited and temporary losses. If, on the other hand, God exists and we choose atheism, we will enjoy the short-lived pleasures of sin, but they will not make up for our eternal loss in hell. If God does not exist, the Christian has only suffered a slight loss, and the atheist has only a minimal advantage. In the light of eternity, it is therefore far wiser to believe in Christ.

However, the evidence for God's existence is much stronger than for atheism, as we have seen in Part One of the book. The probability that God and eternity are real is far better than an even 50/50 chance. The odds are more like 80/20. While the evidence for various pagan gods like Zeus is close to zero, the evidence for the Christian God – from creation, design, morality, and Christ's life, death and resurrection – is powerful. Therefore, we should choose Christ.

We have a choice to make: to turn to Christ or to continue on living in our own way. 'He who believes in the Son has everlasting life; and he who does not believe the Son shall not see life, but the wrath of God abides on him (John 3:36). Jesus said, 'What will it profit a man if he gains the whole world and loses his own soul' (Mark 8:36).

God is eternal. Our lives are short. We should put our trust in Jesus Christ for eternal salvation. We should live wisely, fearing God and serving Him, knowing that we are not here for long. 'Only one life, 'twill soon be past, only what's done for Christ will last'.

Chapter 23

God is love

My great uncle, T. Ernest Wilson was a missionary in Angola in central Africa. Before becoming a missionary, he had been a carpenter in the world's biggest shipyard, Harland and Wolff in Belfast, Northern Ireland, where the Titanic had been built. In 1925 at age 23, he went to Africa with little more than the clothes on his back, trusting God to look after him and supply his needs. He spent forty years in Angola among the Songo tribe, reduced their language to writing, compiled a grammar and a dictionary, commenced the translation of the Bible into their language, and started churches in twenty areas of that part of the country.

This is a story that I heard Uncle Ernest once tell about a man from a different tribe, the Chokwe. Ernest was travelling with African carriers on one of his long journeys, the men camping at night in a ring with fires to keep off the wild animals. They came to a village one evening, and Ernest went and saw the headman and asked him to gather the people for a meeting. The headman blew a horn and the people gathered from all directions into a palaver house, with a roof held up on poles and a fire burning in the middle. Ernest sat on a stool, and the people sat with the men on one side, the women on the other, and the children squatting at the adults' feet.

Ernest read to them from the Bible in John 3:16: 'For God so loved the world that He gave His only-begotten Son, that whoever believes in Him should not perish but have everlasting life'. Then Ernest explained the Christian message as simply as he could to these people who had never heard it before.

When he had finished, the headman asked if he could ask a question: 'Where does the white man say the sun goes at night, into a hole in the earth, or into a hole in the water?' Ernest felt discouraged; all the headman was interested in was basic astronomy. So he went outside and picked up two pieces of fruit, and tried to explain what the white man believed about astronomy. When he had finished, the headman looked at him strangely, and asked, 'Do you mean that we are standing on a ball going round the sun?' Ernest said yes. The headman looked at him again and said, 'That is just crazy – we don't believe anything like that. The sun either goes into a hole in the earth or a hole in the water'. Ernest was upset at having wasted time talking about such things, but he was not interested in arguing.

While he was sitting there talking, though, he saw something come crawling along the ground. This was lion country, and he had a rifle lying at his feet. He bent down and picked up the gun, loaded it, and pointed it at this object coming towards him. But what came into the light of the fire was a human being, and he sat up at looked at Ernest. He had a normal head, broad shoulders and a magnificent torso, but his legs were withered, with nothing but skin and bone. He had great big callouses on his knees and also on his knuckles from dragging himself around.

Ernest asked him, "Who are you?"

"My name is Salwichika", he replied. (The word salwichika means 'father of abandonment').

"What happened?"

"Bwana ('Sir'), I used to be a man like other men – I could walk, I could work, I could hunt, I was married with two boys, but one day I got a terrible pain in my neck, and down into my spine and legs". (Although he didn't know it, he had contracted polio). "I became very ill, and I had to lie down in my hut, and if an old lady had not come and put some food next to my head, I would have starved to death. They thought I was going to die, and they came and took my wife and sold her as a slave, and they took my two boys, and I don't know where they are. But I didn't die, I got better, but I couldn't walk – I could only crawl around on my hands and knees".

Ernest said to him, "Salwichika, would you like to hear what I have been telling the people?"

"Bwana, what is it?"

So Ernest repeated John 3:16 to him in his Chokwe language: 'For

God so loved world that He gave His only-begotten Son, that whoever believes in Him should not perish but have everlasting life'.

Ernest asked him, "Do you understand that?"

"Bwana, I understand the words, but I don't understand the meaning. What does it mean?"

So Ernest went through John 3:16 line by line, explaining it like he would to a child. Then, he said, "Do you understand now?"

Salwichika clapped his hands, and said, "Yes, thank you, I think I do understand now". He gave the native greeting, dropped to his hands and knees and crawled out into the night. Ernest went back to the campfire and slept for the night.

The next morning, Ernest and the carriers left at dawn on a journey of 120 miles up into the Songo country. About a year passed, and they were building up there in Songo country, when Ernest saw something at the edge of the clearing that looked like an animal. They had been having trouble with baboons, and Ernest went into the house to get his gun, and he was just ramming a cartridge into the breech, when he saw that this was not an animal but a human being crawling on his hands and knees. Ernest stood there with gun in hand, and waited until the man came. When he came, the man sat up and smiled and said, "Do you know me?"

Ernest said, "I do, you're Salwichika, the father of abandonment. Where have you come from?"

"I came from the place where you met me".

"Do you mean to say you have come 120 miles?"

"Yes, that is where I have come from".

"How long has it taken you to get here?"

"It has taken me about nine months to come here".

"You haven't been crawling for nine months, have you?"

"No, not exactly, when I came about 20 miles, my hands and knees had broken down into sores, and I had to wait until they healed, so when they healed I continued". Salwichika had done the journey in five stages.

"How did you feed yourself?" Ernest could see his bow and arrows tied on his back. Salwichika followed the game paths and hid in the long grass. He would shoot a deer, tie it on his back and carry it into the village to exchange it for a meal from the native women. Ernest could hardly believe the evidence of his eyes and ears.

Finally, when he had got over his astonishment, Ernest asked, "Whatever brought you here? It has taken you nine months and 120 miles to get here – whatever has brought you all this way?"

"Bwana, I can never forget that story that you told me. You didn't know it, but that night, when I got home, I was like a wounded animal. I was like something with a spear in its heart. As I lay in my little hut and turned it over in mind, that God loved the world – I had never heard that before. You see, I thought that nobody loved me. My name is the father of abandonment, and I never thought that anybody loved me. I decided that I must hear those words again". Salwichika had crawled 120 miles to hear that God loved him. Ernest got out two stools, and when they were seated, told him the story of God's love again.

Some time later, Salwichika said, "Bwana, the first time I heard that story I was like a wounded animal, but after the second time I am healed. I know that God loved me and that He sent his Son to die for me, and that Jesus is my Saviour".

John 3:16

I once heard a little girl repeat the words of John 3:16 as follows: 'God loved the world sooooo much that He gave His only Son …', her little voice rising and falling as she lengthened out the little word 'so'. She highlighted the main point of the verse: how great God's love is. Here are seven things about how great God's love for us is:

1. God's love is great because He is great. He is the everlasting God, the All-mighty Maker of the heavens and the earth. Many young girls dream of a handsome Prince falling in love with them. But how much more amazing it is that the Great God should love such insignificant specks of dust as us. David put it like this, 'When I consider Your heavens, the work of Your fingers, the moon and the stars, which You have ordained, what is man that You are mindful of him, or the son of man that You visit (i.e. pay attention) to him' (Psalm 8:3-4). The distance between us and the High King of Heaven is so great, it is a marvel that He should notice us, or think

upon us. We are so insignificant, yet God says that He loves us.

2. God's love is amazing when we think about who He loved: *the world*. Our world is full of war, greed, foolishness, corruption and shame. There is nothing particularly noble, lovely or worthy in us to attract the love of God. Yet He loves us. There is nothing in us to deserve it. God's love is unmerited and pure – there is no selfishness in it, nothing to gain, no ulterior motive, or hidden agenda, for we cannot provide Him with anything in return. He loves us not because we are lovely, but because 'God is love' (1 John 4:8, 16). Here is a love that is causeless; it springs from the depths of God's eternal heart of love, rather than being prompted by something beautiful in us. God is holy and righteous, yet He still loves us though we are far from perfect. In fact, it is worse than this: God loves us even though we have turned against Him and become His enemies. John puts it this way, 'In this is love, not that we loved God, but that He loved us and sent His Son to be the propitiation [sacrifice] for our sins' (1 John 4:10). God loved us, even though we are unlovely, rebels, disobedient, breakers of His laws, and guilty sinners.

3. The greatness of God's love is seen in His gift: 'God loved the world so much that He gave *His only Son*'. The way to measure love is by looking at what it is prepared to give. Here we see the intensity of God's love. God so loved the world that He sent His Son to death on the Cross. The hymnwriter Samuel Crossman (1624-83) said it like this:

> *My song is love unknown, my Saviour's love to me,*
> *Love to the loveless shown, that they may lovely be.*
> *O who am I, that for my sake,*
> *My Lord should take frail flesh and die.*

> *He came from His blest throne, salvation to bestow,*
> *But men made strange and none the longed-for Christ would know*
> *But O my Friend, my friend indeed,*
> *Who at my need His life did spend.*

Philippians 2:5-8 remind us of the depth to which God's Son was prepared to go for us: 'being in the form of God ... He made Himself of no reputation, taking the form of a slave, and coming in the likeness of men, and being found in appearance as a man, He humbled Himself and became obedient to the point of death, even the death of the cross'. There was a chimney-sweep who once heard a Christian speaking with a group of people, saying that God loved us so much that He gave His only Son. The dirty chimney-sweep burst into the well-dressed company and said, 'I have got seven sons, and I would not give the worst of them for the best of you'. God could not have given anything greater for us. We see the intensity of God's love in Christ's cry of dereliction on the cross: 'My God, my God, why have You forsaken me?' God loved us so much He was prepared to turn His back upon His Son. Isaiah prophesied of Christ's sufferings: 'Yet it pleased the Lord to bruise Him, He has put Him to grief, when You make His soul an offering for sin ...' (Isaiah 53:10).

4. The greatness of God's love is seen in the fact that He loves all of us, for John 3:16 says that God so loved *the world*, not just one nation, or class of people, or the people of one religion, or the good people. God's love is boundless – He loved the whole world. The rich and poor, the great and the small are no different to him. The colour of a person's skin makes no difference to God. There is no one that God does not love. Even the worst of us can take God's Word for it that He loves us. There is no one so bad that God does not love him, or so deep in problems, that God's love cannot save him.

5. The greatness of God's love is seen in the fact that He has made it so simple for us to be saved: 'whoever *believes in Him* shall not perish'. God's love is free. God does not require us to offer a sacrifice for our sins, or to pay money for our crimes, or demand certain religious rituals of us. God has made it so simple that even a child can be saved, simply by believing in His Son. This shows how much God loves us. He has paid the price, and all we have to do is to accept it.

6. The greatness of God's love is also seen in the fact that it is a rescuing love. 'God so loved the world that He gave His only Son, so

that whoever believes in Him *might not perish*'. God had mercy upon us in our great need: we are perishing – dying, and more than that, heading to hell without hope or light. In Ephesians 2:1-3, Paul surveyed the corruption of the human condition, but then in verse 4, described how God intervened in these words: '*But God*, being rich in mercy, because of His great love with which He loved us …'. God intervened and took pity upon us, not only because of our great need, but also out of His great love, and provided a way of escape and salvation.

7. The greatness of God's love is seen in the fact that He has promised eternal life to all who come to Him through Christ: 'God so loved … so that whoever believes in Him should … *have everlasting life*'. God's love is eternal and unchanging, and therefore God's love is the guarantee of eternal life to all who believe. Paul puts it most beautifully: 'that in the ages to come He might show the exceeding riches of His grace in His kindness toward us in Christ Jesus' (Ephesians 2:7). Romans 8:39 reminds us that nothing will be able to separate us from the love of God in Christ Jesus our Lord.

D. L. Moody and the Love of God

One of the greatest preachers of the 19th Century was the American Dwight Lyman Moody. When he visited Britain in 1867 he met a man named Harry Moorhouse. Moody described him as a beardless little man of boyish appearance. Moorhouse offered to come to America and preach for Moody in Chicago, but Moody tried to be as unfriendly as possible. He had heard about him, a 27-year old converted pickpocket from the slums of Manchester, called the Boy Preacher. When Moody got back to Chicago, he received a letter from Moorhouse saying that he had arrived in New York and would preach in Chicago if Moody wished.

Moody wrote him a brief, frosty, note: 'If you come west, call on me', and hoped he wouldn't hear any more of it. Then Moody got another letter saying that Moorhouse was coming to Chicago and would like to preach. When Moorhouse arrived, Moody had to be away for a few days at a convention and he asked the deacons at his church to try Moorhouse out with a small meeting on a Thursday evening.

He said: "there is an Englishman coming here on Thursday who wants to preach; I don't know whether he can or not". On Thursday evening, the preaching was very different from what anyone had heard before, both in the message and the manner, and the deacons got their heads together during the final hymn and announced that Moorhouse would preach again the next evening.

When Moody got back on Saturday he asked his wife about Moorhouse. She said: "he has preached two sermons on John 3:16 and the people liked him very much. He preaches a little different from you – he preaches that God loves sinners".

"Then he is wrong", said Moody.

Here is how Moody described what happened: 'Sunday came and as I went to the church I noticed that everyone brought his Bible' (this was not the custom). 'The morning address was to Christians. I had never heard anything quite like it. He gave chapter and verse to prove every statement he made'.

Moody described the packed evening service. "'Now, beloved friends", said the preacher, "if you will turn to the third chapter of John and the sixteenth verse, you will find my text". He preached the most extraordinary sermon from that text. He did not divide the text into 'secondly' and 'thirdly' and 'fourthly'; he just took the whole verse, and then went through the whole Bible from Genesis to Revelation to prove that in all ages God loved the world. God had sent prophets and patriarchs and holy men to warn us, and He sent His Son, and, after they killed Him, He sent the Holy Ghost. I never knew up until that time that God loved us so much. I used to preach that God was behind the sinner with a double-edged sword ready to hew him down. I preach now that God is behind him with love, and that he is running away from the God of love. This heart of mine began to thaw out; I could not keep back the tears'.

At the end Moody jumped up. "Mr. Moorhouse will speak every night this week. Everybody come. Tell your friends to come". Every night that week Moorhouse announced the same verse as his text, John 3:16, and he preached God's love. At the end of the week he said, "My friends, for a whole week I have been trying to tell you how much God loves you, but I cannot do it with this poor stammering tongue. If I could borrow Jacob's ladder and climb up into heaven and ask Gabriel, who stands in the presence of the Almighty, to tell me how much love the Father has for the world, all he could say would be: 'God so loved the world, that He gave His only begotten Son, that whosoever believeth in Him should not perish but have everlasting life".

The Most Famous Story Ever Told

Probably the most famous story that Jesus ever told is the Parable of the Prodigal Son. Some people have suggested that we should call it the Parable of the Loving Father. It is a story about a man who had two sons, one who stayed at home and worked on the farm, while the other left home to live a wild life. You can find the original version of this story in Luke 15:11-32, where you will see why Jesus was a far better story-teller. This story shows us four ways that God loves us.

Rebellion (vs 11-13)

In Jewish culture, the oldest son received a double-share of the inheritance, which meant in this case he would get two-thirds of his father's possessions. The younger son was due to get only one-third. Doubtless this was part of the reason for the younger son's festering resentment and unhappiness. He came to his father and demanded his share of the inheritance right away, instead of waiting for his father's death. This was unspeakably rude, as much as to say, "I wish you would die so I can enjoy the money".

The younger son was probably not expecting his father to give him the money. Maybe he had planned to storm out of the house if his request had been refused. But the father did not fly into a rage or accuse his son of ingratitude. Instead of refusing the request and reprimanding his son, he handed over the money. No doubt the father was stunned by the son's selfishness and wounded by his rejection. But to show how much he loved him, the father gave the son what he asked for. This was a sizable amount of money – one third of the value of his total estate. It must have been a financial hit to give this money away. Giving it to a son whose actions and attitude didn't deserve it must have been harder still.

Once the son was over the shock of his father's kindness, he announced that he was leaving. Even after being shown such kindness, the headstrong young man was determined to be independent of his father. Packing his bags, he went into a far country – out of range, away from any influence or contact with his father. In the foreign country, he proceeded to spend the money with wild abandon. He made himself plenty of friends with his seemingly endless supply of funds, and enjoyed himself with wine, women and song. He did all the things he was unable to do back home on the farm, and indulged in everything his father would have disapproved of.

Here is the first picture of God's love for us. God has given us life and breath. Despite our rebellion against Him, God keeps on giving the sunshine, the rain, and all the good things of the earth. We take God's gifts, while ignoring the Giver, and without a thought of thankfulness, trying to get as much for ourselves as we can. God loves us despite our desire to get as far away from Him as possible. God loves us even though we want to selfishly do our own thing, ignore His authority and break all His rules. God loves those who do not love Him.

Ruin (vs 14-16)

The younger son's good times did not last. Just when the money was running low, a great famine came on the land. The younger son now began to wish he hadn't wasted all that money on partying. The spent inheritance was originally intended for his security, but he was now exposed to terrible ruin. He had nothing left to buy himself food, and the price of everything was going through the roof. The money gone, all his new friends deserted him; he was on his own. So he decided to get a job, but the only one available was feeding pigs. Worse still, his job did not solve his problems. He was still starving hungry, so hungry that he could have eaten the scraps that the pigs ate. Even the pigs were doing better than him.

Living our own life and selfishly going our own way seems great when things are going well.. But the good times don't last forever, and then we find out who our true friends are. Is there anybody who really loves us? The younger son found out the answer the hard way. Homeless and hungry, at the point of perishing, there was no one who cared in the slightest. He was now at the point of total ruin.

Repentance (vs 17-19)

At this crisis, the young man came to himself, or as we might say, he came to his senses. In his heart, his thoughts turned to home. He remembered his father's house far away, where even the servants were treated kindly and well fed. He remembered the one person who had always loved him: his father. If he was going to survive, his father was the only person he could turn to. The young man prepared his speech: "Father I have sinned against heaven and in your sight – I have taken your money and wasted it, I have disgraced the family name, I have hurt you, and treated your kindness with ingratitude – I am no longer worthy to be called your son. Make me one of your hired workers, the lowest of the servants. At least I will have something to eat. I don't deserve anything more anyway".

This is what repentance is – turning back from our own selfish ways, looking to God and His great love. Repentance is when we are truly sorry for our sins, and not just because of the mess we have made of our life. We truly grieve over our sins, and we show that we are serious about turning away from them by not doing them anymore. Here is the one condition for experiencing God's love – we have to return to Him.

Reception (vs 20-24)

Nothing shows the Father's love more than his reaction to his returning son. How would any normal father respond to seeing a son like this come home? Some fathers might see their son coming and tell him he was a disgrace to the name and an embarrassment to the family. Some might give a lecture about the consequences of our actions. Some might even shout at the son and tell him to go away.

But the father saw the son when he was still a long way off. He was looking out for his son, longing for his return. When the father saw him coming, he didn't stand at the gate with his arms folded. While the son was still walking down the road, he ran out and threw his arms round his son's neck and kissed him. An old man running was not a dignified sight, and to hug a dirty son who smelled of pigs was not pleasant, but the father didn't care. The son started his prepared speech, acknowledging that he had sinned against God and apologizing for treating his father so badly. But before he had even finished, the father was already calling the servants to bring the best clothes, get sandals for his feet and put a ring on his finger. He announced a feast to celebrate his son's safe return and told the servants to get preparations underway.

It has been said that we show how deeply we love something by the joy we display when it is found again. The father's words show how precious his son was to him: "This my son was dead and is alive again; he was lost and is found".

Here we see what God's love is like. There is no one so deep in trouble, so far gone in rebellion and sin, or with such a messed up life that God will not welcome with open arms, when they turn back to Him. He will exchange the smelly clothing of our sins with the clean robes of righteousness – all our wrongs forgiven and forgotten. He will welcome us back, not as servants, but as His sons and daughters, once lost but now found. Then he will prepare for us an everlasting feast of joy and celebration in His kingdom.

God's love is greater than any earthly love. God doesn't extend or limit His love to those who live decent lives or keep His laws. God loves those who do not love Him, but turn away from Him and go their own selfish way. God welcomes the repenting sinner with rejoicing. He does not treat us as we deserve, turning us away. God calls us home to His love, promising we will find forgiveness and joy.

Other Stories, Songs and Statements of God's Love

God's love is seen throughout the whole Bible. But here are some of the most famous parts of the Bible telling of God's love for us:

- Psalm 23 is maybe the most well-known passage in the Old Testament: 'The Lord is my shepherd, I shall not want (i.e. lack anything), He makes me to lie down in green pastures, He leads me besides the still waters, He restores my soul, He leads me in the paths of righteousness for His name's sake' (Psalm 23:1-3). God is pictured as a tender, caring shepherd. This Psalm tells us that God's love is a providing and protecting, guiding and satisfying love.

- The Song of Solomon is a love song written by Solomon, probably about his first love and wife, Pharaoh's daughter. Many Bible scholars suggest this is merely a song about erotic love, but although there is this side to it, it is a story of the fellowship, fears, and faithfulness of young couple falling in love and looking forward to their wedding day. Jewish rabbis and many Christian expositors have held that the song is a picture of God's love for His people. It teaches us that God's love for us is passionate and intense. God's desire is that we should be His, and one day we will be with Him forever.

- Hosea is the story of a prophet who was told by God to marry Gomer, a prostitute, as a picture of God's love for unfaithful Israel. Perhaps Hosea hoped that by marrying Gomer he might reform her, but even after she was married she continued to be unfaithful (no doubt finding being married to a holy man very different from her past life). Having now sunk back into her old ways, she had become a slave, and God tells Hosea to go and rescue her, buying her back to himself as a picture of God's plan of redemption: 'Go again, love a woman who is loved by a lover and is committing adultery, just like the love of the LORD for the children of Israel, who look to other gods and love the raisin cakes of the pagans. So I bought her for myself for fifteen shekels of silver, and one and one-half homers of barley'. God's love for a rebellious world of sinners is beyond our normal understanding of love, going the extra mile, redeeming us even at the price of His own Son's blood. Here is a picture of God's patient, long-suffering and perfect love for us.

- The book of Ruth is another love story in the Bible. It tells how Ruth, a widow, came to live in Israel to care for her mother-in-law Naomi. In doing so, she left behind the gods of her homeland in Moab and put her trust in the true and living God. As a foreigner and a widow, there was little prospect of marriage, and therefore financial security. But God provided her with work that brought in food for herself and Naomi and then a husband, Boaz, a wealthy, godly and kind man, who was prepared to marry her despite her foreign origin. This marriage required that Boaz redeem Ruth and Naomi's family property, paying the price for them to be his. Here is another picture of God's redeeming love for us, a love that reaches out beyond natural barriers, showing kindness to unloved foreigners, rescuing us in our deep need.

- When we come to the New Testament, Paul's letters are full of references to the love of God. Paul greets the Roman Christians in his letter, 'To all who are in Rome, beloved of God' (Romans 1:7). In Romans 5, he writes about the proof of God's love being seen in Christ's death for us: 'for when we were still without strength, in due time Christ died for the ungodly ... God demonstrates His own love toward us, in that while we were still sinners, Christ died for us' (Romans 5:5-8). In Romans 8, he writes, 'He who did not spare His own Son, but delivered Him up for us all, how shall He not with Him also freely give us all things?' (Romans 8:32), and assures us of the unchangeableness of God's love with these words: 'For I am persuaded that neither death nor life, nor angels nor principalities, nor powers, nor things present nor things to come, nor height nor depth, nor any other created things, shall be able to separate us from the love of God which is in Christ Jesus or Lord' (Romans 8:38-39). In Galatians 2:20 we learn that God's love is a personal love. Paul writes, 'the Son of God loved me and gave Himself for me'.

- The love of God is also a favourite subject of John, 'the disciple whom Jesus loved', who rested his head on Jesus' breast at the Last Supper (John 13:23). By referring to himself as the disciple whom Jesus loved, John is not saying that he was special, or claiming to be the favourite disciple of Jesus. Rather, John had simply come to realize that Jesus loved him, and was resting in this great fact. In his first letter, John writes about the love of God. He says, 'By this we know love, because He laid down His life for us' (1 John 3:16), 'Beloved, let us love one another, for love is of God ... He who does not love does not know God, for God is love' (1 John 4:7-8), and, 'we love Him because He first loved us' (1 John 4:19).

Experiencing God's Love

One day in my early twenties, I was on holidays with some friends, sitting on a beach in the evening, singing a children's song.

> I am so glad that our Father in heaven,
> tells of His love in the book He has given,
> wonderful things in the Bible I see,
> this is the dearest that Jesus loves me.

> *I am so glad, that Jesus loves me,*
> *Jesus loves me, Jesus loves me,*
> *I am so glad that Jesus loves me,*
> *Jesus loves even me.*

> Jesus loves me and I know I love Him,
> Love brought Him down my lost soul to redeem,
> Yes it was love made Him die on the tree,
> Oh I am certain that Jesus loves me.

As we sung these words, with the sound of the waves washing up onto the beach in the background, it was almost like the love of God was washing over me. I was 'so glad' that Jesus loved me.

We can only experience and enjoy God's love through the work of the Holy Spirit. This happens as we open our hearts up to God through His Son Jesus Christ. Paul writes that God's love 'has been poured out in our hearts by the Holy Spirit who was given to us' (Romans 5:5). In Ephesians 3:16-19 the same writer prays that the Ephesian Christians 'may be strengthened with power by His Spirit in the inner man that … you may … be able to comprehend with all the saints what is the width and length and depth and height – to know the love of Christ which passes knowledge'. This should be the Christian's desire and prayer: to be filled with the knowledge of Christ's love and in turn to rejoice in thankful praise.

Chapter 24

God is Holy

Of all the misconceptions of the modern Western world about God, perhaps the most common is the idea of God as a grandfather: a good-natured, totally tolerant, slightly absent-minded figure, who exists primarily to ensure our happiness. In this idea, God is just like a human grandparent who smirks at our misbehavior, but frowns when a parent disciplines their child. Similar to a celestial Santa Claus, God knows whether you are being naughty or nice, but He is a kind and gentle soul who gives a Christmas present to everybody no matter what they have done. The one thing that God certainly never does is judge people. As the German poet Heinrich Heine stated sarcastically, 'God will forgive me; it's His job'.

The true God is nothing like this senile and dithering caricature. God is not at death's door, a weak and weary relic. He is the Living God, Lord of all things, undiminished in power and wisdom. He is perfect in every way and His moral perfection is another way of saying that God is holy.

There is great truth to the kind and loving image of God, but that is only half of the story. J. I. Packer writes that the statement, 'God is love' (1 John 4:8, 16) 'is one of the most tremendous utterances in the Bible – and also one of the most misunderstood'[1]. In what way? Yes, God is 'merciful and gracious, longsuffering, and abounding in goodness and truth, keeping mercy for thousands, forgiving iniquity and transgression and sin'. But the same verse continues on to say that God 'by no means clear[s] the guilty, visiting the iniquity of the fathers upon the children and the children's children to the third and the fourth generation' (Exodus 34:6-7).

---

[1] J. I. Packer, *Knowing God*, Hodder and Stoughton, 2014, p.132

Thinking about God's love helps us to understand God's holiness – His moral perfection. Consider what it means for God to be perfectly loving and good. The Bible says that God is love, but what does this mean? Look at two statements in Psalm 11:7 and Psalm 7:11.

The first says, 'The Lord is righteous, He loves righteousness'. Notice that we are told God loves righteousness; the verse does not say that 'God loves everything'. Indeed, it would be impossible for God to love everything. That would mean that God loves totally opposite things at the same time, like mothers caring for their children and murderers abducting and killing them.

For God to be perfectly loving and good means that God cannot love child-molesting, promise-breaking, cheating, lying, stealing or murder. If God loved everything, good as well as bad, He would be morally confused. God would be like a senile grandfather. He certainly would not be perfect. If God loved corrupt policing, or got a laugh out of playground bullying or was blasé about corporate fraud, He would be a moral monster.

Psalm 11:7 states that the Lord loves righteousness, and the flip-side of this is that God does not love wickedness. God only loves actions that are themselves loving, good and true, not cruel and corrupt. If God smiled sweetly upon evil, He would no longer be fit to be the moral Governor of the Universe. He would no longer be loving at all.

Now notice the second verse. Psalm 7:11 extends this logic one step further: 'God is a just judge and God is angry with the wicked every day'. Logically, if God is loving, it means He must judge certain things. In fact, God must hate everything that is not loving and right. Therefore He must be angry with the ways of the wicked, and must one day take action to deal with them. If He refuses to judge the wicked, then again, He is simply smiling upon evil. God Himself has become evil.

Leonardo da Vinci said, 'He who does not punish evil commands it to be done'. If there were no recompense for evil, God would be condoning, commending and ultimately sponsoring evil. God would not simply be morally delinquent. He would be morally repulsive.

Therefore, we conclude that for God to be loving means that He must also hate everything that is not itself loving and righteous. For God to be loving, it also means that He must punish evil. God's holiness is not the opposite of God's love. God's holiness is the exact same thing as God's love; it is God's perfect commitment to what is loving and good.

God's holiness not only means that God is morally perfect and completely without sin. It also means that God is separate from sin and everything that is evil. The result of God's holiness is that we, as sinners, are cut off and separated from God.

Christ's Anger

Consider an incident from the life of Christ that illustrates the relationship between God's love and anger. Jesus was in a synagogue on the Sabbath day when the Jewish religious leaders brought in a man with a withered arm. Their purpose was to trap Christ. If He healed this man on the Sabbath day, as was His custom, they could accuse Him of working on the Sabbath, which was against their law. They could then discredit Him as a religious teacher, and say He was a rebellious upstart rather than the Son of God.

We read that Christ 'looked around at them with anger, being grieved by the hardness of their hearts' (Mark 3:5). The first thing to notice here is that Christ was angry. Some people think that it is wrong to ever be angry, but Christ was angry on a number of occasions. One other famous occasion was when He 'cleansed' the temple, throwing out the people trying to make money out of the worship of God. Christ was right to be angry with people turning the temple of God into a den of thieves. Still today, most people are sickened by the hypocrisy of religious hucksters making money out of God. Christ's anger at such corruption is perfectly justified. The same anger was on display in the case of the disabled man in the synagogue: Christ was rightly angry because the religious leaders had no compassion for a man with a severe disability.

This leads on to a second observation: Christ's anger at the religious leaders was simply a reflection of his compassion and care for the man with the withered hand. Christ wanted to heal this disabled man and was rightfully angry at those who actively tried to stop him being healed, or used the man as a pawn in their hypocritical schemes to trap Christ. Again, then, we see that anger at evil is simply the flip-side of genuine love. God's holiness is not a contradiction of God's love. Far from it: God's holiness is just God's love looked at from another angle.

Nowadays, legal theorists frown on the idea of punishment for crime. This is considered a primitive and barbaric ideology. Ironically enough, the government of my home state of New South Wales, originally established as penal colony (a place where criminals were sent as punishment) renamed its Department of Prisons in 1970 as the Department of Corrective Services and its prisons as Correctional Facilities. Punishment is out, rehabilitation is in. But consider this important question: do you think that evil deserves to be punished? If so, as John Blanchard asks,

> 'Where should God draw the line? Should he punish bank robbers, but turn a blind eye to people who fiddle their expenses? Should he clamp down on massive tax fraud, but sweep small items of dishonesty under the carpet? Should he punish perjury, but gloss over white lies? Should he be ruthless with rapists, but lenient with muggers and bullies?'[2]

God cannot just punish 'great crimes', drawing an arbitrary line for 'evil' in the sand. Instead, as we shall see, His holiness is perfect, and therefore His hatred of evil is infinite. God must punish all sin.

The idea of a holy God who brings justice to people who commit evil is today considered distasteful and unwelcome. Such thinking is typical of many who consider themselves morally and culturally sophisticated. In reality, they do not even have the simplest grasp of basic moral logic.

Consider the following situation. A little girl is abducted by a sadistic killer who before murdering her, subjects her to unmentionable atrocities. Having been arrested by the police and put on trial, the defence expends most of its effort telling the story of the defendant's tragic upbringing and childhood traumas, which led to a sordid life of crime and misconduct. The judge lets the criminal escape jail on a technicality and dismisses the case. He dedicates his closing summation

---

[2] John Blanchard, *Does God Believe in Atheists?* Evangelical Press, 2000, p.544

to a speech deploring the primitive desire for retributive punishment, declaring that we all need to spend more time trying to understand the underlying social conditions and government policies that are the true cause of such unfortunate events.

Such a thing would probably not even happen in our lenient and progressive society today – the uproar would be deafening. Neither can God simply turn a blind eye to evil. If God were to 'just forgive', this would mean sweeping evil under the carpet, in effect saying, 'Blessed are the evildoers'.

The Story of Willie Mullan

In the mid-20th century in Northern Ireland there was a well-known preacher called Willie Mullan. He was the youngest of seventeen children. His father had died in the Battle of the Somme in 1916, but his mother was a God-fearing woman who prayed for her children every day. For her youngest son Willie she prayed this: "Lord, bless Willie, save him some day and make him a man of God". However, at the age of 15, Willie Mullan was taken to a pub by two older men, given a drink, and very soon became an alcoholic. At 16, his mother died suddenly of a stroke in Willie's arms. Over his mother's dead body, he promised he would never touch the drink again, but before the end of the day he had broken his word. None of his brothers were willing to have a drunkard living with them, and he became a homeless tramp, begging for money which he would spend on alcohol. He got involved with a gang which spent its time gambling and drinking and, to fund themselves, committed burglaries and crimes.

One day, Willie Mullan was invited by an open-air preacher to a meeting being held in the town of Newtonards and out of politeness he promised to come. The man came to collect him and took him to the meeting. That night the preacher read from Revelation 6, about how the kings of the earth, the chief captains, the great men, the bondmen, and every free man hid themselves in the caves and called on the rocks and mountains to fall upon them, to hide them from the face of Him that sits on the throne, and from the wrath of the Lamb, 'for the great day of His wrath is come'. He preached about God's wrath which is coming upon the world. Willie Mullan thought the preacher was a fool, and didn't go back to hear him again, but the preacher had managed to lodge this passage of the Word of God in his mind, and the message of God's wrath against sin.

About three weeks later, Willie was sent to case out a house that the gang wanted to break into. He described what happened:

'I jumped into a field just to have a look around and see how we could get there, and when the police came see how we could get away. I'd just jumped into the field and was standing in the grass having a good look round the land, when something said to me: 'What about this day of wrath?' I said to myself: 'There's no day of wrath, there's maybe no God, and no heaven and no hell, and no anything!' I was going to plunge on, and then the voice came again: 'What if there should be a day of wrath? What if you should meet God just in the next step or two?'

'When I looked at the green hills and into the valleys and round that just twenty miles of earth that I could see, I knew quite well that there were millions and millions and millions of miles of earth that I had never seen, and God had made the heavens and the earth. I knew there was a God to meet alright just then. I can remember saying these actual words, I said: "Oh God, You're there and I'm a rebel sinner, and You're going to damn me in hell - well, alright, I deserve it". I thought that God had come to damn me.

'You know, like a flash came this word: 'What are you trembling about? Sure, God loves you'. Oh, I just couldn't get that. I stood there, I couldn't get the hold of this: I thought God loved the people that went to church, God loved the people that said prayers, God loved the people that carried their Bibles. I couldn't get this, that God loved a down-and-out, rebel, scarlet, reptile sinner just like me. I couldn't get that, and then like a flash it came: 'This is what these men preached at the corners – that God so loved the world!' Oh, I was beginning to get it: did God love the whole world, except me? I was getting this clear: that God loved the world of sinners lost, and I was just one of them. Then it came like a flash: that God so loved the world that He gave His only begotten Son. You know, I was beginning to follow this right through: that God's lovely Son had come down, and had gone to dark, rugged, bloodstained Calvary, and on the old rugged cross He had died for the ungodly! Oh, how it came into my soul that Christ had died for an ungodly sinner just like me! And He had so finished that atoning work that He rose from the dead and there was a living Saviour for me, and if I would personally trust Him I would never perish but have everlasting life!'

'Just at that moment when the light of the Gospel came in like that I was almost saved – oh, but the devil doesn't give you up like that you know! The devil said to me: "What about your pals? What about the booze? What about the gambling? How are you going to fix up everything that you're in? What about your sin?" I stood in between the two. You know I could take you to the very spot in the field where I stood, and on that side was my sin and my pals and my booze, and on this side was the cross and the Saviour who died and rose again. I knew that if I would only give my life to Him and trust Him, I would really get saved and start for heaven, but I was trembling. I can remember very well what I did, I took my cap off now, and I screwed it into a rope. I stood there, and then I knew I'd got to make this great decision, and I turned very definitely with that old screwed cap in my hand, and I said: "Lord Jesus, on this spot just now I will give You my whole life, and I will trust You now as my own and personal Saviour", and I was saved! I was saved. You know there was no preacher there, and there was no card to sign, and there was nobody to tell me what had happened. I was all alone, but I had met the Saviour'.

To understand why there is such a thing as the wrath of God and a coming judgment when we going to be held to account by God for the wrongs we have done, we need to think more about what it means for God to be holy.

Isaiah's Vision of God's Holiness

Isaiah the prophet lived in prosperous times. The economy was doing well; the men drove about in chariots and horses, while the women dressed in the latest foreign fashions and were decked out in jewellery.

Isaiah prophesied that God was going to judge the nation and bring down their haughty pride. Isaiah proclaimed woes upon the greedy property developers who added house after house to their portfolio of land-holdings. He proclaimed woes upon the pleasure-seeking hedonists who rose early in the morning to spend the whole day partying, downing intoxicating drinks and listening to the latest music. He proclaimed woes upon those who piled their evil deeds high on their carts – metaphorically speaking – taking bribes to let the guilty off the hook while looking the other way when an innocent man was robbed of justice, calling evil good and good evil while mocking the idea that God was going to intervene (Isaiah chapters 2-5).

Isaiah proclaimed, 'the anger of the Lord is aroused against His people' (Isaiah 5:25). God was going to bring foreign armies against the sinful nation who would attack them. Because they had rejected God's law and 'despised the word of the Holy One of Israel' (Isaiah 5:24), all their glory would go up in smoke.

Just as Isaiah's denunciations against the nation's sins reached a crescendo, he had a terrifying vision of God. Isaiah saw the Lord sitting on a throne in the temple in Jerusalem, high and lifted up, and the train of His garment filled the temple. Isaiah also saw seraphim ('burning ones'), mighty angels who attended God; each one of these fiery beings had six wings – with two they flew, with two they covered their face, and with two they covered their feet. They cried to each other, 'Holy, holy, holy is the Lord of hosts; the whole earth is full of His glory' (Isaiah 6:3).

The job of these fiery angels was apparently to constantly advertise God's holiness, not only by their message, but by their very nature. The seraphim were a reminder that God consumes and destroys everything that is corrupt and unworthy of His pure and holy presence. As these powerful angels cried out, the whole building shook, and the temple was filled with smoke. Yet, amazingly, despite the power and glory of these majestic angelic being, they were not worthy to look upon God – they covered their faces in His presence.

Isaiah's response to this vision of God was terror and anguish. The combination of the fiery angels proclaiming God's holiness, the shaking of the smoke-filled temple building, and the sight of God himself left the prophet trembling.

When Isaiah saw this vision, he said, 'Woe is me'. Instead of proclaiming further woes upon everyone else in his nation, Isaiah instantly realized that his own sinfulness made him unfit for God's presence. He was deserving of God's judgment too. He cried out, 'I am undone' – 'I am as good as dead'; 'I am a man of unclean lips, and I dwell in the midst of a people of unclean lips'.

Isaiah tells us that he saw this vision of God in 'the year that King Uzziah died'. Uzziah had been a relatively good king, and as a result of his good government the kingdom had become strong and wealthy. However, at the peak of Uzziah's power, his heart was lifted up with pride, and he had gone into the temple to offer incense to God (see 2 Chronicles 26). This was forbidden to the kings, according to an ancient separation of powers – only priests could go into the temple and perform the sacred ceremonies. As a result of his pride and disobedience, God struck King Uzziah with leprosy. As a leper, King Uzziah was forced into isolation, banished not just from the temple, but from normal society. His son Jotham was forced to assume the day-to-day running of the kingdom.

When Isaiah said 'I am a man of unclean lips', he was using the same word 'unclean' that lepers would shout to warn others to steer clear of the contagious disease. Isaiah realised his sinfulness in God's presence made him (morally and spiritually) leprous – diseased and filthy in God's sight, unfit for God's holy presence. Just like King Uzziah, Isaiah (in his vision) was in God's holy temple when he had no right to be there.

Spiritually, Isaiah was no different to King Uzziah, and deserving of the same judgment. But worse still, Isaiah realised that he was now looking upon God, which even angels dared not do: 'for my eyes have seen the King, the Lord of hosts'. Isaiah realised that he, a sinner, was standing unprotected before the blazing holiness of God's presence.

Instead of dropping dead, Isaiah saw an angel flying towards him, carrying in his hand a burning coal from off the altar. With this coal, the angel touched Isaiah's mouth and said, 'Behold, this has touched your lips; your iniquity is taken away, and you sin purged' (i.e. cleansed away). God had provided a means of forgiveness through a live, burning coal from off the altar, the place of sacrifice. The altar in the temple was a symbol of the fact that only through sacrifice can God's holiness and judgment against our sins be answered and satisfied. God in His grace has made a way for our sins to be forgiven and cleansed – Christ's death. Just as in Isaiah's case, such forgiveness is far more than we deserve, nor is there any reason that we should expect it. It is simply that God, in grace, has taken the initiative and provided a way of forgiveness.

Isaiah's vision was meant to teach two things. First, that God is a holy God who judges sin and punishes evil. Even as good a man as Isaiah, a prophet proclaiming God's message, was sinful and under God's judgment. But secondly, Isaiah's vision teaches us that God is a loving and gracious God, who forgives and cleanses sinners.

This vision of God's holiness was something which Isaiah never forgot. In his book, Isaiah calls God 'the Holy One' twenty-seven times (out of thirty-nine references to this title in the entire Old Testament; interestingly, the Lord Jesus Christ is called 'the Holy One' four times in the New Testament).

Isaiah's vision is perhaps the greatest chapter in the Bible on God's holiness. What does 'holiness' mean? The word 'holiness' carries the idea of something 'set apart', 'separate from the ordinary', 'distinct', 'infinitely better' (in God's case), or 'sacred'. 'Holy' was therefore used to describe sacred things associated with the Jewish temple and its worship. The very heart of the Jewish temple was called the 'holy of holies': the curtained-off room that contained God's throne, the ark of the covenant, where in his vision, Isaiah had seen God. No one was allowed to go in to the Holy of Holies, not even the priests, except for one day in the year. In addition, the word holiness is used in a moral sense, to describe the fact that God Himself, by His nature, is pure and without sin, separate from anything wrong, immoral, or unclean. This was the lesson that God was wanting to teach Isaiah in this notable vision.

Here is A. W. Tozer's description of God's holiness: 'Since God's first concern for His universe is its moral health, that is, its holiness, whatever is contrary to this is necessarily under His eternal displeasure.

To preserve His creation God must destroy whatever would destroy it. When He arises to put down iniquity and save the world from irreparable moral collapse, He is said to be angry. Every wrathful judgement in the history of the world has been a holy act of preservation. The holiness of God, the wrath of God, and the health of the creation are inseparably united. God's wrath is His utter intolerance of whatever degrades and destroys. He hates iniquity as a mother hates the polio that would take the life of her child'[3].

Why is God's wrath real? Simply because God's holiness and purity is so perfect that even the smallest sin is important to God. The prophet Habakkuk said of God, 'You are of purer eyes than to behold evil, and cannot look on wickedness' (Habakkuk 1:13). In God's perfect holiness – His perfect love of what is good and right and His perfect hatred of all that is not – He requires that all sin is atoned for. That means that all sin must be paid for, one way or another. God's infinite holiness is the reason why His wrath and judgment are coming upon all people.

God the Judge

J. I. Packer writes, 'There are few things stressed more strongly in the Bible than the reality of God's work as Judge … The entire New Testament is overshadowed by the certainty of a coming day of universal judgment, and by the problem thence arising: how may sinners get right with God while there is yet time'[4].

The Seriousness of Sin

Gary Haugen, former Director of the UN genocide investigation in Rwanda, said:

'Standing with my boots deep in the reeking muck of a Rwandan mass grave where thousands of innocent people have been horribly slaughtered, I have no words, no meaning, no life, no hope – if there is not a God of history and time who is absolutely furious,

---

[3] A. W. Tozer, *The Knowledge of the Holy*, OM, 1976, pp.140-1

[4] J. I. Packer, *Knowing God*, pp.156-158

absolutely burning with anger towards those who took it in their own hand to commit such acts'[5].

Haugen said, 'If we want to truly know God, we must endeavour to understand the holy God, the God who has made himself known in Scripture, the God who cannot accommodate himself to the sin of injustice, who can't get used to it, who continually suffers with those who are brutalized in body and spirit by the arrogance of humans'[6].

The perfect holiness of God means that it is not just genocide that God is angry about. All sin brings upon us God's wrath. Romans 1:18 says, 'The wrath of God is revealed from Heaven against all unrighteousness and ungodliness of men'. The word 'all' here teaches us that God is not simply furious with great crimes; His anger burns against all unrighteousness.

We see this in certain incidents in the Bible. In the Old Testament we have the case of Achan, who merely disobeyed God by stealing some clothing, gold and silver, and was put to death for it, along with his family who were accessories to the crime. In the New Testament, there is the story of Ananias and Sapphira who lied about the purchase price of some property that they sold, giving the reduced proceeds to the apostles in Jerusalem, and again died for it.

We may think of these as trivial offences, rather than grave and terrible sins, worthy of death. But the Bible teaches that the wages of sin is death (Romans 6:23), and that any sin, small or great, is deserving of death (Romans 1:31). By our sins, we lose our right to live upon God's earth. It is His world, after all, and God did not create it to be polluted and spoiled by our evil. Not only do we forfeit our right to live on God's earth, but we forfeit our right to real life (eternal life) with God too.

Judgment

The Bible teaches that there is judgment to come. 'It is appointed to man to die once, but after this the judgment' (Hebrews 9:27). Romans 2:6-10

---

[5] Gary Haugen, *Good News About Injustice*, IVP, 1999, p.85
[6] Haugen, *Good News About Injustice*, pp.84-85

lay out the basis for the judgment to come:

> God 'will render to each one according to his deeds: eternal life to those who by patient continuance in doing good seek for glory, honor, and immortality; but to those who are self-seeking and do not obey the truth, but obey unrighteousness - indignation and wrath, tribulation and anguish, on every soul of man who does evil, of the Jew first and also of the Greek; but glory, honor, and peace to everyone who works what is good, to the Jew first and also to the Greek'.

The principle is familiar and simple: God will render to (i.e. repay) people for their works, just like an employer pays wages to his workers. If a person has constantly done only what is good in this life, despite all the myriad temptations, distractions and difficulties, he will earn eternal life. That would be no small achievement. Most people would agree that a man or woman who continually lived righteously and did what is good would deserve eternal life as a reward for their hard work.

But the flip-side of this principle is also true: a person who has rebelled against God's ways, is self-seeking, and goes about doing what is not righteous, also deserves wages for his hard work. Shall God pay him nothing for all this effort, doing evil? No. Instead, God values this person's evil works as worthy of eternal punishment on the same set of scales that weighs perfect continuance in good deeds as worthy of eternal life. In other words, the result of God's judgment is either heaven for a perfect life of continual good works, or hell for those who fall short of this standard.

Many argue that hell is not fair, that conscious eternal suffering in hell is not a punishment equal to a few petty crimes on earth. However, this is to misunderstand the real issue: how an infinitely holy God views sin. Hardly anyone disagrees that Adolf Hitler deserves hell, not only for his horrific evils but for his unflinching and defiant attitude. The same applies to Joseph Stalin, who raised his clenched fist to heaven on his death-bed. But God's holiness is infinitely greater than our lukewarm dislike of sin: God sees all sin as abhorrent. God's attitude to all sin is roughly equal to our abhorrence of Adolf Hitler's crimes. Therefore, viewed from God's perspective, Adolf Hitler is only a little worse than the millions of others who died obstinately refusing to repent of their sins, and without the least interest in being reconciled to their Maker. Their entire life was one long rebellion against God, and an ever-hardening refusal to accept His provision of forgiveness, so why should their eternity be any different to Hitler's? Hell was made for the Devil, says Christ, but those who take the Devil's side shall share the Devil's end.

Spurgeon said, 'The Lord never plays at frightening men'. Hell is real because God is perfectly righteous and pure. The issue is not how many works we have done or how heavily they weigh on the scales of this world's justice system, but the true value or worth of these deeds. God's evaluation is that all evil is so abhorrent that it deserves hell. We gladly accept God's valuation of continual good work as deserving eternal life. Our error is to undervalue evil, and not see it as a perfect and holy God sees it, as 'exceedingly sinful' (Romans 7:13). God values sin at its true price. For God, evil has an equal and opposite worth to good: it deserves eternal punishment.

Thomas Aquinas wrote, 'The magnitude of the punishment matches the magnitude of the sin... Now a sin that is against God is infinite; the higher the person against whom it is committed, the graver the sin—it is more criminal to strike a head of state than a private citizen—and God is of infinite greatness. Therefore an infinite punishment is deserved for a sin committed against him' (*Summa Theologica*).

This quote makes it sound as if sin is simply a personal insult to God, but there is more to it than that. Sin is infinitely detestable in itself, and we would see this if only our sensitivity were as finely-tuned as God's. Once upon a time, in the day when a gentleman's word was his bond, lying was so shameful that men would be challenged to duels if they accused others of it. But God's standards are higher still. Because all sin is an offence against what is right, pure and holy, and because God's standard of holiness is absolute perfection, God's hatred of sin is infinite, and God's judgment upon sin is not only inescapable (Romans 2:3), but inveterate – it will never grow old or cold, tire or end.

Furthermore, as Aquinas points out, all sin is not only an offence against God's principles, but it ruins our relationship with Him. God cannot have any fellowship with sin. Isaiah 59:2 says, 'Your iniquities have separated you from your God, and your sins have hidden His face from you'. Just as in the Garden of Eden, Adam and Eve's sin did not annihilate them, but simply resulted in them being expelled from paradise. So too our sins will separate us from God forever.

God the Saviour

Imagine that one morning you woke up to find that your brand new car had been vandalized on your front driveway. Someone had taken a key to it and scrawled deep marks in the paintwork. The bill to repair it would run into the thousands. A few days later the police phoned you up to say that they had caught the culprit in the very act of doing the same thing to another car. Did you want to press charges? Just before you were about to answer, the police said that there was one other thing you ought to know. It was your own son who they had caught.

That changes everything. With some crimes, there are legal aspects and financial costs to think about. But with this case, there is a deeper and even more important issue: your relationship with your rebellious son. If you love him deeply enough, like the father of the prodigal son in Christ's parable, you could choose to forgive him, so that he might see how much you love him. This would involve not pressing charges, so that he doesn't have a criminal record. It would also mean bearing the cost of the repairs yourself rather than making your son pay. Either way, the cost must be borne, either by your son or yourself. But the deeper problem remains: how to win back the love of your rebellious son.

This is what God's plan of salvation is really all about. In His great love, He has sent His Son, who willingly died in our place, taking our sin upon Him and our death that it deserved. God's plan of salvation not only pays the price for our sins, but is a demonstration of God's great love for us. By the cross of Christ, God calls us to Himself, to return to the one we have sinned against, to be reconciled to our Heavenly Father who loves us.

Those who refuse God's offer of forgiveness and salvation are ultimately saying that they prefer not to receive God's love. As J. I. Packer puts it:

> 'The unbeliever has preferred to be by himself, without God, defying God, having God against him, and he shall have his preference. Nobody stands under the wrath of God save those who have chosen to do so. The essence of God's action in wrath is to give people what they choose, in all its implications: nothing more, and equally nothing less. God's readiness to respect human choice to this extent may appear disconcerting and even terrifying, but it is plain that his attitude here is supremely just, and poles apart from the wanton and irresponsible inflicting of pain which is what we mean by cruelty'[7].

In Jesus' parable of the great supper, a man put on a feast at great expense, inviting many guests. But when the time came, the guests didn't show up, and a servant was sent to tell them that everything was ready. The guests made excuses: one had bought a field and needed to go see it, another had bought ten oxen and needed to try them out, while another had married a wife, as if that in itself was reason enough not to come. The servant returned to tell the host the guests weren't coming. The master was angry and sent his servants out to invite the poor, the disabled and the homeless, until eventually his house was filled. The story is a picture of God's plan of salvation – God's free gift of eternal life, joy and peace. The moral of the story, in part, is that those who refuse the invitation will have no reason to complain. They did not want to enjoy eternal life with God. They will only be getting what they themselves chose.

C. S. Lewis made the same argument, writing about God banishing people to hell: 'There are only two kinds of people in the end: those who say to God, "Thy will be done" and those to whom God says, in the end, "Thy will be done".

The good news for us is that, just like in Isaiah's case, God in His grace has made a way of pardon, cleansing and salvation, giving an

---

[7] Packer, *Knowing God*, p.175

infinite person, His own Son, as the sacrifice for our sins, so that we who are unable to live up to God's holy standards may be saved, simply by receiving God's Son.

Chapter 25

God is Glorious

Masoud was born in Afghanistan into a devout Muslim family. As a boy, he was confused about God and had many questions. "Why can't I see God?" he asked. His grandfather travelled on pilgrimage to Mecca and even went inside the Kaaba, the black cube, the most sacred site in Islam. When he returned, Masoud pestered him with questions, asking if he had seen God there, until eventually he got a slap on the cheek. As he grew up, he read lots of books about God, angels, heaven, and hell. In one book, he read that if a person became a martyr, they would go to heaven and see God.

This was one of the reasons Masoud decided to join the Mujahedeen after school, to fight against the Soviet Red army that invaded Afghanistan on Christmas Day 1979. Many times he tried to get killed by fighting the Soviets. He even personally attacked tanks, thinking, 'if I blow up the tank that is good, but if I get killed and go to heaven that is good too'.

He became a small group commander, leading about twenty men, and had a lot of time to read during the day. He read the Koran in Arabic and also Farsi, his own language. As he read the Koran, he became fascinated with one character he found in different places: Jesus. He asked himself, 'Who is this Jesus, son of Mary, who was such a good man that angels took him to paradise?' (Muslims do not believe that Jesus Christ died). Masoud said, 'I want to go to heaven. If I am going to go to heaven, I have to find out more about this man Jesus. But how? The mosques will not tell me anything more than I already know'.

One night, he had a dream. In the dream, there was a man in white, unlike any Muslim imam. The man's arms were outstretched, calling Masoud to come to him. However, there was a great big dark canyon separating them. Masoud thought that the person in his dream was maybe an angel God had sent because he was trying to find out more about Jesus.

Soon after this, he was injured in an attack. Most of his friends died, and he was taken to hospital in Iran. When he recovered, Masoud decided not to go back to Afghanistan. In fact, he had no more desire to die. Instead, he wanted to find out more about Jesus.

He left the Mujahedeen, resigning his command, along with the honour, power, and respected position. His commander came and tried to convince him to come back to Afghanistan to fight, even accusing him of being afraid. But Masoud had no desire to go back. He no longer wanted to die.

He became a refugee in Iran, trying to find people to help him learn about Jesus. For three months, almost every night, he went to a big shrine, praying to God, asking God to show Himself. He was confused about the dream, trying to work out who Jesus was. Suddenly the thought came to him to find Christian people because they worship Jesus. He went to a Christian church, but they were not willing to talk. He was given a phone number, and invited to a man's house, and he talked with him about Jesus. This went on for about six months, and after this the Christians started to trust Masoud, no longer fearing he was a government spy. One guest speaker said, "Jesus Christ is the Son of God – He is God". Masoud was not prepared to accept this. He said, "When did God get married? Who is His wife?" He was very upset and argued at the idea of Jesus being the Son of God until he left the group altogether.

Masoud started a business, travelling between Pakistan, Afghanistan and Iran. He did well in business and got married. He was still searching and found some Christian missionaries, and was given a Bible, and helped to understand more about Jesus. He was still a Muslim, but wanted to be a Christian – sometimes he was not sure what he believed. In fact, he started trying to forget about Jesus, but God would not let him go. He became a believer in Jesus in 2004. In his own words, 'I repented and accepted Him as Son of God. I surrendered not even knowing how but just accepting'.

Masoud looks back now and says that if it wasn't for God's grace he would not be a Christian. In fact, he would not even be alive. Many times he should have died in the war, or in accidents, and he had a difficult life in Pakistan after becoming a Christian; the Muslims killed people who had converted from Islam. Before he was a Christian, he was like one of them: very zealous for Islam, ready to kill any infidels. He was stubbornly resistant to believing in Jesus as the Son of God – a blasphemous idea in Islam. Without God's grace he would never have accepted Jesus as God's Son, but God showed him mercy, and helped him to believe. In fact, looking back, he now believes it was Jesus Christ Himself, reaching out in His grace, who appeared to him in the dream.

After he became a Christian Masoud had to leave Afghanistan – it was too dangerous for his family now he had turned away from Islam. In Pakistan, he joined a church and started serving God, but persecution came when people found out he had converted. Some attempted to kill him, and he escaped from village to village, from city to city. It was a very difficult time, but God eventually opened a door to leave the country.

Despite suffering so much persecution, he had no desire to go back to Islam. He was like a blind man who found the light – and didn't want to return to the darkness. Now, he serves God by telling Muslims about Jesus in Western countries.

Reports of dreams similar to Masoud's among people from the Muslim world are too numerous to be dismissed as lies or fantasy by sceptical Westerners. Many of these people had no contact with Christianity beforehand but as a result of believing in Jesus Christ have suffered great persecution. Their conversion to Christ is genuine. What are these people seeing in their dreams?

God is Glorious

In the Bible, we sometimes read about the glory of God. We read that the God of glory appeared to Abraham, and to the prophets Isaiah and Ezekiel. In the New Testament, the glory of God shone around the shepherds as the angels announced to them the birth of Christ. The apostles Paul and John also saw a vision of Christ in His glory. But God's glory involves much more than a vision of bright heavenly beings.

In this chapter, we will explore what it means for God to be glorious.

'Glory' is a difficult word to understand. In fact, some have suggested that it is impossible to define the word 'glory', because it is like trying to define the word 'beauty'. Rather than worry about definitions, I want to look through Scripture to build up a picture of what God's glory is. God's glory is seen in seven ways in Scripture:

1. In Creation

The Puritan writer Thomas Watson wrote, 'Glory is the sparkling of the Deity'. Psalm 19:1 says, 'The heavens declare the glory of God'. As we look up into the sky, God reveals something to us about Himself. During the day, we see the beautiful blue expanse stretching out over us, the blazing sun, and the white clouds. We see the golden red sunset at evening and at night we see the thousands of stars twinkling. God is speaking wordlessly and by the heavens He shows us His power, His infinity, and His beauty.

Just as the heavens declare God's glory, so too does the earth beneath, showing God's wisdom, care and provision. Psalm 104 is a song about God's works in creation – it tells of the mountains and seas, rivers and trees, and the animals seeking their food from God. Near the end of the psalm, verse 31 says, 'The glory of the LORD shall endure for ever: the LORD shall rejoice in his works' (KJV). In Isaiah 6:3, the angels cry, 'Holy, holy, holy, is the Lord of hosts. The whole earth is full of His glory'. Creation is an advertisement for God, showing us His glory. God's works give us a little glimpse of the Great God behind it all.

2. In His Mighty Miracles

God's glory is linked with His miracles and wonders in a number of places in the Old Testament. In Numbers 14:21-22 God says, 'but truly, as I live, all the earth shall be filled with the glory of the LORD, because all these men who have seen My glory and the signs which I did in Egypt and in the wilderness, and have put Me to the test now these ten times, and have not heeded My voice'. God's glory was seen in the amazing supernatural miracles that He did in Egypt.

God is Glorious

3. In His Judgments

Psalm 29 must have been one of the favourite psalms of the temple musicians in the Old Testament. It was probably very noisy, with cymbals, drums, and trumpets imitating the sounds of thunder, lightning and raging waters. In Psalm 29:1-3, we read:

> Give unto the LORD, O you mighty ones,
> give unto the LORD glory and strength.
> Give unto the LORD the glory due to His name;
> worship the LORD in the beauty of holiness.
> The voice of the LORD is over the waters;
> The God of glory thunders;
> The LORD is over many waters.

In verse 10 it says, 'The LORD sat enthroned at the Flood, and the LORD sits as King forever'. God is called the God of glory in this psalm, and it gives us a picture of God presiding over the Flood. God's glory is here seen in His righteous judgment of a sinful world.

4. In the Declaration of His Character

When Moses asked to see God's glory in Exodus 33, God said He would make all His goodness pass before Moses and He would proclaim the name of the Lord. So God hid Moses in the cleft of the rock, and said, "The LORD, the LORD God, merciful and gracious, longsuffering, and abounding in goodness and truth, keeping mercy for thousands, forgiving iniquity and transgression and sin, by no means clearing the guilty, visiting the iniquity of the fathers upon the children and the children's children to the third and the fourth generation" (Exodus 34:6-7).

In response to Moses asking to see His glory, God surprisingly declares His name and His character: merciful, gracious, longsuffering, abundant in goodness and truth, forgiving iniquity, but by no means clearing the guilty, visiting iniquity upon men to the third and fourth generation. It is God's moral character that is His chief glory.

353

5. *In a Visible Manifestation*

There are also many passages in the Old Testament where God's glory is seen in a visible manifestation of bright shining light. In Exodus 24:16 we read that the glory of God rested on Mount Sinai, and in Exodus 40, it filled the tabernacle, the sacred tent, that had just been set up. Then later it was seen in Solomon's temple, and in the book of Ezekiel, it departed from the Temple at the time of the Babylonian exile.

God's glory is called the Shekinah (meaning 'dwelling') in the Jewish targums, the paraphrases in Aramaic (the language of Syria spoken by Jews after the Babylonian exile), written to help non-Hebrew speaking Jews understand their Bibles.

Why did God have this visible manifestation of His glory, this 'Shekinah glory', in the cloudy pillar and fire in the Old Testament? I suggest the visible presence was intended to remind the Israelites that God is real, not just imaginary. It also taught that God was present with Israel, dwelling among them (the Shekinah). The bright light also taught of His brilliance.

6. *In Christ*

In the New Testament, God's glory is seen in Jesus Christ. When Christ went up into what we call the Mount of Transfiguration, where His appearance changed, His face shone like the sun and His clothes became as white as light, we read that the disciples 'saw His glory' (Luke 9:32). In 2 Corinthians 4:6 we read, 'For it is the God who commanded light to shine out of darkness, who has shone in our hearts to give the light of the knowledge of the glory of God in the face of Jesus Christ'. In John 1:14 we read, 'the Word became flesh and dwelt among us, and we beheld His glory, the glory as of the only begotten of the Father, full of grace and truth'. In Hebrews 1:3, we read that the Lord Jesus is the 'the brightness [or out-shining] of His glory and the express image of His person'.

In the book of Acts, we have a series of visions of the glory of God. In Acts 7:2, when Stephen the first Christian martyr was on trial, he said that 'the God of glory appeared to our father Abraham in Mesopotamia'. Then, at the end of his speech, we read that Stephen himself saw the glory of God and Jesus standing at the right hand of God (verse 55). When Stephen told the council of this vision, they rushed upon him and stoned him to death. But only one chapter later, we read that Saul, also known as Paul [who was responsible for putting Stephen to death] on the road to Damascus to arrest Christians saw a bright light shining about him from heaven (Acts 9:3). What must Paul have thought when he saw this? I think his initial impression would have been that he was seeing the glory of God. What a shock it must have been to this violent enemy of Christianity to hear the voice, 'I am Jesus who you are persecuting'. The God of glory had indeed appeared to him, in the person of the Lord Jesus Christ. Years later, when Paul recounted his conversion story before King Agrippa, he said 'I saw a light from heaven, brighter than the sun, shining around me' (Acts 26:13).

Here we have the supreme manifestation of God's glory, in the person of Christ.

7. *In His Plan of Salvation*

Lastly, when we come over to the New Testament letters, we read of the glory of God in the plan of salvation. In Ephesians 1:6-7, we read 'to the praise of the glory of His grace, by which He has made us accepted in the Beloved. In Him we have redemption through His blood, the forgiveness of sins, according to the riches of His grace'.

The American preacher Donald Grey Barnhouse said that 'God's greatest glory is His grace', and while I don't think that is completely true (Christ Himself is greater), yet there is an element of truth in what he says: God's grace brings God tremendous glory. God's glory is seen in His plan of salvation by grace. In his letter to the Galatians, Paul gives a short summary of the true gospel (as opposed to the false gospel of works), and concludes this gospel summary with the words 'To whom be glory for ever and ever' (Galatians 1:5). God is the one who gets the glory for our salvation, because it was all according to His grace.

The Reformers had five solas, five watchwords: *sola Scriptura* (Scripture alone), *sola gracia* (by grace alone), *sola fidei* (by faith alone), *sola Christus* (through Christ alone) and *soli Deo gloria* (glory to God alone). The New Testament gospel results in glory to God alone.

Romans 11:36 says, 'For of him, and through him, and to him, are all things: to whom be glory for ever. Amen'. That is, it all comes from God, and it is all through God (that is, in Christ) and it should be all to Him, that is, all the glory goes to God, forever and ever, amen.

Thomas Aquinas and the Glory of God

Thomas Aquinas was born in AD 1225 to a noble Italian family and was sent to a monastery by his parents at age 5. At the age of 19 he decided to join the Dominican order of monks, and then to study at the University of Paris. These plans did not please his parents and he was kidnapped on the way to Paris by his brothers, and taken back to the family's castle where he was held captive for a year. Eventually his family let him escape and in 1245 he went to Paris to study under Albertus Magnus. Because he was quiet some other students thought he was stupid, but his teacher prophetically said, 'You call him the dumb ox, but in his teaching he will one day produce such a bellowing that it will be heard throughout the world'.

Aquinas had come to Paris to study at a time when the ancient Greek writings, particularly Aristotle's, were being revived. He was also influenced by Arabic learning and the teaching of the Jewish sage Maimonides. In 1256 he began teaching theology in Paris, then later in Naples and Rome as the Papal theologian. In Rome, Aquinas began his most famous work, *Summa Theologica,* a summary of Christian beliefs, dealing with the doctrines of God, Creation, Man, Ethics, Christ and the Roman Catholic sacraments. It has been called one of the most influential books ever written, and contains Aquinas's Five Ways, his five arguments for God's existence.

Thomas Aquinas incorporated elements of Aristotle's philosophy into his thinking. He believed that the study of nature was important for understanding God, and believing also that human reason was a gift from God, he tried to combine Christian revelation with human logic.

However, in 1273 he had what is believed to have been some sort of vision or supernatural experience of Christ. As a result, he refused to continue writing *Summa Theologica,* saying 'all that I have written seems like straw to me' by comparison, leaving his great work uncompleted.

Aquinas realized this great truth: intellectual arguments about God's existence are not enough. We need to come to know God personally, and to behold His glory. I do not mean by this that we have to visibly see God. Instead, we need to see God's glory with the 'eyes of our heart', as Paul put it in Ephesians 1:18. David put it like this in Psalm 27:4, 'One thing I have desired of the Lord, that will I seek, that I may dwell in the house of the Lord all the days of my life, to behold the beauty of the Lord and to inquire in His temple'.

What is God's Glory?

What do we learn about God's glory from the various passages we have considered in the Bible? We can summarise God's glory under four headings.

1.   **God's Attributes**. The different aspects of God's glory are all displays of God's attributes: His power and wisdom are seen in creation, His righteous judgment at the flood, His longsuffering mercy with Israel, and His grace in His plan of salvation.

2.   **On Display.** These different ways in which God's glory is seen in the Bible are all manifestations, or revelations, or displays of who God is, whether in creation, or in Christ or in His mighty acts, or in His declaration of His name to Moses. God's glory is God's attributes on display.

3.   **Progressively revealed.** God's glory is progressively revealed throughout the Bible. It is seen in creation, then more is seen at the flood, and in the history of Israel, and the full and final revelation of God's glory is seen in our Lord Jesus Christ. Why is it revealed progressively? Because God's glory is many-sided.

4.   **In Perfection**. Not only are God's attributes displayed in all these different ways, His attributes are seen in perfection. Thus, creation does not reveal us a small God, but a majestic, almighty, eternal and infinite God. God's miraculous works are again a demonstration of His

supernatural power. Thus, another way we can think of God's glory is to think of it as the display of His perfections and excellences. This is, in fact, how some theologians refer to God's attributes: His perfections.

In summary, God's glory involves God's attributes on display, progressively revealed in perfection. We may define God's glory as the excellence and perfection of His person and His attributes, displayed in many ways, but seen pre-eminently in our Lord Jesus Christ, in whom all the attributes of God are perfectly manifested. A short definition of God's glory is 'God's excellence on display'.

God's Perfection

God's glory is a display of His perfection. Consider for a moment some of God's attributes and how they must all be perfect.

- **God's omnipotence**. For God to be all-powerful, He must also be omnipresent and omniscient. For example, if God was not able to act anywhere and everywhere, then His power would be limited. Again, imagine if God was not all-knowing; if this was the case, He would not be omnipotent either. An army might be very powerful, but if it does not know of the movements of the enemy, it is in the dark and in danger of being taken by surprise and badly damaged. In World War Two, the Americans were attacked at Pearl Harbour by the Japanese, and American naval power was greatly dented. For God to be omnipotent, He must therefore also be omniscient, and omnipresent.

- **God's wisdom**. Wisdom involves not only knowledge, and understanding, but it also involves a moral dimension. We read that the fear of the Lord is the beginning of wisdom and the book of Proverbs speaks much about the righteous and the wicked, because true wisdom is righteous. If a man was highly intelligent but very corrupt, he would only be cunningly clever. There would be no guarantee that he would use his cleverness for good. J. I. Packer writes, 'Wisdom without power would be pathetic, a broken reed;

power without wisdom would be merely frightening'[1]. It would be terrifying if God was all-powerful without being all-wise.

- **God's goodness**. If God is not morally perfect, He could not be God at all. If there was any evil in Him, He would become unfair or cruel, and would cease to be worthy of being the rightful Ruler of all.

Thus, God must possess all His attributes in perfection. This is what Scripture teaches:

- God's life is infinite – He is eternal
- God's power and knowledge are infinite: 'Great is our Lord, and mighty in power; His understanding is infinite' (Psalm 147:5)
- God's greatness in infinite: 'Great is the LORD, and greatly to be praised; and his greatness is unsearchable' (Psalm 145:3)
- God's way is perfect, His work is perfect, His will is perfect, His law is perfect, and He is perfect in knowledge[2].

W. E. Hoste defines God as 'a Personal Being, *Infinite* in Holiness, Power, Wisdom and Goodness, Self-existent and Self-sufficieint, Who in His essence is Spirit, Light, and Love, the Great Source, Author and Sustainer of all things'[3].

More than this, all God's attributes are in perfect balance and harmony. We see this in our Lord Jesus Christ. He read He was 'full of grace and truth' (John 1:14), in Him are 'hidden all the treasures of wisdom and knowledge' (Colossians 2:3), and 'in Him is no sin' (1 John 3:5). In Christ, we have perfection in every possible direction. That is glory.

Hoste goes on to say that with God, 'all is in perfect proportion and relation. His holiness is bound up with His love, "God is light" and "God is love". His respect for the moral freedom of His creatures is balanced by His Sovereignty; His long-suffering by His wrath; His mercy by His judgment. God unites in Himself all the antitheses. He is the High and Lofty One who inhabits eternity, yet dwells in time "with him also that is

---

[1] J. I. Packer, *Knowing God*, Hodder and Stoughton, 2005, p.101

[2] Psalm 18:30, Deuteronomy 32:4, Romans 12:2, Psalm 19:7, Job 37:16

[3] W. E. Hoste, *Studies in Bible Doctrine*, Pickering and Inglis, 1932, p.1

of a contrite and humble spirit" (Isaiah 57:15). Exalted in unapproachable sublimity, yet is he "not so far even as to be near"; pervading everything, yet above and distinct from everything; a just God, "of purer eyes than to behold iniquity", yet a Saviour, "the justifier of him which believeth in Jesus"[4].

The Ontological Argument for God

The Ontological (definition: relating to 'being') argument for God's existence was set out by Anselm of Canterbury in AD 1078. Anselm argued that because God is defined as the greatest conceivable Being, and nothing greater than God could be conceived (because if we could think of something greater than God, then *that* would be God), then God must really exist, because if He was only imaginary, then something greater could exist: a real version of God (just as $100 in my hand is greater than $100 in my imagination). In other words, since our definition of God includes perfection, God would be less than perfect if He did not actually exist – a contradiction in terms, which proves that God must in fact exist.

Philosophers have debated this argument over the centuries. Many ordinary people find it confusing; it seems a philosopher's word-trick. Others see this argument as too simple, and that proving God's existence by definition must involve a circular argument.

In fact, we could simplify the argument by saying that God exists, by definition. That is, because God is the eternal and self-existent One, if God were not eternal He would only be a creature, and not truly God. Seeing a non-eternal God is a contradiction in terms, God must be eternal, and therefore exist. But this makes the statement 'God exists' seem tautological (saying the same thing twice), and for all the truth it contains, it leaves a lot to be desired in a proof of God's existence.

Not many people have been converted to belief in God through the ontological argument. And one wonders why it took 1078 years after Christ for this proof of God's existence to come to light. Nevertheless, many Christian philosophers think that the Ontological argument is

---

[4] Hoste, *Studies*, p.22

valid. Another form of the argument by philosopher Alvin Plantinga is as follows:

1. It is possible that a maximally great being exits.
2. If a maximally great being exists, then it exists in some possible world (i.e. some world that could conceivably exist).
3. If a maximally great being exists in some possible world, then it exists in every possible world (because it would not be maximally great if it only existed in some worlds).
4. If a maximally great being exists in every possible world, then it exists in the actual world.
5. If a maximally great being exists in the actual world, then a maximally great being actually exists.
6. Therefore, a maximally great being exists.

Some have objected to the Ontological argument by saying we could use it to prove a maximally great island exists, or a maximally great unicorn exists, or even a maximally great Darth Vader (the powerful villain in the *Star Wars* movies) exists. However, islands and unicorns are not omnipresent, all-powerful and all-knowing, therefore they cannot be maximally great Beings. Neither is Darth Vader a maximally great Being, seeing he is not perfectly morally good. God (a maximally great Being) must be perfect in every way.

The only way to disprove this logical argument would be to show that the first step is false (for every other step follows logically), by proving that it is impossible for God to exist, or that the idea of God is absurd. Some atheists try to do this by arguing that some aspects of perfection are incoherent (e.g., God's omnipotence is impossible for He cannot create a rock so big He cannot lift it, or His omnipotence is incompatible with His being unable to lie or sin), however, as we have seen in the chapter on God's power, these arguments involve errors in understanding God. Therefore, seeing it is possible that God, a maximally great Being, exists, the Ontological argument says that God really does exist.

Whether this argument convinces you that God exists or not, we have seen in this chapter that God cannot be anything less than perfect.

Worshipping God

What should our response be to God's glory? We should worship. Just as we stand and silently admire a glorious sunset, or sit back and breathe in a beautiful piece of music, how much more should we not bow down and adore the Creator who made music and sunlight, and gave us eyes and ears to take it all in?

Worship is, sadly, a much-debased word today, meaning little more among some Christians than a certain style of music. Worship is, in fact, not really about music at all. William Temple, the Archbishop of Canterbury during World War Two, defined worship as follows:

'To worship is to quicken the conscience by the holiness of God, to feed the mind with the truth of God, to purge the imagination by the beauty of God, to open the heart to the love of God, to devote the will to the purpose of God. All this is gathered up in that emotion which most cleanses us from selfishness because it is the most selfless of all emotions – adoration'.

The *Westminster Shorter Catechism* says that 'man's chief end is to glorify God, and to enjoy him forever'. We exist to worship and glorify God. 'Give to the LORD the glory due His name; bring an offering, and come before Him. Oh, worship the LORD in the beauty of holiness' (1 Chronicles 16:29).

We should also trust a perfect God. If His will, His work, His word, and His way are perfect, then we can confidently trust and obey an infinitely wise, loving and powerful God.

Thirdly, just as Moses' face shone after he came down from Mt. Sinai where He met God, so we should be transformed by beholding the glory of the Lord. Paul writes: 'But we all, with open face beholding as in a glass the glory of the Lord, are changed into the same image from glory to glory, even as by the Spirit of the Lord' (2 Corinthians 3:17). We should become more like our Lord Jesus Christ.

PART THREE:

Objections to God

Chapter 26

Faith is Belief without Evidence

Atheists today regularly define faith as believing in something for which there is no evidence. Mark Twain said, 'Faith is believing what you know ain't so'. Some internet atheists even define faith as 'believing in something which does not exist'.

This view of faith has been popularized particularly by the prominent atheist Richard Dawkins, who says faith is a kind of mental illness, a 'way of non-thinking' and one of the world's great evils. Here is Dawkins on faith:

> 'Faith is the great cop-out, the great excuse to evade the need to think and evaluate evidence. Faith is belief in spite of, even perhaps because of, the lack of evidence'[1].

The ironic thing about Dawkins' definition is that there no evidence to back it up. Alister McGrath tells a story in his book, *Dawkins' God*:

> When I debate these issues in public, I regularly get asked why Christians blindly trust in God, in the absence of any supporting evidence. I ask if they would be kind enough to tell me where they find such a ludicrous idea, and to justify it from a serious Christian writer of note. I am usually greeted with an embarrassed silence. Yet on occasion, I get the answer: "Well, that's what Richard Dawkins says." The audience usually laughs. They get the point'[2].

Asking an atheist for a definition of faith is as useless as asking Genghis

---

[1] From "A Scientist's Case Against God", *The Independent*, 20 April 1992.
[2] Alister McGrath, *Dawkin's God: Genes, Memes and the Meaning of Life*, Blackwell Publishing, 2005, pp.117-8

Khan for a definition of compassion. The reason the atheist definition of faith is so poor is because atheists have no interest in truly understanding it. But there is more to it than simply the fact that atheists are clueless about faith; the definition has been deliberately invented to misrepresent faith.

In Lewis Carroll's *Through the Looking Glass*, there is a conversation between Humpty-Dumpty and Alice which runs as follows:

"I don't know what you mean by 'glory'", Alice said.

Humpty Dumpty smiled contemptuously. "Of course you don't – till I tell you. I meant 'there's a nice knock-down argument for you!'"

"But 'glory' doesn't mean "a nice knock-down argument"", Alice objected.

"When I use a word", Humpty Dumpty said in a rather scornful tone, "it means just what I choose it to mean – neither more nor less".

"The question is", said Alice, "whether you can make words mean different things".

Sadly, we can't make words mean just what we choose them to mean. But this is precisely what Dawkins is doing: inventing a definition of faith, without any evidence to back it up, that twists its meaning so he can attack faith as irrational.

So what is faith? I am going to give you two definitions of faith, one from the Bible and the second from a theologian called Griffith-Thomas. But since definitions are not easy to immediately digest, I will give an illustration of faith that will help us unpack and explain the definitions.

My favourite story that illustrates faith involves a little girl who interrupted her father while he was reading his weekend newspaper to ask him if he would build her a doll's house. The father lowered his newspaper and smiled at her. 'Yes darling', he said. Then he picked up his paper and continued reading. Later, through the window he saw his daughter putting a pile of clothes down on the lawn in the back garden. After a while he saw her take some cups and saucers and add them to her pile of clothes. Then he saw her put some plates and cutlery down on the grass. He put down his paper, went in to the kitchen, and asked his wife, 'What is she doing?' His wife replied, 'She obviously believed what you said about building the doll's house'.

Now keep that little story in mind as we look at the definition of faith given by the theologian W. H. Griffith-Thomas. He wrote,

Faith affects the whole of man's nature. It commences with the conviction of the mind based on adequate evidence; it continues in the confidence of the heart or emotions based on conviction, and it is crowned in the consent of the will, by means of which the conviction and confidence are expressed in conduct.

Griffith-Thomas uses four phrases based on the letter 'c' to define faith: conviction of the mind, confidence of the heart, consent of the will, and expressed in conduct.

Think of the way the little girl in the story clearly showed conviction. That is, she was convinced her father was going to build a doll's house. Then secondly, she had confidence. She trusted her father's promise to build a doll's house. She obviously had experience of his love towards her, his ability to make things himself, and his way of keeping his word.

Thirdly, she took action. Her faith expressed itself in conduct. She starting behaving as if a doll's house would very soon appear in her back garden.

The consent of the will is slightly harder to see in the story of the doll's house. When the little girl heard her father promise to build a doll's house, she could either choose to believe her father or not. If she doubted him, she might ask him whether he really meant it, or she might even just go and watch television. Instead, she chose to believe him. Our will is involved in making decisions and in choosing between alternatives; it is the basis for action. The little girl demonstrated 'consent of the will' by actively taking steps to prepare for the coming doll's house.

So, as Griffith-Thomas put it, faith starts with conviction of the mind, is followed by confidence (or trust) of the heart, it is expressed in conduct (or actions), all of which demonstrate the consent (or, choice) of the will.

The Bible's definition of faith is given in an entire chapter, Hebrews chapter 11. Here is the first verse of the chapter: 'Faith is being sure of things hoped for and certain of things not seen' (NIV[3]).

Being 'sure' and being 'certain' are the first things to notice here. They are the same as Griffith-Thomas' 'conviction of the mind'. But notice, there are other aspects of faith that go beyond mere intellectual conviction. Being sure of things *hoped for* and things *not seen* involves an element of trust or 'confidence of the heart', to use Griffith-Thomas' language. As we read through the rest of Hebrews chapter 11 we find people like Noah and Abraham who trusted God's promise about things coming in the future, things which they hoped for but had not yet seen. We also read about many Bible characters who expressed their faith by their conduct, and who made choices to obey God.

Only a century ago, a knowledge of Greek and Latin were pre-requisites for entrance to Oxford University, where Dawkins was a student. Sadly, by Dawkins' day, the language requirements had been dropped. A century ago, nobody said the sort of silly things that Dawkins does about faith. Had Dawkins understood Greek – the language of the New Testament – he would have been aware that the Greek word the New Testament uses for faith (*pistis*) is derived from a verb *peitho*, which means 'to persuade'. In other words, someone believes in something (or has faith – they mean exactly the same thing in Greek) because they are persuaded about the thing they believe in. Faith involves an element of persuasion, and people are usually persuaded of something because it has some evidence or it makes some logical sense. Faith is therefore based, to some extent, on 'reason'.

Notice that Griffith-Thomas says that conviction of the mind is 'based on adequate evidence'. We are convinced by evidence of some sort or other. A little child might believe something because their mother told them so. Adults usually require better reasons, but rarely will a person

---

[3] The NIV translation of this verse is both accurate and understandable. Compare it with the translation by William Tyndale in 1522, the first translation of the New Testament from Greek into English: 'Fayth is a sure confidence of thynges which are hoped for and a certayntie of thynges which are not sene'.

believe something for no reason whatsoever.

Faith has its reasons. For example, many people believe in God because it seems unreasonable to think that the universe just made itself, or that living beings created themselves. Other people believe that Jesus really was the Son of God, and that His resurrection is the most reasonable explanation of the evidence.

It is true that faith goes beyond intellectual reasoning. We could define faith as 'reasonable trust'. Faith is based on evidence and reason, but involves an element of trust as well. However, faith is not anti-intellectual. Atheists like Dawkins are peddling a false and twisted definition by saying that faith is belief in something without evidence.

Faith is not a cop-out, either. Faith is very common – everybody has it. The financial system depends on confidence ('credit' comes from the Latin word '*credo*', I believe). A run on a bank occurs when people have no more faith in it. Similarly, athletes need to have 'self-belief' to win. Anybody getting married has to have faith in their spouse, too.

Some non-Christians speak of faith as a mystical gift that religious people have ('I wish I had your faith'), as if faith were something that some people have, but not others. The same people are quite prepared to allow doctors to operate on them or to fly in aeroplanes, putting their confidence, trust – or faith – in the ability of surgeons and pilots and the technology they use. All people have faith – in many different things.

Even atheists have faith, because when someone says "I believe (something)", they are just saying "I consider this to be true". Alister McGrath writes:

'Christopher Hitchens declares boldly that New Atheists such as himself do not hold any beliefs. "Our belief is not a belief". This astonishing statement is one of the best examples of blind faith I have come across – a delusion that makes his whole approach vulnerable'[4].

The atheist 'definition' of faith is an example of what happens when people talk about something they don't really understand. As Michael

---

[4] https://www.abc.net.au/religion/there-is-nothing-blind-about-faith/10101704

Ruse, an atheist philosopher, wrote, 'Richard Dawkins in *The God Delusion* would fail any introductory philosophy or religion course. Proudly he criticizes that whereof he knows nothing ... *The God Delusion* makes me ashamed to be an atheist'[5].

---

[5] https://www.beliefnet.com/columnists/scienceandthesacred/2009/08/why-i-think-the-new-atheists-are-a-bloody-disaster.html

Chapter 27

Who Made God?

One of the most common arguments against God is the question: "If God made the world, who made God?" We will look at five different ways of answering this question that all arrive at the same conclusion.

The Counter-Question Answer

I have a friend who teaches children the Bible, and he often gets asked the question 'Who made God?' (There is nothing wrong, by the way, with children asking the question; it shows evidence that they are thinking).

My friend answers this question by asking another question: "If God was made by someone, would He still be God?" The children take a little while to process this question, but eventually answer, "No, of course not". Even children work can this out. If someone made God, then God would be merely another creature, like us, and would no longer be God.

My friend's counter-question shows that there is something wrong with the original question. However, it does not explain precisely where the flaw in the question lies.

The Four Options Answer

When I am asked the question, "Who made God?", I often try to help people think through a number of options.

Let us assume nothing and just start with our physical universe, and survey the options for where it came from. There would appear to be four possible answers:

1. Everything could have come into existence from nothing. But the problem with this answer is that it is irrational. You can't get something from nothing. Nothing does not have any power to create a universe, nor does it have any materials from which to build it. 'From nothing, nothing comes'.

2. Some atheists argue that the universe is eternal. Carl Sagan used to say, 'The cosmos is all there is or ever was or ever will be'. The problem with this answer is that nothing in the universe keeps going forever. Batteries run down, shoes wear out, cars need refueling, and no one has yet invented a perpetual motion machine. Our universe will eventually die too. If our universe were infinitely old, it would long ago have suffered 'heat death', like a bonfire running out of wood. The second law of thermodynamics, one of the fundamental laws of science, states that the tendency of natural processes is towards entropy (or, disorder), which means that everything in the universe is slowly running down. To put it another way, the universe is like an old-fashioned watch, still ticking. The fact that it is running down means it must once have been wound up, that is, had a beginning. Only unchanging things are eternal, and as our universe is constantly changing, it cannot be eternal.

3. A third option is that the universe is the result of an infinite regression of causes – a chain of events going backwards forever. In other words, A was caused by B, which was caused by C, and so on, forever and ever. The atheist Bertrand Russell told a story about a lecture in which the speaker was interrupted by a woman who said that the world was a flat plate that rested on the back of an elephant. The speaker asked what the elephant was standing on, and the woman replied that it was standing on the back of a giant tortoise. He then asked what the giant tortoise was standing on, to which the woman replied that it was 'tortoises all the way down'. The audience laughed. Just as we cannot have an infinitely tall tower of tortoises, it is similarly illogical to believe in an infinite regression of causes for our world, a chain of events going backwards indefinitely. An infinite regression of causes faces the same problem as an eternal universe: nothing in the physical realm is infinite.

Therefore, there cannot be an infinite chain of universal causes going backwards forever.

4. This leads us to the fourth option. If we cannot have an infinite regression of causes, there must have been a First Cause. This First Cause must itself have been Uncaused (for if it was caused, it would not be the First cause). The buck has to stop somewhere. God is the Uncaused Cause. In fact, this is how we define God – the eternal, uncaused Creator. Take a simple illustration. If we imagine a row of dominoes that we can knock over, there must be a first domino in the line that starts off the cascade of toppling dominoes. The chain of dominos cannot go on forever; it must start and finish somewhere. Even if we have a circle of dominoes, we must touch one domino to start off the toppling process. But there must also be a cause – outside of the system – to set up the dominoes and knock the first one down. In our experience, it is usually a human being who builds the row of dominoes, and it is usually a human finger that knocks down the first domino. In the universe, a cause outside the system means a supernatural Creator who is outside of nature altogether. God is the Cause of all things, outside the system, a spiritual being, not part of the physical Universe.

Here again we see that the answer to the question, "Who made God?" is: Nobody made God, for God must be eternal. He is the Creator, not the created. The question, 'Who made God?' does not make sense because God is, by very definition, eternal. He is the First Cause, Himself Uncaused. To ask "Who made God?" is to misunderstand what the word 'God' means. It is like asking, 'Who is the bachelor married to?' The question itself has no answer because it is nonsensical. Therefore, we conclude again that God – if He exists – must, by definition, be eternal.

The Two Options Answer

Some atheists respond to the idea that God is eternal by saying that either God is eternal or the universe is eternal – and they choose to believe that the universe is eternal.

There is one thing the atheist gets right here, and it provides us with a key insight: there must be something that is eternal. The atheist is also right that there are only two options: either the universe is eternal or God is eternal. However, the universe cannot be eternal, because our universe had a beginning. We have already seen some of the reasons why the universe is not eternal: it is running down, and using up its available energy. Only unchanging things are eternal, and our universe is not unchanging.

Therefore, based on the two options, we conclude that God must be eternal. This again means that nobody made God.

The Einstein Answer

This answer was not given by Albert Einstein, yet his scientific work helps us understand the answer to the 'Who made God?' question.

Einstein's theories of relativity showed that time is part of the fabric of the universe, just as much as matter, energy, space and the laws of physics. Einstein's work also helped scientists to accept that the universe had a beginning. Therefore, the fact that the universe had a beginning means that time did not exist before the universe.

What this also means is that, if God made the universe, then God transcends time. He is not only outside of creation, but He is outside of time too. The word we use for this is eternal: God is timeless. God is not governed or bound by time. He simply exists, forever. That means that God had no beginning, nor was He created by anything or anyone.

So here is the fourth answer to the question: the fact that time had a beginning means that God is eternal, without beginning. Therefore the question, 'Who made God?' does not make any sense.

The Kalam Cosmological Argument

The Kalam cosmological argument is an argument for God's existence derived from medieval Islamic philosophy, often set out as follows:

1. Whatever had a beginning had a cause
2. The universe had a beginning
3. Therefore, the universe had a cause

This argument is often used to prove that God is the cause of the universe. But while the argument is logically valid, it has two problems.

First, the kalam cosmological argument seems (to an ordinary person) to be a philosopher's trick. We would normally expect the first premise to say something like 'Whatever exists must have a cause' (instead of 'whatever *had a beginning* must have a cause'). To this shorter premise the atheist would reply, 'then God needs a cause too'. When the theist replies, 'but God is eternal, He did not have a cause', ordinary folk think that a special exception is being made for God.

The first premise of the kalam cosmological argument thus appears to be starting out by making a special exception for God that lets him off the causality hook from the get-go. It appears to allow us to state that God is eternal, without any reason or proof. Like any other special exceptions – like a teacher's pet in class, or an athlete in a sporting contest – this special exception seems to be unfair. It also appears to assume exactly what needs to be proved, that God is eternal.

Now, of course, the first premise is not really a trick, and it does not really make a special exception for God. The first premise is instead better understood as the logical conclusion to an earlier train of argument that we saw in our Four Options Answer:

    (a) the universe cannot have come into existence with no cause, and

    (b) the universe cannot be eternal, and

    (c) the universe cannot be the result of an infinite regress, therefore

    (d) there must be a first cause, itself uncaused.

This opens up the possibility of a thing which is uncaused, i.e., eternal – a special exception to the law of cause and effect. We call this First Cause, Itself Uncaused (and therefore eternal), God.

But this leads on to my second problem with the kalam cosmological argument: it assumes too much prior knowledge (the impossibility of an eternal universe or an infinite regress). It crams too many prior logical arguments and conclusions into its first step without unpacking them all slowly and carefully. If the kalam cosmological argument had seven or eight steps, carefully retracing all the earlier steps we have taken in the Four Options Answer, the ordinary man in the street would have far less impatience with it. As a result, when the kalam cosmological argument is set out in a simplistic (but actually very complex) three-step form, it only convinces people who already understand these earlier logical steps. It does not help the ordinary person understand the situation clearly enough (without a lot of extra explanation), and thus it lets the atheist debater slip off the hook too easily.

By the way, some atheists complain that all this argument proves is that there must be a cause for the universe, not that there is a God. But the cause of the universe is its Creator (therefore infinitely powerful, to have made it from nothing), outside of time (eternal), not part of the physical universe, i.e. spiritual (immaterial), and creative (able to make decisions, i.e. personal). A personal, powerful, eternal, spiritual Being is exactly how we talk about God. Even though this argument does not tell everything about our Creator, or what He is like (e.g. loving or holy), it still shows there is a God.

Who Designed the Designer?

In his book, *The God Delusion*, Richard Dawkins repeatedly asks, 'Who designed the designer? Astonishingly, Dawkins views this as 'the central argument of my book'[1]. Dawkins' question is just another way of phrasing the question "Who made God?". As we have seen, to ask who made God is a logical blunder, because God cannot have been made (or designed) by anyone – He is, by definition, eternal. Dawkins' question is therefore a nonsense question, as ridiculous as asking what flavour is jealousy.

Dawkins changes the question to "Who designed the Designer?" so he can make the following argument: to posit God as the ground of all being is a nonstarter, for 'any God capable of designing a universe, carefully and foresightfully tuned to lead to our evolution, must be a supremely complex and improbable entity who needs an even bigger explanation than the one he is supposed to provide'. Thus the God hypothesis is 'very close to being ruled out by the laws of probability'.

Now, of course, Dawkins detests design in the universe, and so his

---

[1] Richard Dawkins, *The God Delusion*, pp.157-8

question is an attempt to undermine any design argument. But to see why Dawkins' argument is problematic, let us imagine what would happen if the first human astronauts to land on Mars found a spacecraft on the far side of the planet. The fact that they don't know who designed it would hardly be any evidence against the fact that it was designed. The spacecraft obviously did not assemble itself into existence, did it? We do not need to know the name of the designer to reliably identify design when we see it. Archaeologists do this all the time. When they find shards of pottery or copper coins or gold jewellery buried in the ground they infer that ancient craftsmen deliberately designed these implements.

But when faced with design in the universe (the fine-tuning of the laws of nature) or the impossibility of the naturalistic origin of life (the cell), or evidence of design in the biosphere (the marvels of the human body), Dawkins tries to evade the evidence of design by insisting that we cannot infer design until we explain who designed the designer. This question is unreasonable. If we were to refuse to admit a spaceship was designed until someone answered Dawkins' question, we would be sent off for psychiatric assessment.

Furthermore, Dawkins' argument can be turned back on himself. If the universe made us, who made the universe? And if the universe, being a highly complex and improbable arrangement of matter, requires an even more complex thing to bring it into being, then what created the universe, and where did it come from? Dawkins' question just leads to another infinite regression. By the logic of his own argument, if highly complex things are improbable, then our highly complex universe should not exist at all. On the other hand, if highly complex and improbable things (like the universe) exist, then it is possible for God to exist too.

Dawkins tries to argue that God must be more complex than anything He has designed. But Dawkins is wrong: God is not 'complex', He is infinite – almighty, all-knowing and eternal. God is not part of the material universe, and therefore questions about His 'complexity' are not reducible to probabilistic evaluation. Mathematical probability only applies to things we can count or measure, so it is not clear how we could ever estimate God's probability mathematically. Dawkins does not put a number on it because he would be just making it up. Therefore, it seems that Dawkins is not really making a probability argument after all. He is just playing with words, rephrasing his belief in atheism another way.

The fact that we regularly reason from design to a designer, the way archaeologists reason from arrowheads to ancient craftsman, means there is no problem with reasoning from design in the universe to a Designer. Dawkins is letting his dislike of God get in the way of common sense. He attempts to make a logical argument, but he is really just rearranging his prejudices. Dawkins' argument is therefore just a cop-out, an excuse for not facing up to the powerful evidence for design.

God is necessary, for the universe cannot have created itself, and something outside of nature – eternal and immaterial – with great power and wisdom created it. God *must* exist.

Conclusion

For a little child to ask the question, "Who made God?" is perfectly reasonable, and the answer is simple: God is the Creator, not the created; He is the First Cause, Himself uncaused, and therefore eternal. If children cannot understand these concepts, give them time. But for adults to think that the question 'Who made God?' (or Who designed the Designer?') is a powerful objection to God is an embarrassing reflection upon modern society's ability to engage in serious thought. Little wonder that the philosopher William Lane Craig, after dealing with Dawkins' 'Who designed the Designer' question, wrote:

> Several years ago my atheist colleague Quentin Smith unceremoniously crowned Stephen Hawking's argument against God in *A Brief History of Time* as 'the worst atheistic argument in the history of Western thought'. With the advent of *The God Delusion* the time has come to relieve Hawking of this weighty crown and to recognize Richard Dawkins's accession to the throne[2].

---

[2] William Lane Craig, "Dawkins's Delusion", in *Contending with Christianity's Critics*, ed. Ed Copan and William Lane Craig, B&H, 2009, p.5

Chapter 28

Religion causes Wars

By contrast with the two previous objections to God, we come here to an argument that is weighty and serious. Religion has caused wars, ancient and modern. Back in the 1970s, 80s and 90s, the Northern Ireland 'troubles' were proof that religion causes wars. Following the attacks on the Twin Towers in New York in 2001, the focus shifted to Islamic terrorism. Before all this, there were the Salem witch trials, the Spanish Inquisition[1], and the Crusades. Sam Harris wrote that religion is 'the most prolific source of violence in our history'[2].

It is true that religion has added to the world's suffering, and not just by wars. Other shameful things have been done even in the name of Christianity, including the awful persecution of Jews in Europe in the middle ages, and more recently the abuse of children by paedophile priests. Televangelists living in luxury have not helped, flying about in private jets while siphoning money from their audiences. Institutional religion is always going to be a problem because 'power corrupts'. But we must not blame institutions, for they are all made up of individuals, and individuals are the real culprits behind every crime. The problem goes right to the very heart of each one of us. In *The Gulag Archipelago*, the Soviet Nobel Prize winning novelist Aleksandr Solzhenitsyn wrote:

It was granted to me to carry away from my prison years on my bent back, which nearly broke beneath its load, this essential experience: how a human being becomes evil and how good. In the intoxication of youthful successes I had felt myself to be infallible and I was

---

[1] About 3000-5000 people were killed in the Spanish Inquisition.
[2] Sam Harris, *The End of Faith: Religion, Terror and the Future of Reason*, W. W. Norton, 2004, p.27

therefore cruel. In the surfeit of power I was a murderer and oppressor. In my most evil moments I was convinced that I was doing good and I was well supplied with systematic arguments. It was only when I lay there on the rotting prison straw that I sensed within myself the first stirrings of good. Gradually it was disclosed to me that the line separating good and evil passes not between states nor between social classes nor between political parties, but right through every human heart, through all human hearts. And that is why I turn back to the years of my imprisonment and say, sometimes to the astonishment of those about me, bless you, prison, for having been a part of my life.

The problem of evil not only passes through all human hearts. As Jesus said, the problem of evil comes 'from within, out of the heart of man' (Mark 7:21). We are all to blame – whether atheist or Muslim or Christian. 'All have sinned and fall short of the glory of God' (Romans 3:23). The human heart is the problem – not religion. False religion, it hardly needs stating, is not going to solve the problem of human wickedness, and in some cases it has even made problems worse, adding to the body count. Only God's solution can fix the problem, and as the first stage of that rescue plan He sent His Son, and at the cross, God dealt with sin so that we can be forgiven and transformed. Even Christians are not perfect; we are fallen sinners too.

Is Religion the Main Cause of War?

Someone has said, if religion has killed its thousands, then politics has killed its tens of thousands. World Wars One and Two resulted in the deaths of over 65 million people, yet neither of them had much to do with religion. The twentieth century saw over 70 major conflicts, collectively resulting in about 200 million deaths, but few of these were religious. The *Encyclopedia of Wars* lists 121 wars (out of a total of 1763 wars between 8000 BC and AD 2000) under 'Religious Wars' (6.9%)[3], and if wars connected to Islam are removed, the figure drops to 3%.

---

[3] Charles Phillips and Alan Axelrod, *Encyclopedia of Wars*, Facts on File, 2005

Religion Causes Wars

David Berlinski, a secular agnostic Jew, comments: 'there is this awkward fact: the twentieth century was not an age of faith. Lenin, Stalin, Hitler, Mao, and Pol Pot will never be counted among the religious leaders of mankind'[4]. Politics has been far more deadly than religion. Shall we put an end to politics as well as religion? Most atheist regimes have been more than happy to do precisely this, getting rid of democracy and installing totalitarian dictatorships for the furtherance of their agendas.

Some respond to the mention of two world wars by suggesting that we need to get rid of nation-states and have a one-world government. But no one suggests we should ban football matches because of violence between rival fans. The problem of war and violence lies deeper than nation-states or football fan clubs, or religion. The problems that fuel tribalism – pride, envy, greed, injustice and oppression – come from the human heart. These are what cause the world's conflicts, whether in the home, the workplace, or between states. Tribal politics, national pride, or ethnic grievances are a better explanation for most of the terrible wars of human history. My family originally comes from Northern Ireland, and as anyone who knows Northern Ireland will affirm, the main problem is political and national rather than religious. John Blanchard writes, 'None of the bombing, shooting and burning in the Balkans and Northern Ireland was aimed at getting people to change their religious ideas'[5].

Christopher Hitchens said that organized religion is "the main source of hatred [in the world]"[6]. (Having called religion the main source of hatred, Hitchens also ironically declared at the same debate: 'I think it [religion] should be treated with ridicule and hatred and contempt. And I claim that right'). No wonder some people refer to atheists like Hitchens as 'hatheists'. The Nobel Prize-winning atheist physicist Steven Weinberg said: 'Religion is an insult to human dignity. With or without it you would have good people doing good things and evil people doing

---

[4] David Berlinski, *The Devil's Delusion: Atheism and its Scientific Pretensions*, 2nd ed., Basic Books, 2009, p.19

[5] John Blanchard, *Does God Believe in Atheists?* Evangelical Press, 2000, p.519

[6] Christopher Hitchens, "Be It Resolved: Freedom of Speech Includes the Freedom to Hate", debate at University of Toronto, 15/11/2006

evil things. But for good people to do evil things, that takes religion'[7].

Berlinski rebuts this claim: 'Just who has imposed on the suffering human race poison gas, barbed wire, high explosives, experiments in eugenics, the formula for Zyklon B, heavy artillery, pseudo-scientific justifications for mass-murder, cluster bombs, attack submarines, napalm, intercontinental ballistic missiles, military space platforms and nuclear weapons? If my memory serves, it was not the Vatican'[8]. These evils were the fruit of science. Shall we ban science because of the evils it has begotten?

Berlinski adds: 'What Hitler did not believe and what Stalin did not believe and what Mao did not believe and what the SS did not believe and what the Gestapo did not believe and what the NKVD did not believe and what the commissars, functionaries, swaggering executioners, Nazi doctors, Communist Party theoreticians, intellectuals, Brown Shirts, Black Shirts, gauleiters, and a thousand party hacks did not believe was that God was watching what they were doing. And as far as we can tell, very few of those carrying out the horrors of the twentieth century worried overmuch that God was watching what they were doing either. That is, after all, the meaning of a secular society'[9].

Atheism is the Greatest Evil the World has Ever Seen

It would be easier to listen to atheist criticisms of religion if atheists were willing to accept that atheism itself has been one of the greatest causes of mass-murder in world history. More than 100 million people were killed by officially atheist regimes in the last 100 years. Estimates of those killed under Stalin range from 10 to 20 million, while Mao is thought to have been responsible for the deaths of between 40 to 60 million people in China. All these were their own countrymen, killed in peacetime. Stalin said that, 'One death is a tragedy; a million is a statistic'. Mao nonchalantly declared that he was not worried if half of China's 600

[7] From an address at the Conference on Cosmic Design, American Association for the Advancement of Science, Washington, D.C., April 1999
[8] David Berlinski, *The Devil's Delusion: Atheism and its Scientific Pretensions*, Basic Books, 2009, p.21
[9] Berlinski, *The Devil's Delusion*, pp.26-7

million people died in a nuclear war, for there would still be 300 million left. As to witch trials, as the historian Paul Johnson has noted, Mao's Cultural Revolution was the greatest witch-hunt in history – up to 20 million people died (by comparison, only 20 people were executed at the Salem witch trials of 1692-3). For atheist mass-murderers, killing millions of people was little different to mowing the grass.

Christopher Hitchens in his book, *God is Not Great: How Religion Poisons Everything*, manages to somehow turn a blind eye to the atrocities of atheism. Weinberg would have been more truthful if he had stated that atheism was the worst sponsor of evil the world has ever seen.

Atheist regimes specially targeted Christian churches for persecution. Once in power in Russia, the communists murdered over 4000 priests and 3000 nuns in 1922. Children were indoctrinated in the schools against Christianity, Christmas was banned, Christians lost their jobs, the regime changed to a five-day week in order to replace the Christian seven-day week and break Sunday observance, church bells were confiscated to stop the call to religion, then they launched campaigns of the forcible closure of churches altogether, and the arrest of priests[10].

Aleksandr Solzhenitsyn was sent to a gulag (labour camp) for criticizing Stalin's conduct of World War Two in a private letter. He became a Christian during his imprisonment and said, 'If I were asked today to formulate as concisely as possible the main cause of the ruinous Revolution that swallowed up some sixty million of our people, I could not put it more accurately than to repeat: Men have forgotten God; that's why all this has happened'[11].

Karl Marx said that religion was the opium of the masses. Perhaps it would be better to say that atheism is the opiate of the mass-murderers. Czeslaw Milosz (1911-2004), the former atheist and Nobel Laureate in Literature (1980) said, 'The true opium of the people is a belief in nothingness after death – a huge solace of thinking that for our betrayals, greed, cowardice, murders we are not going to be judged'[12].

Richard Dawkins tweeted after a 2012 debate with John Lennox:

---

[10] Peter Hitchens, *The Rage against God*, Zondervan, 2010, pp.179-192
[11] Templeton Prize address, 1983
[12] Czeslaw Milosz, in his essay, *Discreet Charms of Nihilism*

John Lennox, in all seriousness, thought he could get away with the old "Stalin was an atheist, therefore . . . " trick. Not doubting the fact. Stalin was an atheist. Problem lies in the "therefore". Stalin was short man with moustache, therefore mass murderer.

Dawkins here denies there is any connection between atheism and mass-murder. The problem for Dawkins is that atheism – not moustaches – appears to be the common denominator of all the twentieth century's worst mass-murderers.

The connection between atheism and mass-murder is obvious. First of all, real atheists do not believe that morality is real. Dawkins himself said it: 'there is no good or evil'. Next, atheists 'believed no God was watching them', so that there is no final accounting with God to fear. Dostoevski said, 'Without God, everything is permitted'. There is no need to show restraint if you are an atheist dictator and your revolution is in peril. You can just kill everyone you think might be a threat, which is precisely what Stalin and Mao did.

Dawkins regularly reacts with fury at accusations that atheism prompted the twentieth centuries worst villains: "Oh, now that's ridiculous. First, atheism had nothing to do with Hitler and Stalin. Stalin was an atheist and Hitler was not"[13].

The Australian non-religious journalist, Andrew Bolt, commenting upon Dawkins' outburst, observed:

Hitler was indeed violently anti-Christian, if not atheist. Check what he said in private conversations recorded at the time and later published in Hitler's *Table Talk*: 1941-1944.

From July 1941: 'National Socialism and religion cannot exist together. The heaviest blow that ever struck humanity was the coming of Christianity. Bolshevism is Christianity's illegitimate child. Both are inventions of the Jew'.

From October, 1941: 'Christianity is a rebellion against natural law, a protest against nature. Taken to its logical extreme,

---

[13] Australian Broadcasting Corporation, *Q & A Program*, debating Cardinal George Pell, April 2012

Christianity would mean the systematic cultivation of the human failure'.

True, Hitler told his intimates it was not "opportune" to "hurl ourselves now into a struggle with the churches". "The best thing is to let Christianity die a natural death".

So in public he paid lip service to churches, although that didn't fool one famous atheist, who in 2006 grudgingly admitted: "It could be argued that, despite his own (public) words Hitler was not really religious but just cynically exploiting the religiosity of his audience".

And which atheist said that? Why, Dawkins himself. How odd[14].

It wasn't just the twentieth century atheist regimes that thought that 'no God was watching'. The leaders of the glorious, 'enlightenment' (i.e. anti-religious) regime of revolutionary France were sceptics and deists who firmly believed that God, if He existed, took no interest in the affairs of men. God may be necessary to explain our existence, they thought, but for all practical purposes He does not exist. What was the result? The poet Wordsworth wrote:

All perished, all—
Friends, enemies, of all parties, ages, ranks,
Head after head, and never heads enough
For those that bade them fall[15].

Christianity's Conscience

Christianity is very different to all this. Jesus preached, 'Blessed are the peacemakers' in His Sermon on the Mount (Matthew 5:9). The crowds that followed Him hoped He would mount a Messianic military revolt against Rome, but instead Jesus simply 'went about doing good and healing all who were oppressed by the devil' (Acts 10:38). Jesus told

---

[14] Andrew Bolt, *Delusions of Despots go to Richard Dawkins' head in God debate*, https://www.dailytelegraph.com.au/news/opinion/delusions-of-despots-go-to-richard-dawkins-head-in-god-debate/news-story/958666c40d17c840661acb4f26c59ff6
[15] Wordsworth's *1805 Prelude*, Book 10

Pilate, 'My kingdom is not of this world. If My kingdom were of this world, My servants would fight' (John 18:36). He told His disciples to put away their swords when He was about to be arrested, 'for all who take the sword will perish by the sword' (Matthew 26:52). He never authorized wars in His name, whether of conquest or defence. Instead, He told His disciples their mission was to go into all the world and preach the gospel. Christ Himself did not have a penny to His name at His death, only the coat He wore. He repeatedly raged against the money-changers in the temple, and He sent His disciples out to preach without money, without supplies, without salary, without subscriptions, without any of the slimy schemes of modern Christian money-rakers.

Because of its belief that all human beings have been created in the image of God, Christianity is against murder and insists on the right to life of all – the disabled, the sick, the weak, even the unborn. It declares the equal value of all men and women in God's eyes.

It is also important to state that some of the worst crimes of Christianity are perversions of true Christianity. The Roman Catholic church's policy of celibacy for priests and its attendant epidemic of child sexual abuse is one example. But the New Testament never insists on celibacy, nor even speaks of a special 'priestly' class or hierarchical power-structure. The terrible medieval persecution of Jews throughout Europe is another; these crimes of anti-Semitism were a repudiation of the true spirit of Christian love. While we may rightly blame these Christians for what they have done, we cannot blame Jesus Christ. Neither did Christ ever authorized any such actions as the crusades, by word or deed. They were not even justified by the common defence that Muslim armies earlier wiped out the Christian civilisations of the Middle East and North Africa, for Christ Himself taught His followers not to return evil for evil. These episodes remind us that misguided and mistaken religion allied with worldly power is as dangerous as any other malign force. However, true religion is about love, not power.

To conclude, the boot is really on the other foot. Atheism has more blood on its hands than any religion the world has ever seen. It is the height of hypocrisy to point the finger at anyone else.

Chapter 29

The Problem of Evil and Suffering

The problem of evil and suffering has been described as the only argument against God worth considering. The Roman philosopher Lucretius stated: 'If God designed the world it would not be, a world so frail and faulty as we see'.

Atheists point to evil and suffering in the world and ask, How can we believe in a God if He allows terrible things to happen? For example, on Boxing Day 2004, a tsunami in the Indian Ocean resulted in the deaths of over 200,000 people in Indonesia, Sri Lanka, India, Thailand and other countries. Either God is not powerful enough to stop such things, or He does not care enough to stop such things, or (says the atheist) He simply does not exist.

The atheist actor Stephen Fry was challenged by an interviewer with why he didn't believe in God. Fry replied by giving the example of a four year old child with bone cancer. The argument against God from evil and suffering is emotionally sensitive, passionate and powerful. What is the Christian response?

Atheism offers no Answer

As challenging as the problem of evil and suffering is for the Christian, it also presents a difficult dilemma for the atheist. If God does not exist, then the universe is nothing more than matter and energy. But if so, where do we get the ideas of 'good' and 'evil' from? As quoted earlier in the book, Richard Dawkins wrote: 'the universe we observe has precisely the properties we should expect if there is, at bottom, no design, no purpose, *no evil and no good*, nothing but blind pitiless indifference'[1].

---

[1] Richard Dawkins, *River out of Eden, A Darwinian view of life*, Basic Books, 1995, p.133,

As we saw in an earlier chapter, Dawkins finds the question of whether Hitler did something wrong 'a genuinely difficult question'. Dawkins also has no problem, in principle, in eating human pedestrians killed on the road (i.e. cannibalism) – after all, we are just animals – nor does he object to killing children up to one year old[2]. This is the morality of atheism.

Norm Geisler tells a story about an atheist student who submitted an essay arguing that there is no such thing as objective morality, and that all morality is relative: 'it's all a matter of personal opinion – you like chocolate, I like vanilla', and so on. The essay was bound in a blue folder.

The professor returned the essay, marking it F for fail, with a note saying that he did not like blue folders. The student complained and demanded an explanation. The professor replied that he did not like blue folders, and so he had marked the essay as a fail. The student protested: "that's not fair – you haven't marked the paper on its arguments". The professor replied, "Wait a minute ... wasn't your paper the one that said there is no such thing as fairness, rightness, and justice? Didn't your paper argue that it's all a matter of taste?" "Yes", replied the student. "Fine, then", said the professor, "I don't like blue. You get an F".

The student finally grasped the point. He believed in objective morality after all, in particular, that he should be treated fairly[3]. The attempt to reduce morality to a matter of personal taste is a failure.

The problem for the atheist is that there is no such thing as evil unless there is also good, and there is no such thing as good or evil in a materialistic, atheistic universe. Where are the molecules of evil that we can weigh and count, or the force of good that we can measure? Good and evil are moral and spiritual entities rather than material substances.

The prominent Oxford atheist Professor Peter Atkins called human beings 'slime on a planet'. But we do not weep and wail as we wipe the slime off a bathroom surface, so why should anyone shed any tears if people are killed by a tsunami? Killing millions of people is no different

---

emphasis added

[2] Peter Singer, *The Genius of Darwin: The Uncut Interviews*, 2009

[3] Norman Geisler and Frank Turek, *I Don't Have Enough Faith to be an Atheist*, Crossway, 2004, pp.173-4

to disinfecting a bathroom of bacteria. Atheist dictators did not shed any tears as they killed millions of people in the 20th century. If human beings are nothing more than bags of chemicals which bubble up into existence for a short time and then disappear forever, there is no reason for crying at the spilling of blood any more than the spilling of milk.

Atheism therefore has this difficulty: it provides no basis for good and evil. This is not to say that all atheists are horribly evil. The problem is that atheism renders evil an illusion. Atheists cannot protest against evil, because they are protesting against an illusion. There is no such thing as good or evil unless God also exists, who is Himself the source and embodiment (so to speak) of goodness.

Serious atheists understand this. Richard Dawkins was interviewed by Britain's *Daily Telegraph* in 1992. He said, 'Suppose that some child is dying of cancer, we say, "Why is this child dying; what has it done to deserve it?" The answer is, there's no reason why … there's no reason other than a series of historical accidents which led to this child dying of cancer. No reason to ask why'. When reminded that people still ask the question, Dawkins replied, 'That's their problem'.

On another occasion, Dawkins was involved in a debate with Jaron Lanier who said, 'There's a large group of people who simply are uncomfortable with accepting evolution because it leads to what they perceive as a moral vacuum, in which their best impulses have no basis in nature'. Richard Dawkins replied: 'All I can say is, That's just tough. We have to face up to the truth'[4].

So, in answer to Stephen Fry's question about a four year-old with cancer, atheism's reply is simply, 'Tough! That's his problem'.

If God is a fairytale, as the atheist insists, then so too are good and evil. And while we are on fairy tales, who's to say that witches with a taste for children are wrong? If Dawkins feels it is okay to eat human roadkill, then surely witches may eat children. After all, morals are nothing more than personal tastes. Who's to say that a man is doing wrong when he kills, cooks and eats another man? As serial-killer (and cannibal) Jeffrey Dahmer put it, "If it all happens naturalistically, what's

---

[4] "Evolution: the dissent of Darwin", *Psychology Today*, Jan/Feb, 1997, p.62

the need for a God? Can't I set my own rules? Who owns me? I own myself"[5].

Atheism reduces all talk of 'evil' and 'suffering' to sentimental nonsense and nostalgic superstition. Complaining about the 'unfairness' of life is like a child bawling when he doesn't get what he wants. The idea that something is not 'right' with the world – and that we should protest against it – is a delusion, a hangover from our religious and superstitious past.

Therefore, atheists need to stop protesting about evil and suffering and face up to the harsh headwind of life's pointlessness. Indeed, we should stop celebrating compassion, sheltering invalids, fighting unfairness, or protecting the weak. We should instead do whatever it takes to get what we want out of life, and let the devil take the hindmost.

The problem with this atheistic view is the fact that morality is real. We are deeply troubled by injustice and evil, particularly when it concerns our own money, property and family.

The atheist says that we are just animals lately emerged from the jungle, that ethics is just aesthetics, morals are just tastes and changeable fashions. But we know deep down in our hearts that all such talk is desperate nonsense. Morality is real because good and evil are undeniable. If we were just animals or chemicals, why should right and wrong even trouble us?

The atheist argument against God from suffering and evil is thus self-defeating. By protesting the existence of suffering and evil in the world, the atheist saws off the branch he is sitting on: he admits that good and evil are real. The atheist's cry of pain shows that good and evil – and therefore moral and spiritual entities – are real.

The Christian Answer to Evil and Suffering

What is the Christian answer to the problem of evil and suffering? How do we reconcile a world that is full of suffering with a God who is good? There are six things that can be said.

---

[5] *Jeffrey Dahmer: The Monster Within*, A&E documentary, 1996.

The Problem of Good

The first thing to be said is that it is an exaggeration to say that the world is full of suffering. Yes, there is plenty of suffering in the world, but there are also many wonderful things. Life is fundamentally good.

Life on earth is not unremittingly bleak and miserable. It would be more accurate to say that while life contains suffering, there are also many incredibly beautiful things to enjoy. We can tell jokes, fall in love, marvel at the birth and growth of happy children, experience deep and rewarding friendships, learn about an amazing variety of interesting subjects, play sport, invent games, go on holidays to wonderful places, walk up mountains with beautiful views, taste a wonderful variety of different foods, or listen to emotionally moving music.

Where do all these good things come from? If, on atheist reasoning, all the evil and suffering proves there is no God, then the opposite presumably also is true: good and beautiful things are evidence that a good God does exist.

Lord Hailsham, Lord Chancellor of England, called this 'the problem of good' and said, 'it is this which led me to God in the first place':

'the real problem is not the problem of evil, but the problem of good, not the problem of cruelty and selfishness, but the problem of kindness and generosity, not the problem of ugliness, but the problem of beauty. If the world is really the hopeless and meaningless jumble which one has to believe it to be if once we reject our value judgments as nothing more than emotional noises ... evil then presents no difficulty because it does not exist... But how, then, does it come about that we go through life on assumptions which are perfectly contrary to the facts, that we love our wives and families, thrill with pleasure at the sight of a little bird ..., that we rage at injustice inflicted on innocent victims, honour our martyrs, reward our heroes, and even occasionally, with difficulty, forgive our enemies and do good to those who persecute us and despitefully use us? No, it is light which is the problem, not darkness... The thing we have to explain is the positive, not the negative'[6].

Humans possess many amazing capabilities that allow us to enjoy the good things of this world. Our abilities to appreciate the beauty of a sunset or enjoy the symphony of an orchestra or be stimulated by intelligent thought (like the question of whether God exists) or even our own conscious self-awareness – all these things not only show the great gulf fixed between us and the animals, but are inexplicable on the theory that we developed these abilities by means of 'survival of the fittest'.

David Berlinski writes, 'Do we understand why alone among the animals, human beings have acquired language? Or a refined and delicate moral system, or art, architecture, music, dance, or mathematics? This is a severely abbreviated list. The body of Western literature and philosophy is an extended commentary on human nature, and over the course of more than four thousand years, it has not exhausted its mysteries. "You could not discover the limits of soul" Heraclitus wrote, "not even if you traveled down every road. Such is the depth of its form"'[7].

God not only made all the beautiful things on our small planet, but He made us with the capabilities to explore and enjoy them. And for all that, what thanks does He get? We are an ungrateful lot, and the Bible says that such thanklessness is one of our chief sins.

The atheist exaggerates his case, complaining that the world is full of suffering. He makes it sound as if the only thing we could ever eat was cold porridge, trapped in an atheist prison-state like East Germany or North Korea. Stephen Fry laments a four-year-old child with bone cancer. Fair enough, but he himself did not have bone cancer as a four-year-old (and neither did 99.9999% of all other children who ever lived).

Leonardo Da Vinci famously drew a picture called the Vitruvian Man, with his arms extended to show that the width of our outstretched arms is exactly equal to the height of our body. The result is that the human form fits within a square. Further, with our arms extended at an inclined angle, our body also fits within a circle centred on our navel. Da

[6] Lord Hailsham, *The Door Wherein I Went*, Collins, 1975, p.41-2
[7] David Berlinski, *The Devil's Delusion*, Basic Books, 2009, p.158

Vinci's drawing was intended to demonstrate the amazing symmetry, elegance and natural beauty of the human frame. The Vitruvian man has been suggested as a way of describing human beings to possible visitors from outer space.

Stephen Fry's vision of humanity, by contrast, holds up a four-year-old with bone cancer. It is a rather melancholy mindset, unbalanced and unrelieved by any benefits of life on earth. Even if someone does not believe in the Devil, one can hardly imagine a cattier argument against God. This is the outlook of someone poisoned by atheism's bleakness, looking for the very worst possible case as representative of life on earth.

But it is, as the atheist replies, still a fact that bone cancer occurs. What is the Christian answer to why there is suffering and evil in the world?

There has been a Mutiny

There is a story about a Christian on board a ship who went to speak to the captain. The captain said, 'I don't believe in God. If my ship were in as much of a mess as the world is, I would lose my job'. The Christian replied, 'The reason the world is in a mess is because there has been a mutiny'.

The second thing the Christian says is that, in the beginning, our world was not like this. In the opening chapter of Genesis, God six times pronounced various things 'good'. Then finally, we read that 'God saw everything that He had made, and indeed it was very good' (Genesis 1:31). Our world was originally created a paradise. Things did not stay that way, of course; man rebelled against His Maker, bringing sin, death and the curse into the world.

If God is the ultimate source of everything good and truly happy, then the problem with our world is that the relationship between the Creator and His creatures has been ruptured. We are cut off from our One true happiness, from the source of the Good Life.

G. K. Chesterton put it this way: 'The strongest saints and the strongest skeptics alike took positive evil as the starting point of their argument. If it is true (as it certainly is) that a man can feel exquisite happiness skinning a cat, then the religious philosopher can make one or two deductions. He must either deny the existence of God, as all atheists do; or he must deny the present union between God and man, as all Christians do'[8].

The world's evil and suffering stand as a stark monument to a broken relationship between creation and its Creator. How could it be otherwise? If the tenants in a house refuse to pay the rent or move out, why should the homeowner continue to maintain the house, pay the bills or repair the damages caused by their wild partying? Why should God simply allow His creature's mutineering ways to be rewarded with uninterrupted enjoyment of paradise after the great divorce?

The Meaning of Death

As a result of our mutiny against God, death has come to our world. In Genesis, Adam and Eve were expelled from the garden paradise and were denied access to the tree of life. The result: death eventually came.

God created this world, not simply for the happiness of human beings, but with the desire that He might share with us in the enjoyment of it, in harmony and friendship. With mankind's rebellion against its Maker, that relationship was ruined, and without God, humanity was cut off from the source of life itself. 'My people have committed two evils; they have forsaken Me, the fountain of living waters and have hewn for themselves cisterns – broken cisterns that can hold no water' (Jeremiah 2:13). The Psalmist sung to God, 'With You is the fountain of life; in Your light we see light' (Psalm 36:9). Instead of God, light and life, we now have death, darkness and the Devil dominating the world.

God is not only the ultimate source of all life, He is also the ultimate source of all true happiness. He invented all the things that bring us joy. He is the One who created the beauty of a sunset, the wonder of music, and the One who designed a man and woman to fall in love.

With the Creator of Life rejected, death – the absence of life – has taken His place. There is little point in complaining about untimely deaths, for death comes to all. Furthermore, many of the sad things in

---

[8] G. K. Chesterton, *Orthodoxy*, Hendriksen, 2006, p.10

life have been caused by man's inhumanity to man, corruption, greed, and foolishness.

Death is the most democratic institution upon earth. No one born on earth escapes alive. Robert Bolt, the British playwright put it this way:

'even at our birth, death does but stand aside a little. And every day he looks towards us and muses somewhat to himself whether that day or the next he will draw nigh'.

A four-year-old dying is terribly sad, but the sudden death of a friendly 94-year old also comes as a shock and brings us pain. And who is to say that a four year-old with cancer suffers more pain than all the emotional, relational and physical distress of a normal 94-year life?

But even 100 years is just a momentary flicker by comparison with the life of the stars. The flame of our lives, however short or long, is quickly extinguished, and its length is meaningless in the context of endless time.

Jesus was challenged on one occasion by two disasters: Pilate the governor killing some Galileans who had come to worship God in Jerusalem and a tower falling and killing eighteen people. By implication, the question was, Why did God allow this to happen? Jesus replied, 'Do you think that these people were worse sinners than all Galileans or those dwelling in Jerusalem. I tell you no, but unless you repent you will all likewise perish' (Luke 13:15). After dismissing the idea that these people were suffering from some sort of karma, or because they specially deserved death, He went on to warn of something far worse than death that hangs over all our heads: to perish in hell. We are all sinners under God's wrath, awaiting His judgment. Death is a terrible thing, but Jesus put this short life in perspective, telling us we need to turn back to God in repentance to be saved from something far worse than just death.

In the end, death comes to all, and therefore to argue that God cannot exist because some deaths are unfair or untimely is absurd. What would the atheist prefer – to live forever in perfect happiness? That is exactly what God promises to those who love Him!

The Suffering of God

Michael Frost tells a story about the Australian evangelist John Smith, who founded the God's Squad motor cycle ministry as an outreach to outlaw 'bikie' gangs. John Smith was speaking at a religious education class in a high school in Melbourne, Australia. After his message, the students were allowed to write out questions on cards to be passed up to the speaker to answer publicly. Most of the questions were about whether the Christian faith was reasonable or not. But one of the questions read, 'Where was God when I was raped?'

After the question was read out, John Smith was unable to answer and instead great big tears started rolling down his cheeks into his moustache. The whole group of students fell silent as he wept on the stage. Michael Frost writes, 'There was no need for any theological answer after that. Where was God when I was raped? The answer was expressed in those big salty tears'[9]. Michael Frost titled the story, 'The Tears of God'.

God's Spirit is not simply seen in the tears of John Smith. God's Spirit is also seen in the actions of His people, building hospitals to care for the sick and dying, providing refuges for the elderly, disabled and orphans, feeding the hungry and befriending the downtrodden. Above all, God's Spirit is seen in the words and actions of Jesus Christ, who 'went about doing good, and healing all who were oppressed by the Devil' (Acts 10:38).

There is another story, a parable about Judgment Day, in which billions of people stand before God's throne. Most shrank back in fear, but some were defiant.

"What right does God have to judge us?" said a young girl, pulling up her sleeve to show a number tattooed on her arm in a Nazi concentration camp. "We were tortured and killed".

Another young man lowered his collar, showing a rope burn: "What about this? Lynched for no crime other than being black!"

"It wasn't my fault", said a pregnant schoolgirl.

Across the vast assembly complaints rang out against God for the

---

[9] Michael Frost, "Tears of God", *Australian Stories for the Soul*, Strand, 2001, pp.55-6

suffering and evil He had allowed in the world. "What does God know about pain or hunger or fear or hatred? How fortunate God is to live in heaven where all is bliss".

Finally, a delegation was sent forward, comprised of people who had suffered the most. A Jew, a young black man, someone from Hiroshima, a man who suffered terribly from arthritis, a child born with deformities.

Before God could be allowed to judge, He must suffer what they had suffered. God should feel what it is like to live on earth. Let Him be a Jew. Let Him be born to a single mother. Give Him a work so difficult that even His family will think Him out of His mind when He tries to do it. Let Him be betrayed by His closest friends. Let Him face false charges, be tried by a prejudiced jury and convicted by a cowardly judge. Let Him be tortured, flogged, mocked, and spat upon. Then let Him die alone in agony.

As each part of the sentence was announced, loud roars of approval went up from the crowds of people standing in front of God's throne. But when at last the sentence had been pronounced, there was a long silence. Suddenly everyone realized that God had already served His sentence.

One of the greatest comforts for the Christian in suffering is the fact that God cares about us. Peter wrote, 'Casting all your care upon Him, for He cares for you' (1 Peter 5:7). How do we know God cares? Because Christ has suffered, and knows what it is like. The letter to the Hebrews says of Christ that, 'in that He Himself has suffered, being tempted, He is able to aid those who are tempted ... for we do not have a High Priest who cannot sympathise with our weaknesses, but was in all points tempted as we are, yet without sin'[10]. We might not understand the reason for our suffering, or be able to see any light in the darkness, but the Christian is encouraged by the truth that God cares.

It is also true that it is in suffering that the Christian often finds Christ drawing nearest. John Stott wrote:

'I could never myself believe in God, if it were not for the cross ... In

---

[10] Hebrews 2:18, 4:15

the real world of pain, how could one worship a God who was immune to it? I have entered many Buddhist temples...and stood respectful before the statue of the Buddha...a remote look on his face, detached from the agonies of the world. But each time after a while I have had to turn away. And in imagination I have turned instead to that lonely, twisted, tortured figure on the cross, nails through hands and feet, back lacerated, limbs wrenched, brow bleeding from thorn pricks, mouth dry and intolerably thirsty, plunged in God-forsaken darkness. He laid aside his immunity to pain. He entered our world of flesh and blood, tears and death. He suffered for us. Our sufferings become more manageable in light of his. There is still a question mark against human suffering, but over it we boldly stamp another mark, the cross which symbolizes divine suffering'[11].

Why?

But surely, we ask, shouldn't God intervene and stop terrible suffering? John Blanchard points out that not only would God have to manipulate the laws of physics, He would also 'need to control thoughts and actions that were the indirect causes of suffering':

'After my weekly game of golf I drive to pick up my wife from another appointment. Imagine that I am delayed by those playing in front of me, then find that I am running behind schedule. Dashing out of the clubhouse to the car park, I accidentally knock over a lady member who hits her head so violently on a concrete kerb that she sustains irreparable brain damage. How should God have intervened to prevent subsequent years of suffering? By causing the players in front of me to play better or faster? By making me choose an earlier starting time? By shortening the time it took me to shower and change after the game? By steering the lady into the clubhouse through a different door? Would you honestly accept the idea of a God who manipulated things in this way, squeezing out every atom of

---

[11] John Stott, *The Cross of Christ*, IVP, 2006, p.326

your independence or choice?'[12].

Blanchard quotes Francis Bridger's book *Why Can't I Have Faith?*, 'We should be reduced to such a state of physical, social and psychological instability that life would fall apart, paradoxically bringing even more suffering in its train'.

But why did God allow evil and suffering to come into the world in the first place? One answer is that there is something of higher value than physical happiness.

Cicero, in his work *De Officiis* (On Moral Duties), argued that if happiness and pleasure are the highest goals of life and pain the only evil, then we should 'rake together from every quarter objects to delight the senses'. But (he continued) where then would be prudence, or justice, or fortitude – the courage and patience that endures pain or labour or adversity – or temperance (self-restraint)? Rome would have been a weak and unimportant state if it had not considered as virtues things like duty, faithfulness, honesty, kindness, courage and not doing wrong to others. In the words of one commentator on Cicero, virtue for its own sake was 'the only antiseptic that preserved Roman society from utter and remediless corruption'. The Romans would have been slaves, not only to every vice of selfish savages, but to every other nation.

Ask yourself this: would you be happier to be presented with a gold medal at the Olympics for doing nothing – that is, even though you were a lazy slob and a couch-potato, not in the least athletic, and did not compete in any event at all? Or would you prefer to win a gold medal after years of training, struggle, sweat and pain? Or to change the dream, would you be happier if you won a million dollars in a lottery, or if you earned a million dollars by working hard at some difficult idea that paid off, and helped others along the way? Shallow and selfish people prefer to win the lottery, but experience shows that they tend to waste the money nearly as soon as they get it and ruin their relationships in the process. A life without struggle and suffering sounds lovely at first, but that sort of happiness is ultimately not satisfying.

---

[12] John Blanchard, *Where was God on September 11?* Evangelical Press, 2002, p.19

Furthermore, suffering has some benefits. Suffering produces maturity. Malcolm Muggeridge, the agnostic British journalist who converted to Christianity, wrote:

'Contrary to what might be expected, I look back on experiences that at the time seemed especially desolating and painful with particular satisfaction. Indeed, I can say with complete truthfulness that everything I have learned in my seventy-five years in this world, everything that has truly enhanced and enlightened my existence, has been through affliction and not through happiness. In other words, if it ever were to be possible to eliminate affliction from our earthly existence by means of some drug or other medical mumbo jumbo, as Huxley envisaged in *Brave New World*, the result would not be to make life delectable, but to make it too banal and trivial to be endurable. This, of course, is what the Cross signifies. And it is the Cross, more than anything else, that has called me inexorably to Christ'[13].

Think of one of the most famous stories in the Bible. Joseph, the favourite of his father, was hated by his own brothers, who wanted to kill him. They changed their mind and instead sold him as a slave to make a bit of money. He was taken in chains to the land of Egypt, where he spent years separated from his father, who was heartbroken at the brothers' news that his son had been attacked by a wild animal. In Egypt, Joseph was falsely accused of a crime, thrown into prison, and left to rot. Unexpectedly, he was brought out of prison, and called before Pharaoh, where he explained exactly what needed to be done to save Egypt and the surrounding lands from a terrible famine. As a result he was elevated to the position of Prime Minister of the land. Finally, he was re-united with his own father and family, whose lives he also saved from starvation.

Would Joseph, looking back on his life, having saved the land of Egypt and his own family from dying in the famine, be happy with the way things had turned out? Would he have been satisfied that God was

---

[13] Malcolm Muggeridge, *Homemade*, July, 1990

able to bring good things out of apparent disasters?

The truth is that he would not have been able to save the known world in his day if he had not been sent to Egypt, thrown into prison, and been in the right place to tell Pharaoh exactly what to do. The Bible records that Joseph, rather than holding a grudge against his once-evil but now repentant brothers, instead said to them: 'do not be grieved or angry with yourselves because you sold me here, for God sent me before you to preserve life' (Genesis 45:5). Later he said, 'you meant evil against me, but God meant it for good, in order to bring it about as it is this day, to save many people alive' (Genesis 50:20).

Pain and trouble are worth it if they have a purpose, and the New Testament repeatedly tells us that God brings good things out of trials for those who love and trust Him. James says, 'Count it all joy when you fall into various trials, knowing that the testing of your faith produces perseverance' (James 1:2-3). Paul puts it this way, 'all things work together for good for those who love God' (Romans 8:28).

Suffering also calls us to humble ourselves and turn to God. C. S. Lewis wrote about the value of suffering: 'God whispers to us in our pleasures, speaks in our consciences, but shouts in our pains. It is His megaphone to rouse a deaf world ... No doubt pain as God's megaphone is a terrible instrument; it may lead to final and unrepented rebellion. But it gives the only opportunity the bad man can have for amendment. It removes the veil; it plants the flag of truth within the fortress of the rebel soul'[14].

The idea that there are some things that are more valuable than physical happiness might sound ridiculous in our shallow, hedonistic age. However, consider the matter of freedom. The reason why freedom is more valuable than happiness is that it is only freedom that that allows us the highest of all forms of happiness.

C. S. Lewis explained it like this: 'God created things which had free will. That means creatures which can go either wrong or right. Some people think they can imagine a creature that was free but had no possibility of going wrong; I cannot. If a thing is free to be good it is also

---

[14] C. S. Lewis, *The Problem of Pain*, William Collins, 2015, pp.91, 93-4

free to be bad. And free will is what has made evil possible. Why, then, did God give them free will? Because free will, though it makes evil possible, is also the only thing that makes possible any love or goodness or joy worth having. A world of automata – of creatures that worked like machines – would hardly be worth creating. The happiness which God designs for His higher creatures is the happiness of being freely, voluntarily united to Him and to each other in an ecstasy of love and delight compared with which the most rapturous love between a man and a woman on this earth is mere milk and water. And for that they must be free'[15].

Paradise Restored

Our world has so many problems. We get upset to see video footage of a cheetah running down an antelope and ripping out its throat. We are disturbed by the pollution and destruction of the natural environment. No politician seems able to solve our social problem of crime, poverty, addiction, and injustice. We are saddened when a terrible disease takes away a life. We are worried by the threat of nuclear war. What is the answer to these problems?

The Christian answer is that God's purpose is to bring about His Kingdom on earth. It will be a restoration of paradise, only far more beautiful than the first. That is why the Bible ends in the book of Revelation, just as it began in Genesis, with a garden paradise, not in heaven but on earth.

Isaiah the prophet gives us a glimpse of this coming Kingdom of God. There are seven main characteristics:

1. **No more war**: 'they shall beat their swords into plowshares, and their spears into pruning hooks; nation shall not lift up sword against nation, neither shall they learn war anymore' (Isaiah 2:4).
2. **The reign of the rightful King**: 'unto us a Child is born, Unto us a Son is given; And the government will be upon His shoulder. And His name will be called Wonderful, Counselor, Mighty God,

---

[15] C. S. Lewis, *Mere Christianity*, pp.47-8

Everlasting Father, Prince of Peace. Of the increase of His government and peace There will be no end, Upon the throne of David and over His kingdom, To order it and establish it with judgment and justice From that time forward, even forever. The zeal of the LORD of hosts will perform this' (Isaiah 9:6-7)

3. **Social justice**: 'with righteousness He shall judge the poor, and decide with equity for the meek of the earth; He shall strike the earth with the rod of His mouth, and with the breath of His lips He shall slay the wicked. Righteousness shall be the belt of His loins, And faithfulness the belt of His waist' (Isaiah 11:4-5)

4. **Natural harmony**: 'The wolf also shall dwell with the lamb, the leopard shall lie down with the young goat, the calf and the young lion and the fatling together; and a little child shall lead them. The cow and the bear shall graze; their young ones shall lie down together; and the lion shall eat straw like the ox' (Isaiah 11:6-7).

5. **Environmental restoration**: 'The wilderness and the wasteland shall be glad for them, and the desert shall rejoice and blossom as the rose; it shall blossom abundantly and rejoice, even with joy and singing. The glory of Lebanon shall be given to it, the excellence of Carmel and Sharon. They shall see the glory of the LORD, The excellency of our God' (Isaiah 35:1-2).

6. **No disease**: 'Then the eyes of the blind shall be opened, and the ears of the deaf shall be unstopped. Then the lame shall leap like a deer, and the tongue of the dumb sing' (Isaiah 35:5-6).

7. **Everyone will know God**: 'the earth shall be full of the knowledge of the LORD As the waters cover the sea' (Isaiah 11:9).

Norman Geisler put it most memorably: 'I will admit that this world is not the best possible world, but it might be the best way to get to the best possible world'[16].

The Yale historian Kenneth Scott Latourette said, 'Christianity, while acknowledging the presence of suffering, declares that life can be

---

[16] Norman Geisler and Frank Turek, *I don't have Enough Faith to be an Atheist*, Crossway, 2004, p.400

infinitely worth living and opens the way to eternal life in fellowship with God Who so loved the world that He gave Himself in Christ'.

Today, life on earth is not only cursed with emptiness and futility but it ends in death. One day, this world itself will be rescued. Again, this calls for faith in God who has made this promise. Paul puts it this way: 'For the creation was subjected to futility, not willingly, but because of Him who subjected it in hope; because the creation itself also will be delivered from the bondage of corruption into the glorious liberty of the children of God. For we know that the whole creation groans and labors with birth pangs together until now' (Romans 8:20-22).

Paul says that life on earth is futile, empty and meaningless. How could it be otherwise, when the original design for human existence – fellowship with God – has been ruined by our rebellion? However, as Paul assures us, the futility we feel not only gives us desires for something more satisfying, but those desires for paradise will one day be satisfied, if we are prepared to lay down our arms, and turn back to our Creator.

God does not intend the world finally to be futile. The atheist cries out in protest at evil and suffering, and questions why God has not removed all our problems, creating in their place a paradise on earth. Strangely, when the Christian replies that this is precisely what God is in fact promising to those who love Him, the atheist responds by calling this escapism, 'pie in the sky when you die', George Orwell's Sugarcandy Mountain.

Dinesh D'Souza writes, 'All I am trying to show here is that the only way for us to really triumph over evil and suffering is to live forever in a place where those things do not exist. It is the claim of Christianity that there is such a place and that it is available to all who seek it. No one can deny that, if this claim is true, then evil and suffering are exposed as temporary hardships and injustices. They are as transient as our brief, mortal lives. In that case God has shown us a way to prevail over evil and suffering, which are finally overcome in the life to come'[17].

---

[17] Dinesh D'Souza, *What's so Great about Christianity*, Tyndale, 2007, p.283

Conclusion

The problem of evil and suffering is probably the best argument that atheism has against God. Suffering and evil are the most painful parts of our existence, and cast doubt on God's wisdom and ways. However, as we have seen, the atheist argument has seven major problems:

1. The argument undercuts atheism itself by treating good and evil as real entities (whereas, in an atheist universe, they are mere illusions),
2. It ignores the many evidences of God's goodness in Creation.
3. It is explained by our human rebellion against our Creator.
4. Death, the ultimate evil, comes to all, so to complain that some suffering is untimely or unfair is absurd.
5. God has come and experienced the worst of all human suffering – being crucified. To argue that He doesn't love us or care is not true.
6. For God to intervene to stop evil would be to violate our human dignity and freedom, for He would have to override our decision to rebel against Himself.
7. God's promise is that He will one day destroy all evil and suffering and restore paradise for those who love and trust Him.

God's ways are a mystery to us, particularly in times of suffering and difficulty. They call for faith when we do not have all the answers. We might even say that arguments over the problem of evil and suffering are a lot like arguments about God in general. God is invisible, so that we cannot be certain that He exists. Similarly, the evenly-balanced contest between good and evil means that we cannot be certain that Christianity is true. We are forced to go beyond mere arguments and reason, and must exercise faith in God, or (as some people do) reject God. Ultimately, even an atheist has to make a decision based on intuition, or preference, or (as they would call it) 'blind faith'.

Chapter 30

Darwinian Evolution

There are many Christians who believe in evolution. This shows it is not necessary to believe that Genesis is literal history to be a Christian. A Christian is simply someone who believes that 'God so loved the world that He gave His only begotten Son', and confesses Jesus Christ as Lord, believing He has been raised from the dead[1].

Nevertheless, evolution is the reason many atheists give for why they do not believe in God. Richard Dawkins was an Anglican until midway through his teens, at which point he became an atheist: 'The main residual reason why I was religious was from being so impressed with the complexity of life and feeling that it had to have a designer, and I think it was when I realised that Darwinism was a far superior explanation that pulled the rug out from under the argument of design. And that left me with nothing'[2].

Many Christians have an emotional reaction to evolution, almost amounting to fear. They worry it will undermine their faith, and maybe disprove or dethrone God. They are therefore reluctant to look into the details and evaluate the evidence for it. Of course, the reverse is also true of many people (and not just Christians): they accept evolution largely for superficial, cultural reasons, without understanding the science.

Evolution, when all boiled down, teaches that 'living beings created themselves' (Wolfgang Smith)[3]. Does evolution actually possess such fantastic creative powers? That depends on two things: a convincing explanation and compelling evidence. Does evolution have a convincing

---

[1] John 3:16, Romans 10:9
[2] Simon Hattenstone, "Darwin's child", *The Guardian*, 10 February 2003
[3] Wolfgang Smith, *Teilhardism and the New Religion*, Tan Books and Publishers, 1988, p.24

explanation for how such miracles happen, and can it show compelling evidence to prove it has produced such wonders? To truly understand evolution, however, we need to realize that convincing explanations and compelling evidence are not strictly necessary.

Richard Dawkins wrote, 'Even if there were no actual evidence in favor of the Darwinian theory ... we should still be justified in preferring it over all rival theories'[4]. That sounds very strange – wasn't it Richard Dawkins who said that blind faith is believing in something for which there is no evidence? But to understand why Dawkins would still believe in evolution even if there were no evidence, listen to Harvard Professor Richard Lewontin. In a review of his fellow atheist Carl Sagan's book, *The Demon-Haunted World*, Lewontin wrote:

'Our willingness to accept scientific claims that are against common sense is the key to an understanding of the real struggle between science and the supernatural. We take the side of science in spite of the patent absurdity of some of its constructs, in spite of its failure to fulfill many of its extravagant promises of health and life, in spite of the tolerance of the scientific community for unsubstantiated just-so stories, because we have a prior commitment, a commitment to materialism.

It is not that the methods and institutions of science somehow compel us to accept a material [i.e. atheistic] explanation of the phenomenal world, but, on the contrary, that we are forced by our *a priori* adherence to material causes to create an apparatus of investigation and a set of concepts that produce material explanations, no matter how counter-intuitive, no matter how mystifying to the uninitiated. Moreover, that materialism is absolute, for we cannot allow a Divine foot in the door'[5].

Ordinary readers might be surprised to learn that, in the final analysis, evolution is not really about following the evidence wherever it leads, or

---

[4] Richard Dawkins, *The Blind Watchmaker*, Norton, 1986, p.287
[5] Richard Lewontin, *The New York Review of Books*, Jan 9, 1997, pp.28, 31

an open-minded, objective, search for the truth. As Lewontin clearly states, no matter how absurd or ridiculous the materialistic (i.e. atheistic) explanation for life on earth, 'we cannot allow a Divine foot in the door'. Now, of course, atheists say the exact same thing about creationists: no amount of scientific evidence will shift them from their faith position. But by Lewontin's own admission, evolutionary science also has 'a prior commitment', an unshakable allegiance, to materialism. No amount of evidence can or ever will change the conclusion. Because any input from God is excluded from the outset, something like evolution *must* be true by default. Therefore, living beings created themselves.

A Little Historical Background

It is important to understand the historical context to Lewontin's quote and particularly the 'struggle' between science and the supernatural (i.e. God) that Lewontin refers to.

In the same book review, Lewontin tells how he first met Carl Sagan, at a public creation-evolution debate in Little Rock, Arkansas, in 1964. Sagan and Lewontin's opponent was a creationist Ph.D. biology professor. Lewontin reports that, 'despite our absolutely compelling arguments, the audience unaccountably voted for the opposition'. Nothing to do with the quality of the arguments or the speakers, no, but somehow a public audience in the most scientifically advanced nation on earth (in the same decade they first put a man on the moon) voted against evolution. It was not just happening in Arkansas either.

On the presidential campaign trail in 1980 Ronald Reagan said about evolution: "Well, it is a theory. It is a scientific theory only, and it has in recent years been challenged in the world of science—that is, not believed in the scientific community to be as infallible as it once was". By the 1980s a number of states in the USA had passed legislation mandating that equal time be given to teaching evolution and 'creation science'.

In fact, Darwinian evolution was under sustained attack on two fronts by the 1980s. On the one hand, there were many evolutionary scientists who had started to publicly air their doubts, not about evolution *per se*, but about Darwin's explanation – selection and mutation – as well as the evidence of the fossil record. They did not doubt *that* evolution had happened, but *how*. Søren Løvtrup, although an evolutionist, could write, 'Someday the Darwinian myth will be ranked the greatest deceit in the history of science'[6]. The famous Harvard palaeontologist (and Marxist) Stephen Jay Gould, pointed out that the fossil record contradicted Darwinian gradual evolution, and suggested a new theory called Punctuated Equilibrium, arguing that evolution happened in very short sharp (almost revolutionary) leaps forward followed by vast ages of time when nothing seemed to change. Gould called Darwinism "effectively dead"[7].

The in-house debate over how evolution had occurred – by sudden large jumps or by slow and gradual change – became quite heated, with Darwinian gradualists calling the new theory 'evolution by jerks', and the critics calling the gradualist position 'evolution by creeps'. The big problem with Gould's theory, to Darwinian gradualists like Richard Dawkins, was that it was virtually indistinguishable from creationism: new creatures appeared fully-formed out of nowhere and thereafter never changed. Gould's response was simple: this is exactly what the fossil record shows. (The in-house debate still continues today, by the way, 40 years later[8]).

---

[6] Søren Løvtrup, *Darwinism: The Refutation of a Myth*, Croome Helm, 1987, p.422

[7] Stephen Jay Gould, "Is a New and General Theory of Evolution Emerging?" *Paleobiology* 6, 1980, pp.119-30

[8] In 2007, Eugene Koonin published a paper titled, 'The Biological Big Bang Model for the Major Transitions in Evolution', arguing that 'major transitions in biological evolution show the same pattern of sudden emergence of diverse forms at a new level of complexity'. In other words, evolution by jerks. The paper argued that Darwinian gradualism failed to explain 'pretty much everything' (David Berlinski's own summary in *The Devils Delusion*, p.193). The reaction of the Darwinian faithful was brutal and swift, but as the fighting was dying down, biologist Shi V. Liu wrote that 'we must realize that Darwin's fetal mistakes have ... misled science into a dead end', but nevertheless, 'we may still appreciate the role of Darwin in helping scientists [winning an] upper hand in fighting against the creationists' (http://www.biology-direct.com/content/2/1/21/ comments #284660). In November 2016, at the meeting of perhaps the world's most prestigious scientific institution, the Royal Society, titled "New Trends in Evolutionary Biology", the first presentation by the distinguished Austrian evolutionary theorist Gerd Müller argued that 'the theory largely avoids the question of how the complex

On the other flank, creationists were making increasingly successful attacks on evolution in scientific debates. The most famous was the nationally televised debate in the US in 1981 between Dr. Duane Gish and Dr. Russell Doolittle, professor of biochemistry at the University of California, San Diego. The *Washington Post* report the next day was titled, "Science Loses One to Creationism", with the sub-heading, quoting Doolittle (as overheard by a journalist after the debate), 'How am I going to face my wife?' *Science* magazine described the debate as a rout.

Gish was a world-class scientist who co-authored no less than six scientific papers with two Nobel Prizewinning chemists, Vincent du Vigneaud and Wendell Meredith Stanley, synthesizing peptides, the most advanced chemistry of the time. (By contrast, Richard Dawkins did his Ph.D. research on chickens pecking seeds). Gish engaged in over 300 formal debates, mostly on university campuses, and was so successful that evolutionary opponents in the US eventually refused to take him on. In his debates, Gish summarised the major scientific problems with evolution (the origin of the universe, the origin of the first life, mutations, natural selection, fossils) so clearly and succinctly that the losers later resorted to name-calling, mocking his presentation as the Gish Gallop. Few could match Gish, and eventually evolutionists realized it was wiser to stop debating than allow creationist arguments to gain traction. Gould, writing to Dawkins, said about creationists, 'what they seek is the oxygen of respectability', and [debating them] would 'give them this oxygen by the mere act of engaging with them at all'[9].

Dawkins himself (along with another leading evolutionary biologist, John Maynard-Smith) had debated two creationist Ph.D. scientists at the famous Oxford Union Debating Society in 1986, where Dawkins got so worried about losing he made an impassioned extra, unscheduled speech pleading with the audience not to vote for his opponents, because such a result would give credibility to religious fundamentalists (breaking

---

organizations of organismal structure, physiology, development or behavior — whose variation it describes — actually arise in evolution'. In other words, Müller argued the Darwinian theory still has no real explanation for 'pretty much everything'.

[9] As related by Dawkins in *The Devil's Chaplain*, 2003

the rules of the debate by bringing up the issue of religion). The evolutionary biologists won the vote, but a sizeable number of the audience voted against Dawkins, after which he vowed never again to debate creationists. Rather than debate, evolutionists instead turned to writing popular books, where they could say what they liked without fear of rebuttal or cross-examination. Very few public creation-evolution debates have been held in the last thirty years.

Richard Dawkins' 1986 book, *The Blind Watchmaker*, was perhaps the point at which the tide started to turn. Explaining Darwinian evolution to the non-scientific world with brilliant rhetoric, Dawkins not only showed how Darwinian evolution explains the appearance of design in biology without a Designer, thus rebutting creationism, but also disposed of the alternative evolutionary theories to Darwinism like Punctuated Equilibrium. Dawkins went on to write a number of follow-up books about Darwinian evolution, before his 2006 block-buster *The God Delusion* moved on to more general atheist arguments.

When Richard Lewontin said that science's commitment to materialism was 'absolute', he meant intellectually: no contrary evidence ever could or would penetrate the citadel of the mind. But there is another sense in which Lewontin's words came true. The commitment to atheism was 'absolute' in the sense that his fellow atheists would do whatever it took to triumph in the struggle with creationism. Lewontin's totalitarian tone was not entirely surprising; he was a Marxist, after all.

Western society prizes the idea of freedom of speech, of free and fair debate. Our parliamentary systems require an opposition who provide scrutiny of government policies. Our court system works on the principle that both prosecution and defendant get to present their case, and to cross-examine the other. The business world uses financial auditing – independent accountants are called in to check the records. Journalism involves inviting interviews or comment from both parties to a dispute.

The 'struggle' against creationism was different. We have already mentioned the suppression of debate, and we might perhaps have some sympathy for the evolutionists' excuse: debating is an artform that depends on rhetoric as much as facts, but why should a two hour debate not give enough time to set out the evidence for evolution properly?

Instead of debate, evolutionists turned to publishing books promoting Darwinian evolution to the public – where the other side of the debate was not given a word at all.

The best debaters are not afraid to expose their audience to the strongest arguments of their opponents before answering them. But instead of allowing the public to hear about the controversy, Darwinian evolutionary biologists insisted there was no debate at all; the science was settled. Rather than allowing the public to hear any scientific weaknesses of the theory, they simply switched off their opponents' microphone. In addition to presenting their case in books for the public, the evolutionary establishment also discouraged doubt by other means.

Richard Dawkins wrote in a book review in the *New York Times* in 1989: 'It is absolutely safe to say that if you meet somebody who claims not to believe in evolution, that person is ignorant, stupid or insane (or wicked, but I'd rather not consider that)'.

Matt Ridley, in his book *Red Queen: Sex and the Evolution of Human Nature*, opted for a patronizing approach: 'to those who believe that the world was made in seven days by a man with a long beard and that therefore human nature cannot have been designed by selection but by an Intelligence, I merely bid a respectful good day'.

Isaac Asimov, in his 1984 article, 'The Threat of Creationism', tried an alarmist approach, writing that 'creationism seems like a bad dream, a sudden reveling of a nightmare, a renewed march of an army of the night risen to challenge free thought and enlightenment'. This was the article that law professor Phillip Johnson of University of California, Berkeley, read while on sabbatical in London, and realized that maybe there was something to the creation-evolution debate after all (he was not particularly interested in it before). If Asimov had to resort to such facile name-calling instead of simply laying out the scientific evidence and allowing his audience to evaluate it on its merits, what was he trying to cover up? As a result of his year's researches, Johnson went on to write *Darwin on Trial*, launching the Intelligent Design movement.

Many evolutionary biologists, adamant that two-hour debates were not long enough to clearly state their case, were happy instead to trot out one-line slogans like 'Evolution is a fact, not a theory', 'There is no scientific debate over evolution', or 'no "serious scientist" doubts evolution'. Internet atheists continue this tradition, adding to these slogans their own original and often obscene abuse of creationists and God, confirming that anti-religious sentiment sustains the theory as much as scientific evidence.

The atheistic science establishment also found ready allies in the culture war. Leftists in the entertainment industry and big names in popular culture, like *Simpsons* cartoons and the *Friends* sitcom, regularly caricatured creationism as an intellectual joke, the equivalent of not believing in gravity.

But the 'absolute' commitment to atheistic explanations went further, with the harassment and firing of creationist teachers and university professors who aired doubts or criticisms of evolutionary theory, and the denial of degrees and admittance into graduate programs of students with creationist beliefs despite excellent academic results. Dr. Jerry Bergman's *Slaughter of the Dissidents* (2008) documented many of these cases, and Ben Stein's 2008 film *Expelled: No Intelligence Allowed* brought the more prominent examples to the notice of the wider public.

Atheist Professor P. Z. Myers wrote:

Here I am, a biologist living in the 21ˢᵗ century in one of the richest countries in the world, and one of the two biology teachers in my kids' high school is a creationist. Last year, the education commissioner in my state tried to subvert the recommendations for the state science standards by packing a hand-picked 'minority report' committee to push for required instruction in Intelligent Design creationism in our schools. All across the country, we have these lunatics trying to stuff pseudoscientific religious garbage into our schools and museums and zoos. This is insane ... Our only problem is that we aren't martial [i.e. violent] enough, or vigorous enough, or loud enough, or angry enough. The only appropriate responses should involve some form of righteous fury, much butt-kicking, and the public firing and humiliation of ... [Darwin skeptic] teachers, many schoolboard members, and vast numbers of sleazy far-right politicians'[10].

De-platforming of opposition, suppression of debate, stifling of contrary evidence as inadmissible by definition, repetition of trite slogans, and purges of opponents, have all been acceptable tactics in the 'struggle'. It sounds almost like the Soviet Union in Stalin's hey-day.

Do not think that I rehearse this history to 'play the victim card' or to gain sympathy. The bully-boy tactics and stifling of scrutiny does not prove Darwinian evolution wrong, nor does the sneering attitude. These might simply indicate a lack of good breeding and manners. The reason for the history is simply to encourage readers, many of whom may feel unqualified to judge a scientific debate, to take a look at the evidence for themselves.

At the end of this chapter, I will go one step further and show how there is no possible scientific evidence that could ever falsify or invalidate evolution. Why? Because the commitment to atheism is absolute. Dawkins lets us into the real meaning of evolution: 'Darwin made it possible to be an intellectually-fulfilled atheist'[11]. Atheism is what sustains evolutionary theory, not evidence.

Evolution's Explanation and Evidence

There is a story of a university science professor who held up a glass beaker containing a yellow liquid before his students in their first lecture. He asked them to observe very carefully what he did, and then to copy him, one by one, as the beaker was passed around the room. First, he lifted the beaker up under his nose and smelled the liquid. Then he dipped his finger in the beaker. Then he licked his finger. He passed the beaker to his students and watched as it went round the room.

Eventually, the beaker was returned to the professor. He asked them what they thought the liquid was. One student called out, 'Urine' and the professor said, 'That is correct'. A groan went up from the room.

---

[10] P. Z. Myers, "While We're at it, Let's also Fire the Math Teachers who Can't do Algebra", *Pharyngula*, August 1, 2005, p.2

[11] Richard Dawkins, *The Blind Watchmaker*, p.6

'However', continued the professor, 'if you observed very carefully you will have noticed that I dipped *this* finger in the beaker, but I licked this finger off instead'. The lecturer reinforced the point that careful observation is one of the most important qualities in science.

Here we are going to look at the four main arguments for evolution. The ordinary layman might protest that he is not qualified to judge such scientific matters, but the evidence itself is not very hard to understand. As we are going to see, there is evidence for Darwin's theory. However, there are also major difficulties and unresolved problems. Sorting the truth from the spin is more necessary in this matter than anywhere else in modern science because so much rides on the debate.

The crucial requirement for understanding the debate is something most people already possess: careful observation, allied with critical-thinking skills. Most people are happy to watch a magician perform – we enjoy observing carefully and trying to work out how the trick is being performed. The skills of careful observation and critical thinking are all we need here.

Natural Selection

I remember being in a junior high school class in my early teens when an openly Christian teacher was challenged by questions from two students. One asked, "What's wrong with premarital sex?", the other, "What about the peppered moths?"

At the time, I had never heard of peppered moths, but I got the impression that the question had something to do with evolution and was a powerful argument against Christianity. The teacher did not answer the question, and it was not till a few years later that I heard a scientist explain the story of the peppered moths. How he answered the question really helped me understand what evolution was really all about.

Here is the story of the peppered moths, found in most biology textbooks. Before the Industrial Revolution in England these moths, *Biston Betularia*, were mostly light coloured. Birds which ate them found the light-coloured moths hard to spot as they rested, camouflaged, on the light-coloured tree trunks. The moths were thus less likely to be eaten.

After the Industrial Revolution had darkened the trees with soot, the moths turned dark, and so were again able to hide themselves on the trunks. The Peppered Moths had evolved from a light colour to a dark colour. This is one of the most famous textbook cases of evolution in action.

What the scientist explained to me – the catch – was that there were both light and dark varieties of moths before the Industrial Revolution, as well as after. The way the story is often told makes it seem that natural selection caused a new type of moth to appear after the Industrial Revolution. However, the truth is that both varieties of moth were already in existence at the beginning[12].

Here is a little analogy the scientist used to explain what really happened to the peppered moths. He put it this way: to claim that the moths evolved into a different colour is like saying that every time Israel and the Arab nations have a war, the Arabs are evolving into Jews (because there are usually relatively less Arabs and relatively more Jews afterwards).

My classmate at school seemed to be very impressed by the story of the peppered moths. And so have millions of other people. But once I heard the full story, I realized that no actual moths evolved from light to dark colours. The genetic information for light and dark coloured moths existed before the Industrial Revolution. All that changed were the relative proportions of light and dark coloured moths as birds ate more of one sort than the other under the different conditions.

The story of the peppered moths is a classic case of natural selection in action, but the story does not explain the origin of the light or dark colours, let alone the origin of the moths from some other different animal. In the words of famous evolutionist and genetics pioneer, Hugo de Vries, natural selection explains the survival of the fittest, not the arrival of the fittest. This is why it is called natural selection, not natural creation.

The same is true of other text-book cases of natural selection.

---

[12] Not all evolutionists hide the fact that both varieties of peppered moth existed before the Industrial Revolution. See Boyce Rensberger's *Washington Post* article, "How Science Responds When Creationists Criticize Evolution", Jan 8, 1997.

Another classic example is the finches in the Galapagos Islands, the size of whose beaks changed due to drought conditions (the seeds were tougher to crack and so birds with smaller beaks died out). However, all the different beak sizes were present *before* the drought came. Natural selection again caused changes in a population, but only by eliminating species struggling to survive the drought – not by creating new species. Natural selection is a culling mechanism, not a creative force.

Many atheists claim that natural selection is the greatest scientific idea ever discovered. Daniel Dennett, the atheist philosopher, wrote, 'If I were to give an award for the single best idea anyone has ever had, I'd give it to Darwin, ahead of Newton and Einstein and everyone else … the idea of evolution by natural selection'[13]. Dennett explains that 'contemporary biology has demonstrated beyond all reasonable doubt … that natural selection – the process in which reproducing entities must compete for finite resources and thereby engage in a tournament of blind trial and error from which improvements automatically emerge – has the power to generate breathtakingly ingenious designs'[14].

But now that we have seen how it actually works – by elimination, not creation – it turns out that natural selection is not a source of biological diversity at all. It is like a young man who responds to an advertisement for a Ferrari for sale at an amazing low price and turns up at the address to find that there is indeed a bright red, shiny, Ferrari, but when he asks to take it for a drive, he is told the car won't go. The reason for the amazing low price is revealed: there is no engine under the bonnet. This is the problem with evolution: it has no engine, no mechanism, no answer to the question of how 'living beings created themselves'. Just like the young man and the Ferrari, natural selection turns out to be a big let-down; it is all show and no go. It promises miraculous things with effortless ease, but (as discerning buyers know) there's always a catch to such claims. The fact that so many people who consider themselves part of the 'smart-set' believe in evolution by natural selection only shows how easily duped some folk are by scientific-sounding language.

[13] Daniel Dennett, *Darwin's Dangerous Idea*, Simon and Shuster, 1995, pp.20-21
[14] Daniel Dennett, "Show Me the Science", *New York Times*, Aug. 28, 2005

Granville Sewell (Professor of Mathematics, University of Texas, El Paso) put it best: 'Darwin's attempt to explain the origins of all the magnificent species in the living world in terms of the struggle for survival is easily the dumbest idea ever taken seriously by science'[15].

Natural selection is a fact – it can explain some things in nature. However, it fails to explain the creation of all the wonderful varieties of life. Darwin's great mechanism for the origin of species is therefore true but trivial. It is not the means by which evolution could occur. That's why early-20th-century evolutionists were forced to look elsewhere for the source of biological variation. The solution they discovered was mutations.

Mutations

We are familiar with mutations from movies like *X-Men* or the *Teenage Mutant Ninja Turtles*. In these fictional stories, mutations give certain characters super-powers. But in the real world, genetic mutations are copying mistakes in the DNA that cause diseases and disabilities like cystic fibrosis, haemophilia, or Downs Syndrome.

There is a joke (which might offend some people) about three men who went fishing in a boat on a lake one day when, all of a sudden, an angel appeared. When the men got over the shock, one said to the angel,

"I have had a bad back since I was hit by shrapnel in the Vietnam War … would you be able to help me?"

"Sure" said the angel and touched his back. Straight away, his back was healed, and the man felt relief for the first time in years.

The second man wore thick glasses and had a hard time reading and driving. He asked the angel if he could do anything to help him. The angel smiled, reached out and took the glasses and threw them into the lake. As soon as they hit the water, the man was able to see perfectly again.

When the angel turned to the third man, he put out his hands defensively. "Don't touch me, I'm on a disability pension".

---

[15] Granville Sewell, *In the Beginning and other Essays on Intelligent Design*, Discovery Institute Press, 2010

We all probably know people who suffer from a disability, and most deserve all the help and support that they get. But there are some people on benefits who are not very disabled. To understand the second part of the evolutionary explanation, we need to keep in mind the words 'disability benefits'. Hold on to that expression and we will see its relevance soon.

Evolutionary scientists nowadays admit – when pressed – that natural selection has no creative power. Instead, they assure us that mutations (copying mistakes in our DNA) provide the source of new variations from which natural selection can select favourable traits, and generate all kinds of the wonderful new varieties of life on earth.

When genetic mutations were discovered in the early 20th century, there was a frenzy of mutation breeding (using radiation and chemicals) to fast-forward evolution. However, few programs continue today because bombarding fruit-flies with radiation or chemicals, causing mutations, has only produced thousands of disabled, defective and dead flies.

This is where we come back to the concept of disability benefits. Mutations are disabilities, but some mutations come with benefits. Mutations in humans tend to cause terrible birth defects, genetic diseases and death. But some mutations are not lethal, and some mutations may even be beneficial.

Notice what the following creatures have in common: flightless birds, sightless fish, tailless cats, seedless grapes and wingless beetles. All these organisms have lost something. The lack of wings, eyes, and seeds may even have benefits: consumers prefer to eat grapes without seeds, fish without eyes do not get them damaged and infected by bumping into walls in dark underwater caves, and wingless beetles do not get blown off windy islands into the sea.

These organisms enjoy 'disability benefits'. In evolutionary terms, natural selection would enable wingless beetles to outbreed flying beetles and therefore take over the island. However – and here is the crucial point – none of these mutations involve gains. They all involve losses. Mutations have not added wings or eyes where none existed beforehand.

Take a common mutation that evolutionary biologists promote as proof that mutations can be beneficial. Sickle-cell anaemia is terrible disease, resulting in about 100,000 deaths per year world-wide. Sickle-cell anaemia is a genetic condition that results in an abnormality in haemoglobin, the molecule that carries oxygen in the bloodstream. Sickle-cell anaemia has one benefit, however: it protects carriers from malaria, an even deadlier disease, which causes over 500,000 deaths per year world-wide. Sickle-cell anaemia provides an advantage if a person lives in a malaria-prone region of the world. However, it is only beneficial in the way an amputation is welcomed by someone with gangrene. It is a disability with one benefit.

The same applies to other cases of mutations promoted as evidence by evolutionary biologists: bacterial resistance to antibiotics, malarial resistance to anti-malaria drugs, or the uptake of citrate by *E.coli*. Every single one of these cases involves a mutation breaking something, although this disability nevertheless results in a side-benefit.

As evolutionary biologist (and one-time wife of prominent atheist Carl Sagan) Lynn Margulis explained: 'Darwinists say that new species emerge when mutations occur and modify an organism. I was taught over and over again that the accumulation of random mutations led to evolutionary change – led to new species. I believed it until I looked for evidence'[16]. She stated elsewhere, 'New mutations don't create new species; they create offspring that are impaired'[17]. Trying to evolve new creatures by mutations is like throwing an old-fashioned rotary dial phone at a wall in the hope it will turn into a modern smartphone.

All domestic dogs are thought to be descended from wolves via mutations and selective breeding. All dogs can interbreed, and still belong to the same canine family. But dogs are damaged wolves. Some purebreds have serious health issues arising from genetic mutations. But domesticated dogs come with a benefit: they are 'man's best friend'. The mutations that make them our friends have left dogs at a disadvantage, unable to compete with wolves out in the wild. The dogs' genetic losses are our gains.

---

[16] Dick Teresi, "Lynn Margulis", *Discover*, April 2011
[17] Darry Madden, "UMass Scientist to Lead Debate on Evolutionary Theory," *Brattleboro Reformer*, February 3, 2006.

Biochemist Michael Behe writes: 'mutation easily breaks or degrades genes, which, counterintuitively, can sometimes help an organism to survive, so the damaged genes are hastily spread by natural selection'[18].

Evolutionary biologists also point to cases of polyploidy, the doubling of genes by a mutation, or mutations in 'hox' genes (which act like a switch, e.g. turning on an extra leg which grows out of a fruit fly's head). These duplications, it is theorized, might then be free to mutate into something more useful. But even duplications of existing genes do not create anything new. They just copy something and place it somewhere else. Students do not get double the marks for handing in two copies of homework to teachers. There is no scientific evidence of extra legs changing into something new and useful. A useless leg is a drag on fitness, rendering the fruit-fly less able to survive. Natural selection would tend to eliminate it.

Both mutation and natural selection are real, scientifically observable processes, but neither have the power to produce evolutionary changes of the sort that will turn frogs into princes. Mutations are going in the wrong direction; they cause damage, decay and disorder. If evolution is going to turn bacteria into brain surgeons, not only must it create new raw materials (nerve cells, bones, blood cells, skin, muscle, etc.), but it also needs to 'engineer' combinations of these structures to produce new organs of incredible co-ordination (like kidneys, livers, tongues, fingers, or ears).

Mutations do the very opposite. Evolutionary biologists claim that time is the saviour here: given enough time, eventually enough beneficial mutations will produce new structures. But lots of mutations over millions of years will not build new structures. Dr. Lee Spetner put it this way, 'Whoever thinks macroevolution can be made by mutations that *lose* information is like the merchant who lost a little money on every sale but thought he could make it up in volume'[19]. Pierre-Paul Grassé, Professor of Evolution at the Sorbonne for over thirty years and President of the French Academy of Sciences, wrote:

---

[18] Michael Behe, *Darwin Devolves: the New Science about DNA that Challenges Evolution*, HarperOne, 2019, p.10
[19] Lee Spetner, *Not by chance!* The Judaica Press, 1997

'The opportune appearance of mutations permitting animals and plants to meet their needs seems hard to believe. Yet the Darwinian theory is even more demanding: a single plant, a single animal would require thousands and thousands of lucky, appropriate events. Thus, miracles would become the rule: events with an infinitesimal probability could not fail to occur .... There is no law against day dreaming, but science must not indulge in it'[20].

So here are two problems: firstly, natural selection does not create new things (it kills them off), and secondly, mutations do not build new and improved biological structures (they break them). Evolution is running in exactly the wrong direction. It is not evolution, it is devolution. How 'living beings created themselves' remains unclear, because Darwinian evolution explains nothing of the sort.

Common Descent

Evolutionary biologists are aware of the problems with natural selection and mutation – their inability to create genuine biological novelty. Of course, few publicly advertise the flaws in their theory – that would give too much ground to creationists.

Why then do most biologists still believe in evolution, despite the fact they have no working explanation or mechanism for the creation of new animals and plants? The reason is this: there is still one argument that convinces them that evolution is a fact, despite the failure of natural selection and mutations. That piece of evidence is common descent.

What do we mean by 'common descent'? Evolutionary theory argues that all animals and plants are related to each other and descended from each other, in a giant 'tree of life'. Evolutionary biologists are convinced that all life is related for a number of reasons.

One piece of evidence for common descent came from the field of embryology in 1868. The German zoology Professor Ernst Haeckel (1834-1919), published *Natürliche Schöpfungs-geschichte* ('The Natural

---

[20] Pierre-Paul Grassé, *Evolution of Living Organisms*, Academic Press, 1977, p.103

History of Creation') in which he provided an important additional argument to support Darwin's new theory of evolution: evidence that the human embryo goes through different animal stages. The human embryo starts out as one cell like an amoeba, then has gill slits like a fish, a yolk sac like a chicken and a tail like a monkey. Haeckel argued that this proves that humans share a common descent from other animals.

However, it turned out the drawings were faked by Haeckel to make human embryos look more similar to other animals than they really are. He drew the pictures from memory and made them all look the same size, exaggerating the similarities. Human embryos only bear superficial similarities to animal embryos (e.g. there are no actual gill 'slits', which were claimed as proof we evolved from fish) and the embryonic structures are not 'useless leftovers' from our animal ancestors, but perform essential functions in the development of the embryo.

Despite Haeckel's malpractice being exposed in 1874 by Professor Wilhelm His, and the university of Jena convicting him of fraud, Haeckel's drawings and his theory of 'embryonic recapitulation' (i.e. our animal ancestry is retraced in our embryonic form) have persisted to this day as evidence for evolution in modern biology textbooks.

The publication in 1997 by embryologist (and evolutionist) Dr Michael K. Richardson of photographs showing what human and animal embryos really look like demonstrated the scale of Haecke's forgeries of the evidence. Stephen Jay Gould wrote that Haeckel 'exaggerated the similarities by idealizations and omissions', with drawings characterised by 'inaccuracies and outright falsification'[21]. Michael Richardson said 'It looks like it's turning out to be one of the most famous fakes in biology'[22].

Another argument for common descent is that humans share 99% of their genes with chimps, as Richard Dawkins stated in *The Blind Watchmaker*[23]. However, this claim was made before scientists were able to fully sequence human and chimp genomes (2005). Other studies

---

[21] Stephen Jay Gould, "Abscheulich! - Atrocious! - the precursor to the theory of natural selection", *Natural History*, March 2000.
[22] Elizabeth Pennisi, "Haeckel's Embryos: Fraud Rediscovered" *Science* 277 (1997) p.1435
[23] Richard Dawkins, *The Blind Watchmaker*, W.W. Norton, 1986, p.263

arrived at a similar figure by only comparing the most similar regions of the genome (ignoring other regions which were not). Recent studies based on comparisons of actual gene sequences have shown that the figure is more likely in the range of 81% to 87%[24]. The 99% figure is a myth.

Another common evidence for common descent is 'vestigial organs'. One hundred years ago there were about 180 parts of our bodies that were said to be 'vestigial', that is, useless leftovers from our evolutionary animal ancestors. Examples included our tonsils, appendix and even the very important pituitary gland. Darwin himself originally promoted the idea that the human appendix was a left-over organ from our ancestors[25]. This was used as evidence for common descent, the idea that we descended from animals.

However, medical science has gradually discovered the purposes of all these organs. Our appendix is not a useless left-over from when we used to eat grass like cows, but is full of lymphoid tissue that fights infection, just like the tonsils (one organ at each end of the digestive system). Recent research suggests it is a safe house for good bacteria[26]. In other words, it is part of our immune system. Our previous scientific ignorance (and its apparent evidence for evolution) has disappeared with increasing medical knowledge. It is true that there are creatures with 'devolved' features, for examples, flightless birds with small, useless wings. These may be vestigial in the true sense, but are not strong evidence that birds share common ancestry with all other creatures.

Perhaps the main evidence for common descent is the fact that different creatures have the same bodily structures, slightly modified, to perform different functions. Thus, the cat, the bat, the whale and the human all have similar bone patterns in their forelimb/wing/flipper/arm,

---

[24] Jeffrey Tomkins and Jerry Bergman, "Genomic monkey business – estimates of nearly identical human – chimp DNA similarity re-evaluated using omitted data", *Journal of Creation* 26(1):94–100, April 2012, see https://creation.com/human-chimp-dna-similarity-re-evaluated

[25] Charles Darwin, *The Descent of Man*, J. Murray, 1871, pp.17–33

[26] Bollinger, R.R., Barbas, A.S., Bush, E.L., Lin, S.S. and Parker, W., "Biofilms in the large bowel suggest an apparent function of the human vermiform appendix", *J. Theor. Biol.* 249(4), 2007, pp.826–831

despite the fact that they use it to do different things: run, fly, swim and handle. Another example is that all animals are built on a DNA-based genetic code. These similarities show that all animals are related, and we can further classify these animals into groups in a hierarchical fashion. This suggests a branching tree of life, with all organisms related to each other by 'descent with modification'.

There is no dispute over the biological similarities. The issue is rather with the logic of this argument. Did an albino human and albino donkey get their albinism from a common ancestor? No, because there may be other reasons for animals having things in common. Some evolutionary theorists have even used analogies from motor cars to try to prove common descent or 'descent with modification'. For example, Professor Tim Berra, in his book *Evolution and the Myth of Creationism*, points to the development of the Corvette from 1953 to 1978 which 'evolved through a selection process acting on variations that resulted in a series of transitional forms and an endpoint rather distinct from the starting point. A similar process shapes the evolution of organisms'[27].

The problem with Berra's analogy is that every one of the Corvettes were designed by engineers, whose cars were constrained by common functional requirements (all cars need to have engines, wheels, seats, etc.) and simply followed basic design principles with artistic variations over time. The development of the Corvette illustrates the exact opposite of mindless, materialistic evolution: it illustrates creation by intelligent (motor vehicle) designers.

In a similar way, it can be just as easily argued that the reason why many animals have similarities is that they were designed to do similar things. Functional constraints mean that all animals must have certain common features (moving, air-breathing, food-eating, etc.), just like all cars have wheels and engines.

The fact that both intelligent design and common descent can account for the same effects means, logically-speaking, that the argument fails to eliminate intelligent design as an explanation for similarities between animals. Similarities can equally be explained by either cause –

---

[27] Tim Berra, *Evolution and the Myth of Creationism*, Stanford University Press, 1990, pp.118-119

divine creation or common descent. Therefore, the logic of the argument from similarity is not conclusive one way or the other.

Furthermore, there are other scientific problems with the evolutionary argument from similarity, the main one being that many animals share remarkable similarities even though they belong to unrelated branches of the 'tree of life'. Both bats and porpoises use sonar systems (although unrelated), while the eyes of humans and squid are similar. Evolutionary biologists look at these cases and call them 'convergent evolution', meaning that evolution converged on the same designs in unrelated branches of the tree of life. But this is just another way of saying that these similarities cannot be explained by descent from a common ancestor. Therefore the evolutionary claim that *only* common descent can explain similar designs is false. The common descent argument fails the logic test.

Fossils

The final – and most important – evidence for evolution is fossils, the remains of animals and plants buried in the earth's rock layers. Fossils show how life on earth has gradually changed over time. Carl Dunbar, a palaeontologist (someone who studies ancient forms of life in the fossils) wrote, 'Although the comparative study of living animals and plants may give very convincing circumstantial evidence, fossils provide the only historical documentary evidence that life has evolved from simpler to more and more complex forms'[28].

In Darwin's day, the fossil record was a problem for his theory. Darwin wrote that 'the number of intermediate and transitional links, between all living and extinct species, must have been inconceivably great' because evolution happened gradually by 'infinitesimally small modifications' over hundreds of millions of years. He asked ,

'Why then is not every geological formation and every stratum full of such intermediate links? Geology assuredly does not reveal any such finely graduated organic chain; and this, perhaps, is the most obvious

---

[28] Carl O. Dunbar, *Historical Geology*, John Wiley and Sons, 1949, p.52

and gravest objection which can be urged against my theory. The explanation lies, however, in the extreme imperfection of the geological record'[29].

However, in the 150 years since Darwin, many millions of fossils have been collected. A plaque in the Smithsonian Institute in Washington DC in the 1990s stated that the museum contained forty million fossils. Evolution took enough time for billions of fossils to form. Indeed, there are fossil-bearing beds of rock which contain millions of fossils in them. The *Journal of Paleontology* reported that 'Robert Broom, the South African palaeontologist, estimated that there are eight hundred thousand million skeletons of vertebrate animals in the Karroo formation'[30]. What does the evidence from the fossils show 150 years after Darwin?

Here is one way to help you understand and evaluate the fossil evidence for evolution. Imagine if someone told you that out of the 400 weather stations around the world meteorologists use to measure whether global temperatures are rising or not, there were 390 that said the temperature was increasing, but there were 10 weather stations that said it was not. What would you say to someone who argued that the 10 weather stations with no increase in temperature proved that global warming is a hoax? (Now, before anyone gets angry, please understand I am painting an entirely imaginary scenario here – I have no idea how many weather stations are used to tell us about global temperatures. I also realise that the science of meteorology is far more complex than this). However, my question is whether we should prefer the evidence of the 390 weather stations or the 10 weather stations? The answer, of course, is that we should go with what the 390 tell us. We should follow the 97.5% of the evidence, rather than the 2.5%.

This is precisely the situation we are faced with the fossils. The fossil evidence for evolution is equivalent to the 10 weather stations, or 2.5% (and this is actually being generous). 97.5% of the evidence is against evolution.

---

[29] Charles Darwin, *On the Origin of Species*, John Murray, 1859, p.171
[30] Norman D. Newell, "Symposium on Fifty Years of Palaeontology: Adequacy of the Fossil Record", *Journal of Palaeontology*, 33, May 1959, p.492

Perhaps you don't believe me? Listen to Stephen Jay Gould, the most famous palaeontologist of his day, who wrote, 'The extreme rarity of transitional forms in the fossil record persists as the trade secret of palaeontology'[31]. Elsewhere he wrote, 'All palaeontologists know that the fossil record contains precious little in the way of intermediate forms, transitions between major groups are characteristically abrupt'[32]. In other words, instead of a finely-graded, slowly changing chain of life among the fossils (as Darwin predicted), the record instead shows extremely few intermediates between different types of animals.

Niles Eldredge is another famous evolutionary palaeontologist, a partner with Gould in the theory of Punctuated Equilibrium. He wrote,

'No wonder palaeontologists shied away from evolution for so long. It seems never to happen. Assiduous collecting up cliff faces yields zigzags, minor oscillations, and the very occasional slight accumulation of change over millions of years, at a rate too slow to really account for all the prodigious change that has occurred in evolutionary history. When we do see the introduction of evolutionary novelty, it usually shows up with a bang, and often with no firm evidence that the organisms did not evolve elsewhere! Evolution cannot forever be going on someplace else. Yet that's how the fossil record has struck many a forlorn palaeontologist looking to learn something about evolution'[33].

Palaeontologists have now collected billions of fossils, and while evolutionary biologists point to a few potential cases of 'missing links' – transitional (or in-between) fossils – the important fact to bear mind is that the overwhelming majority of fossils (97.5%) should actually be intermediaries – missing-links – if evolution were true. Instead, it is exactly the opposite. The fossil record shows virtually no evidence that animals have gradually evolved into each other.

To see a snapshot of the situation with the fossil record, consider the

---

[31] Stephen Jay Gould, "Evolution's Erratic Pace", *Natural History* 86, May 1977, p.14

[32] "The Return of the Hopeful Monsters", *Natural History*, 86(6), 1977, pp.22-30

[33] Niles Eldredge, *Reinventing Darwin*, Orion Publishing, 1996, p.95

family tree of dinosaurs, including all the familiar favourites: 1. Stegosaurus (rows of plates on its back and spikes on its tail), 2. Triceratops (three-horns on its head), 3. Brachiosaurus (long neck and long tail), 4. Tyrannosaurus Rex, 5. Archaeopteryx, and 6. Birds[34].

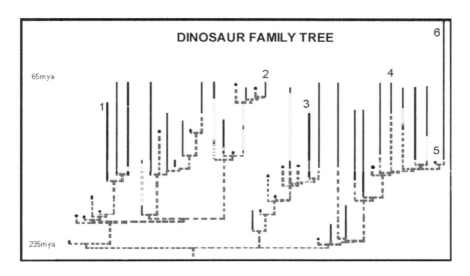

Here we have the evolutionary family tree of about forty different types of dinosaurs. The graph plots their fossils from 235 million years ago till 65 million years ago, when the dinosaurs disappeared. Billions and billions of dinosaurs would have lived during this period of 175 million years, enough for many fossils to form. The question is whether there is any fossil evidence of dinosaurs gradually evolving from one sort of dinosaur into another, and leaving fossil evidence of this gradual change in the rocks. If evolution is true, there should be many examples of transitional fossils.

The vertical lines on the chart show the fossil evidence for all the forty or so different types of dinosaur. But notice that while most of the vertical lines are solid black (indicating actual fossils), all the horizontal lines are dotted (indicating theorized evolutionary connections). In other words, the dotted lines show where there are no actual fossils.

The graph shows that all the distinctly separate types of dinosaurs

---

[34] Modified from Paul Sereno, "The Evolution of Dinosaurs", *Science* (284), 25 June 1999

stayed the same over time. They did not change. The chart also shows that there are no transitional fossils between the dinosaurs. All the horizontal transitions are imaginary lines. It is also important to remember that many dinosaurs have very distinctive fossils. But there are no fossils showing the gradual origin of triceratops' horns, stegosaurus' plates and spikes, or other dinosaurs' prominent bony features.

There is no evidence of any dinosaurs merging into other dinosaurs, nor evolutionary intermediates, transitioning over time. Nor are the dinosaurs alone in this. Graphs of similar orders of animals and plants are the same, showing no evidence of evolutionary transitions among the fossils. There are no evolutionary links.

Dr Colin Patterson, Senior Paleontologist at the British Museum of Natural History, was asked why he had included no transitional forms in his book on evolution. He replied:

'... I fully agree with your comments on the lack of direct illustration of evolutionary transitions in my book. If I knew of any, fossil or living, I would certainly have included them ... Yet Gould and the American Museum people are hard to contradict when they say there are no transitional fossils ... I will lay it on the line there is not one such fossil for which one could make a watertight argument'[35].

If life evolved gradually, with lots of infinitesimally small changes, over hundreds of millions of years, the majority of newly discovered fossils should be transitional or in-between fossils, producing a gradual spectrum of continuous change. The crucial evidence proving evolution – which the fossil record does not show – would be that the majority of fossils are transitional forms that fit in between modern-day species.

Evolutionists reply by pointing to the fossil equivalent of the 10 weather stations that say global temperatures are not rising. They argue that there are some very good cases of 'missing links'. In fact, we see one of the best cases in the chart above. The second-last column on the right represents one of evolutionary biology's most famous creatures,

[35] Dr. Colin Patterson, letter to Luther D. Sunderland, 10 April, 1979, as published in *Darwin's Enigma*, Master Books, 1984, p.89.

Archaeopteryx, which is considered a transitional fossil between reptiles (like dinosaurs) and birds (the final column on the far right of the chart).

Archaeopteryx was discovered in Germany in 1861 (two years after Darwin's *Origin of Species*). *Archaeopteryx* shared certain features of birds (wings, feathers, a beak) and certain features of reptiles (teeth, a long tail, and a claw on the wings), and was immediately hailed as evidence demonstrating the evolution of reptiles into birds.

However, even if we were to accept *Archaeopteryx* as a reptile-bird transition (and there are good reasons to doubt this[36]), there is still a major problem. There have now been about twelve fossil specimens of *Archaeopteryx* discovered and all show exactly the same form. On the chart above, they all sit on the one spot. This begs the question why they aren't at slightly different stages of evolutionary development from a reptile into a bird. If the evolutionary transition from reptiles to birds took a few million years (because there had to be many major anatomical changes), then we would expect a few different forms of reptile-birds to show up, forming a gradual chain of slowly changing features from the reptilian form to the bird form. Instead, all of the *Archaeopteryx* fossils found show the exact same form.

Evolutionists make much noise about a few ambiguous cases of fossils like *Archaeopteryx* that possibly qualify as transitional. Atheist Professor Jerry Coyne in his book, *Why Evolution is True* argues that there is plenty of evidence for transitional fossils: the evolutionary transition from fish to amphibians, from amphibians to reptiles, from reptiles to mammals, from dinosaurs to birds [i.e. *Archaeopteryx*], from artiodactyls (a cow-like creature) to whales (i.e. whales evolved from swimming cows!), and the evolution of humans from smaller apelike ancestors. That's Coyne's case: six examples of fossil intermediates. But if evolution were true, there should be intermediates everywhere.

---

[36] *Archaeopteryx* was a bird: it had avian lungs, a large wishbone for flight and feathers. Some other fossil birds also had teeth, and claws and long tails. Alan Feduccia, a bird expert says: 'Paleontologists have tried to turn *Archaeopteryx* into an earth-bound, feathered dinosaur. But it's not. It is a bird, a perching bird. And no amount of 'paleobabble' is going to change that' (Virginia Morell, "Archaeopteryx: Early Bird Catches a Can of Worms", *Science* 259, 1993, pp.764–65).

Leaving aside the debate over these 'intermediates', some of which are dubious reconstructions from fragmentary and ambiguous fossils, we need to keep our eyes on the big picture. Coyne focuses only on the data that supports his theory. He does not tell his readers the inconvenient truth that 97.5% of the evidence is against it.

Professor George Gaylord Simpson, perhaps the most influential palaeontologist of the 20th century, stated:

'This [lack of evolutionary fossil transitions] is true of all thirty-two orders of mammals... This regular absence of transitional forms is not confined to mammals, but is an almost universal phenomenon, as has long been noted by paleontologists. It is true of almost all classes of animals, both vertebrate and invertebrate...it is true of the classes, and of the major animal phyla, and it is apparently also true of analogous categories of plants'[37].

What evolutionary biologists like Jerry Coyne are doing by pointing to six possible cases of 'missing links' is what trial lawyers call 'selective citation of evidence', or 'cherry picking'. Here's another way to think of it. Imagine if someone told you that once upon a time there was a land-bridge that stretched all the way across the Pacific Ocean, from California to China. If anyone asked for proof, this person pointed to the Hawaiian islands. No one would believe them, of course, because the Pacific Ocean is vast (60 million square miles), and the Hawaiian Islands are a mere pin-prick on the map (10,000 square miles in area, or 0.0016% of the Pacific Ocean).

This is a situation precisely comparable to the fossil evidence for evolution. The claim that the few possible fossils of 'intermediates' proves evolution true is as laughable as saying that the eight Hawaiian islands are proof of an ancient 10,000km land bridge across the ocean that once connected California to China.

If gradual evolution over long ages were true we would find that the vast majority of fossils – more than 90%, many millions of our museum's

---

[37] G. G. Simpson, *Tempo and Mode in Evolution*, Columbia University Press, 1944, pp.105, 107

fossils – were transitional, not a few 'maybes'. The entire fossil record would be one huge continuum of changing life-forms.

Jerry Coyne is a master of misdirection. He points to six cases of possible transitional fossils to cover the failure of the fossil record to turn up the predicted millions of missing links. Atheists like Coyne are quite happy to misrepresent the true nature of the fossil evidence, which completely contradicts the theory of gradual evolution.

The Cambrian Explosion

Perhaps the biggest fossil problem for evolution is the 'Cambrian explosion', sometimes called biology's 'big bang'. The Cambrian explosion is the sudden appearance of the earliest forms of animal life in the fossil record. The earth is believed to have been formed 4.5 billion years ago, and for the first 4 billion years there was no multicellular life. The only things in the fossils are microscopic single-celled creatures like bacteria. Then about 600 million years ago, virtually all the animal phyla appeared. Phyla are the major groups of animals: chordates (including vertebrates), clams, snails, sponges, jellyfish, arthropods (spiders, insects, crabs, centipedes), and worms. There are about 300 different creatures in the Cambrian rocks, and all appear in the fossil record without any evolutionary ancestors. Instead of Darwin's story of gradual development, all animal phyla appeared abruptly in the fossil record in the Cambrian rocks. Evolutionist Jeffrey Schwarz writes that the major animal groups 'appear in the fossil record as Athena did from the head of Zeus – full blown and raring to go'[38].

Many of these Cambrian animals are extremely advanced, with eyes every bit as sophisticated as modern eyes, legs, brains, digestive systems, kidneys and backbones (even a fish-like creature, *Metaspriggina,* has recently been found in the Cambrian). That means that there is no evidence that eyes and all the rest of these organs gradually evolved at all. The evidence is precisely what we would expect if they had been created by God from nothing. Richard Dawkins writes:

---

[38] Jeffrey H. Schwartz, "Homeobox Genes, Fossils, and the Origin of Species, *Anatomical Record (New Anatomist)* 257, 1999, pp.15-31

'the Cambrian strata of rocks, vintage about 600 million years, are the oldest in which we find most of the major invertebrate groups. And we find many of them already in an advanced state of evolution, the very first time they appear. It is as though they were just planted there, without any evolutionary history. Needless to say, this appearance of sudden planting has delighted creationists'[39].

Agnostic David Berlinski writes, 'If life progressed by an accumulation of small changes as Darwin suggests ... the fossil record should reflect [this] ... But before the Cambrian era, a brief 600 million years ago, very little is inscribed in the fossil record; but then ... an astonishing number of biological structures ... come into creation at once'[40].

There are millions of 'Cambrian' fossils entombed in the rocks all over the world, and there should be billions of ancestors, showing the gradual development of all the different forms of life over previous periods of millions of years. But not one of the ancestors of any of these 300-odd Cambrian animals has ever been found. The Cambrian rocks show that life did not evolve into existence, it exploded!

This is exactly the sort of evidence that should cause us to doubt that evolution ever happened. But giving up evolution because of contrary evidence is simply never going to happen.

Evolution is Not Falsifiable

What would evolutionary biologists possibly accept as evidence against the theory? Richard Dawkins was once asked this question and answered, 'if there was a single hippo or rabbit in the Precambrian, that would completely blow evolution out of the water. None have ever been found'[41]. Of course, Dawkins was not being entirely sincere, for if a fossil rabbit was found in Precambrian rocks, Dawkins could simply say that the rocks had been incorrectly classified[42].

---

[39] Richard Dawkins, *The Blind Watchmaker*, p.229
[40] David Berlinski, "The Deniable Darwin", in *The Deniable Darwin and Other Essays*, ed. David Klinghoffer, Discovery Institute, 2009, p.42
[41] C. Wallis, "The Evolution Wars", *Time*, 7 August 2005
[42] Some finds have been dismissed as a result of contamination (as in the case of the

But, in principle, fossils found in the wrong rock layers, hundreds of millions of years out of their proper evolutionary order, is the sort of evidence that should falsify evolution. What this would show is that the entire geological column, and with it the evolutionary history of life, is false.

This is precisely what happened in spectacular fashion in 1990, when a Tyrannosaurus Rex skeleton was dug up and the bones brought to the Montana State University's lab. As researchers studied the leg bone, it was noticed that some parts inside had not completely fossilized. There were blood vessels and even blood cells with nuclei. Dr. Mary Schweitzer said:

'The lab filled with murmurs of amazement, for I had focused on something inside the vessels that none of us had ever noticed before: tiny round objects, translucent red with a dark center. Then a colleague took one look at them and shouted, "You've got red blood cells. You've got red blood cells!"'[43]

Schweitzer reported: 'It was exactly like looking at a slice of modern bone. But, of course, I couldn't believe it. I said to the lab technician: "The bones, after all, are 65 million years old. How could blood cells survive that long?"' She explained: 'If you take a blood sample, and you stick it on a shelf, you have nothing recognizable in about a week. So why would there be anything left in dinosaurs?' She said: 'I just got goose bumps, because everyone knows these things don't last for 65 million years'[44]. Cells usually degrade soon after the death of the organism, so how could they last this long?

In 2000, another T-Rex leg bone, which had to be broken to be

---

Roraima pollen found in Precambrian rocks, P.B.H. Bailey, "Possible microfossils found in the Roraima Formation in British Guiana", *Nature* 202:384, 25 April 1964), or just ignored (as in the case of six-legged, composite-eyed insects found in the Precambrian deposits of the Salt Range in Pakistan (B. Sahni, "Age of saline series in the Salt Range of the Punjab", *Nature* 153:462–463, 1944; B. Sahni, "Microfossils and the Salt Range thrust", *Proceedings of the National Academy of Sciences, India, Section B* 16:i–xix, 1945)

[43] M. Schweitzer and I. Staedter, "The Real Jurassic Park", *Earth*, June 1997, pp.55–57

[44] B. Yeoman, "Schweitzer's Dangerous Discovery", *Discover* 27(4):37–41, 2006, p.39

transported back to the lab, was found to contain soft tissues that were still flexible. More discoveries since 1990 have turned up evidence of unfossilised dinosaur material, including real (not fossilized) bone, haemoglobin, other fragile proteins, and soft tissue such as flexible ligaments and stretchy blood vessels. In 2013, Schweitzer even reported DNA: 'These data are the first to support preservation of multiple proteins [viz. actin, tubulin, PHEX, histone H4] and to present multiple lines of evidence for material consistent with DNA in dinosaurs'[45].

Dinosaur soft tissues have now been reported in over 50 secular publications. One report states: 'The researchers also analyzed other fossils for the presence of soft tissue, and found it was present in about half of their samples going back to the Jurassic Period, which lasted from 145.5 million to 199.6 million years ago…'[46]

Dr. Schweitzer said that it was difficult to publish the findings in the scientific literature: "I had one reviewer tell me that he didn't care what the data said, he knew that what I was finding wasn't possible … . I wrote back and said, 'Well what data would convince you?' And he said, 'None.'"[47] In fact, Schweitzer found it difficult to believe the results herself. She said that she repeated one experiment seventeen times before she would believe the evidence before her eyes[48].

Some scientists expressed disbelief that these structures could have survived so long, and suggested other theories to explain the phenomenon. Perhaps the blood vessels were actually more recent bacterial biofilms and that the red blood cells were iron-rich spheres called framboids? These theories have since been disproven[49].

Schweitzer even tells how she noticed that a Tyrannosaurus Rex skeleton (from Hell Creek, Montana) had a similar smell to a human cadaver in the lab which had recently died after chemotherapy. When

[45] Mary Schweitzer and 3 others, "Molecular analyses of dinosaur osteocytes support the presence of endogenous molecules", *Bone* 52(1):414–423, 2013
[46] S. Pappas, "Controversial *T. Rex* soft tissue find finally explained", livescience.com/41537-t-rex-soft-tissue.html, 26 November 2013
[47] Yeoman, "Schweitzer's Dangerous Discovery", *Discover*
[48] Mary Schweitzer, *Science* 307:1852, 25 March 2005
[49] https://www.discovermagazine.com/planet-earth/slime-versus-dinosaur

she mentioned it to her mentor, the famous palaeontologist Jack Horner, he replied, 'Oh yeah, all Hell Creek bones smell'[50].

In 2012, at the Western Pacific Geophysics Meeting in Singapore, August 13–17, Dr Thomas Seiler, a German physicist, presented a paper on behalf of a team of researchers in which they gave Carbon-14 dating results from many bone samples from eight dinosaur specimens. All carbon-dates ranged from 22,000 to 39,000 years. However, Carbon-14 only lasts thousands of years before it decays and disappears (it has a half-life of 5,730 years). It has a maximum life of about 100,000 years, not millions of years. If dinosaurs really were millions of years old, there should not be one atom of Carbon-14 left in these bones.

What was the reaction to this Carbon-14 research paper? Afterwards, all mention was removed from the conference website. It was as if the paper had never been presented. Rather than debate the shocking findings, organisers resorted to censorship and cover-up. The conference presentation is still available on Youtube[51].

What is the response of evolutionists generally to the evidence of soft tissues in dinosaur fossils? Their answer is that unfossilised soft tissues must obviously be able to last for hundreds of millions of years! Kevin Padian, past-president of the National Centre for Science Education (the main US organisation dedicated to fighting creationism) states, 'Chemicals that might degrade in a laboratory over a short period need not do so in a protected natural chemical environment ... it's time to readjust our thinking'[52]. The problem for Padian is that the dinosaur fossils found in Hell's Creek were exposed not only to heat and cold, but also groundwater. Scientists ordinarily place biological samples in the deep freeze to preserve them, but the dinosaur soft tissues were not 'protected' in any way.

Evolutionary scientists like Mary Schweitzer are looking hard for some sort of mysterious process that might preserve soft tissues for hundreds of millions of years. Maybe they will find one, but at the

---

[50] Yeoman, "Schweitzer's Dangerous Discovery", *Discover*

[51] https://www.youtube.com/watch?v=QbdH3l1UjPQ.

[52] David Perlman, "T. Rex Tissue Offers Evolution Insights", *San Francisco Chronicle*, April 13, 2007.

moment, all they have is blind faith in evolution and its long ages. Their refusal to accept the simple and obvious answer staring them right in the face – that the dinosaur tissue is not millions of years old – show the lengths to which evolutionary thinking will go rather than deny the theory. This episode shows that there is no possible way to invalidate the theory of evolution. It does not matter what evidence is presented, it will never be accepted as a falsification of evolution.

Radiometric Dating

But surely radiometric dating proves that the earth is very old, and evolution is true? Radiometric dating works by measuring the rate at which radioactive elements decay into other elements. However, consider the following analogy: if a candle burns at 3cm per hour, how long has a 17cm tall candle been burning? The answer is that we cannot work this out without knowing how tall the candle originally was. Similarly, radiometric dating methods require three assumptions:

1. The initial amounts of the elements are known.
2. No elements leaked in or out of the rocks being dated.
3. The radioactive decay rate has always remained constant.

To see how crucial these assumptions are, consider two examples. In 1980, Mt. St. Helens in the USA erupted, and five samples from rocks from the cooled lava flows gave five different dates from 0.34 to 2.8 million years old, although they were in reality less than 10 years old. Similarly, thirteen samples from Mt. Ngauruhoe in New Zealand were dated from <0.27 as high as 3.5 million years, despite coming from 20th century lava flows. The wrong dates were the result of a false assumption, namely that the only argon measured in the rocks was a result of the radioactive decay of potassium into argon, and that all initial argon (a gas) had escaped from the lava before the rocks cooled. If all the argon had not escaped from the molten lava, the initial conditions (zero argon) are wrong, and a highly inflated date is produced, as seen here[53].

---

[53] See creation.com/radio-dating-in-rubble, creation.com/excess-argon-within-mineral-concentrates, and creation.com/radioactive-dating-failure.

Similarly, other radioactive elements are able to leak into or out of rocks (like uranium, which is soluble in water), violating assumption 2, and producing false dates. Scientists often invoke such contamination problems to dismiss dates that do not align with expected outcomes. In other words, dates from radioactive decay are more like a lottery than the squeaky-clean science the public is told they are. In reality, scientists play 'the dating game' and pick the dates they prefer.

The Alternative Paradigm

What do I make of the dinosaur soft-tissue discoveries, and the hidden assumptions involved in dating rocks and fossils? I believe they call into question the entire paradigm, or worldview, of evolution.

Bear in mind that the earth is covered in vast rock layers stretching hundreds of thousands of square kilometres. Some, like the Carboniferous coal seams, stretch half-way across North America and then all the way across Europe. The decaying vegetation that turned into coal in these sedimentary rock layers was not laid down in a small, shallow lake. In South Australia there is the famous Ediacaran sandstone layer, a geological formation which extends over thousands of square kilometres, full of thousands of fossilised jellyfish. If the rock layers were laid down slowly over millions of years, any dead bodies of animals would have been scavenged, rotted and disappeared before a fortnight was out, long before they would have been able to be fossilised. Instead, these fossils have been suddenly buried intact under massive amounts of sediment. What sort of amount of water was able to transport huge volumes of sand over hundreds of thousands of square kilometres, enough to bury alive hundreds of thousands of jellyfish, entombing them in rock that hardened rapidly, before they had time to start decaying in the sun? Here is what geology assuredly reveals: billions of dead things, buried in rock layers, laid down in water, all over the earth. That sounds like a massive flood, exactly what the Bible describes in Noah's day.

The alternative to the evolutionary worldview is that the geological column is the record of the sudden cataclysmic burial of a myriad creatures, starting with those on the bottom of the oceans (in Cambrian rocks) then (as we proceed upwards) fish, amphibians, reptiles and land creatures. The rock layers are not the result of slow and gradual processes, but of catastrophic processes associated with Noah's flood.

I don't want to be too dogmatic on this point, because I realise other Christians take a different view, but four facts support an OUYEAH (Old Universe, Young Earth and Humans) creationist position. That is, I believe that life on earth is a recent creation while the universe itself is old. First, natural physical mechanisms allow for a young earth in an old universe. Einstein's theories of time dilation due to gravity have shown that time can be distorted by gravity, so that billions of years may pass in outer space while time stands virtually still at an 'event horizon' near to the centre of an early expanding universe.

Secondly, scientists now happily accept the idea of cosmic inflation, the mysterious (some might say, miraculous) expansion of the early universe at much faster than the speed of light, multiplying in size millions of times over. If cosmic inflation is possible, anything is, even OUYEAH. If God stretched out the universe at a speed faster than light (on Day Four of Creation), there is no longer any problem, in principle, with how it is possible to see light from far-distant stars.

Thirdly, there are serious problems with the evolutionary dating scheme of long ages on earth, and not just the problem of smelly, stretchy, unfossilised dinosaur soft tissues (see the article in the footnotes[54]). Here's a little joke: homeowners are told that the best modern synthetic paint lasts about fifteen years before it needs re-coating, but ancient cave paintings have lasted 50,000 years. Oh yeah.

Fourthly, the biblical reasons for a recent creation of life are very strong: Jesus' statement that 'from the beginning of the creation, God made them male and female' (Mark 10:6), the statement in Exodus 20:11 that Israel was to keep the Sabbath because 'in six days God created the heavens and the earth … and rested the seventh day', Paul's statement that Adam's sin brought death into the world (Romans 5:12) and that creation was not originally subject to the futility, corruption, groaning and pain that it currently experiences (Romans 8:19-23), with the promise of a new creation reversing of the effects of the curse (Isaiah

---

[54] https://creation.com/age-of-the-earth

35), including an end to carnivory (Isaiah 11:6-9). It is hard to see, on this reading, how animal death and bloodshed, sickness and predation (which we see in the fossil record) could have been called 'very good' (Genesis 1:31) by God before Adam's sin, or how the 'last enemy' (1 Corinthians 15:26) to be destroyed in God's program for bringing in a new creation could be death if God created death in the first place.

Conclusion

Darwinian evolution has no credible explanation for how 'living beings can create themselves', nor does it present the sort of compelling evidence from the fossil record that shows it has actually happened. Evolution is not even falsifiable. The commitment to atheism by scientific elites is absolute.

Malcolm Muggeridge wrote about the public and science:

'Towards any kind of scientific mumbo-jumbo we display a credulity which must be the envy of African witch-doctors. While we shy away with [ridicule] from the account of the creation in the Book of Genesis, we are probably ready to assent to any rigmarole by a Professor Hoyle about how matter came to be, provided it is dished up in the requisite jargon and associated, however obliquely, with what we conceive to be 'facts'[55].

Dr. Michael Denton (an agnostic) wrote, 'Ultimately, the Darwinian theory of evolution is no more nor less than the great cosmogenic myth of the twentieth century'[56].

The last word, though, must go to Richard Dawkins. When asked, "Is evolution a theory, not a fact?", he replied, 'Evolution has been observed. It's just that it hasn't been observed while it's happening'[57].

---

[55] Malcolm Muggeridge, *Jesus Rediscovered*, Fontana, 1969, p.47

[56] Denton, Michael, *Evolution: A Theory in Crisis*, Burnett Books, 1985, p.358

[57] "Battle over evolution", Bill Moyers interviews Richard Dawkins, *Now*, 3 December 2004, PBS network

Chapter 31

God is a Moral Monster

In one of Richard Dawkins' more explosive outbursts he raged: 'The God of the Old Testament is arguably the most unpleasant character in all fiction: jealous and proud of it; a petty, unjust, unforgiving control-freak; a vindictive, bloodthirsty ethnic cleanser; a misogynistic, homophobic, racist, infanticidal, genocidal, filicidal, pestilential, megalomaniacal, sadomasochistic, capriciously malevolent bully'[1].

Dawkins portrays God as evil, but the glaring problem with this paragraph is that Dawkins himself believes that there is no such thing as good or evil. (Remember: Dawkins said that in our universe of 'blind pitiless indifference' there are 'no good or evil'). So how can Dawkins accuse God of being evil – if evil does not exist? We have gone over this ground twice already, in the chapters on C. S. Lewis and Morality (Part One) and the Problem of Suffering and Evil (Part Three). In atheism, morality is an illusion. So, Dawkins's argument here is completely incoherent and self-contradictory.

Nor is Dawkins a shining model of moral guidance to follow. Remember, again, that Dawkins said he had no problem, in principle, with eating human roadkill (i.e. cannibalism), or with abortion up to one year old – killing little children. Dawkins also said, 'What's to prevent us from saying Hitler wasn't right? I mean, that is a genuinely difficult question'.

Based on these comments, Richard Dawkins would hardly appear to be in any position to lecture others on morality. It would be safer to say that Dawkins is one very morally-confused individual. We see evidence of Dawkins' moral muddle-headedness in the first complaint on his list

---

[1] Richard Dawkins, *The God Delusion*, p.31

about God: jealousy. Dawkins here fails to understand a very basic moral issue. Consider the question: is it right or wrong for a husband to be jealous if another man starts trying to steal the heart of his wife or girlfriend? In such a situation, jealousy is a perfectly appropriate and right emotion. No one finds fault with an artist if she gets jealous because someone has copied her work of art and tried to say it was their own creation. In these situations, jealousy is perfectly appropriate. Similarly, God is perfectly entitled to feel jealousy when His creatures start falling down and worshipping carved tree trunks or the moon or animals as God their creator. The praise and worship rightly belongs to the great Creator.

The fact that the Bible teaches us to love our neighbor, to care for the poor, the widow and the orphan, or to not murder or steal or lie, should also cause us to pause a moment and consider whether Dawkins is not presenting a caricature of the God of the Bible.

Atheists hardly command the moral high-ground. Malcolm Muggeridge wrote: 'I've spent a number of years in India and Africa where I found much righteous endeavour undertaken by Christians of all denominations; but I never, as it happens, came across a hospital or orphanage run by the Fabian Society [a British socialist organization], or a humanist [i.e. atheist] leper colony'[2].

The Flood and the Canaanite Genocide

The main problem Dawkins identifies with biblical morality is that God decrees the death of certain people in the Old Testament. However, as the Creator of all living things – the One who gave people life – God has the right to take life back. Car drivers who break the rules of the road have their driving licences taken off them, doctors or lawyers lose their registration for professional malpractice, even schoolchildren may be expelled from school, but the same principle leaves Dawkins outraged when God applies it to our lives. Does God not have the right to act as the Moral Governor of the Universe?

This is something that many modern people get wrong. The Bible

---

[2] Malcolm Muggeridge, *Jesus Rediscovered*, Fontana, 1969, p.139

teaches that by committing any sin – not just terrible atrocities but any sin – we forfeit the right to live on God's earth (see Romans 1:32). God did not create the world to be polluted by our corruption and wickedness. The fact that He allows rebels and law-breakers to continue living in His world, polluting it with our greed, perversion, violence, and falsehoods, great and small, is a testament to God's longsuffering mercy, and His desire that we should turn back to Him in repentance (2 Peter 3:9). But God has the right, not only to take human life if He wishes, but to fold up the entire universe and throw it on the celestial scrapheap if He so pleases.

Dawkins takes particular exception to the story of Noah's flood: 'the moral of the story of Noah is appalling. God took a dim view of humans, so he (with the exception of one family) drowned the lot of them'[3].

What Dawkins strangely omits to mention is the fact that the biblical account explicitly states that God did so because the world was full of violence and corruption. Surely even Dawkins takes a 'dim view' of domestic violence, of people being stabbed and shot on the streets, or world wars? Rather than let the world sink into a sewer of complete savagery, God destroyed it with a flood and started again. Bear in mind that God gave people plenty of time to change their ways – over 100 years – and plenty of warnings through Noah. They had the opportunity to repent and reform. God gave them more than a second chance. The world in Noah's day fully deserved the judgment when it came. God also made a way of escape for anyone who wished to be saved via Noah's ark. It is hard to see how God can be faulted.

The same goes for the story of the Canaanite wars, a story similar to Noah's flood on a smaller scale and over a longer period. The Canaanites were not a society of honest peasants, humble and quiet. Here was an entire culture completely given over to depraved evil. The most notorious sin of the Canaanites was human sacrifice: burning alive their babies as offerings to their gods. But they were also guilty of many other things the Bible labels abominations including incest and bestiality, for which sins God said that the land was going to 'vomit them out' (Leviticus 18). In

---

[3] Richard Dawkins, *The God Delusion*, pp.237-8

this case, God gave the Canaanite society nearly 400 years to repent and turn away from these evils, from Abraham's day till Moses' time. He also gave fair warning of their impending destruction – Israel was forty years in the wilderness coming from Egypt to the Promised Land. In fact, a few of the Canaanites took the warning seriously and cut a bargain with Israel (like Rahab and the Gibeonites), but the vast majority of the Canaanites refused to come to terms with the Israelites, or to abandon their ingrained culture, and instead chose to attack Israel, fighting to the death until they were destroyed. Nor was God being racially discriminatory in the matter: He threatened that the land would also vomit the Israelites out if they copied the Canaanites, which is what eventually happened, with the result that Israel went into exile in a foreign land for their sins.

Atheists point out that there were many children killed in Noah's flood and the Canaanite wars; it is the taking of innocent life that particularly makes God a 'moral monster'. The problem, however, with the people before the flood and the inhabitants of Canaan was not just individual sinners, but a culture of evil that permeated everything in society from the top to the bottom: politics, the economy, religion, the arts and family life. Once rampant sexual hedonism and violence have saturated society, the problem becomes the fact that their collective identity was inseparable from their crimes and sins. In the two cases concerned, the collective culture had become an engulfing atmosphere of evil. Their collective culture had become so ingrained, it was a self-perpetuating system which permeated society beyond the point of return.

The Bible uses a proverb to describe the spread of evil: 'a little leaven (i.e. yeast) leavens the whole lump (i.e. of dough)'[4]. In other words, evil has a tendency to spread and completely corrupt. A more modern illustration would be a disease like cancer and the way it spreads throughout the body until it kills a person. Even Richard Dawkins has a word for this: the 'meme' – an element of culture that is passed from person to person by non-genetic means. When the culture itself has become completely toxic there is nothing left to rescue. Evil is

---

[4] 1 Corinthians 5:6, Galatians 5:9

contagious, because for some people it is delicious and desirable. When a culture glamourizes and glorifies it, it must be entirely removed just like cancer, or it will keep on spreading. God said that these cultures were irredeemably evil – saturation point had been reached and there was nothing left to save.

The nearest example we have to this sort of culture of evil in modern times is in Nazi Germany and in Soviet Russia. However, in the case of the two biblical societies, the situation was worse, for whereas Nazi Germany and Soviet Russia were totalitarian states where everyone was forced to adopt the culture, in the biblical cases everybody was a willing participant in the evils they enjoyed.

God gave these two societies centuries to change their ways, but this grace only showed how ingrained and entrenched the intergenerational evil had become. God's judgment, when it fell, was entirely justified.

Abraham's Sacrifice of Isaac

Dawkins' view of God as a moral monster becomes particularly problematic once we look at the few forays Dawkins makes into biblical interpretation and exposition. In fact, if Dawkins has actually read the Bible, he has completely lost the plot. As the leading modern preacher of fundamentalist atheism, Dawkins has mastered the foam-flecked sermon-style, but his ability to read and intelligently understand the biblical text leaves a lot to be desired. This is hardly surprising, for he is not a Christian and has neither very much acquaintance with the Bible nor love for it. He seems to lack the patience to try to understand what it is saying, nor does he demonstrate any interest in interacting with the breadth and depth of scholarship on biblical interpretation. His attempts at exposition are amateurish in the extreme; plenty of Sunday School children regularly do better.

Dawkins argues that God is filicidal in that He told Abraham to sacrifice his son Isaac (see Genesis 22). But even children in Sunday School do not get as confused as Dawkins at hearing this story. If we read the entire story of Abraham, starting ten chapters earlier in Genesis, we realize that all through his life, Abraham was being tested in faith. God called him to leave his homeland in Chaldea (modern-day southern

Iraq) to live in a land that God would give him, and Abraham left all, not knowing where he was going. God promised him a family even though his wife was barren and old. Miraculously, God gave Abraham and Sarah a son, Isaac, in their old age. God protected Abraham through various famines and wars, and patiently put up with Abraham's mistakes when he distrusted God and tried out his own ideas, making a mess of things. But finally, after God had kept all His promises and Abraham's faith was strong, he was put to one final test. It is obvious that God did not desire Isaac's death. Killing Isaac not only went against every moral rule in the book, but was also contrary to God's direct promises to make a great nation out of Abraham's special son. In fact, the very first verse of the story is a plot spoiler, alerting us to the fact that God was testing Abraham. So, when Abraham went ahead and obeyed God, and was poised to plunge the knife into his son, God intervened and stopped the test. "Now I know", said God, "how much you trust Me". The idea that the Bible somehow condones or encourages the killing of children has never crossed the minds of any Jews or Christians for three thousand years.

When our youngest son turned three, he was given (among other birthday presents) a bag of chocolate frogs. He was allowed to eat one each day. Being partial towards chocolate frogs, I asked him a few days after his birthday if I could have one. "No!" he responded angrily. This upset me a little, firstly because I didn't get a chocolate frog, and secondly because he seemed a bit too selfish. So a few days later I asked again, and got the same response. But a few days later I asked again, and this time, to my surprise, he said, "Of course you can!". However, this time, I did not take the chocolate frog. I was so happy that my little son was prepared to share that I didn't need a chocolate frog. "You can have them all", I said.

A similar thing is happening with God and Abraham. God was not interested in the least in seeing Abraham kill Isaac. But God wanted to see how much Abraham trusted and loved God.

Dawkins makes some other muddled attempts at biblical interpretation, like the idea that the Bible approves of certain terrible sins simply because it records them (as if a newspaper were encouraging murder because it emblazons it on its headline). The Bible records the failings of many of its main characters, like Moses' murder or David's adultery, for the simple reason that it paints its characters 'warts and all'. One of the Bible's main messages is that all have sinned (Romans 3:23), without exception. Anyone who imagines that God is condoning such behavior is so out of their depth at interpreting the Bible that they need a course in reading literature.

Alister McGrath sums up the situation: 'The God that Dawkins does not believe in is "a petty, unjust, unforgiving control freak; a vindictive, bloodthirsty ethnic cleanser; a misogynistic, homophobic, racist, infanticidal, genocidal, filicidal, pestilential, megalomaniacal, sadomasochistic, capriciously malevolent bully". Come to think of it, I don't believe in a God like that either'[5].

McGrath goes on to remind Dawkins that the picture Christians see when they think of God is Jesus. Nor is Jesus different from the God of the Old Testament, as if God has a Jekyll and Hyde split-personality. God is described as compassionate or merciful more times in the Old Testament than in the New, and the Jesus of the gospels is so angry with corrupt religion that he makes a whip and chases out the money-changers in the temple. Both have zero tolerance for sin, and both nevertheless reach out in grace to the worst of sinners, offering pardon and reconciliation.

Slavery

Many modern critics of Christianity protest that the Bible condones slavery. Slavery is found often in the Old Testament while in the New, the apostles Peter and Paul do not condemn it, but instead call upon Christian slaves to obey their masters (Colossians 3:22, 1 Peter 2:18).

However, this criticism reveals a double-standard. When Christians today speak up for their moral principles, secularists often get upset. They accuse Christians of trying to establish a theocracy, or they warn about the need to keep church and state separate. But then they turn

---

[5] Alister McGrath, *The Dawkins Delusion: Atheist Fundamentalism and the Denial of the Divine*, SPCK, 2007, p.46

round and accuse the earliest Christians of the exact opposite: of *not* trying to impose their morality upon others (in the case of slavery).

Let me put it this way: which is worse, kidnapping or murder? Murder, obviously. But slavery usually involves kidnapping, so if murder is a greater evil, why do Christianity's critics get upset when Christians campaign against the murder of unborn little children (abortion)?

Christianity's critics cannot have it both ways. Do they wish Christians to campaign to try to impose their morality upon the godless? Presumably not. But why then do they criticize the early Christians for not protesting against slavery, or gladiatorial blood-sports, imperialistic wars, crippling taxation, torture, death by crucifixion, infanticide (usually of girls), or other evils of Roman society?

The policy of the apostles, following Jesus Himself, was to avoid political activism altogether, and simply preach the gospel. This is because the gospel message is the only thing which has the power to truly overcome evil and change people inwardly. The gospel message that Christ preached said that all people are slaves – to sin – and only the Son can set us free (John 8:32-36). As far as politics was concerned, Jesus said, 'My kingdom is not of this world' (John 18:36); he refused to get involved on the explosive question of whether Jews should pay tax to Caesar, instead replying, 'Render to Caesar the things that are Caesar's and to God the things that are God's' (Mark 12:17). The apostles likewise argued that the Christian's citizenship is in heaven (Philippians 3:20) and taught that we are to set our minds on heavenly things (Colossians 3:1). They preached that Christ was going to judge this world for its evils and set up a kingdom on earth at His return which would do away with all these wrongs.

The Bible also provides the only real basis for any moral condemnation of slavery. It declared that all people are made in the image of God (Genesis 1:26), it graphically pictures the pain and suffering of the Jewish slaves in Egypt and proclaims their exodus as divinely-authorized, it abolished slavery as an institution within the nation of Israel in the Old Testament (although certain forms of slavery were allowed[6]), it teaches that all people come from one man (Acts 17:26), that the gospel is for all people everywhere (Matthew 28:19), that the Holy Spirit came upon all Christians, slave as well as free (Acts 2, 1 Corinthians 12:13), and calls all Christians brothers and sisters.

That the Christian gospel is not a political program might disappoint some Christians who praise William Wilberforce and other evangelicals who abolished the slave trade in the 19th century (after prolonged opposition from secularists of the day). But for non-Christians it should come as a genuine relief. Do they really want the roll-out of an entire Christian moral agenda, which goes a long way beyond abolishing slavery? Do they want to ban gambling or Sunday trading, or start putting homosexuals in jail, or burning witches or stoning to death adulterers? Admittedly, none of these are actual New Testament social policies (for it doesn't have any political plan), but you get the picture: turning Christianity into a political program is to pervert the gospel itself. Some Christians like the idea of imposing Christian moral standards upon the godless by law, but coercing unbelievers to live as Christians is no more helpful in the long run than forcibly baptizing pagans.

The idea that the Bible is pro-slavery is an atheist delusion: God nowhere commands it, nor was it part of His design in creation, and the gospel is the only force in history that has ever been able to overthrow it.

Hell

The final complaint atheists have against God is that He sends people to hell. We have already shown why it is perfectly righteous for God to send people to hell in our chapter on God's holiness (Part Two), and we will not repeat the argument here. However, why should God not send the Devil to hell, or those who have defiantly chosen the Devil's side? As C. S. Lewis puts it, what real alternative is there?

---

[6] For example, voluntary and temporary servitude to repay debts; Israelites were also permitted to have non-Israelite slaves (Numbers 25:44ff). This aligns with the fact that in the Old Testament it was impossible to ban all sin. For example, divorce was permitted (Deuteronomy 24:1-4), even though it was against God's original purpose (Genesis 2:24, Malachi 2:16).

'In the long run the answer to all those who object to the doctrine of hell, is itself a question: What are you asking God to do? To wipe out their past sins and, at all costs, to give them a fresh start, smoothing every difficulty and offering every miraculous help? But He has done so, on Calvary. To forgive them? They will not be forgiven. To leave them alone? Alas, I am afraid that is what He does'.

The same people who complain about hell also tend to say that the atonement is immoral. Why did God have to send His Son to die for our sins? Why couldn't He just forgive us all? The question hardly needs a reply: God cannot just sweep evil under the carpet. To do so would make Him complicit in evil, like a judge smirking as murderers go free from court, as if they had done no wrong. God, as a perfectly moral Being, requires that justice is done, and not only for murders; no evil will be left unpunished. But atheists defiantly refuse to repent of their many sins, and throw back God's offer of forgiveness in His face, trampling underfoot the blood of His Son. In so doing, they show how richly they deserve their coming judgment.

In *The Great Divorce*, Lewis describes a busload of people on a day trip from hell to visit heaven. None of them enjoy it when they get there. They are all addicted to their self-centred delusions:

'Hell begins with a grumbling mood, always complaining, always blaming others... You may even criticise [this mood] in yourself and wish you could stop. But there may come a day when you can no longer. Then there will be no 'you' left to criticise the mood or even enjoy it, but just the grumble itself, going on forever like a machine'.

Elsewhere, Lewis said, 'It is not a question of God 'sending us' to hell. In each of us there is something growing, which will BE hell unless it is nipped in the bud' (*God in the Dock*). Unless we turn back to God, and start to be slowly transformed into His beautiful likeness, we are already well on the way to becoming just like the Devil of hell, full of bitterness and selfish pride, every day fighting against the truth and the love of God, until one day He lets us go where we truly belong.

Chapter 32

Christianity is Bigoted, Exclusive, Intolerant and Oppressive

M any people today ask, How can one religion be right and the others wrong? Aren't all religions valid ways to worship God and love others? The claim of Christianity to be the truth – the only way to God – is a bigoted and intolerant attitude.

I once drove past a church billboard which had two lines. The first said: *There is no truth!* The second line was a question: *Is that true?* The first line dogmatically stated a truth, which therefore contradicted itself. Some today argue that there are no such things as facts – there are only interpretations. But isn't that just an interpretation, then, too? Or is it a fact? These examples highlight the problem with the idea that there is no such thing as absolute truth and that everybody's view is equally valid.

In *Revenge of the Sith* (one of the *Star Wars* movies), Obi Wan Kenobi (the good guy) said: "Only a Sith deals in absolutes" (Siths are the bad-guys). The problem with this statement is that it too deals in absolutes. This would make Obi Wan Kenobi a Sith, with grave consequences for the plot-line of the entire *Star Wars* series of movies.

Many people believe in religious relativism: all religions in their own ways believe in the same God and teach people to be loving. But this is not true; many religions are very different. Some religions teach that God exists (Christianity, Judaism, Islam) while others do not believe in God (Buddhism, Confucianism). Christianity teaches that Jesus is God's Son, while others (Islam and Judaism) say He was not. Christians believe that Jesus rose from the dead, whereas Jews and Muslims do not believe this and Muslims do not even believe that Jesus died (they say that God would not have allowed this to happen to such a good man, and God instead substituted someone else for Him on the cross, while God took Jesus to heaven). Muslims believe that it is permissible to wage *jihad*, holy war[1], whereas Christ said, 'Blessed are the peacemakers' (Matthew 5:9) and forbad his followers to take up the sword to defend Him.

Even most atheists agree that not all viewpoints are equally valid. An atheist who does not believe in God and a Christian who does believe in God cannot both be right.

G. K. Chesterton wrote, 'It is not bigotry to be certain we are right, but it is bigotry to be unable to imagine how we might possibly have gone wrong'. The schoolboy who says that 2 plus 2 equals 4 is not bigoted; he has just done his homework.

The same applies to religion. If the answer to one simple question is 'yes' – Is Jesus Christ God's Son who died for our sins and rose again? – then Christianity is true and atheism, Judaism, Islam, Buddhism, Hinduism, Confucianism and all the rest are false.

Many people today say it is arrogant to try to convert others to a particular religion, but aren't the same people trying to convert you to their way of thinking about proselytising? The same sceptics have little hesitation in bringing up reasons why we should doubt God's existence. Atheists are not slow to try to convert others to their belief that there is no God. The atheist magician Penn Jillette even says this:

'I don't respect people who don't proselytize. If you believe that there is a heaven and hell, or that people could be going to hell, or not get eternal life, and you think it's not really worth telling them this because it would make it socially awkward ... How much do you have to hate somebody to believe that everlasting life is possible and not tell them that?

I mean, if I believed, beyond the shadow of a doubt, that a truck was coming at you, and you didn't believe that truck was bearing down on you, there is a certain point where I tackle you. And this is

---

[1] 'Fight those who believe not in Allah nor the Last Day, nor hold that forbidden which hath been forbidden by Allah and His Messenger, nor acknowledge the religion of Truth, (even if they are) of the People of the Book, until they pay the Jizya with willing submission, and feel themselves subdued' (*Quran*, 9:29)

more important than that'[2].

Truth, by its very nature, is exclusive – not all answers to certain questions are right. Jesus said, 'I am the way, the truth and the life, no one comes to the Father except by Me' (John 14:6). On the one hand, therefore, Christianity is exclusive. But on the other hand, Christ is inclusive. He doesn't turn away anyone. His offer of eternal life is not limited to people of one nationality, or skin colour, or social class, or gender, or sexual orientation. Salvation is for all people everywhere. Christ says, 'Come to Me, all you who labor and are heavy laden, and I will give you rest. Take My yoke upon you and learn from Me, for I am gentle and lowly in heart, and you will find rest for your souls' (Matthew 11:28-29).

Talking about religion may be socially awkward and even divisive, yet Christians are told in the Bible not only to speak the truth, but to do it lovingly and humbly: 'always be ready to give a defense to everyone who asks you a reason for the hope that is in you, with gentleness and respect' (1 Peter 3:15).

Thou Shalt not Judge!

One of the most-quoted, but least understood, Bible verses today is Matthew 7:1, where Jesus said, 'Judge not, that you be not judged'.

In 2009, beauty queen Carrie Prejean's answer to a question thrown at her by homosexual judge Perez Hilton about same-sex marriage got her into a lot of hot water and probably cost her the Miss USA contest. After saying that she believed that marriage was between a man a woman, Prejean was given a hard time in the media.

Even professing Christians criticized Prejean, like Miley Cyrus, the one-time squeaky-clean teenage TV star of Hannah Montana fame. Here is what Cyrus said in a Twitter conversation with Perez Hilton about the Miss USA row: 'God's greatest commandment is to love. And judging is not loving. That's why Christians have such a bad rep'.

In case you missed the irony, Miley Cyrus was criticizing (a.k.a.

---

[2] https://www.youtube.com/watch?v=6md638smQd8

'judging') Carrie Prejean for 'judging' other people. It was Carrie Prejean who was being judged – literally in the Miss USA competition, and morally for her viewpoint on homosexual marriage. Whenever someone says "Do not judge!" they are in fact themselves judging someone for holding an opinion.

Again, this example shows that all moral viewpoints cannot be equally valid and true. Those who say that no one should impose their morality upon others seem quite happy to impose this particular moral view on others.

Just as all religions take different views on certain subjects (like the resurrection of Jesus), so many people take different views of morality. They cannot all be correct. While it is far from the only example, the question of homosexuality provokes different answers. Christianity, Islam and Judaism teach that it is a perversion of proper sexuality, but on the other hand it is now considered a secular sin to say this.

Whereas only a generation ago homosexuality was a crime in certain states and countries, now Christians are increasingly losing their jobs for saying that they think it is sinful. The much-publicized case of Israel Folau, the Australian rugby star is just one among many.

All Moralities are Not Created Equal

Christians (among many others) believe that the safest and most healthy environment for a child to grow up, and therefore ultimately to produce a stable society, is in a family with their biological parents. Rutgers University sociologist David Popenoe states: 'Few propositions have more empirical support in the social sciences than this one. Compared to all other family forms, families headed by married biological parents are the best for children'[3].

US President Barack Obama, in his 2008 Father's Day speech, lamented the fact that one half of black children in the USA now grow up without a father: 'children who grow up without a father are five times more likely to live in poverty and commit crime, nine times more likely to drop out of schools, and twenty times more likely to end up in

---

[3] David Popenoe, *War over the Family*, Transaction Publishers, 2008

prison'.

It's not just children in single-parent families that suffer. Divorce has consequences too: children from broken homes earn lower grades at school, have more psychological problems, tend to be more aggressive, are more likely to commit suicide or end up in prison[4].

What about children growing up with same-sex parents? The claim that there is no evidence that children growing up with gay or lesbian parents suffer poorer psychosocial outcomes is simply not true. Studies by Sullins, Allen and Regnerus have found that children raised in same-sex households have more than twice the rate of significant emotional problems compared with children raised in opposite-sex parents, and nearly four times those of children raised by married, biological parents, as well as a 65% graduation rate from school compared to children living in opposite sex marriage families[5].

G. K. Chesterton wrote that 'the first two facts which a healthy boy

---

[4] Studies in the early 1980's showed that children in repeat divorces earned lower grades and their peers rated them as less pleasant to be around *(Andrew J. Cherlin, Marriage, Divorce, Remarriage –Harvard University Press 1981)*. A study of children six years after a parental marriage breakup revealed that even after all that time, these children tended to be "lonely, unhappy, anxious and insecure" *(Wallerstein "The Long-Term Effects of Divorce on Children", Journal of the American Academy of Child and Adolescent Psychiatry 1991)*. Seventy percent of long-term prison inmates grew up in broken homes *(Horn, Bush, "Fathers, Marriage and Welfare Reform")*. Children of divorce, particularly boys, tend to be more aggressive toward others than those children whose parents did not divorce *(Emery, "Marriage, Divorce and Children's Adjustment", 1988)*. People who come from broken homes are almost twice as likely to attempt suicide than those who do not come from broken homes. *(Velez-Cohen, "Suicidal Behavior and Ideation in a Community Sample of Children", Journal of the American Academy of Child and Adolescent Psychiatry 1988)*. Children of divorced parents are roughly two times more likely to drop out of high school than their peers who benefit from living with parents who did not divorce *(McLanahan, Sandefur, "Growing Up With a Single Parent: What Hurts, What Helps", Harvard University Press 1994)*.

[5] Paul Sullins, "Emotional Problems among Children with Same-sex Parents: Difference by Definition", *British Journal of Education, Society & Behavioural Science*, 2015, 7(2): pp.99-120; Allen D., "High school graduation rates among children of same-sex households," *Review of Economics of the Household* 635 (2013); Regnerus M., "How different are the adult children of parents who have same-sex relationships? Findings from the New Family Structures Study," 41 *Social Science Research* 752 (2012) iv

or girl feels about sex are these: first that it is beautiful and then that it is dangerous'. Like many other things, including fire and sharp knives, sex is powerful but it can also cause great harm. More people get hurt today by broken relationships than by fire or sharp knives, and the main problem with relationships is selfish people. Is it really any wonder that a culture that promotes hedonism, narcissism, pleasure-seeking and self-fulfillment has the most relationship breakdown? The progressive Western world view today teaches we should prohibit guns but put no fences around sex. The Judeo-Christian view is that in the realm of relationships, self-control in the short term leads to long-term benefits.

Margaret Thatcher said socialism collapses because 'eventually you run out of other people's money'[6]. Similarly, self-centredness is not a successful long-term strategy for individuals or society, and hedonism is ultimately self-harming. The unrestrained sexual free-for-all promoted by 'progressives' not only hurts the most vulnerable in society, its children, but more than this, the sexual morality of rampant promiscuity ultimately leads to civilizational collapse.

The Oxford social anthropologist J. D. Unwin surveyed 86 tribes, societies and civilizations in his 1934 book, *Sex and Culture*. He wanted to see if there was a link between sexual freedom and cultural flourishing (measured in terms of architecture, art, science, engineering, literature, and agriculture). Unwin did not appear to be religiously inclined, but his finding was that unleashing sexual freedom always led to the collapse of a culture three generations later, so that the culture was destroyed from within, or conquered or taken over by a more energetic one. Unwin writes:

'The history of these societies consists of a series of monotonous repetitions [i.e. of the pattern of decline and collapse following sexual freedom] ... Sometimes a man has been heard to declare that he wishes both to enjoy the advantages of high culture and to abolish compulsory continence [i.e. sexual restraint]. The inherent nature of the human organism, however, seems to be such that these desires are

---

[6] Speech to the British Conservative Party Conference (10 October 1975)

incompatible, even contradictory … [like] the foolish boy who desires both to keep his cake and to consume it. Any human society is free to choose either to display great energy or to enjoy sexual freedom; the evidence is that it cannot do both for more than one generation'[7].

Philosopher Kirk Durston writes, 'Unwin makes it clear that he does not know why sexual freedom directly leads to the decline and collapse of cultures, although he suggests that when sexual energy is restrained through celibacy or monogamy, it is diverted into more productive social energy'[8].

These findings align with the view that the same Creator who gave us sexual desires in the first place also put boundaries around sex for our ultimate good.

Intolerant Indoctrination

Emma Thompson is a British actress who became an atheist in her teens. She said: 'I was quite keen on Jesus and toyed with Christianity in my teens. I went to Bible classes with the vicar who lived next door, and I remember saying: "My uncle is a homosexual, would he be allowed into heaven?" The vicar paused, and at that moment I knew I was done with religion'[9]. In another interview with a gay magazine, she added: "I thought, 'That's ridiculous! It's perfectly normal, so what do you mean it isn't allowed?'".

In a 2008 interview with *The Australian* newspaper Thompson said, 'I'm an atheist; I suppose you can call me a sort of libertarian anarchist. I regard religion with fear and suspicion. It's not enough to say that I don't believe in God. I actually regard the system as distressing: I am offended by some of the things said in the Bible and the Koran, and I refute them'.

Thus, on the one hand, Thompson complains about Christian morality, but then turns around and campaigns for her own version of

[7] Unwin, *Sex and Culture*, Oxford University Press, 1934, p.412

[8] Kirk Durston, "Why Sexual Morality May be Far More Important than You Ever Thought", https://www.kirkdurston.com/blog/unwin

[9] *Guardian*, https://www.theguardian.com/lifeandstyle/2018/aug/25/emma-thompson-dieting-screwed-up-my-metabolism-i-regret-ever-going-on-one-

morality, imposing 'progressive' values with self-righteous fervour. Thompson's new morality is, of course, just the old immorality.

It is not just Emma Thompson who wants to impose her moral values on others. Children in government schools in many Western countries are now being indoctrinated in the LGBTQI lifestyle. The World Health Organization Regional Office for Europe currently recommends teaching 4-6 year-olds ways to explore their sexuality and gender identity, while 9-12 year-olds are to be taught about their first sexual experience and gender orientation. The 'All about Me' sex education curriculum (including graphic descriptions of sexual activities but no mention of marriage) is being rolled out in England in 2020[10]. All children are required to attend classes designed to 'smash hetero-normativity', under the guise of protecting homosexual children from bullying. All children are being proselytized in the homosexual lifestyle and children under the age of 10 are being hyper-sexualized.

It is commonly argued today that homosexuality is normal, natural, that gays are born that way, and that they can't change. But homosexuals only make up about 2% of the population[11] (so homosexuality is not normal, statistically). Neither is it natural – animals occasionally practise it, yes, but the same is true even of cannibalism, so we can't take animals as a guide to behaviour. The 'natural order' is that males and females were designed for each other. Gays are not born that way either – there is no 'gay gene' or biological basis for homosexuality (studies of identical twins with identical genes, exploring whether genetics or environmental influences cause people to become gay, show that it happens largely because of unique life experiences[12]). And gays can change; many with homosexual tendencies in youth are heterosexual later in life[13].

Young children are also being taught that gender is a choice: whether someone is a boy or girl (or up to one hundred other genders) is up to

---

[10]   https://www.christian.org.uk/news/who-wants-kids-under-4-to-be-taught-about-masturbation-and-gender-identity/

[11] In the UK, 1.7% of over 18s are gay according to the 2015 census, while in Australia's 2014 census, the figure was 3%

[12] Bailey, J. Michael (2000), Langström, Niklas (2010), Burri, A (2011)

[13] Sandfort, T. G. M. (1997), Dickson, N., Paul, C., and Herbison, P. (2003)

them to choose. While such gender-bending ideologies are already damaging children's bodies through surgery and hormone treatment in the short term, what LGBTQI advocates do not realise is that in the long run such state-sponsored indoctrination is bound to backfire. Nobody likes being forced to learn something or to behave in a certain way, least of all rebellious teenage kids in school. Legislating to allow biological men who self-identify as women to use female dressing rooms, or to compete in women's sporting contests is ultimately bound to produce rising resentment against LGBTQI people. The irony of the LGBTQI position is that confused children must be allowed to change their biological gender, but gays must not be allowed to help change their homosexual feelings. State-sanctioned persecution and prosecution of families who do not accept LGBTQI sexual orthodoxy is the aim of the LGBTQI lobby. Just who is being intolerant and oppressive?

Atheism as a Fig Leaf

What is the link between atheism and 'progressive morality'? We see the connection quite clearly in Emma Thompson's story: rejection of God and rebellion against traditional morality go hand in hand. The rise to power in Western society of the LGBTQI lobby and the swelling numbers of people identifying as atheists are connected.

On many university campuses, the main reason young people reject God is because, as they openly admit, of their sexually promiscuous lifestyles. As Augustine the famous 5th century Christian said (and he lived exactly the same way in his youth), 'He who denies the existence of God, has some reason for wishing that God did not exist'.

The author Aldous Huxley's reasons for rejecting God were political and sexual freedom. He wrote:

I had motives for not wanting the world to have a meaning; and consequently assumed that it had none, and was able without any difficulty to find satisfying reasons for this assumption... For myself as, no doubt, for most of my contemporaries, the philosophy of meaninglessness was essentially an instrument of liberation. The liberation we desired was simultaneously liberation from a certain political and economic system and liberation from a certain system of morality. We objected to the morality because it interfered with our sexual freedom; we objected to the political and economic system because it was unjust... There was an admirably simple method of confuting these people and at the same time justifying ourselves in our political and erotic revolt: we could deny that the world had any meaning whatsoever'[14].

Bertrand Russell, with whom the book began, had a similar story. While he was a highly educated and intelligent mathematician and philosopher, he was also (and there really is no nice way to say this) a lecherous philanderer and adulterer who engaged in affairs with multiple women, leaving a trail of ruined relationships and emotional wreckage behind him. At various points in his life, he showed a callous disregard for how his utterly selfish actions harmed other people. It is hard to avoid the conclusion that there was a strong connection between Russell's atheism and his debauched lifestyle, rejection of traditional morality and lack of common decency.

The prominent atheist philosopher Thomas Nagel wrote: 'I want atheism to be true and am made uneasy by the fact that some of the most intelligent and well-informed people I know are religious believers. It isn't just that I don't believe in God and, naturally, hope that I'm right in my belief. It's that I hope there is no God! I don't want there to be a God; I don't want the universe to be like that'[15]. Nagel went on to describe his condition as a 'cosmic authority problem'.

The argument against God that claims that religion is intolerant and oppressive is just a fig leaf. God is real and the arguments for God are powerful; the reason increasing numbers of Westerners reject them is not because atheism is convincing, but because it is convenient. Atheism is a fig leaf for their hedonistic immorality.

---

[14] Aldous Huxley, *Ends and Means*, 5th ed., Harper and Brothers, 1937, pp.312, 316
[15] Thomas Nagel, *The Last Word*, Oxford University Press, 1997, pp.130–131

Towards a Truly Pluralistic Society

Is there any hope for our increasingly fragmented and polarized Western society? How do we get on with each other without putting people in prison for holding a different opinion?

There are two sorts of pluralistic societies. First of all, there is Hindu pluralism, which says that there are many roads by which people may pursue the quest for truth or the path to peace. None of them have universal validity; none are absolute truth. All must be tolerated. This, of course, merely brings us back to the internal contradiction with which we started this chapter: someone who says there is no absolute truth has just stated an absolute truth.

The pluralistic society of ancient Rome was similar: tolerance was extended to the worship of all gods, except for Christianity which was prohibited because of its belief that there was only one true God. In AD 203, a Christian noblewoman called Perpetua, the young mother of a nursing infant, was arrested and put to death in Carthage, North Africa, along with five others. Her crime was not so much that she worshipped Christ, but her refusal to worship the Roman emperor.

Roman pluralism adds state coercion to the 'tolerance' mix. The only opinion allowed is the one the state dictates. The call to respect everybody's lifestyle and to be tolerant of all opinions applies to all, unless someone holds to traditional Judeo-Christian morality. Aside from the discrimination and double-standards, what could anyone complain about? This is simply the establishment of a state religion: agnosticism.

The second form of pluralism involves true freedom. Voltaire the French sceptic did not actually say the words commonly attributed to him, but they nevertheless sum up his libertarian attitude: 'I disapprove of what you say, but I will defend to the death your right to say it'.

Christians are in a good position to contribute to a truly pluralistic society, even though they believe they have the truth, because of three factors. First, because Christians believe that everybody is made in the image of God, they are able to have respectful discussions with people of different viewpoints. Because Christians believe, as the United States Declaration of Independence states, that God created all men equal, it is possible to speak to people without condescension, hatred or contempt.

Secondly, because Christians believe that 'all have sinned', including themselves, it is possible for Christians to walk and talk humbly with others, aware of our own failures and the possibility that we are in error. Christians are aware, not least because of many deep theological questions, that we can all learn from others. Thirdly, because Christians are taught to 'love the Lord your God with all your mind' (as well as heart, soul and strength), Christians are encouraged to think through questions in a balanced way, intellectually as well as emotionally. Christians also have a history to fall back on, a civilization that has lasted 2000 years, in which mistakes were made and lessons learned.

Of course, it is possible also for Christians to speak what they believe is the truth, but in a harsh way without love or grace. This is not what Christ modelled or the apostles taught[16]. When it happens it is usually the result of immaturity or insecurity in the faith, or lack of experience interacting and discussing viewpoints with others. The best way to overcome this nervous reaction is simply to engage in more discussion with different people.

It is the lack of interaction, discussion and civil debate in modern society that causes much of the polarization that Western society is experiencing. People hear from their own preferred viewpoints, and live in an echo-chamber (whether left-wing or right-wing), reinforcing their prejudices. When people hide behind the anonymity that the internet allows, or interact on it with people that they are never going to personally meet, they feel more free to abuse and attack others verbally. More personal and preferably face-to-face discussion is the answer.

Modern parliamentary democracies are built on this principle. Parliament is not just for 'voting at my party's beck and call', but for civilized discussion and respectful debate. The result is that, although representatives do not always agree, they are able to express their opinions. It is not an accident that modern parliamentary democracy arose and flourished in Christian countries. It would be an irony if Christians were the only group of people banned from expressing their opinions in a modern pluralistic democracy.

---

[16] John 1:14, 17, Ephesians 4:15

Index

Is the Bible Really the Word of God? The Doctrine of Scripture

The Bible is continually under attack. Critics argue that it is full of mistakes, impossible to understand, and we can't be sure of what it originally said. There are good reasons for believing that the Bible is really the Word of God and that He speaks in living power to us through it.

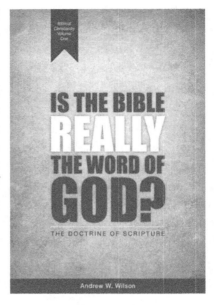

Do Not Quench the Spirit: a Biblical and Practical Guide to Participatory Church Gatherings

For many Christians, going to church is like watching television. Was church really meant to be a spectator sport? The New Testament encourages the use of spiritual gifts by many in the church gatherings. Martyn Lloyd-Jones wrote, 'The notion of people belonging to the church in order to come to sit down and fold their arms and listen, with just two or three doing everything, is quite foreign to the New Testament.

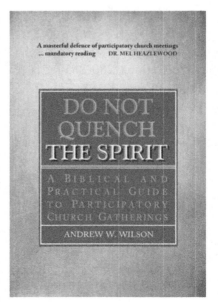

Believer's Bible Doctrine Handbook: Eighty Christian Truths

Providing brief summaries of eighty Christian truths, *Believer's Bible Doctrine Handbook* deals with ten areas of doctrine: Scripture, God, Christ, the Holy Spirit, Man, Sin, Salvation, Sanctification, the Church and Future Events, offering concise expository, practical and historical explanations of all the main doctrines of the Christian faith

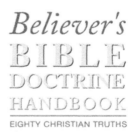

The Most Amazing Prophecy in the Bible: Daniel's Prophecy of the Seventy Sevens

What would be the chances of someone correctly predicting seven events, putting them in the right order, and even saying when they will occur? This is what we find in Daniel's prophecy of the Seventy Sevens. Daniel 9:24-27 is truly the most amazing prophecy in the Bible.

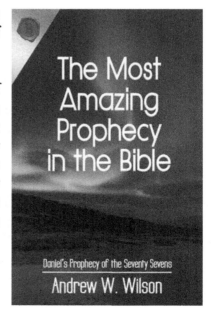